Shojo Beat

Kaze
HIKARU

21

Story & Art by
Taeko Watanabe

Contents

Story Thus Far

It is the end of the Bakufu era, the third year of Bunkyu (1863) in Kyoto. The Shinsengumi is a band of warriors formed to protect the shogun.

Tominaga Sei, the daughter of a former Bakufu *bushi*, joined the Shinsengumi disguised as a boy by the name of Kamiya Seizaburo to avenge her father and brother. She has continued her training under the only person in the Shinsengumi who knows her true identity, Okita Soji, and she aspires to become a true *bushi*.

In order to inspect the Choshu, Kondo and Ito head to Hiroshima in the company of Bakufu officials. The Shinsengumi discover that suspected assassin Sakamoto Ryoma is hiding somewhere in Fushimi, and, under orders from Hijikata, Sei dresses as a woman to infiltrate the Teradaya Inn.

At the inn, a mysterious man named Saitani Umetaro bullies Sei, and she soon discovers he is Sakamoto himself. Fearing for her safety, Okita follows Sei to Fushimi against Hijikata's orders, but in the end, the two fail to apprehend Sakamoto.

Characters

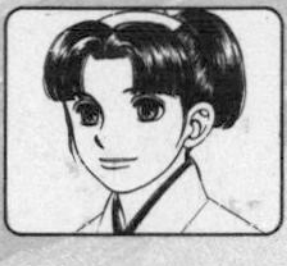

Tominaga Sei
She disguises herself as a boy to enter the Mibu-Roshi. She trains under Soji, aspiring to become a true *bushi*. But secretly, she is in love with Soji.

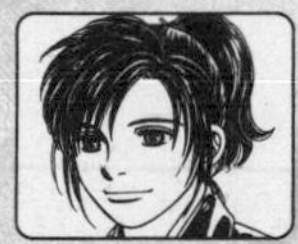

Okita Soji
Assistant vice captain of the Shinsengumi and licensed master of the Ten'nen Rishin-ryu. He supports the troop alongside Kondo and Hijikata and guides Seizaburo with a kind yet firm hand.

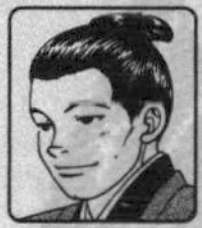

Kondo Isami
Captain of the Shinsengumi and fourth grandmaster of the Ten'nen Rishin-ryu. A passionate, warm and well-respected leader.

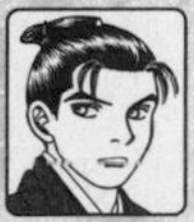

Hijikata Toshizo
Vice captain of the Shinsengumi. He commands both the group and himself with a rigid strictness. He is also known as the "Oni vice captain."

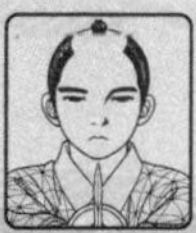

Saito Hajime
Assistant Vice Captain. He was a friend of Sei's older brother. Sei is attached to him in place of her lost brother.

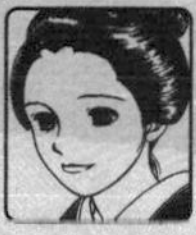

Sato
Formerly known as the Shimabara geisha Akesato. After the death of her love, Yamanami, she has supported Sei as "Seizaburo's lover."

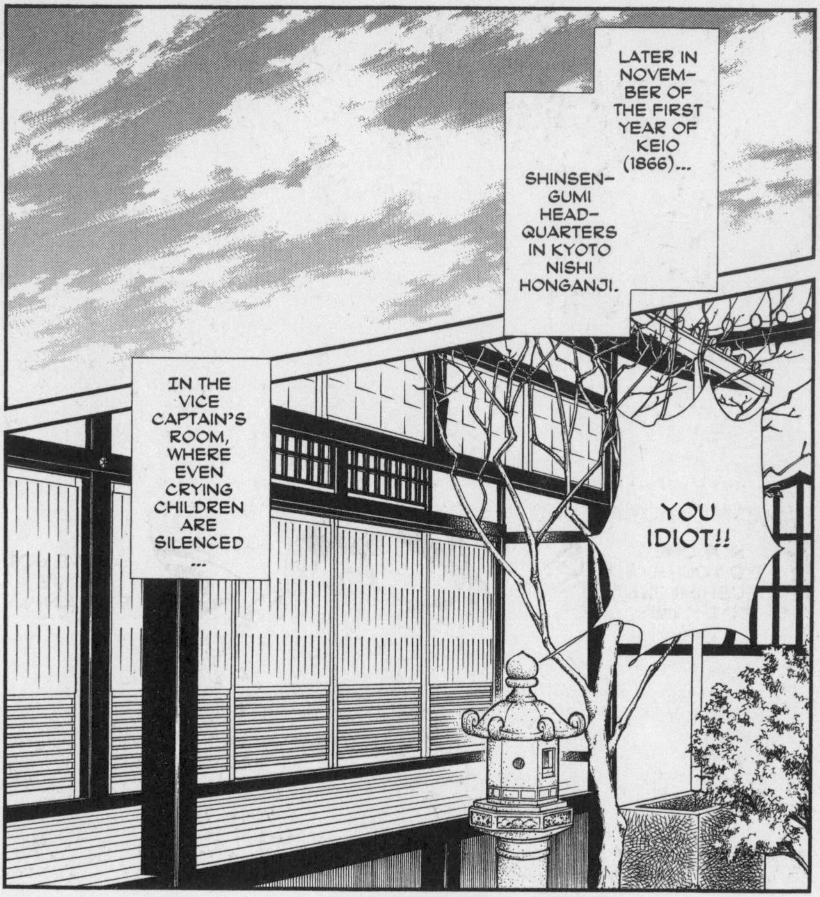
LATER IN NOVEMBER OF THE FIRST YEAR OF KEIO (1866)...
SHINSEN-GUMI HEAD-QUARTERS IN KYOTO NISHI HONGANJI.
IN THE VICE CAPTAIN'S ROOM, WHERE EVEN CRYING CHILDREN ARE SILENCED ...
YOU IDIOT!!

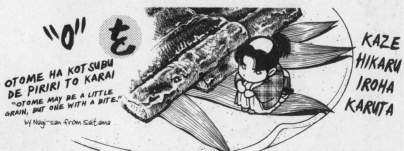

KAZE HIKARU IROHA KARUTA

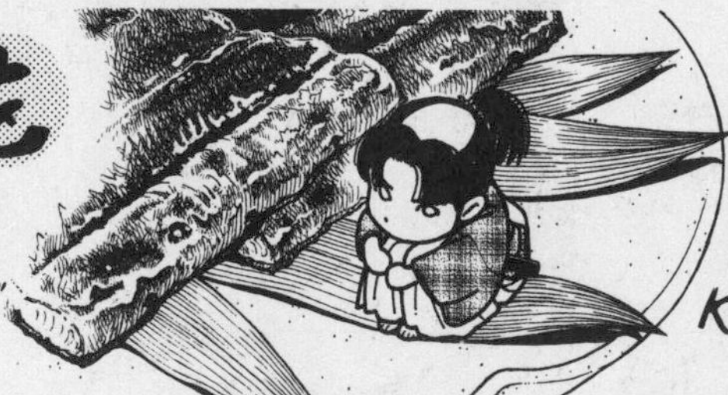

"O" を

OTOME HA KOTSUBU DE PIRIRI TO KARAI

"OTOME MAY BE A LITTLE GRAIN, BUT ONE WITH A BITE."

by Nagi-san from Saitama

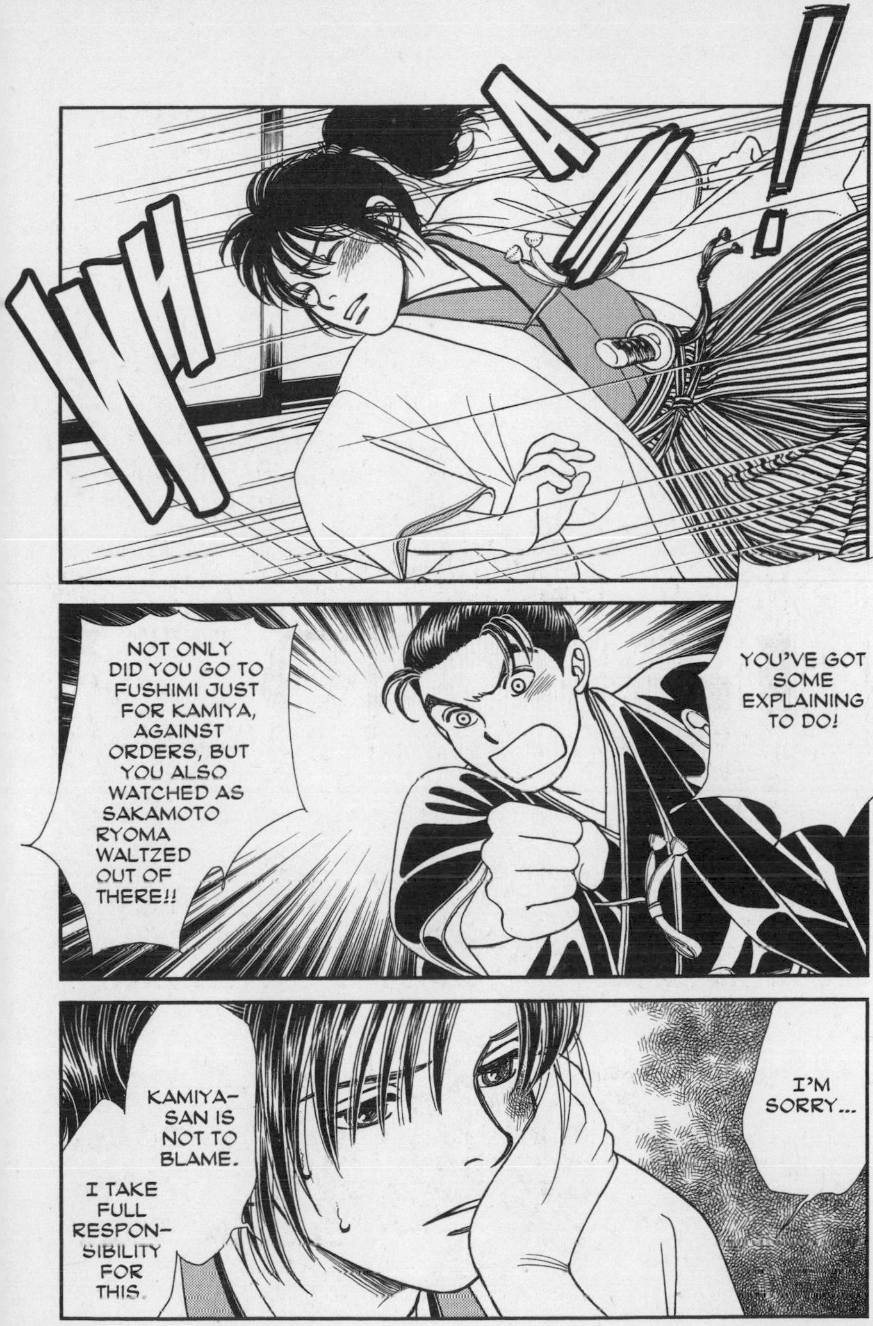
WHA!!
YOU'VE GOT SOME EXPLAINING TO DO!
NOT ONLY DID YOU GO TO FUSHIMI JUST FOR KAMIYA, AGAINST ORDERS, BUT YOU ALSO WATCHED AS SAKAMOTO RYOMA WALTZED OUT OF THERE!!
I'M SORRY...
KAMIYA-SAN IS NOT TO BLAME.
I TAKE FULL RESPON-SIBILITY FOR THIS.

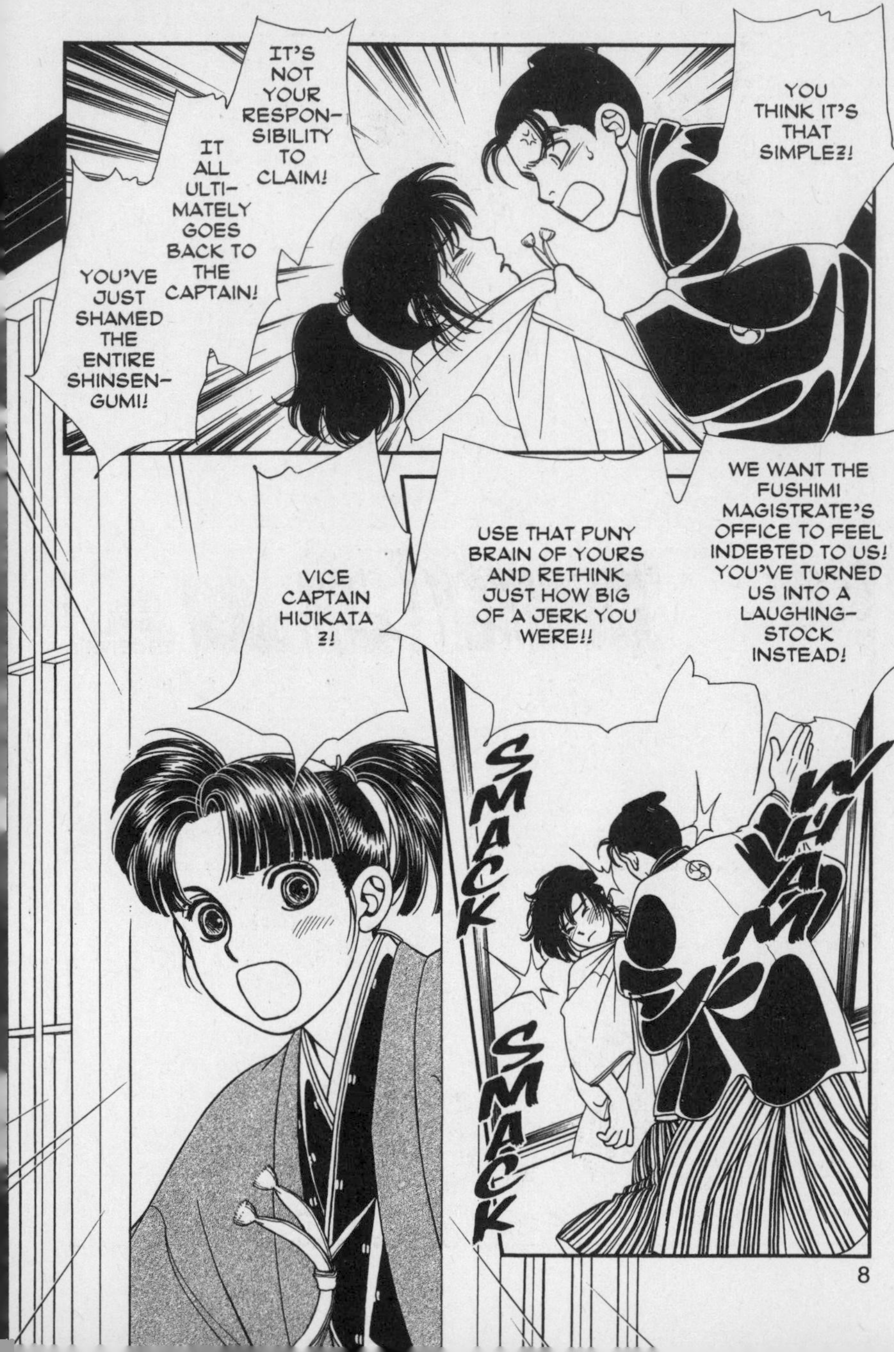
YOU THINK IT'S THAT SIMPLE?!
IT'S NOT YOUR RESPONSIBILITY TO CLAIM!
IT ALL ULTIMATELY GOES BACK TO THE CAPTAIN!
YOU'VE JUST SHAMED THE ENTIRE SHINSENGUMI!
WE WANT THE FUSHIMI MAGISTRATE'S OFFICE TO FEEL INDEBTED TO US! YOU'VE TURNED US INTO A LAUGHINGSTOCK INSTEAD!
USE THAT PUNY BRAIN OF YOURS AND RETHINK JUST HOW BIG OF A JERK YOU WERE!!
WHAM
SMACK
SMACK
VICE CAPTAIN HIJIKATA?!

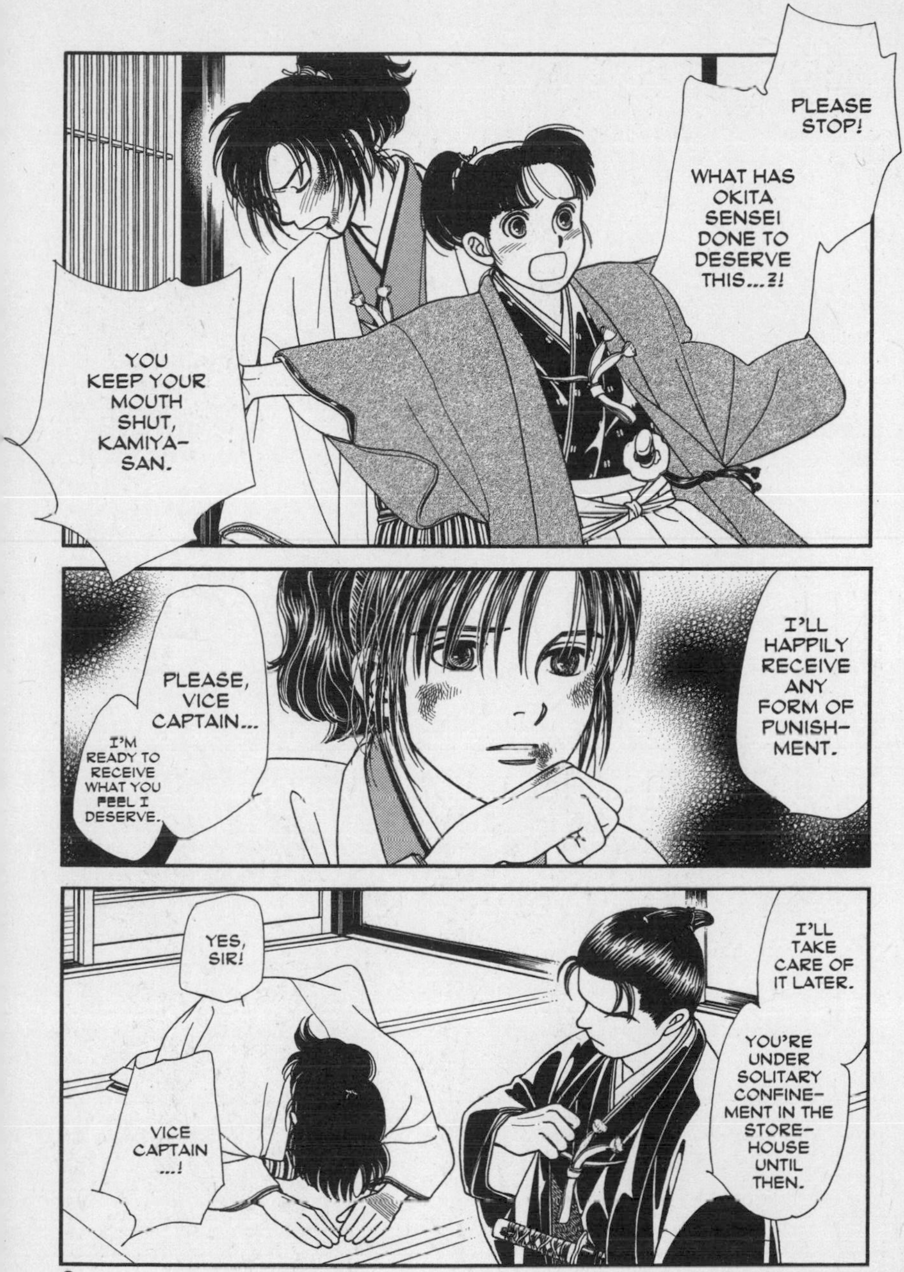
PLEASE STOP!
WHAT HAS OKITA SENSEI DONE TO DESERVE THIS...?!
YOU KEEP YOUR MOUTH SHUT, KAMIYA-SAN.
I'LL HAPPILY RECEIVE ANY FORM OF PUNISHMENT.
PLEASE, VICE CAPTAIN...
I'M READY TO RECEIVE WHAT YOU FEEL I DESERVE.
I'LL TAKE CARE OF IT LATER.
YOU'RE UNDER SOLITARY CONFINEMENT IN THE STOREHOUSE UNTIL THEN.
YES, SIR!
VICE CAPTAIN...!

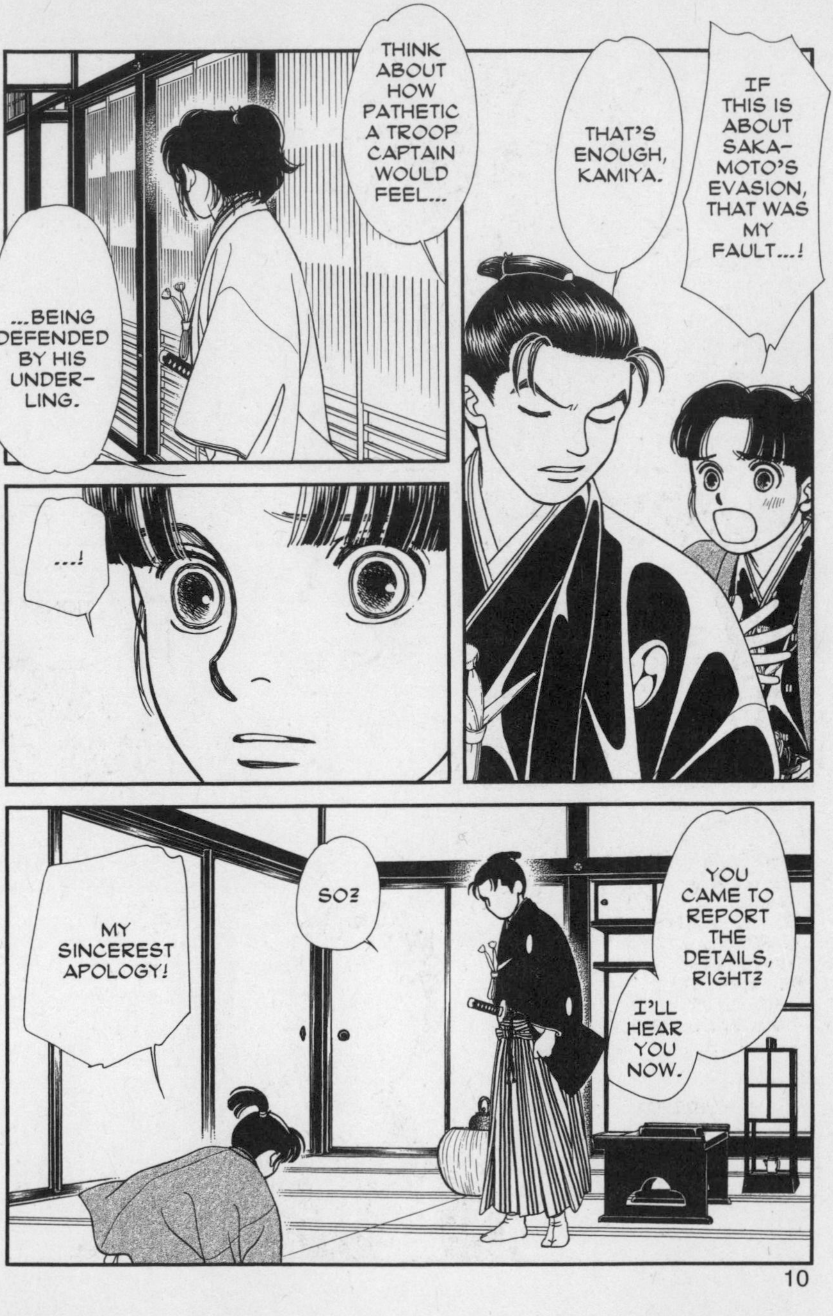
IF THIS IS ABOUT SAKA-MOTO'S EVASION, THAT WAS MY FAULT...!
THAT'S ENOUGH, KAMIYA.
THINK ABOUT HOW PATHETIC A TROOP CAPTAIN WOULD FEEL...
...BEING DEFENDED BY HIS UNDER-LING.
...!
YOU CAME TO REPORT THE DETAILS, RIGHT?
I'LL HEAR YOU NOW.
SO?
MY SINCEREST APOLOGY!

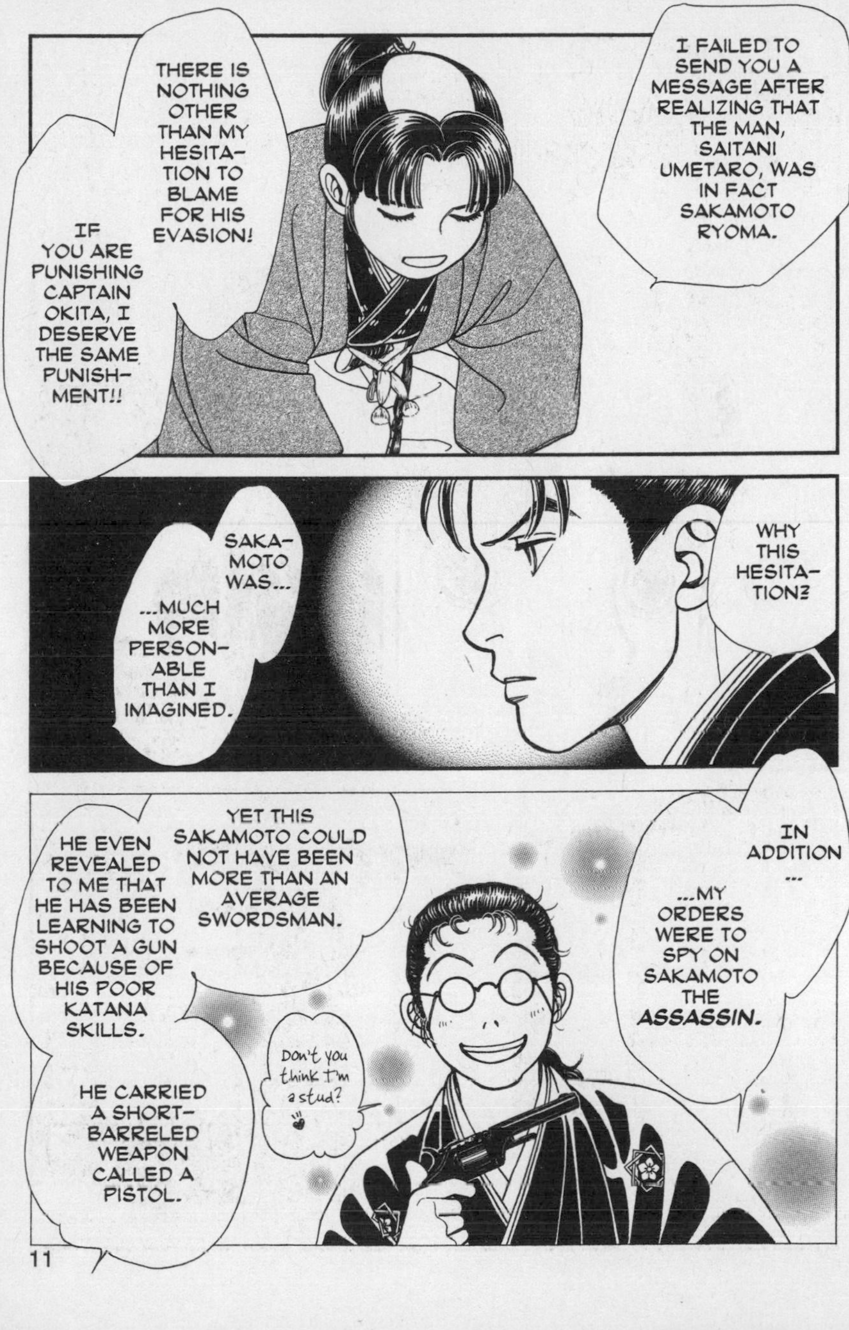
I FAILED TO SEND YOU A MESSAGE AFTER REALIZING THAT THE MAN, SAITANI UMETARO, WAS IN FACT SAKAMOTO RYOMA.
THERE IS NOTHING OTHER THAN MY HESITATION TO BLAME FOR HIS EVASION!
IF YOU ARE PUNISHING CAPTAIN OKITA, I DESERVE THE SAME PUNISHMENT!!
WHY THIS HESITATION?
SAKAMOTO WAS...
...MUCH MORE PERSONABLE THAN I IMAGINED.
IN ADDITION...
...MY ORDERS WERE TO SPY ON SAKAMOTO THE **ASSASSIN.**
YET THIS SAKAMOTO COULD NOT HAVE BEEN MORE THAN AN AVERAGE SWORDSMAN.
HE EVEN REVEALED TO ME THAT HE HAS BEEN LEARNING TO SHOOT A GUN BECAUSE OF HIS POOR KATANA SKILLS.
Don't you think I'm a stud?
HE CARRIED A SHORT-BARRELED WEAPON CALLED A PISTOL.

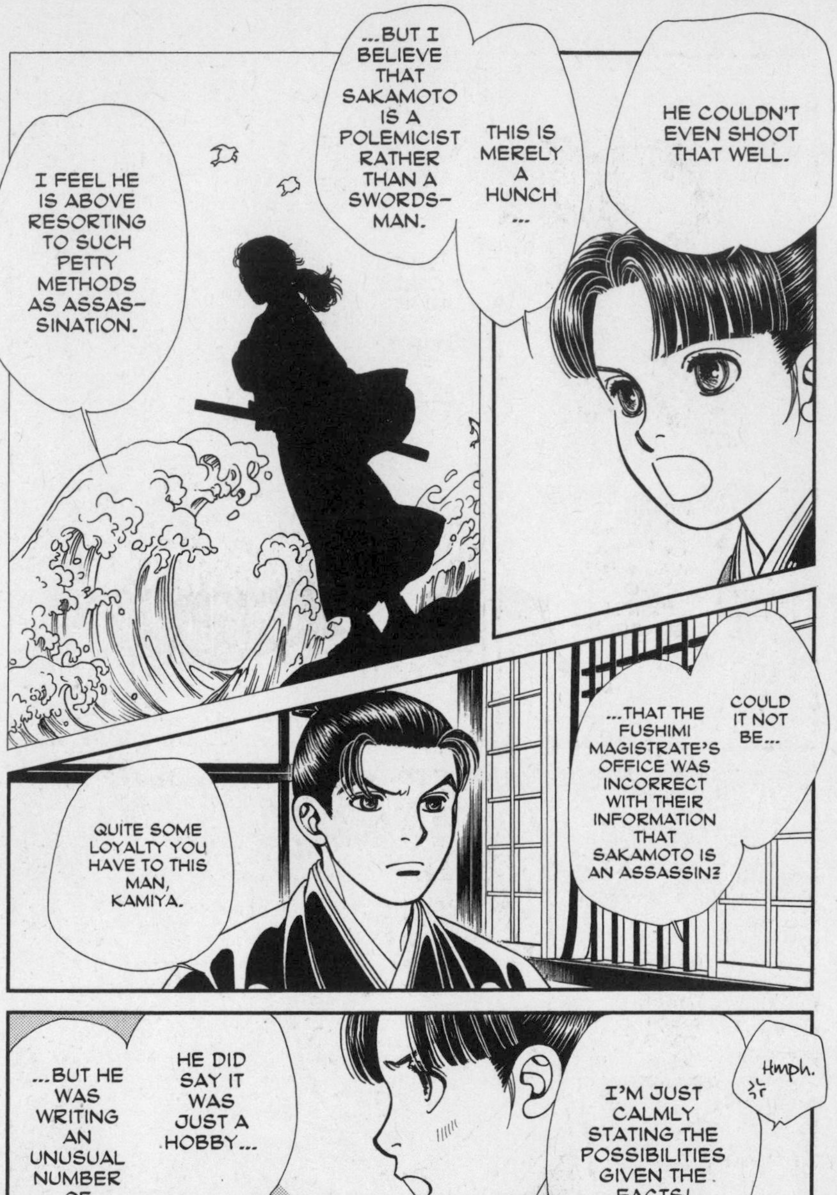
HE COULDN'T EVEN SHOOT THAT WELL.
THIS IS MERELY A HUNCH...
...BUT I BELIEVE THAT SAKAMOTO IS A POLEMICIST RATHER THAN A SWORDS-MAN.
I FEEL HE IS ABOVE RESORTING TO SUCH PETTY METHODS AS ASSAS-SINATION.
COULD IT NOT BE...
...THAT THE FUSHIMI MAGISTRATE'S OFFICE WAS INCORRECT WITH THEIR INFORMATION THAT SAKAMOTO IS AN ASSASSIN?
QUITE SOME LOYALTY YOU HAVE TO THIS MAN, KAMIYA.
Hmph.
I'M JUST CALMLY STATING THE POSSIBILITIES GIVEN THE FACTS!
HE DID SAY IT WAS JUST A HOBBY...
...BUT HE WAS WRITING AN UNUSUAL NUMBER OF LETTERS.

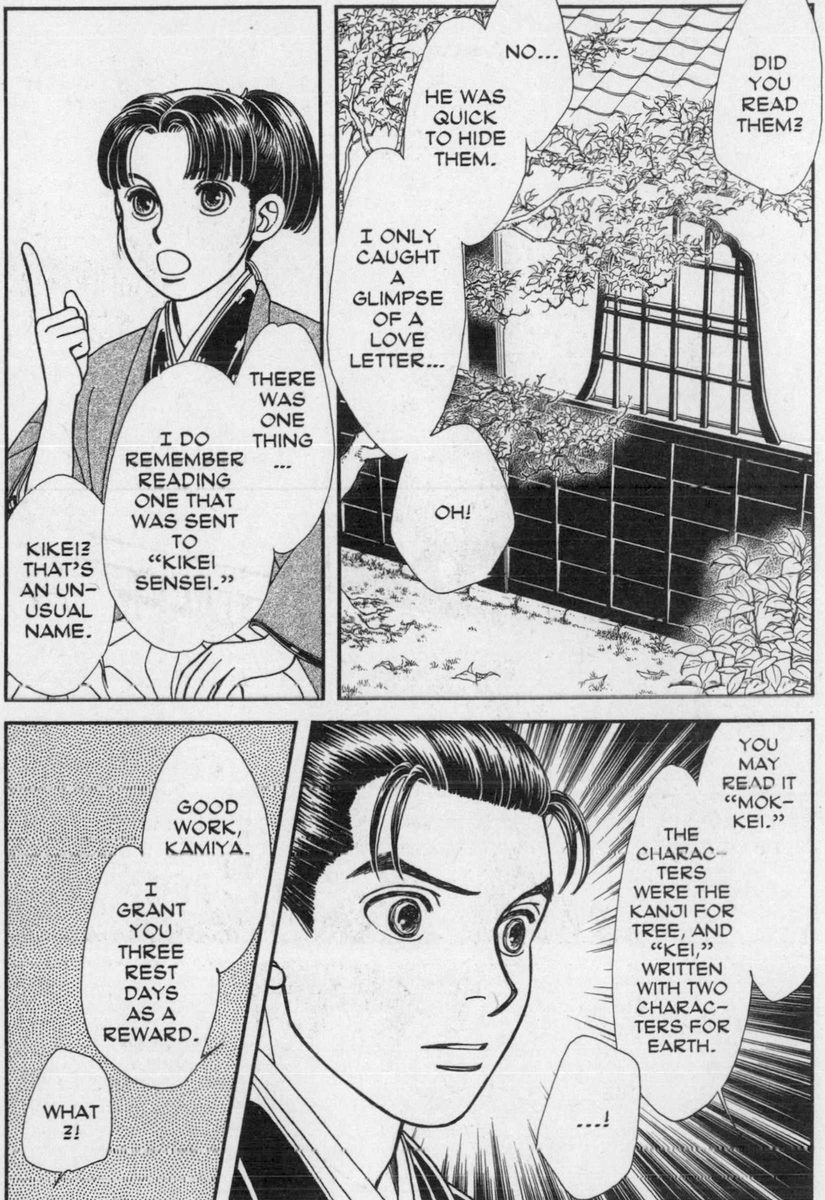
DID YOU READ THEM?
NO...
HE WAS QUICK TO HIDE THEM.
I ONLY CAUGHT A GLIMPSE OF A LOVE LETTER...
OH!
THERE WAS ONE THING...
I DO REMEMBER READING ONE THAT WAS SENT TO "KIKEI SENSEI."
KIKEI? THAT'S AN UN-USUAL NAME.
YOU MAY READ IT "MOK-KEI."
THE CHARAC-TERS WERE THE KANJI FOR TREE, AND "KEI," WRITTEN WITH TWO CHARAC-TERS FOR EARTH.
...!
GOOD WORK, KAMIYA.
I GRANT YOU THREE REST DAYS AS A REWARD.
WHAT?!

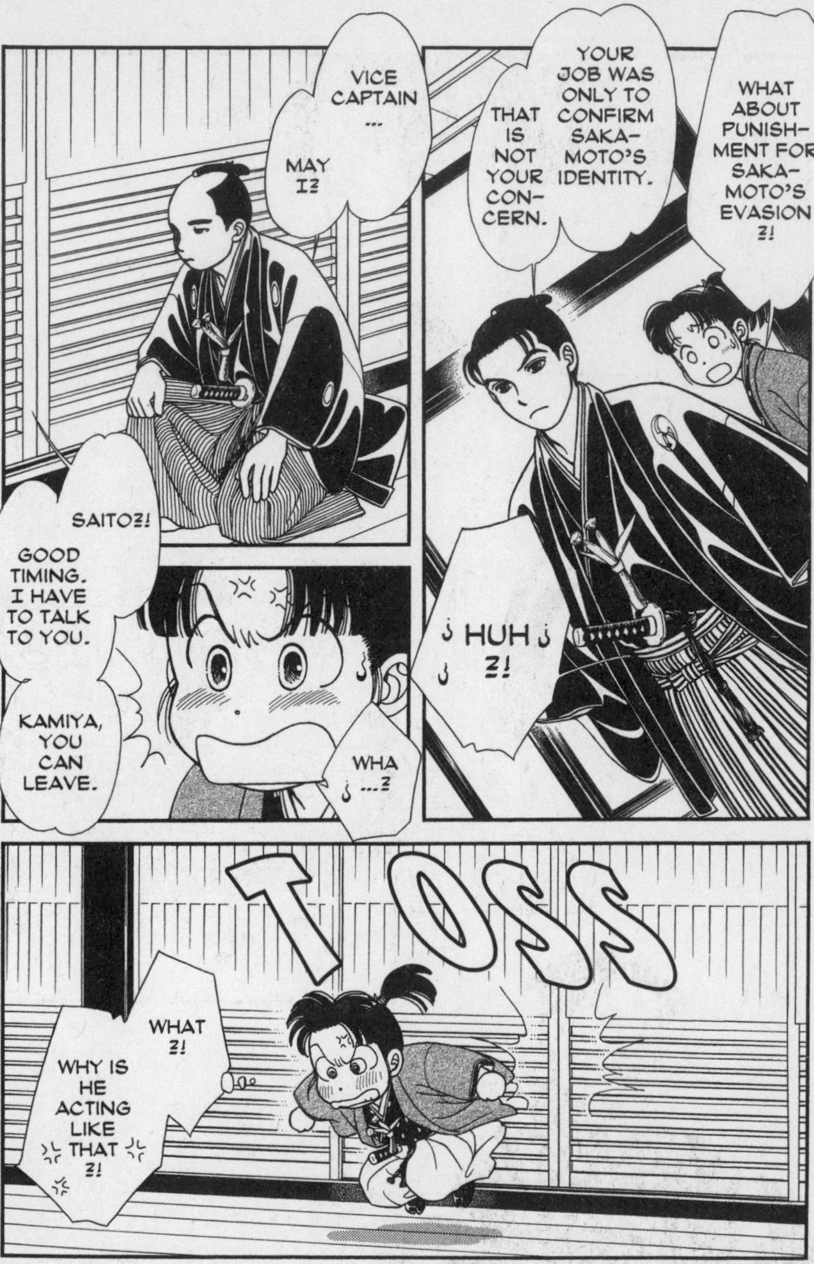
WHAT ABOUT PUNISHMENT FOR SAKAMOTO'S EVASION?!
YOUR JOB WAS ONLY TO CONFIRM SAKAMOTO'S IDENTITY.
THAT IS NOT YOUR CONCERN.
HUH?!
VICE CAPTAIN... MAY I?
SAITO?!
GOOD TIMING. I HAVE TO TALK TO YOU.
KAMIYA, YOU CAN LEAVE.
WHA...?
TOSS
WHAT?!
WHY IS HE ACTING LIKE THAT?!

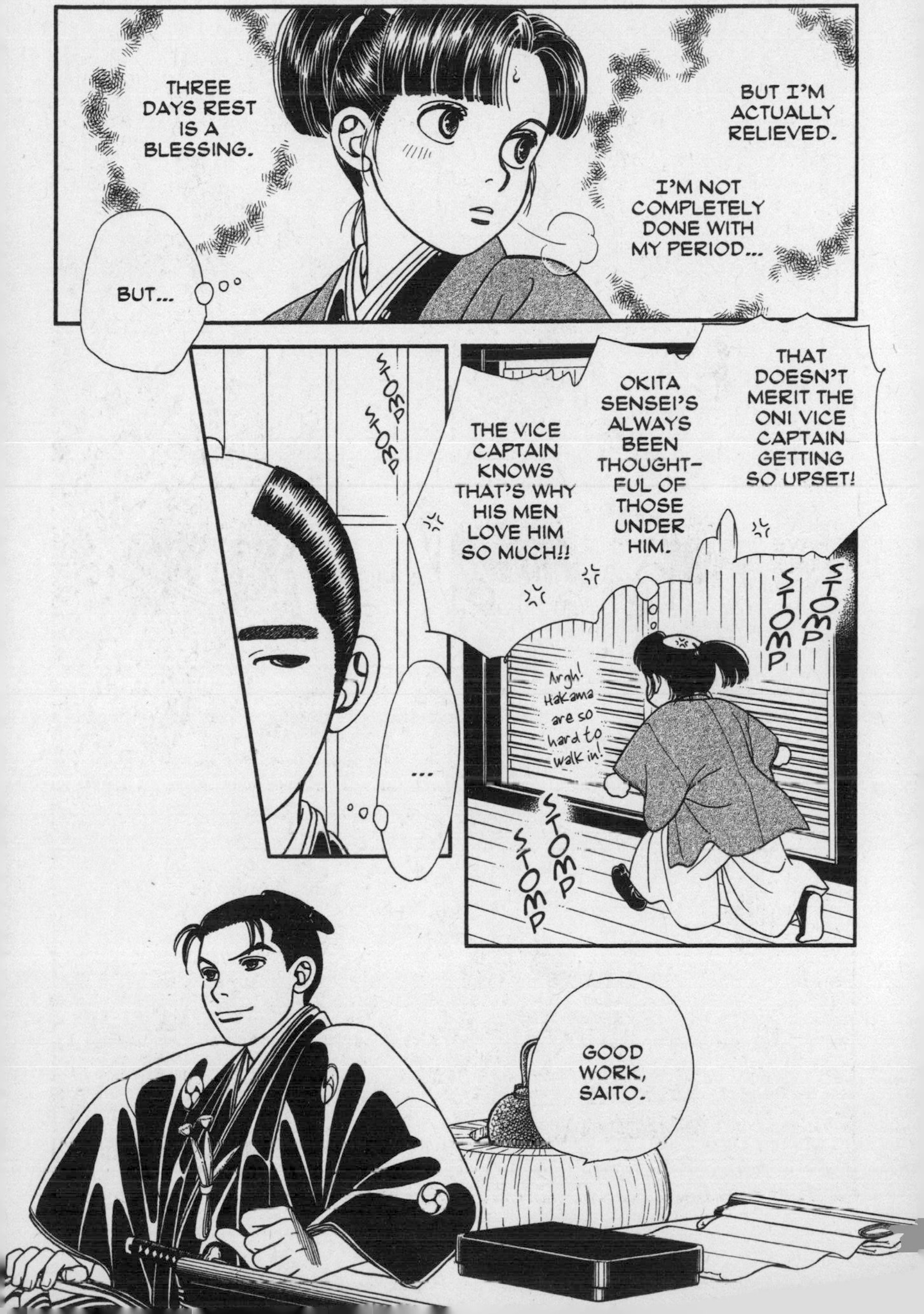
BUT I'M ACTUALLY RELIEVED.
I'M NOT COMPLETELY DONE WITH MY PERIOD...
THREE DAYS REST IS A BLESSING.
BUT...
THAT DOESN'T MERIT THE ONI VICE CAPTAIN GETTING SO UPSET!
OKITA SENSEI'S ALWAYS BEEN THOUGHTFUL OF THOSE UNDER HIM.
THE VICE CAPTAIN KNOWS THAT'S WHY HIS MEN LOVE HIM SO MUCH!!
STOMP STOMP
Argh! Hakama are so hard to walk in!
STOMP STOMP
STOMP STOMP
...
GOOD WORK, SAITO.

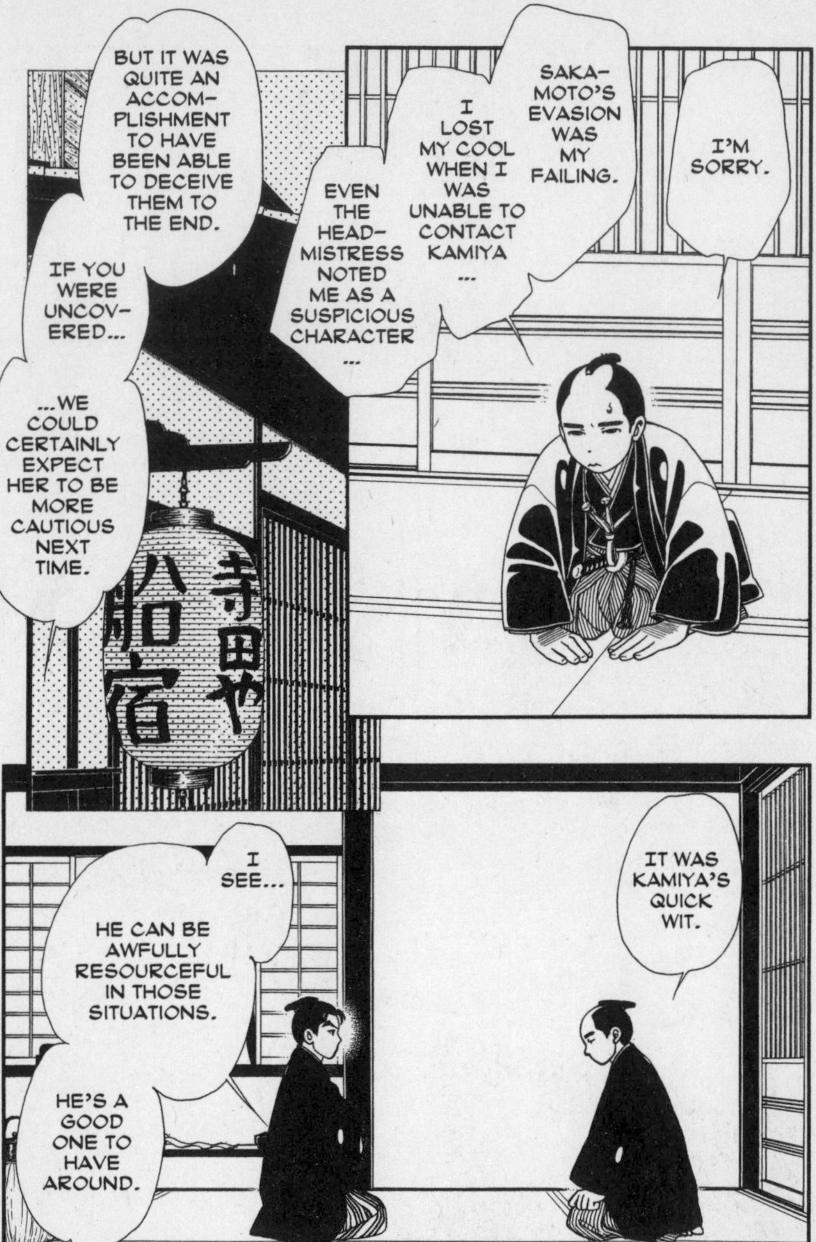
I'M SORRY.
SAKAMOTO'S EVASION WAS MY FAILING.
I LOST MY COOL WHEN I WAS UNABLE TO CONTACT KAMIYA...
EVEN THE HEADMISTRESS NOTED ME AS A SUSPICIOUS CHARACTER...
BUT IT WAS QUITE AN ACCOMPLISHMENT TO HAVE BEEN ABLE TO DECEIVE THEM TO THE END.
IF YOU WERE UNCOVERED...
...WE COULD CERTAINLY EXPECT HER TO BE MORE CAUTIOUS NEXT TIME.
寺田や
船宿
IT WAS KAMIYA'S QUICK WIT.
I SEE...
HE CAN BE AWFULLY RESOURCEFUL IN THOSE SITUATIONS.
HE'S A GOOD ONE TO HAVE AROUND.

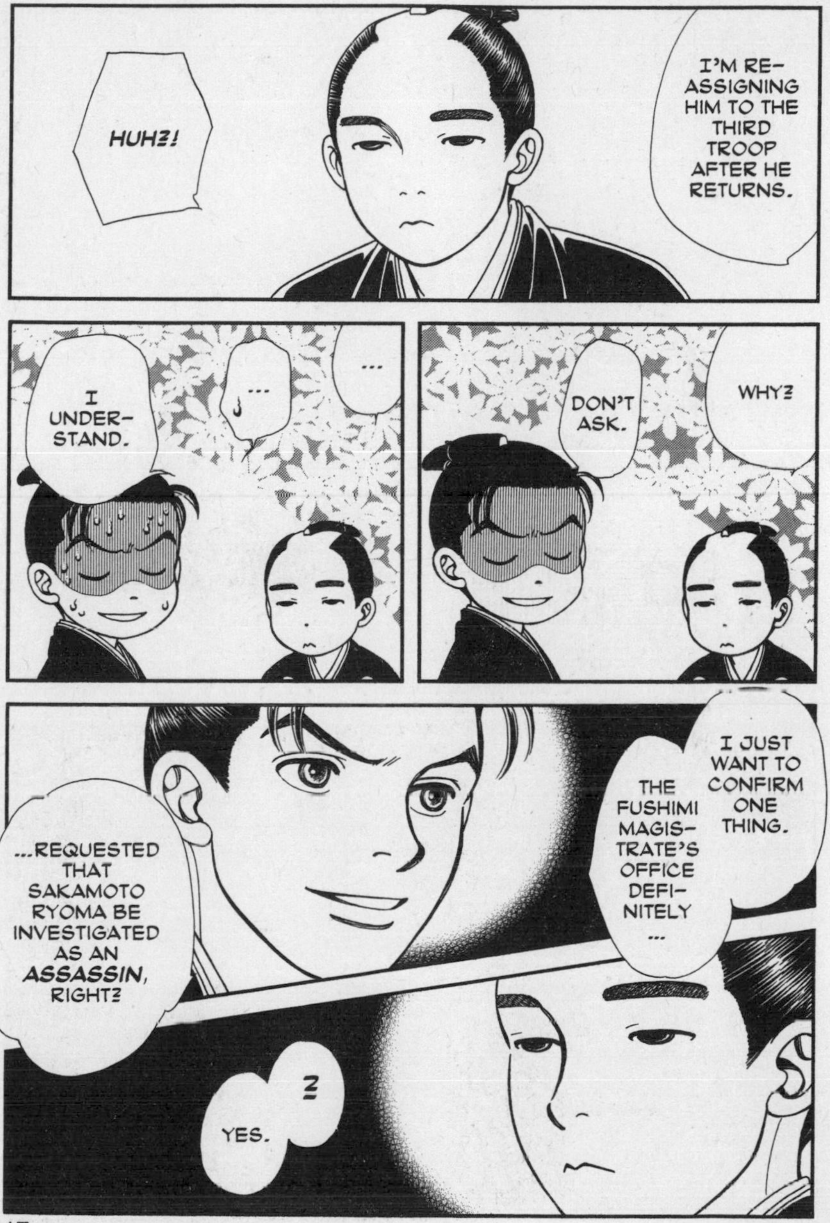
I'M RE-ASSIGNING HIM TO THE THIRD TROOP AFTER HE RETURNS.
HUH?!
WHY?
DON'T ASK.
...
...
I UNDER-STAND.
I JUST WANT TO CONFIRM ONE THING.
THE FUSHIMI MAGIS-TRATE'S OFFICE DEFI-NITELY ...
...REQUESTED THAT SAKAMOTO RYOMA BE INVESTIGATED AS AN ASSASSIN, RIGHT?
?
YES.

Ha.
JUST WHEN I WAS WON-DERING WHY THEY WERE SO HUMBLE IN THEIR REQUEST.
THIS IS EXACTLY WHY NO BAKUFU HIGHER-UP CAN BE TRUSTED.

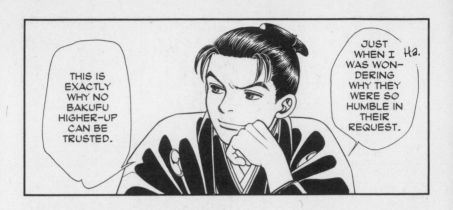

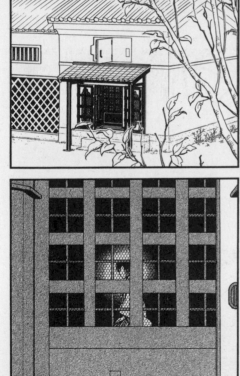

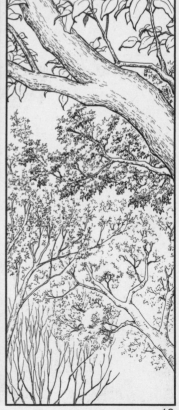

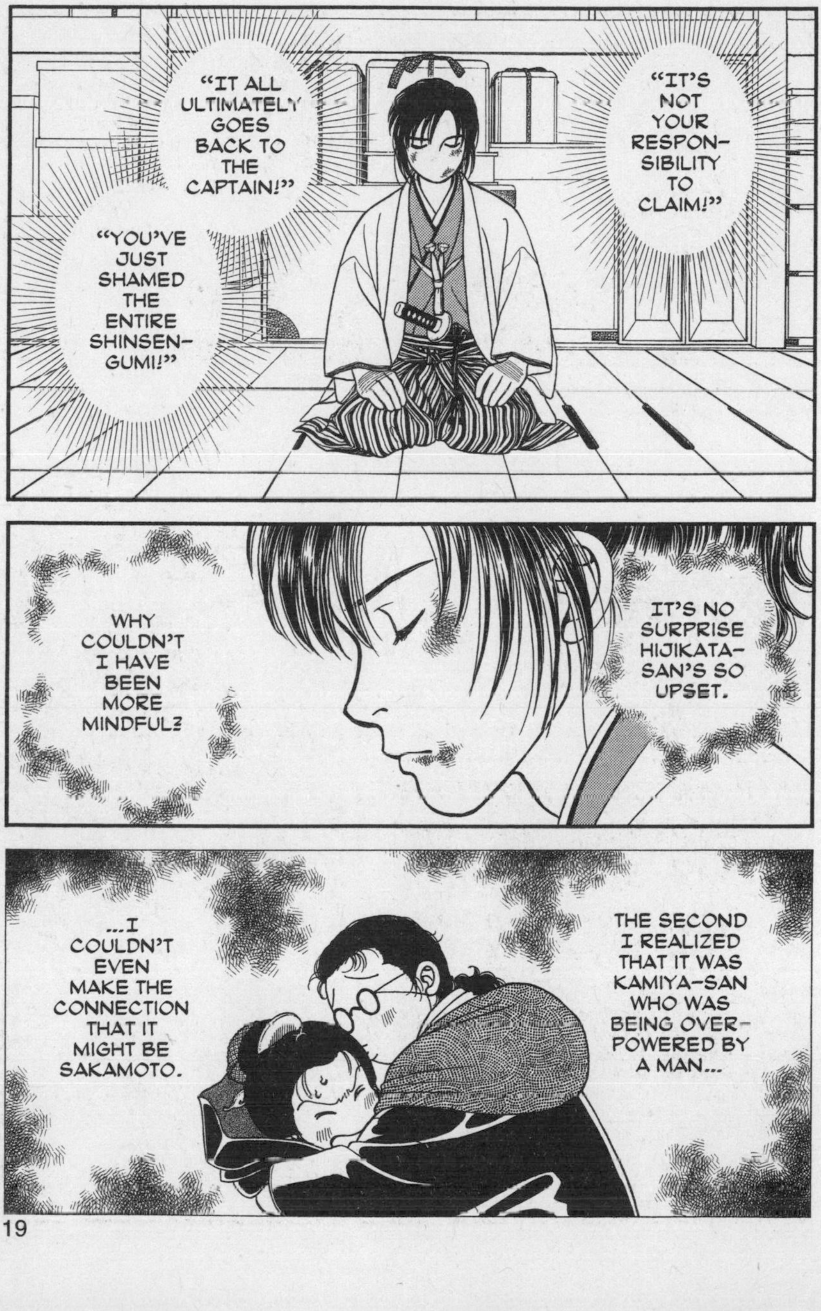
"IT'S NOT YOUR RESPON-SIBILITY TO CLAIM!"
"IT ALL ULTIMATELY GOES BACK TO THE CAPTAIN!"
"YOU'VE JUST SHAMED THE ENTIRE SHINSEN-GUMI!"
IT'S NO SURPRISE HIJIKATA-SAN'S SO UPSET.
WHY COULDN'T I HAVE BEEN MORE MINDFUL?
THE SECOND I REALIZED THAT IT WAS KAMIYA-SAN WHO WAS BEING OVER-POWERED BY A MAN...
...I COULDN'T EVEN MAKE THE CONNECTION THAT IT MIGHT BE SAKAMOTO.

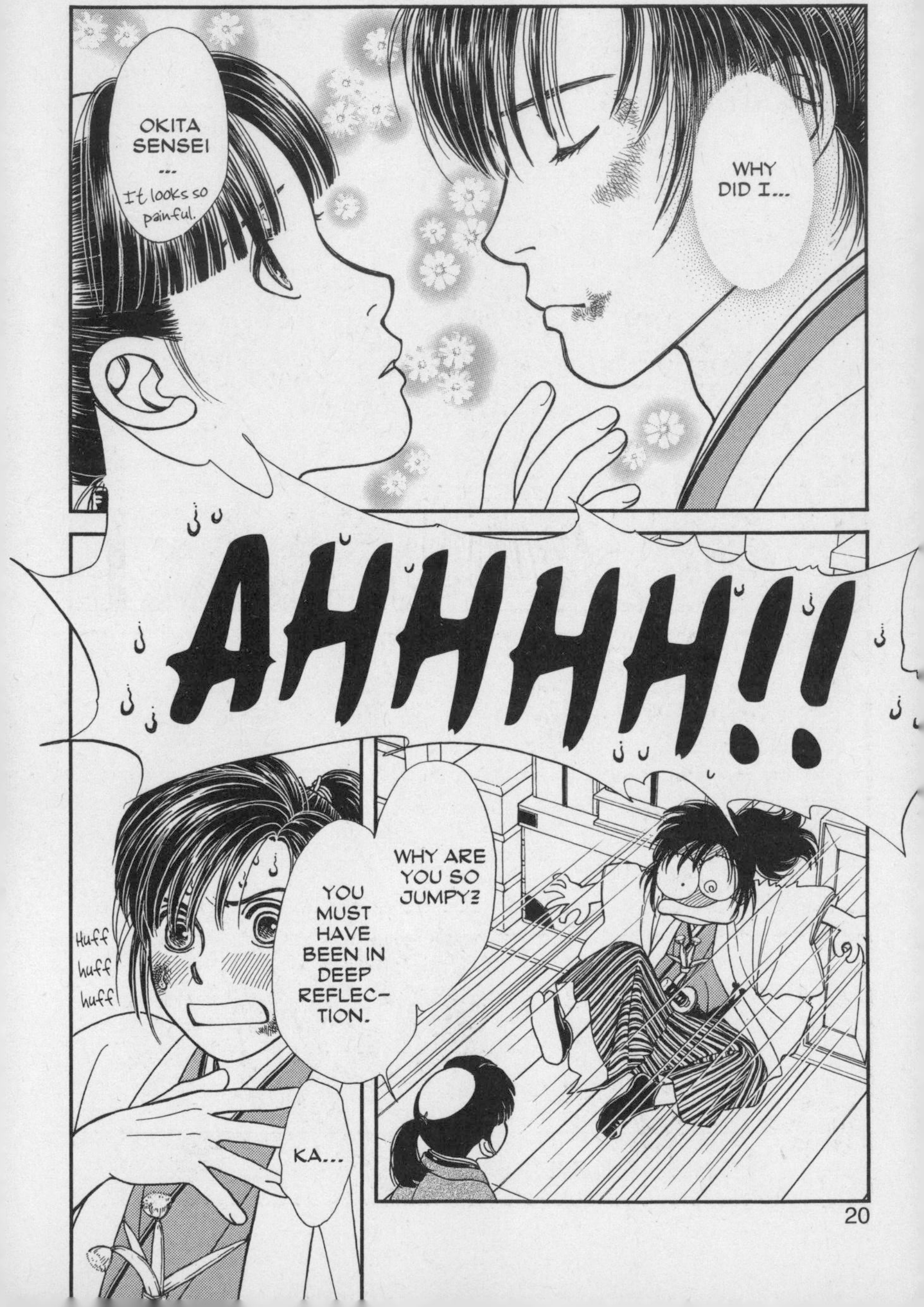
WHY DID I...
OKITA SENSEI
...
It looks so painful.
AHHHH!!
WHY ARE YOU SO JUMPY?
YOU MUST HAVE BEEN IN DEEP REFLECTION.
KA...
Huff huff huff

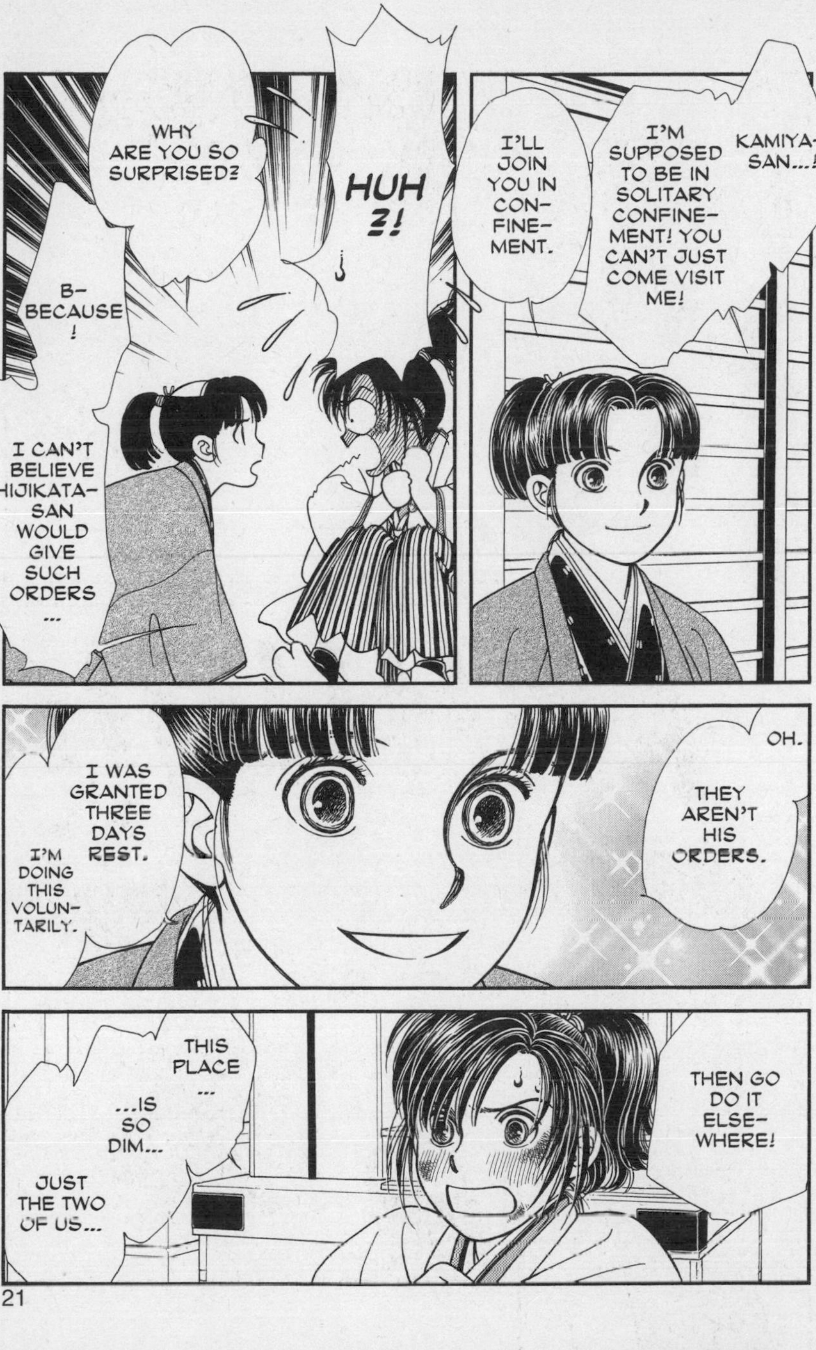
KAMIYA-SAN...!!
I'M SUPPOSED TO BE IN SOLITARY CONFINEMENT! YOU CAN'T JUST COME VISIT ME!
I'LL JOIN YOU IN CONFINEMENT.
HUH ?!
WHY ARE YOU SO SURPRISED?
B-BECAUSE!
I CAN'T BELIEVE HIJIKATA-SAN WOULD GIVE SUCH ORDERS...
OH.
THEY AREN'T HIS ORDERS.
I WAS GRANTED THREE DAYS REST.
I'M DOING THIS VOLUNTARILY.
THEN GO DO IT ELSEWHERE!
THIS PLACE...
...IS SO DIM...
JUST THE TWO OF US...

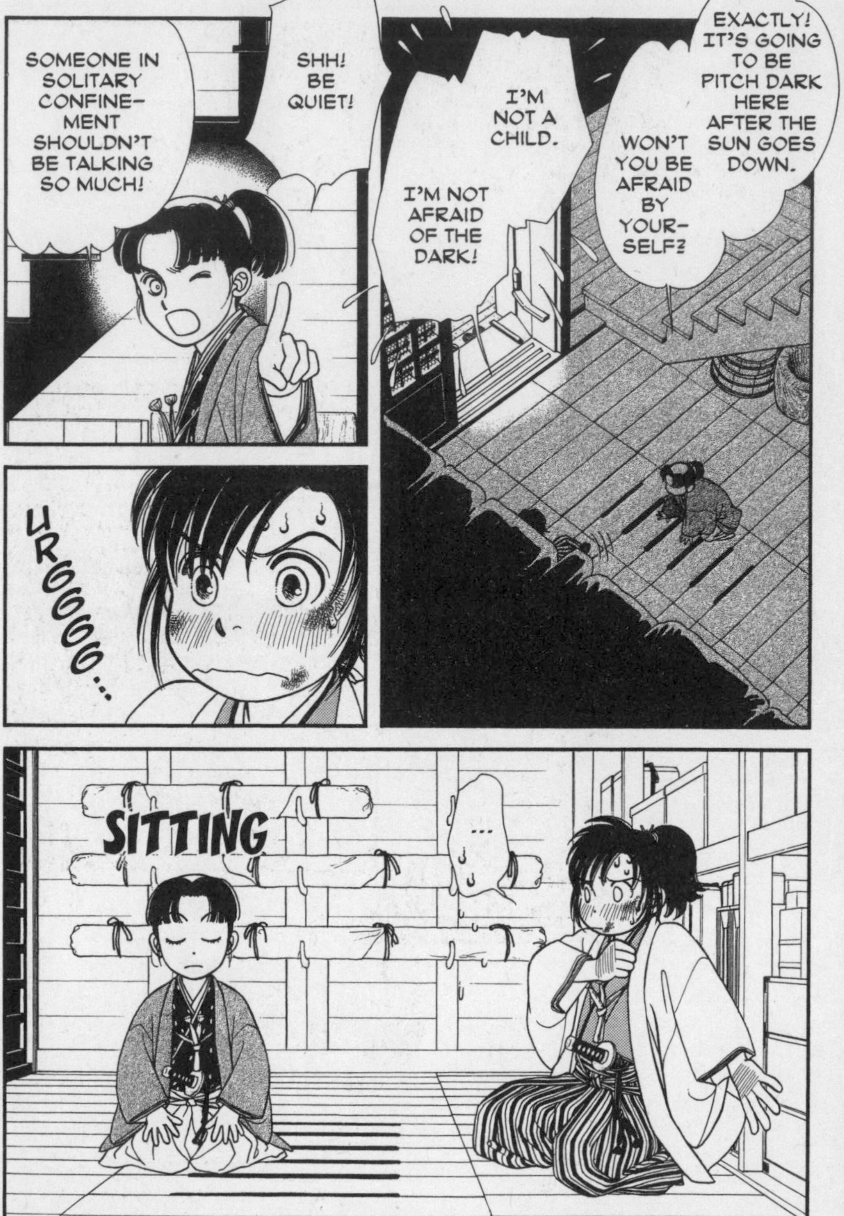
EXACTLY! IT'S GOING TO BE PITCH DARK HERE AFTER THE SUN GOES DOWN.
WON'T YOU BE AFRAID BY YOURSELF?
I'M NOT A CHILD.
I'M NOT AFRAID OF THE DARK!
SHH! BE QUIET!
SOMEONE IN SOLITARY CONFINEMENT SHOULDN'T BE TALKING SO MUCH!
URGGGG...
...
SITTING

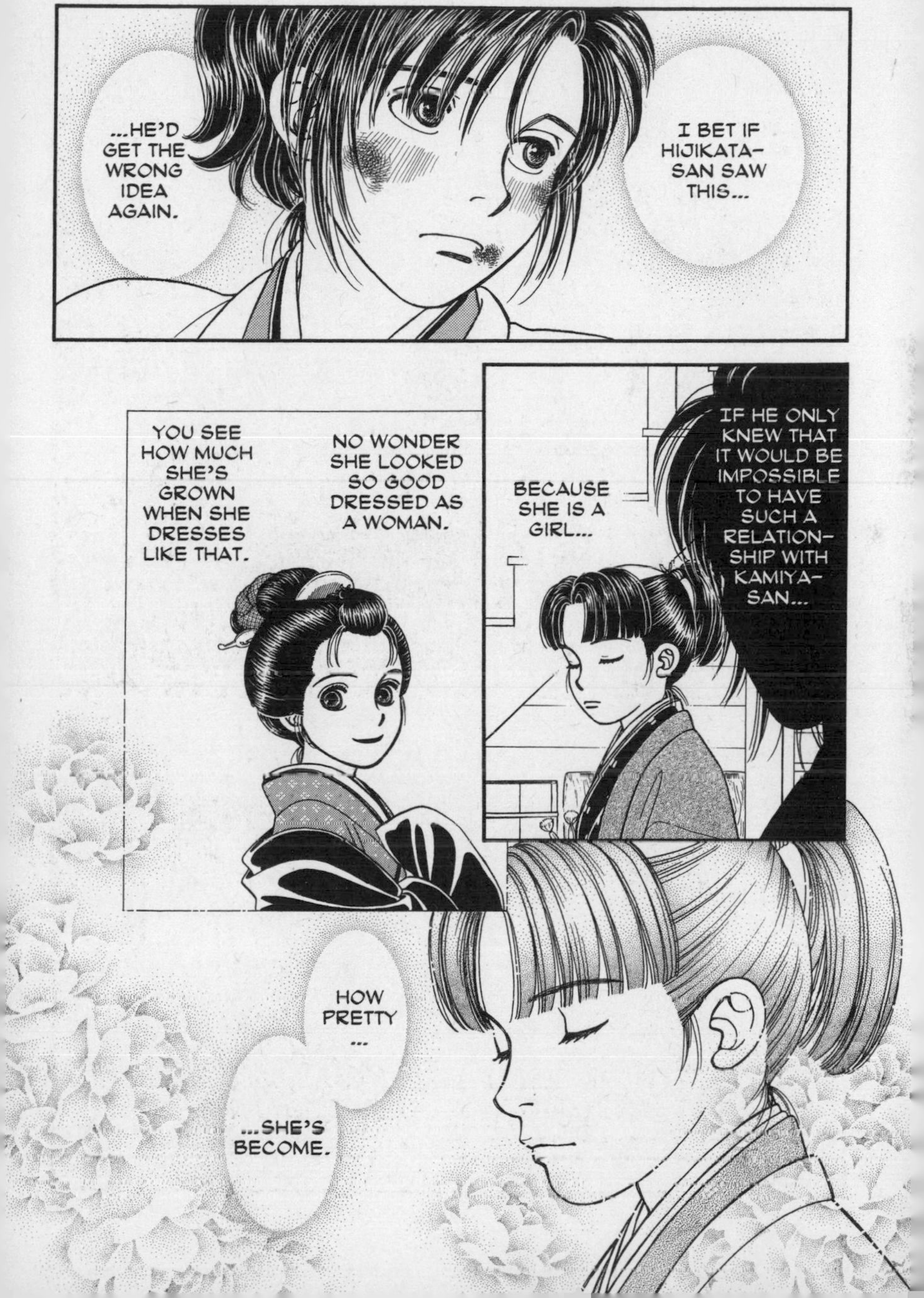
I BET IF HIJIKATA-SAN SAW THIS...
...HE'D GET THE WRONG IDEA AGAIN.
IF HE ONLY KNEW THAT IT WOULD BE IMPOSSIBLE TO HAVE SUCH A RELATIONSHIP WITH KAMIYA-SAN...
BECAUSE SHE IS A GIRL...
NO WONDER SHE LOOKED SO GOOD DRESSED AS A WOMAN.
YOU SEE HOW MUCH SHE'S GROWN WHEN SHE DRESSES LIKE THAT.
HOW PRETTY...
...SHE'S BECOME.

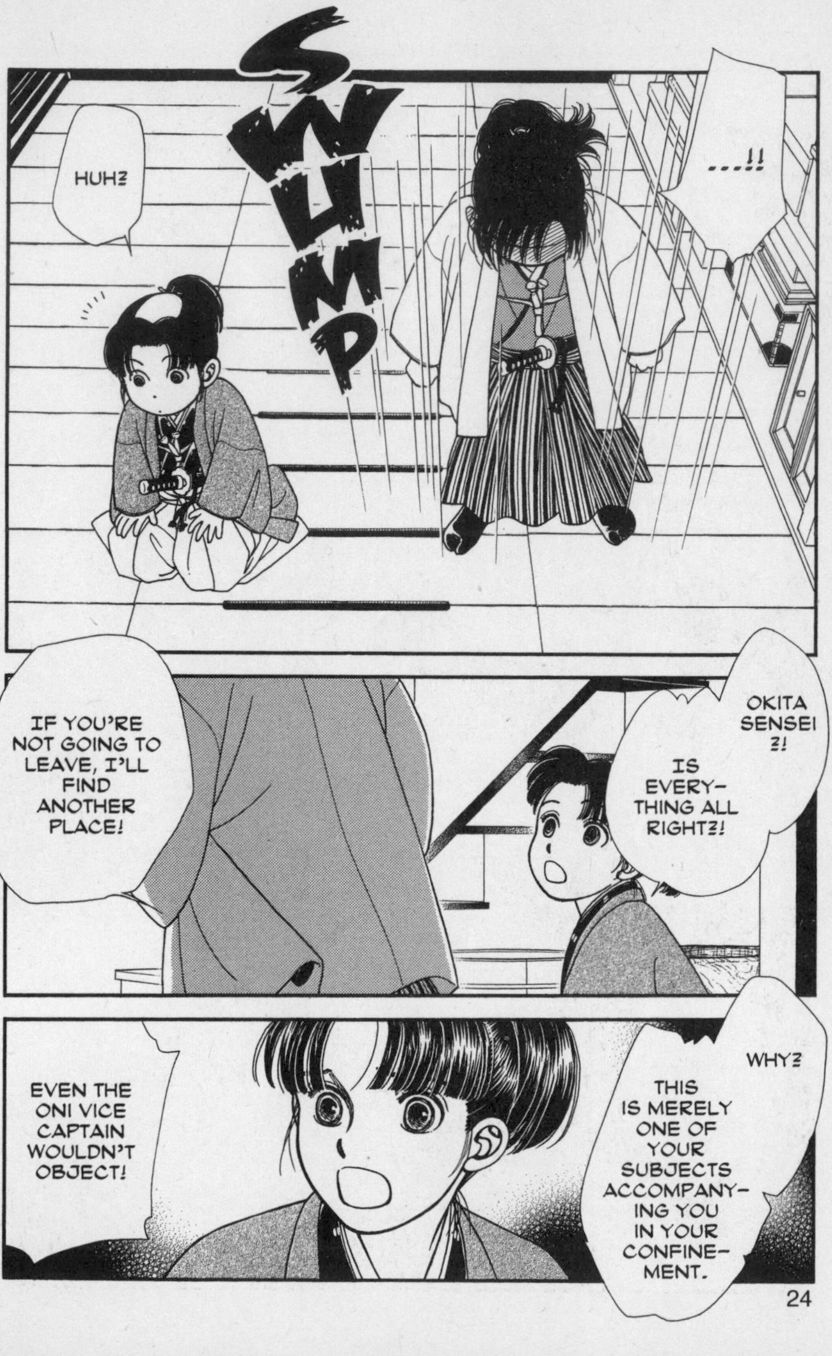
...!!
SWUMP
HUH?
OKITA SENSEI?!
IS EVERYTHING ALL RIGHT?!
IF YOU'RE NOT GOING TO LEAVE, I'LL FIND ANOTHER PLACE!
WHY?
THIS IS MERELY ONE OF YOUR SUBJECTS ACCOMPANYING YOU IN YOUR CONFINEMENT.
EVEN THE ONI VICE CAPTAIN WOULDN'T OBJECT!

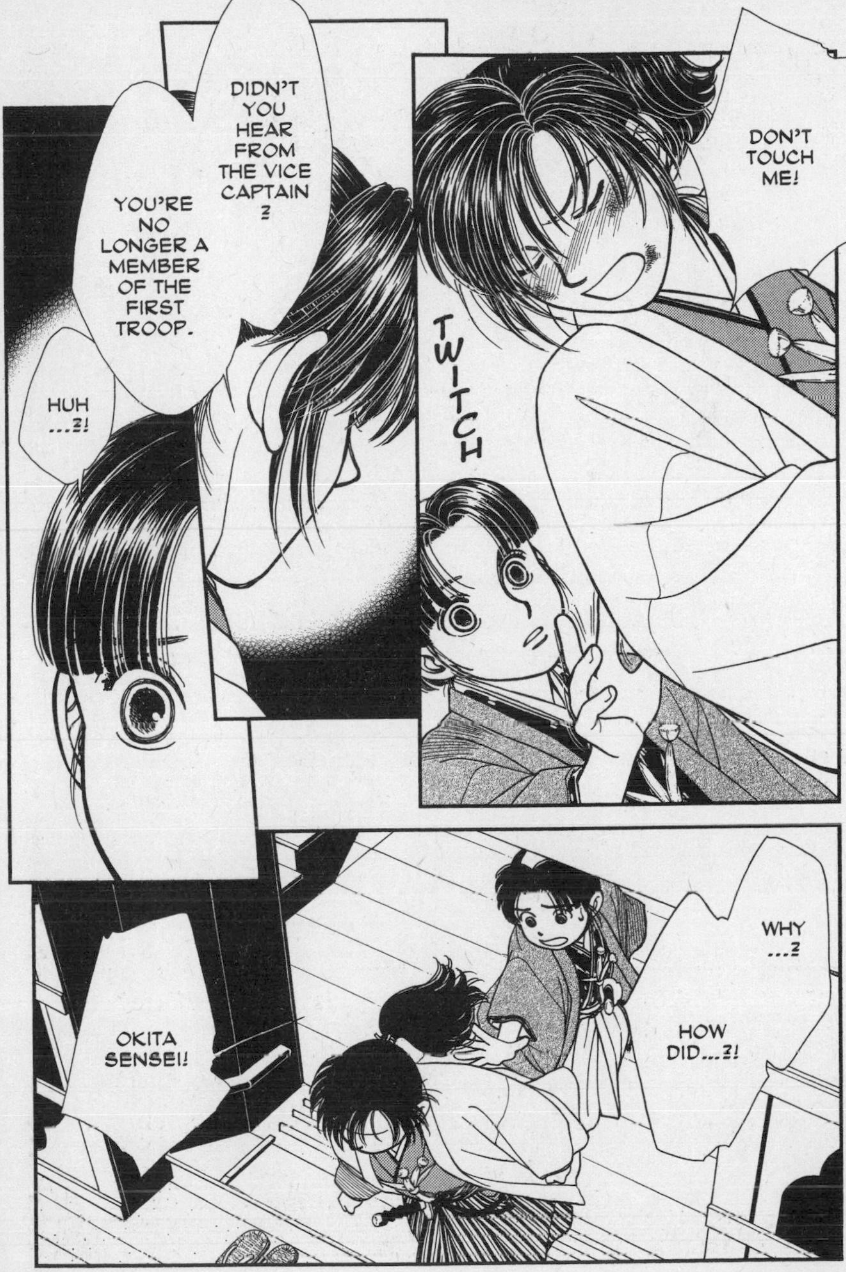
DON'T TOUCH ME!
TWITCH
DIDN'T YOU HEAR FROM THE VICE CAPTAIN ?
YOU'RE NO LONGER A MEMBER OF THE FIRST TROOP.
HUH ...?!
WHY ...?
HOW DID...?!
OKITA SENSEI!

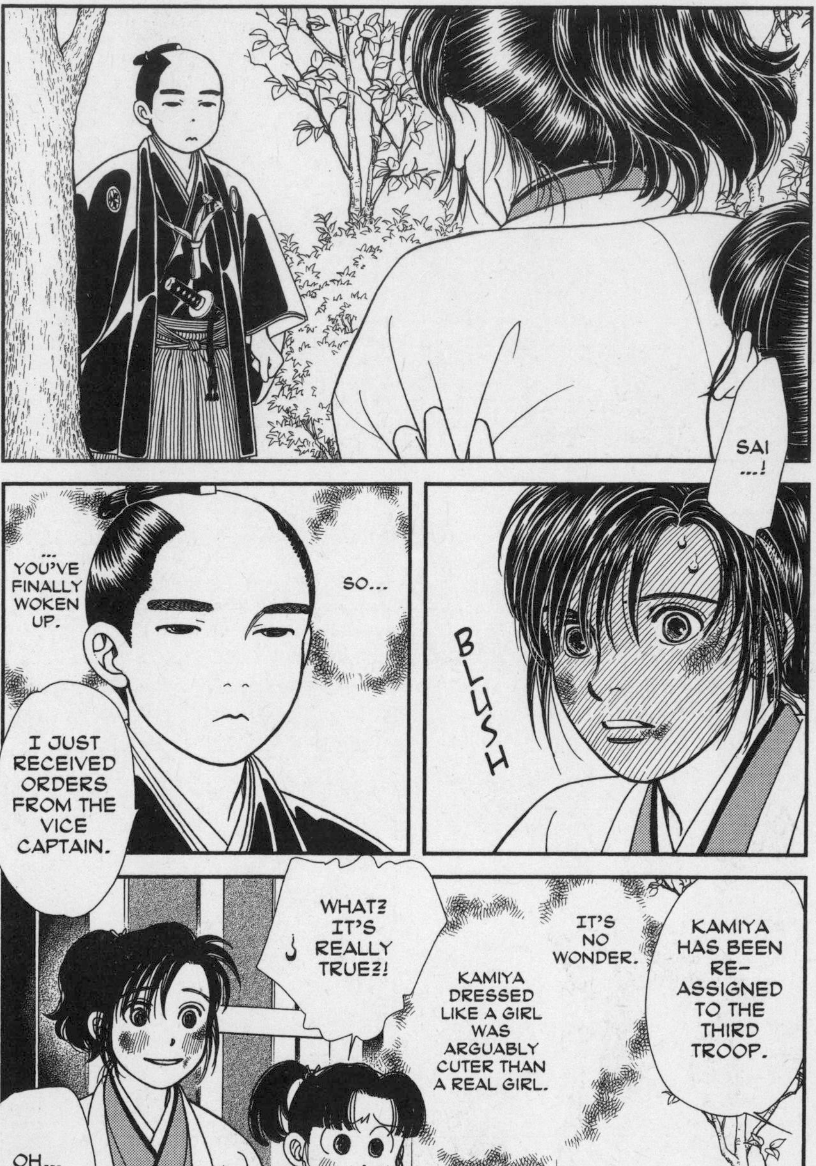
SAI ...!
BLUSH
SO...
... YOU'VE FINALLY WOKEN UP.
I JUST RECEIVED ORDERS FROM THE VICE CAPTAIN.
KAMIYA HAS BEEN RE-ASSIGNED TO THE THIRD TROOP.
IT'S NO WONDER.
KAMIYA DRESSED LIKE A GIRL WAS ARGUABLY CUTER THAN A REAL GIRL.
WHAT? IT'S REALLY TRUE?!
OH... I SEE...

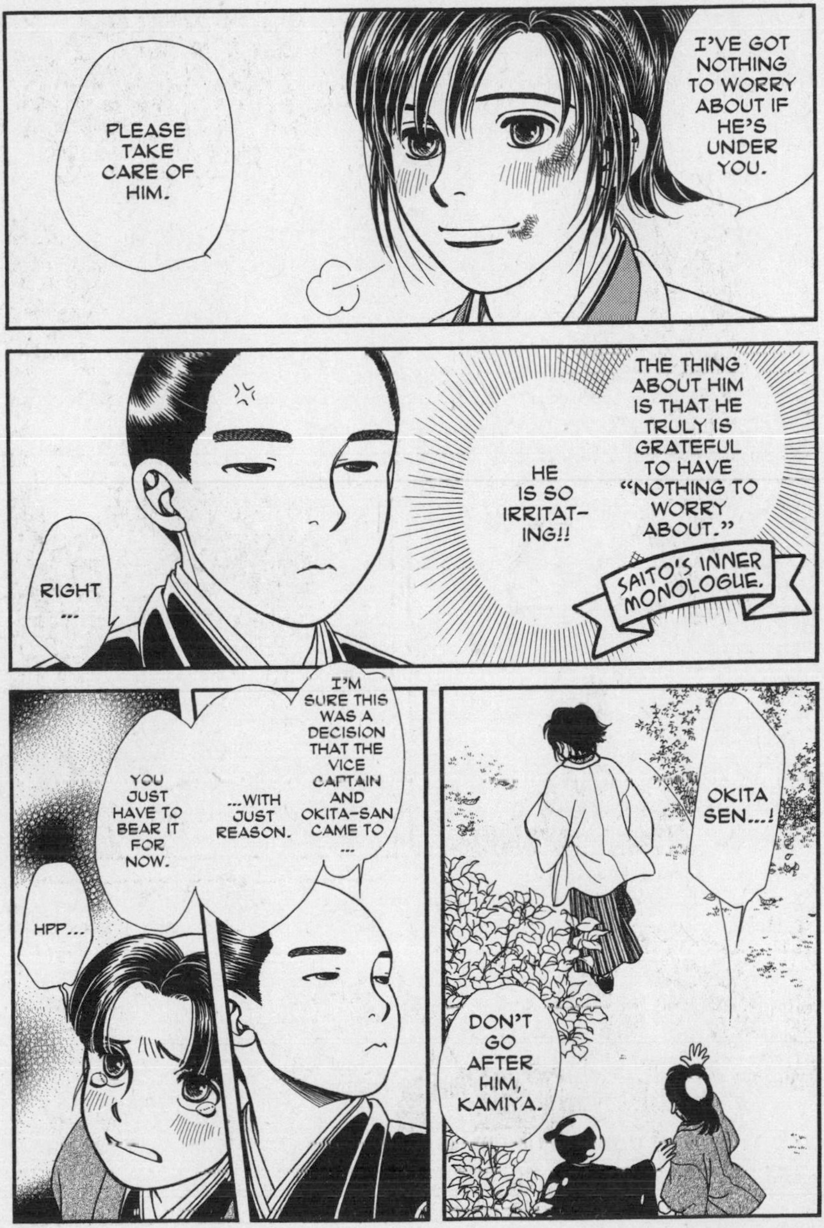
I'VE GOT NOTHING TO WORRY ABOUT IF HE'S UNDER YOU.
PLEASE TAKE CARE OF HIM.
THE THING ABOUT HIM IS THAT HE TRULY IS GRATEFUL TO HAVE "NOTHING TO WORRY ABOUT."
HE IS SO IRRITAT-ING!!
SAITO'S INNER MONOLOGUE.
RIGHT...
OKITA SEN...!
DON'T GO AFTER HIM, KAMIYA.
I'M SURE THIS WAS A DECISION THAT THE VICE CAPTAIN AND OKITA-SAN CAME TO...
...WITH JUST REASON.
YOU JUST HAVE TO BEAR IT FOR NOW.
HPP...

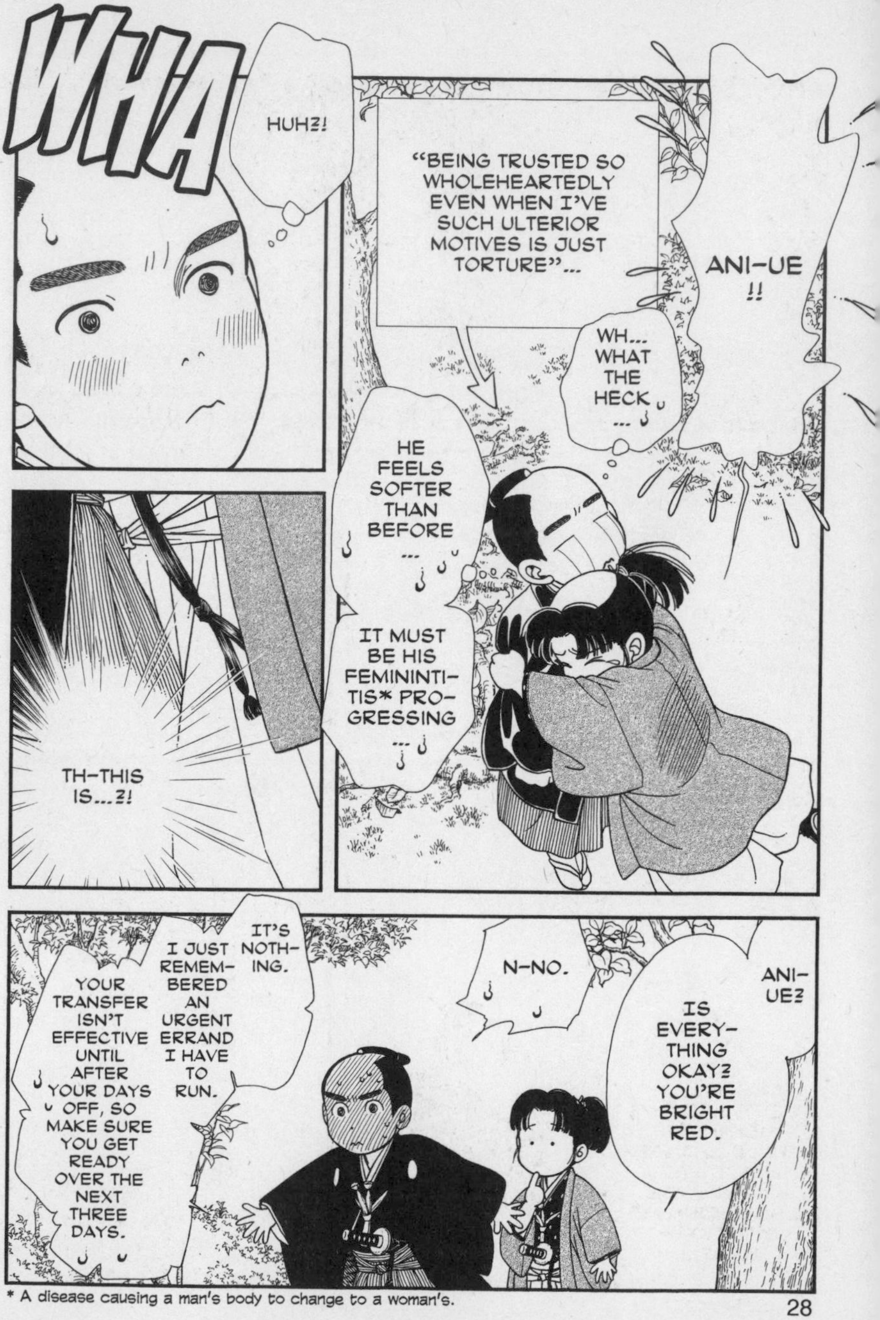
ANI-UE !!
"BEING TRUSTED SO WHOLEHEARTEDLY EVEN WHEN I'VE SUCH ULTERIOR MOTIVES IS JUST TORTURE"...
WH... WHAT THE HECK ...
HE FEELS SOFTER THAN BEFORE ...
IT MUST BE HIS FEMININTITIS* PROGRESSING ...
HUH?!
WHA
TH-THIS IS...?!
ANI-UE?
IS EVERYTHING OKAY? YOU'RE BRIGHT RED.
N-NO.
IT'S NOTHING.
I JUST REMEMBERED AN URGENT ERRAND I HAVE TO RUN.
YOUR TRANSFER ISN'T EFFECTIVE UNTIL AFTER YOUR DAYS OFF, SO MAKE SURE YOU GET READY OVER THE NEXT THREE DAYS.

* A disease causing a man's body to change to a woman's.

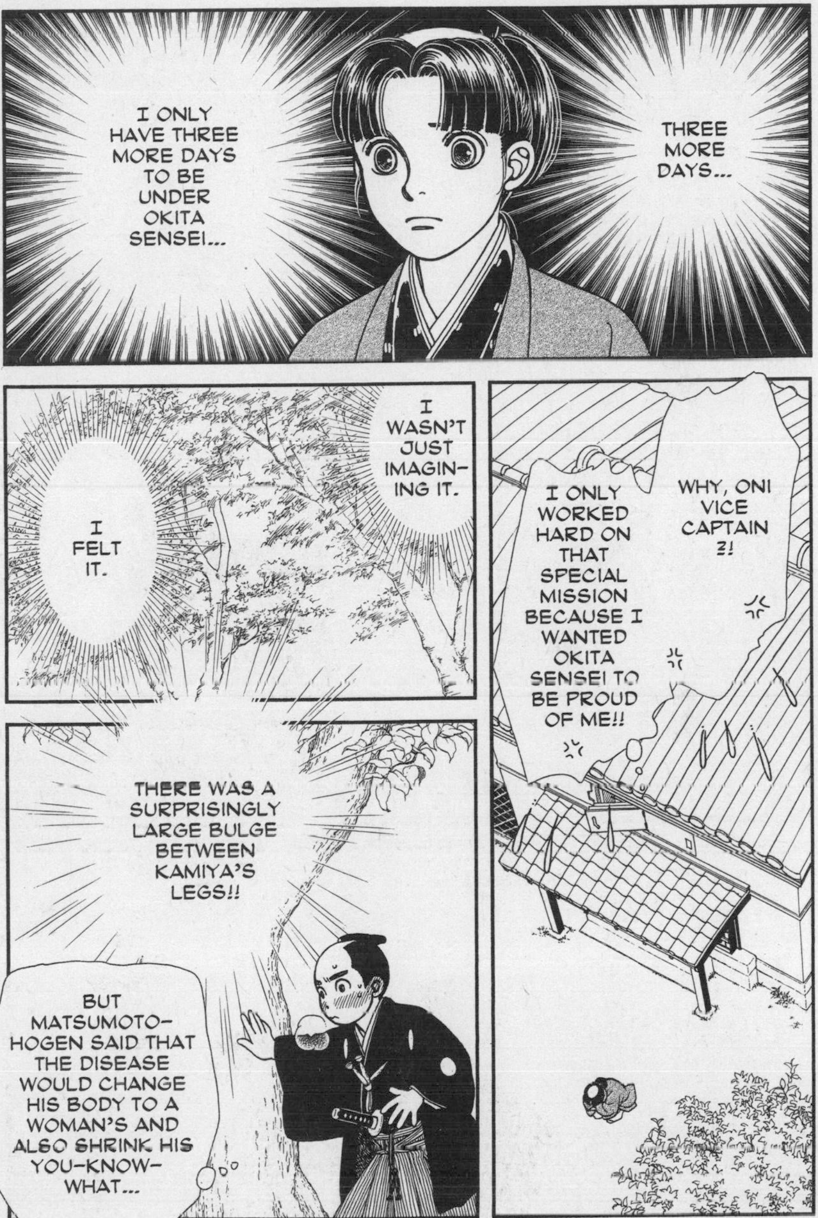
THREE MORE DAYS...
I ONLY HAVE THREE MORE DAYS TO BE UNDER OKITA SENSEI...
WHY, ONI VICE CAPTAIN ?!
I ONLY WORKED HARD ON THAT SPECIAL MISSION BECAUSE I WANTED OKITA SENSEI TO BE PROUD OF ME!!
I WASN'T JUST IMAGINING IT.
I FELT IT.
THERE WAS A SURPRISINGLY LARGE BULGE BETWEEN KAMIYA'S LEGS!!
BUT MATSUMOTO-HOGEN SAID THAT THE DISEASE WOULD CHANGE HIS BODY TO A WOMAN'S AND ALSO SHRINK HIS YOU-KNOW-WHAT...

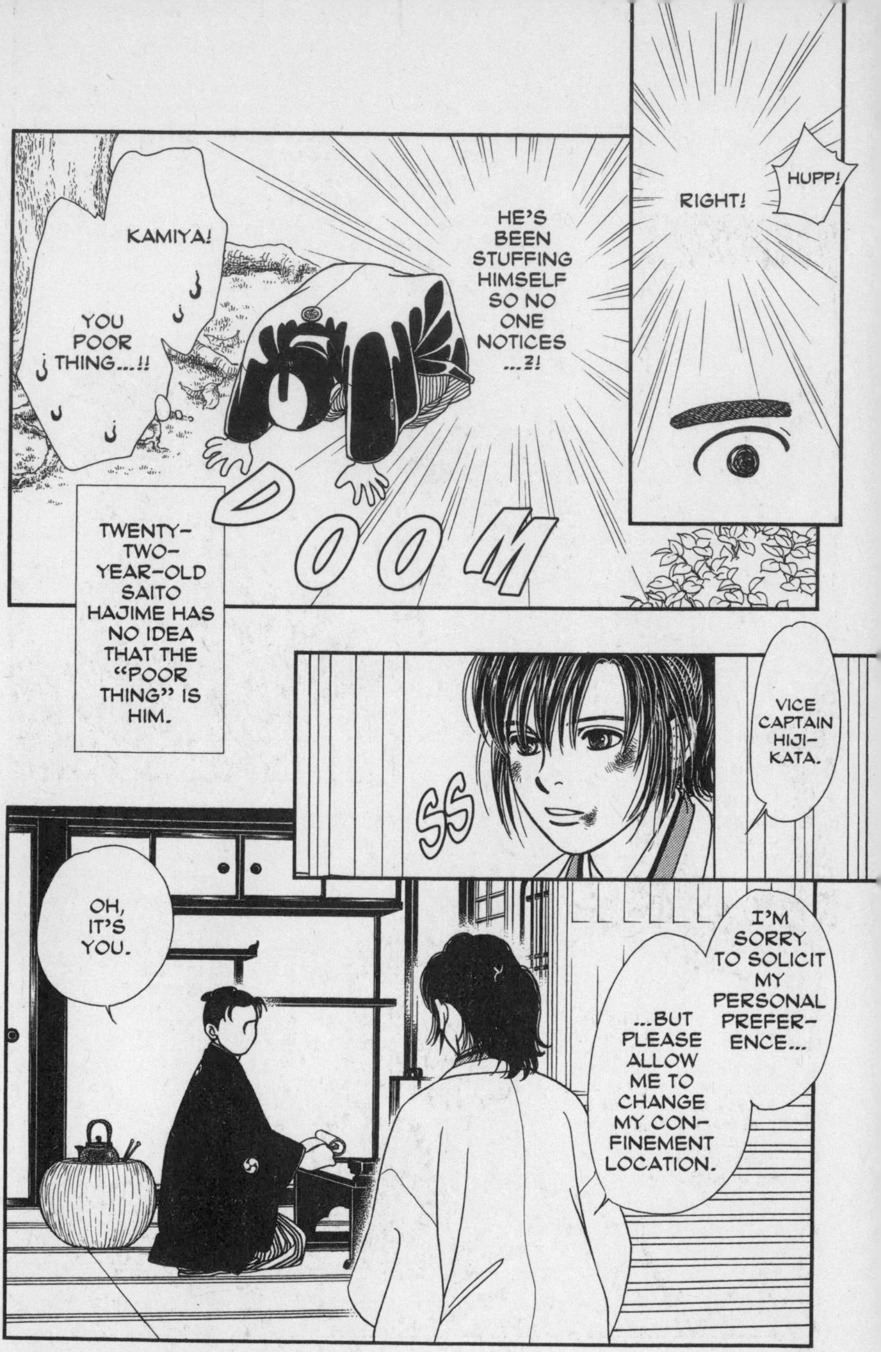
HUPP!
RIGHT!
HE'S BEEN STUFFING HIMSELF SO NO ONE NOTICES ...?!
KAMIYA!
YOU POOR THING...!!
DOOM
TWENTY-TWO-YEAR-OLD SAITO HAJIME HAS NO IDEA THAT THE "POOR THING" IS HIM.
VICE CAPTAIN HIJI-KATA.
SS
I'M SORRY TO SOLICIT MY PERSONAL PREFER-ENCE...
...BUT PLEASE ALLOW ME TO CHANGE MY CON-FINEMENT LOCATION.
OH, IT'S YOU.

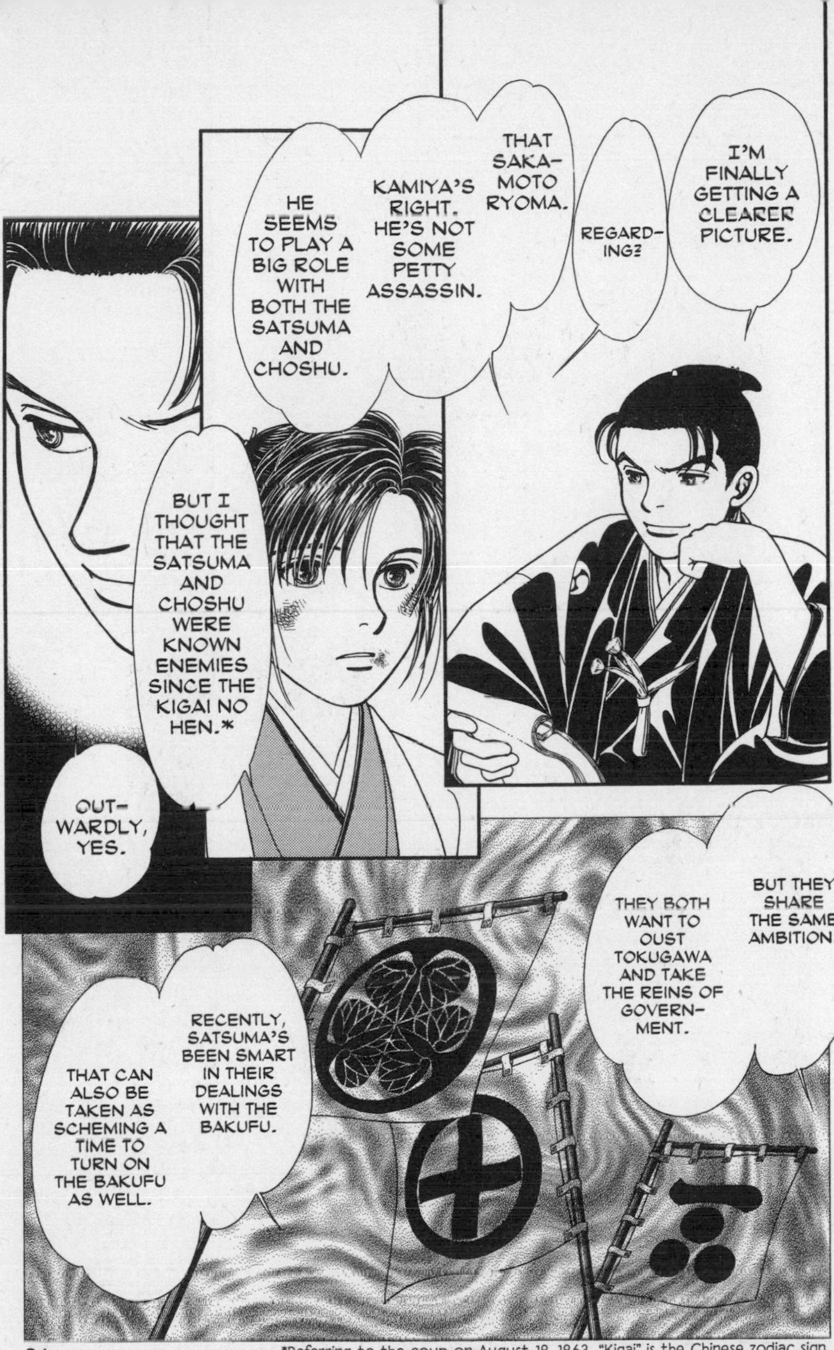
I'M FINALLY GETTING A CLEARER PICTURE.
REGARDING?
THAT SAKAMOTO RYOMA.
KAMIYA'S RIGHT. HE'S NOT SOME PETTY ASSASSIN.
HE SEEMS TO PLAY A BIG ROLE WITH BOTH THE SATSUMA AND CHOSHU.
BUT I THOUGHT THAT THE SATSUMA AND CHOSHU WERE KNOWN ENEMIES SINCE THE KIGAI NO HEN.*
OUTWARDLY, YES.
BUT THEY SHARE THE SAME AMBITION.
THEY BOTH WANT TO OUST TOKUGAWA AND TAKE THE REINS OF GOVERNMENT.
RECENTLY, SATSUMA'S BEEN SMART IN THEIR DEALINGS WITH THE BAKUFU.
THAT CAN ALSO BE TAKEN AS SCHEMING A TIME TO TURN ON THE BAKUFU AS WELL.

*Referring to the coup on August 18, 1863. "Kigai" is the Chinese zodiac sign.

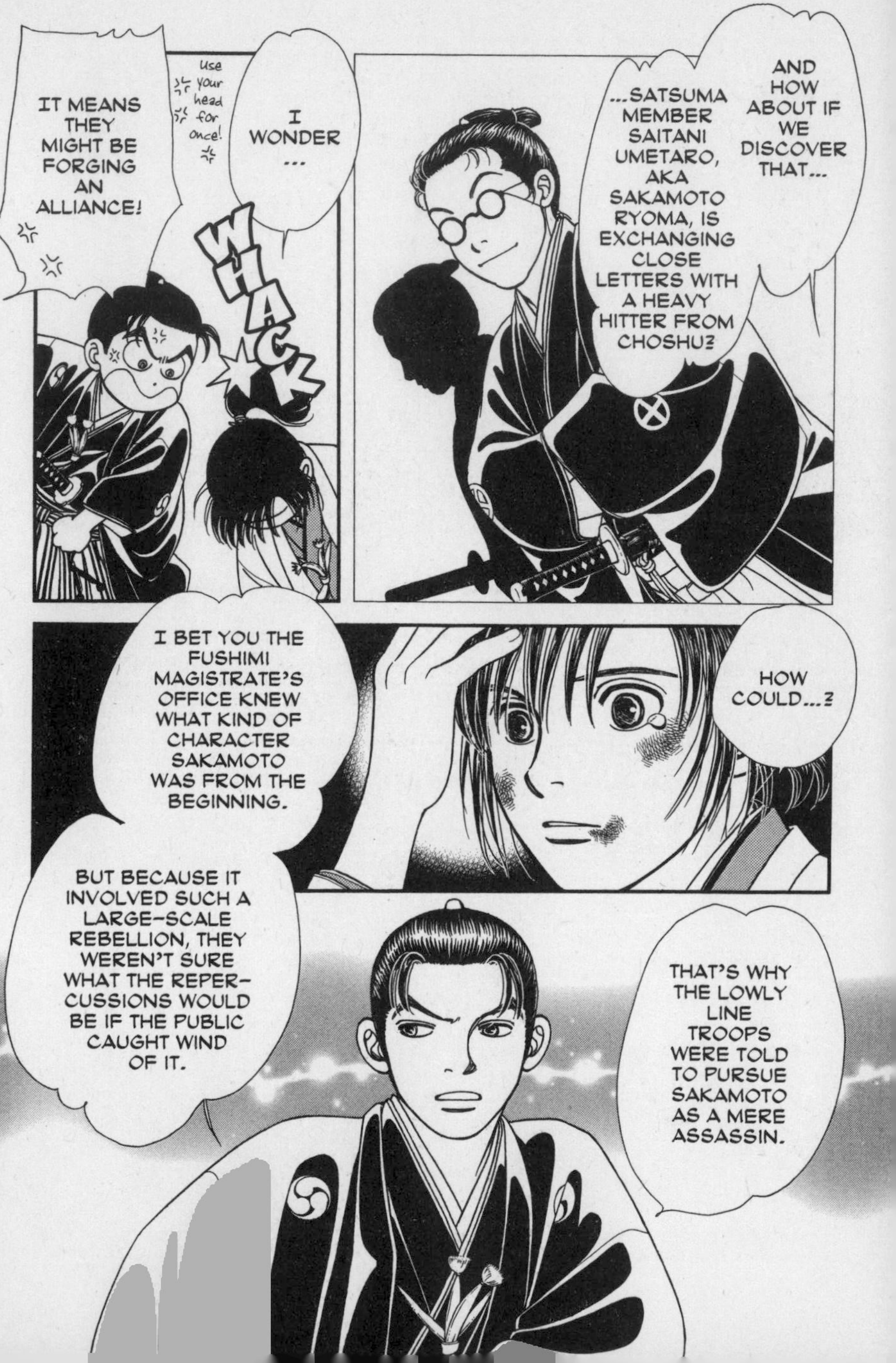
AND HOW ABOUT IF WE DISCOVER THAT...
...SATSUMA MEMBER SAITANI UMETARO, AKA SAKAMOTO RYOMA, IS EXCHANGING CLOSE LETTERS WITH A HEAVY HITTER FROM CHOSHU?
I WONDER...
WHACK
Use your head for once!
IT MEANS THEY MIGHT BE FORGING AN ALLIANCE!
HOW COULD...?
I BET YOU THE FUSHIMI MAGISTRATE'S OFFICE KNEW WHAT KIND OF CHARACTER SAKAMOTO WAS FROM THE BEGINNING.
BUT BECAUSE IT INVOLVED SUCH A LARGE-SCALE REBELLION, THEY WEREN'T SURE WHAT THE REPERCUSSIONS WOULD BE IF THE PUBLIC CAUGHT WIND OF IT.
THAT'S WHY THE LOWLY LINE TROOPS WERE TOLD TO PURSUE SAKAMOTO AS A MERE ASSASSIN.

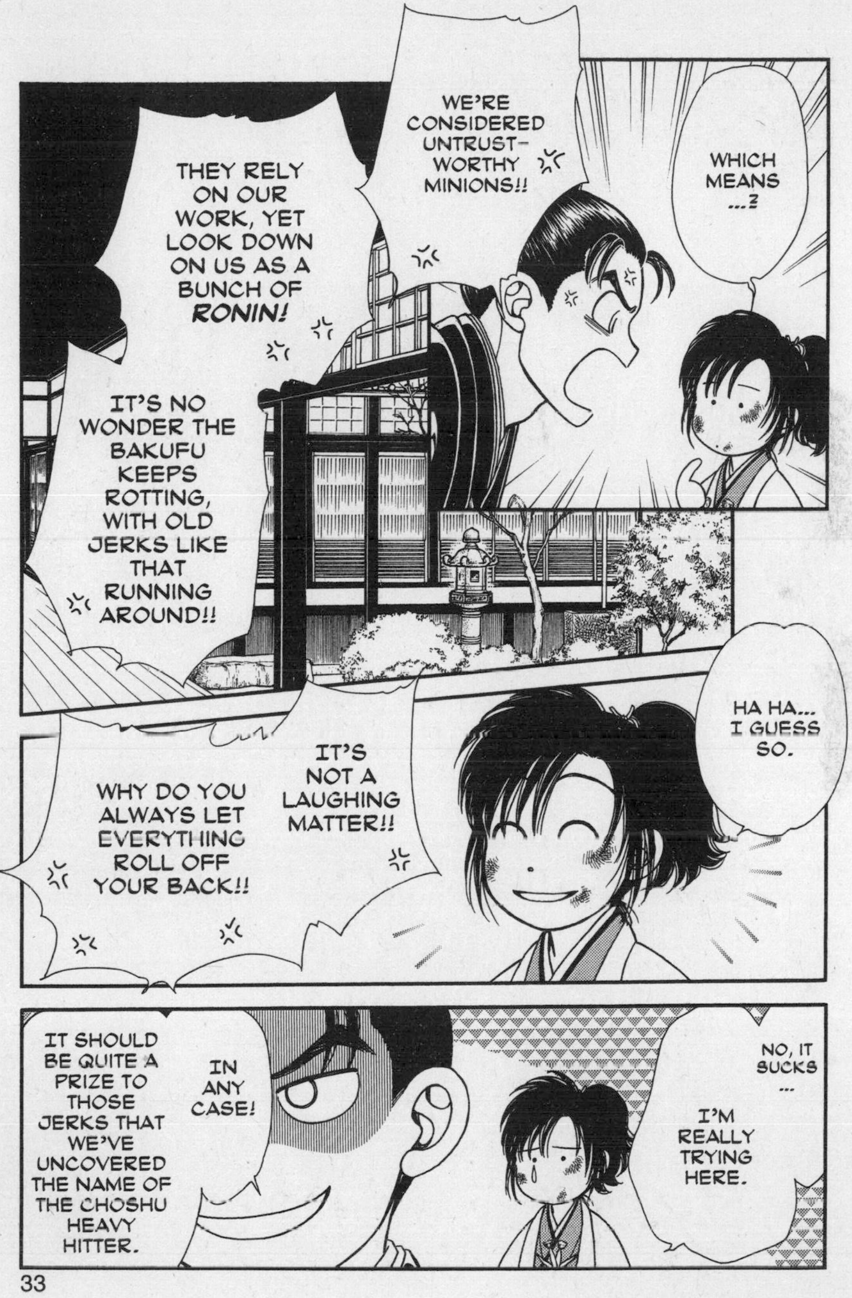
WHICH MEANS ...?
WE'RE CONSIDERED UNTRUST-WORTHY MINIONS!!
THEY RELY ON OUR WORK, YET LOOK DOWN ON US AS A BUNCH OF *RONIN!*
IT'S NO WONDER THE BAKUFU KEEPS ROTTING, WITH OLD JERKS LIKE THAT RUNNING AROUND!!
HA HA... I GUESS SO.
IT'S NOT A LAUGHING MATTER!!
WHY DO YOU ALWAYS LET EVERYTHING ROLL OFF YOUR BACK!!
NO, IT SUCKS ...
I'M REALLY TRYING HERE.
IN ANY CASE!
IT SHOULD BE QUITE A PRIZE TO THOSE JERKS THAT WE'VE UNCOVERED THE NAME OF THE CHOSHU HEAVY HITTER.

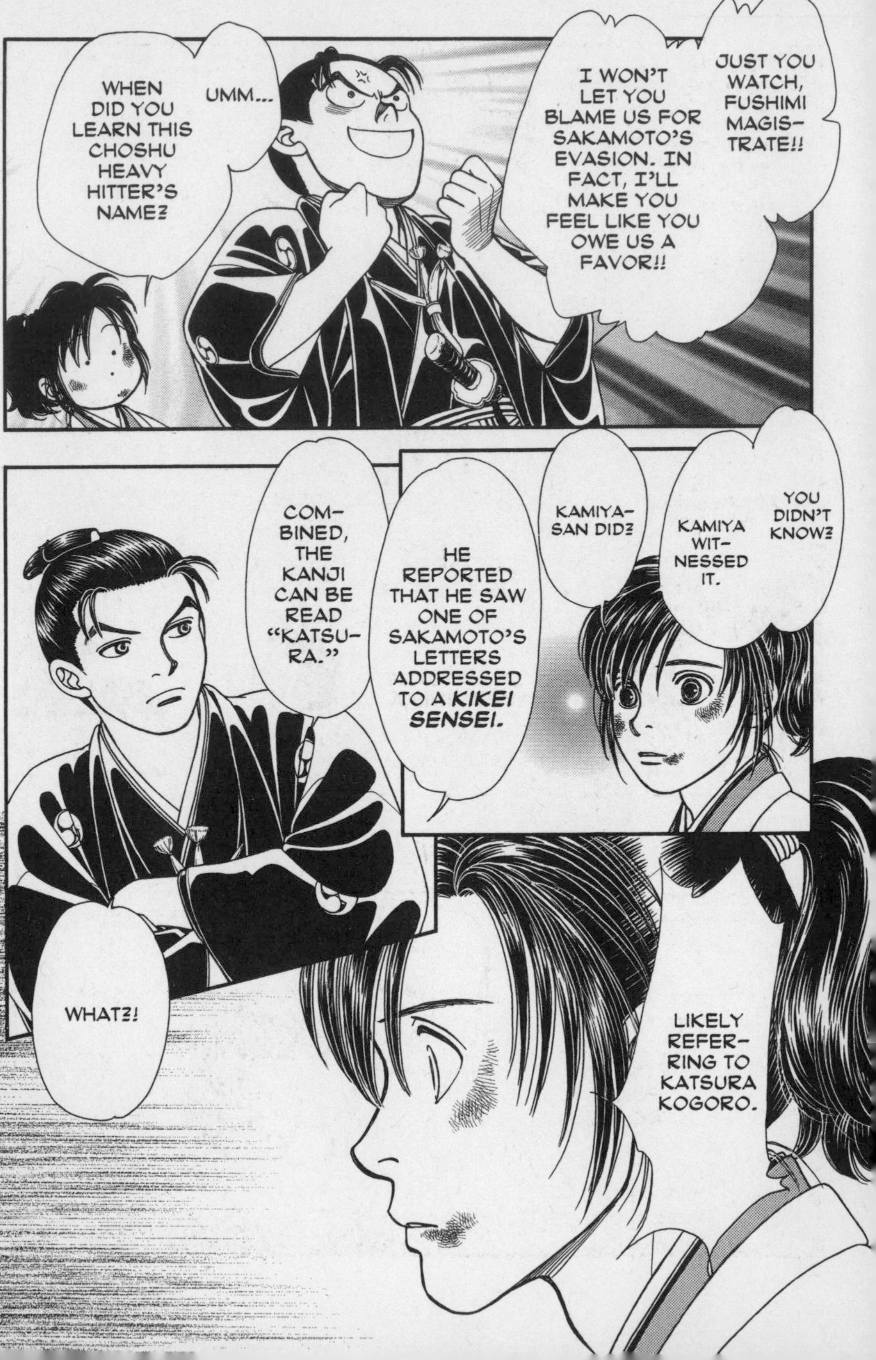
JUST YOU WATCH, FUSHIMI MAGIS-TRATE!!
I WON'T LET YOU BLAME US FOR SAKAMOTO'S EVASION. IN FACT, I'LL MAKE YOU FEEL LIKE YOU OWE US A FAVOR!!
UMM...
WHEN DID YOU LEARN THIS CHOSHU HEAVY HITTER'S NAME?
YOU DIDN'T KNOW?
KAMIYA WIT-NESSED IT.
KAMIYA-SAN DID?
HE REPORTED THAT HE SAW ONE OF SAKAMOTO'S LETTERS ADDRESSED TO A ***KIKEI SENSEI.***
LIKELY REFER-RING TO KATSURA KOGORO.
COM-BINED, THE KANJI CAN BE READ "KATSU-RA."
WHAT?!

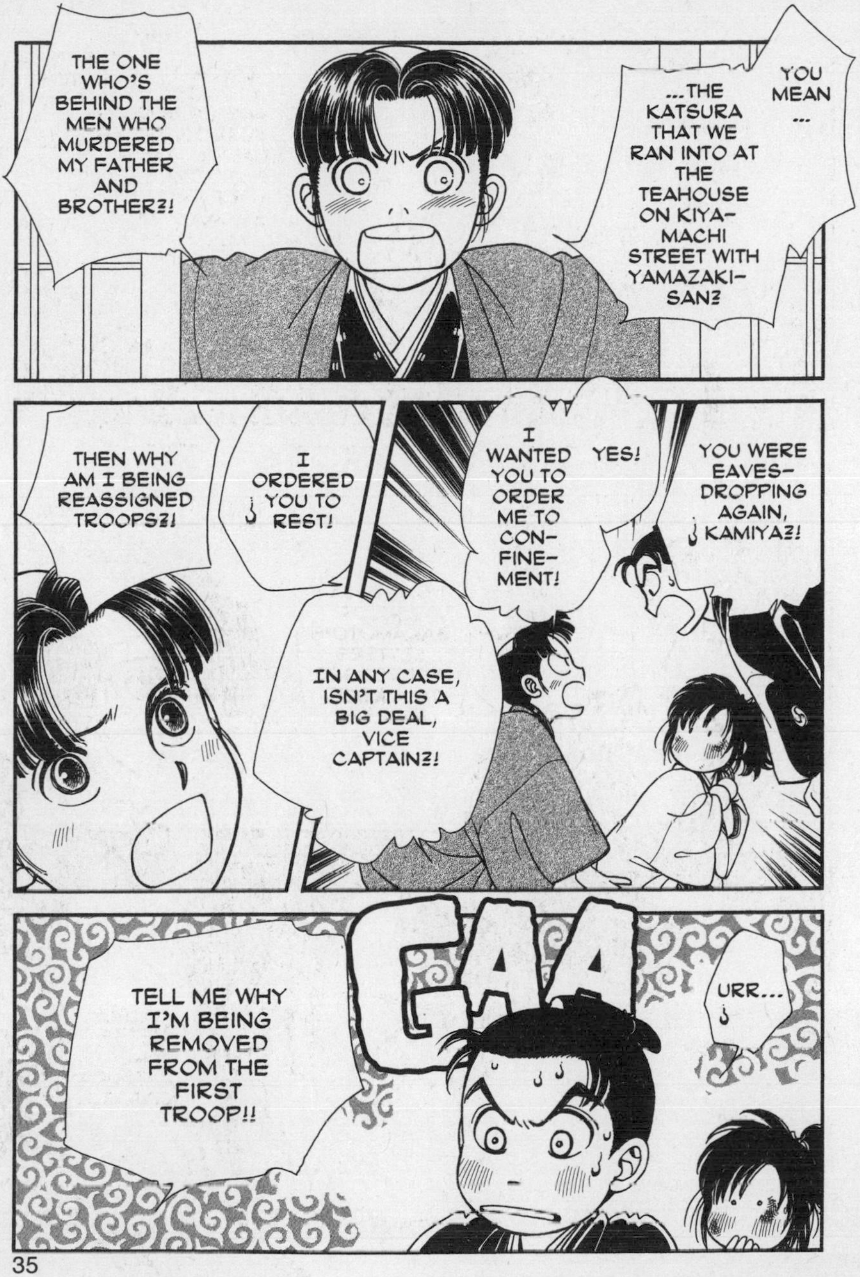
YOU MEAN ...
...THE KATSURA THAT WE RAN INTO AT THE TEAHOUSE ON KIYA-MACHI STREET WITH YAMAZAKI-SAN?
THE ONE WHO'S BEHIND THE MEN WHO MURDERED MY FATHER AND BROTHER?!
YOU WERE EAVES-DROPPING AGAIN, KAMIYA?!
YES!
I WANTED YOU TO ORDER ME TO CON-FINE-MENT!
I ORDERED YOU TO REST!
IN ANY CASE, ISN'T THIS A BIG DEAL, VICE CAPTAIN?!
THEN WHY AM I BEING REASSIGNED TROOPS?!
GAA
URR...
TELL ME WHY I'M BEING REMOVED FROM THE FIRST TROOP!!

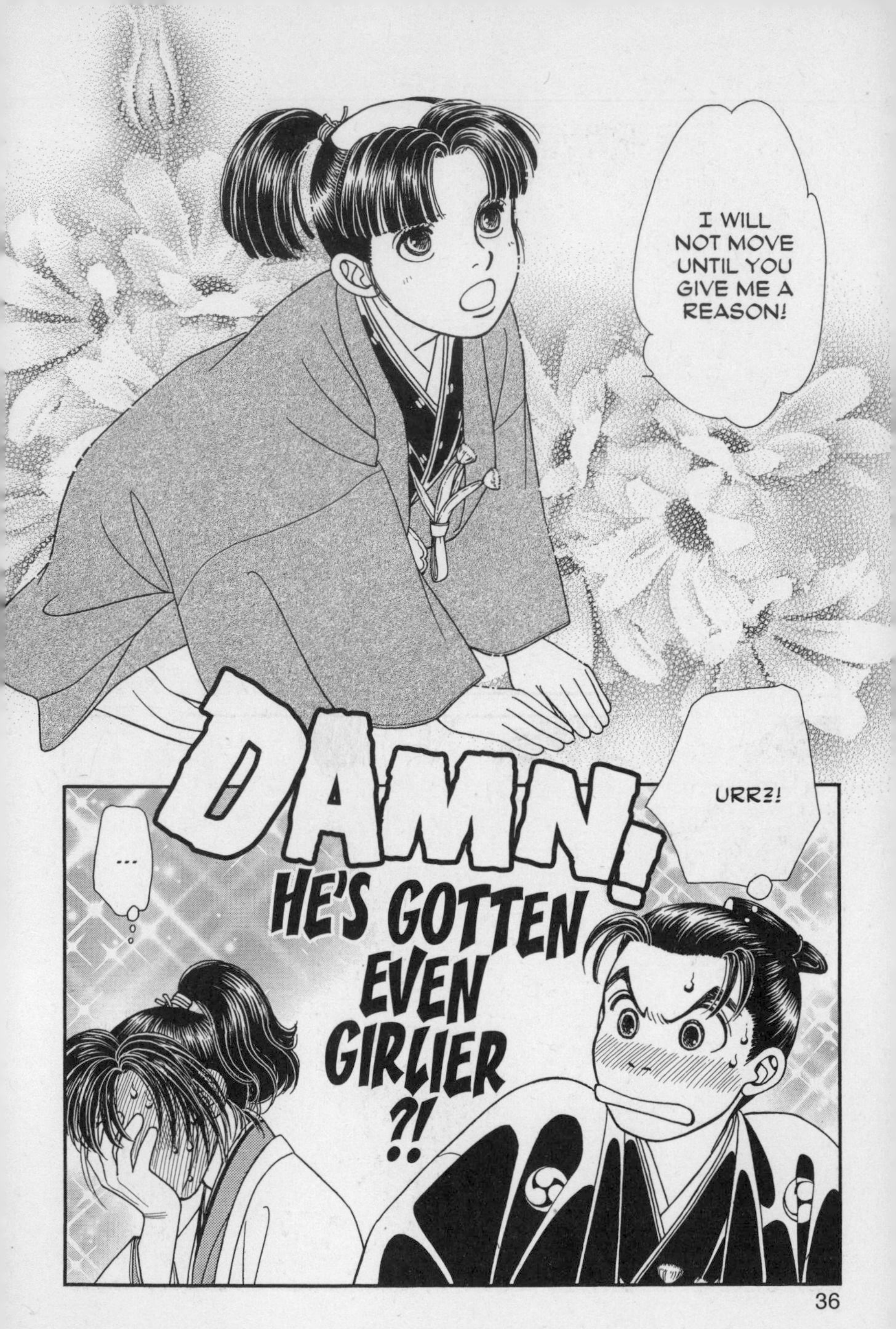
I WILL NOT MOVE UNTIL YOU GIVE ME A REASON!
URRƺ!
DAMN! HE'S GOTTEN EVEN GIRLIER ?!
...

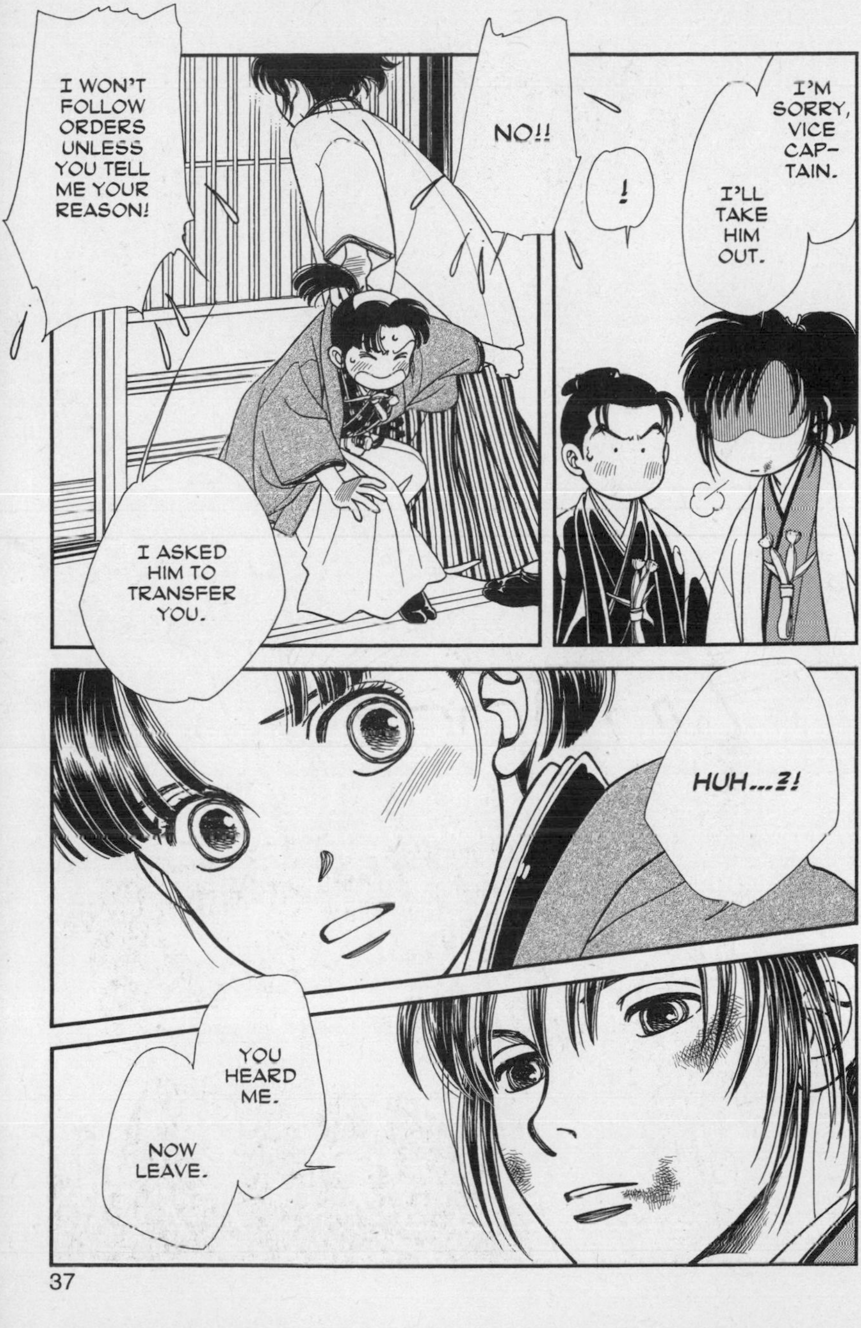

I'M SORRY, VICE CAPTAIN.
I'LL TAKE HIM OUT.
!
NO!!
I WON'T FOLLOW ORDERS UNLESS YOU TELL ME YOUR REASON!
I ASKED HIM TO TRANSFER YOU.
HUH...?!
YOU HEARD ME.
NOW LEAVE.

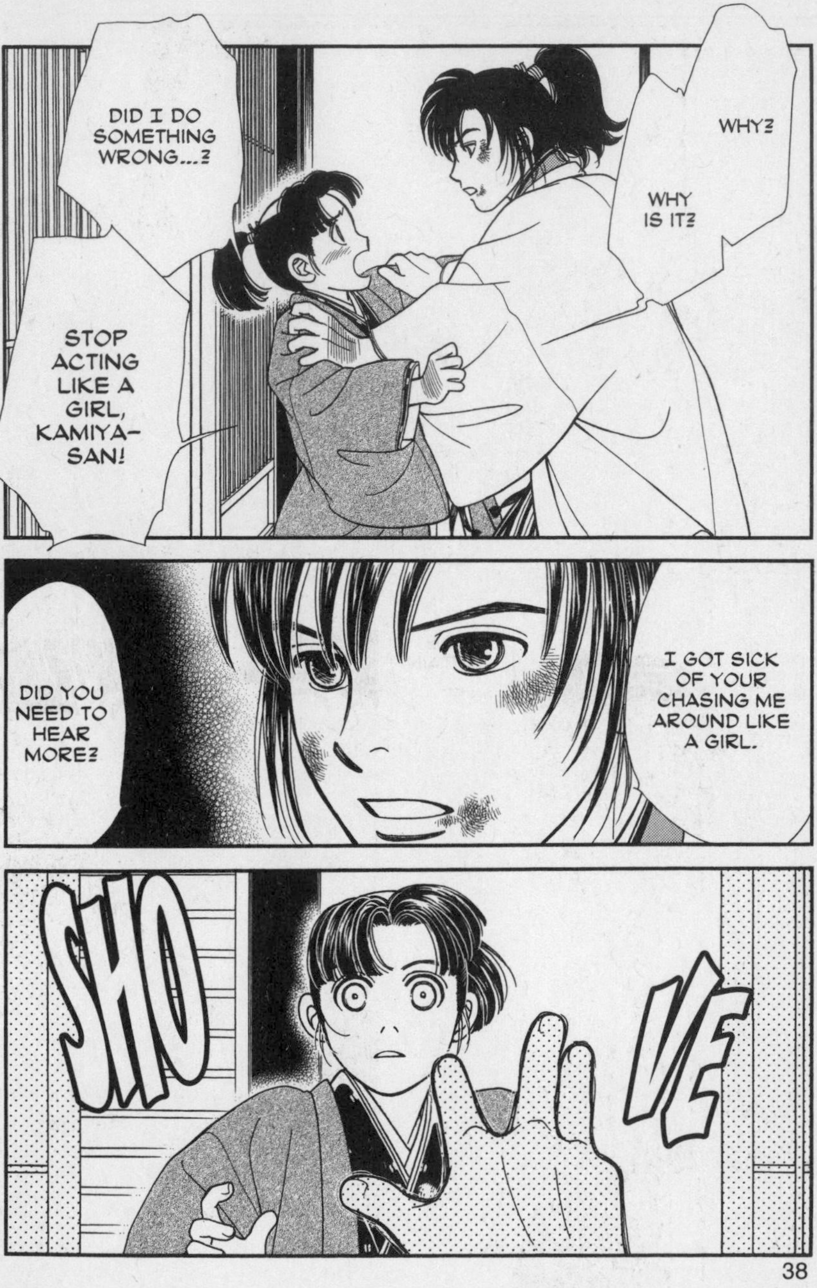
WHY?
WHY IS IT?
DID I DO SOMETHING WRONG...?
STOP ACTING LIKE A GIRL, KAMIYA-SAN!
I GOT SICK OF YOUR CHASING ME AROUND LIKE A GIRL.
DID YOU NEED TO HEAR MORE?
SHOVE

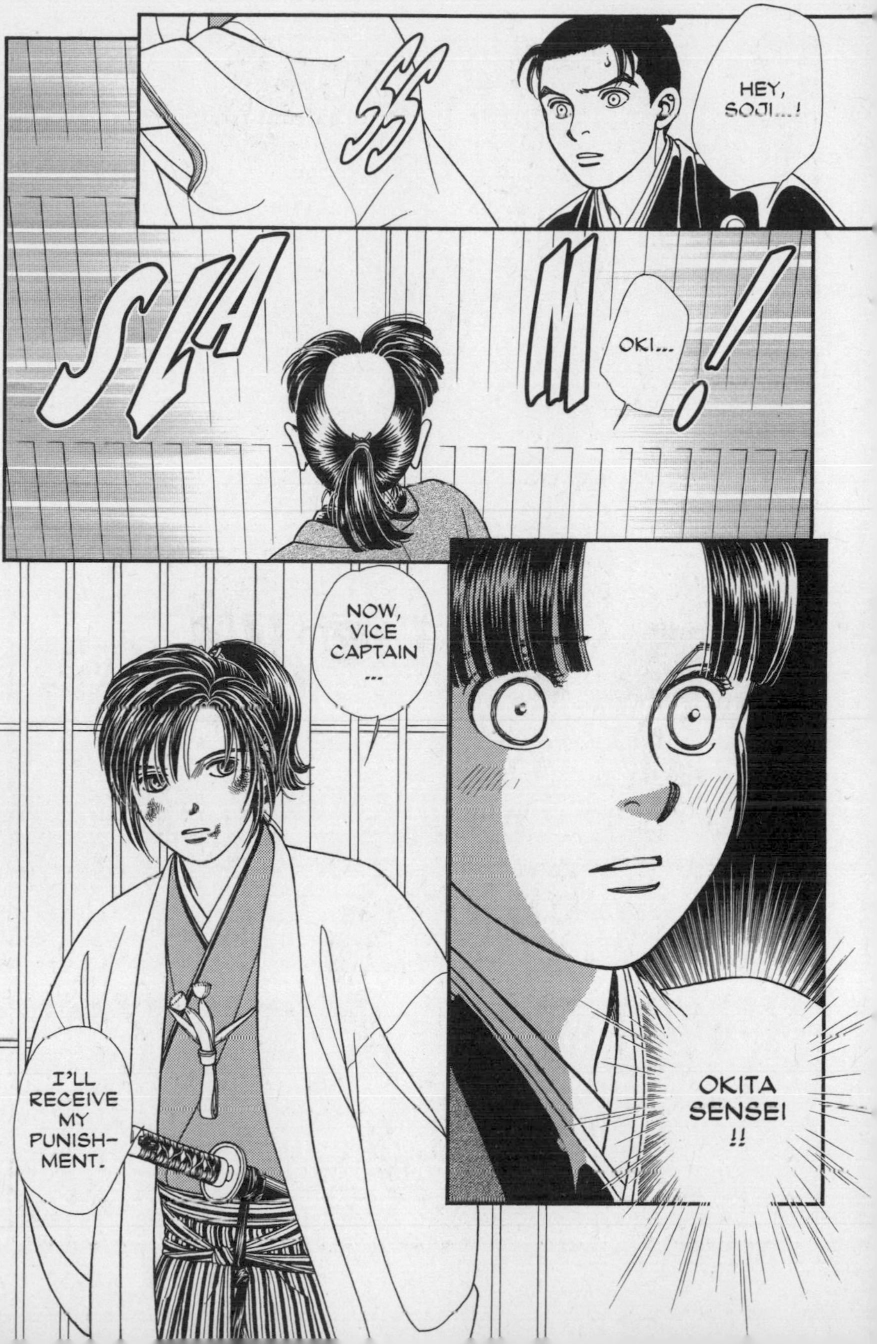
HEY, SOJI...!
SS
OKI...
SLAM!
OKITA SENSEI !!
NOW, VICE CAPTAIN ...
I'LL RECEIVE MY PUNISHMENT.

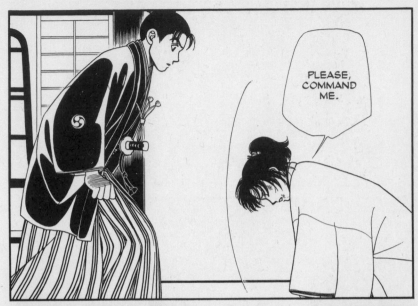

PLEASE, COMMAND ME.
SOJI...!

KAZE HIKARU IROHA KARUTA

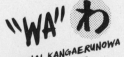

"WA" わ

WAKARANAI KANGAERUNOWA GOHAN MADE
"PUZZLING THOUGHTS LAST ONLY UNTIL THE NEXT MEAL"

by Kuma-san from Fukushima

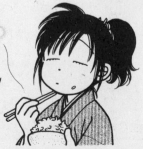

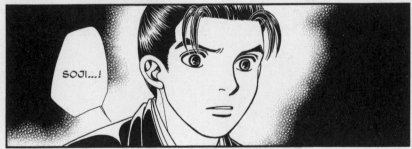

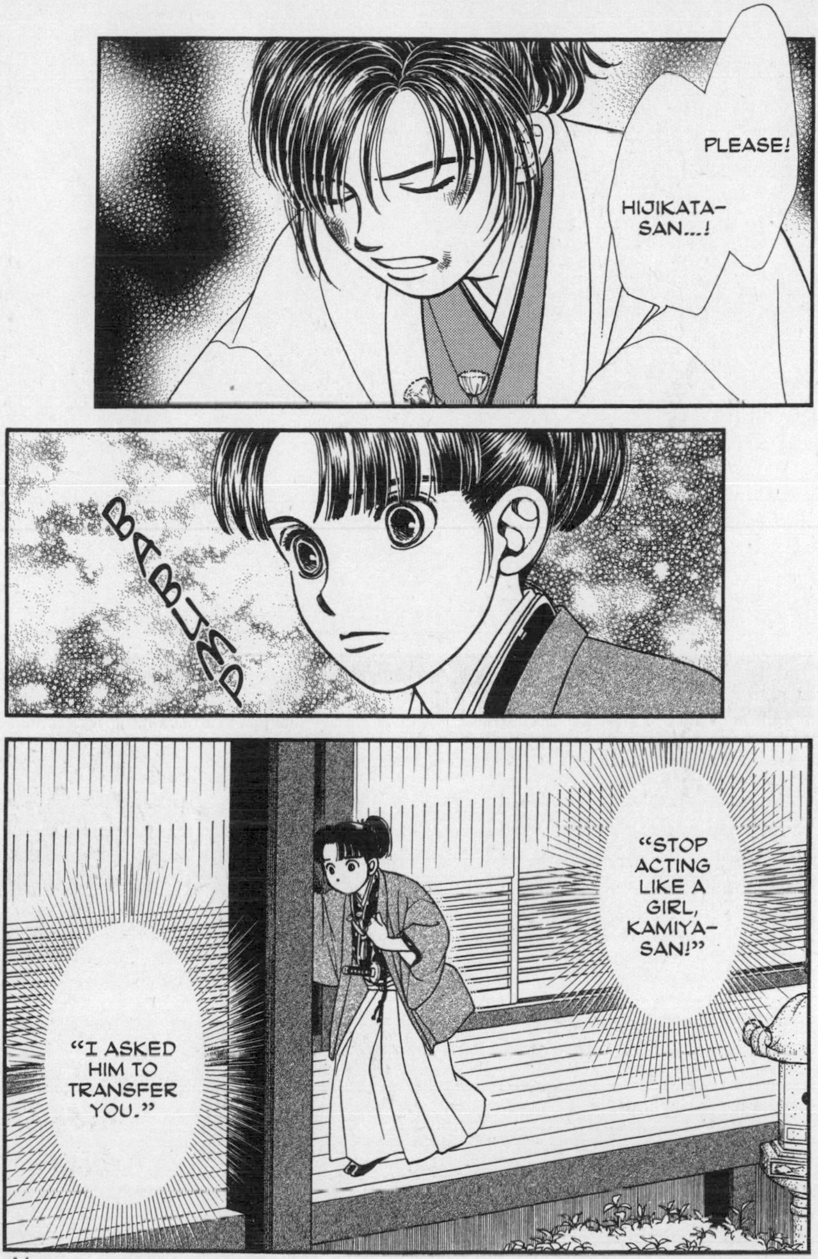
PLEASE!
HIJIKATA-SAN...!
BABUMP
"STOP ACTING LIKE A GIRL, KAMIYA-SAN!"
"I ASKED HIM TO TRANSFER YOU."

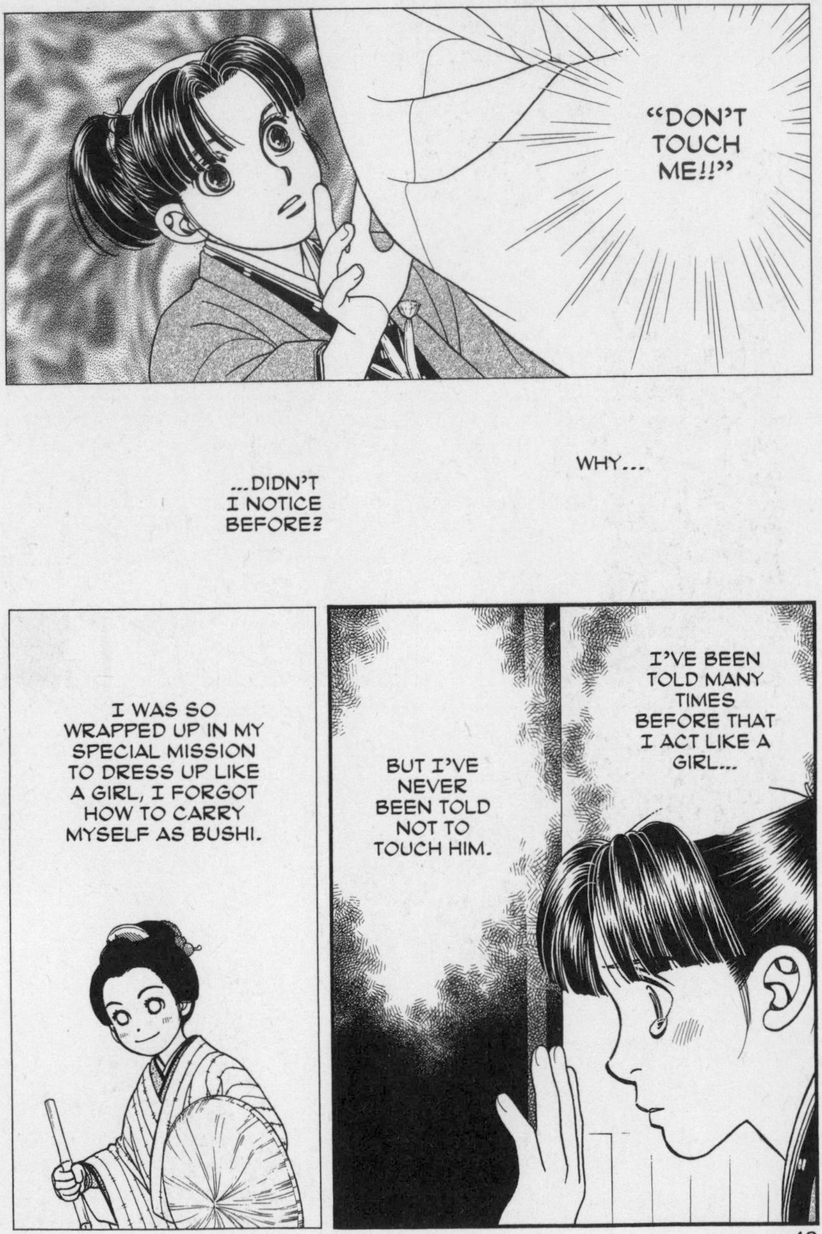
"DON'T TOUCH ME!!"
WHY...
...DIDN'T I NOTICE BEFORE?
I'VE BEEN TOLD MANY TIMES BEFORE THAT I ACT LIKE A GIRL...
BUT I'VE NEVER BEEN TOLD NOT TO TOUCH HIM.
I WAS SO WRAPPED UP IN MY SPECIAL MISSION TO DRESS UP LIKE A GIRL, I FORGOT HOW TO CARRY MYSELF AS BUSHI.

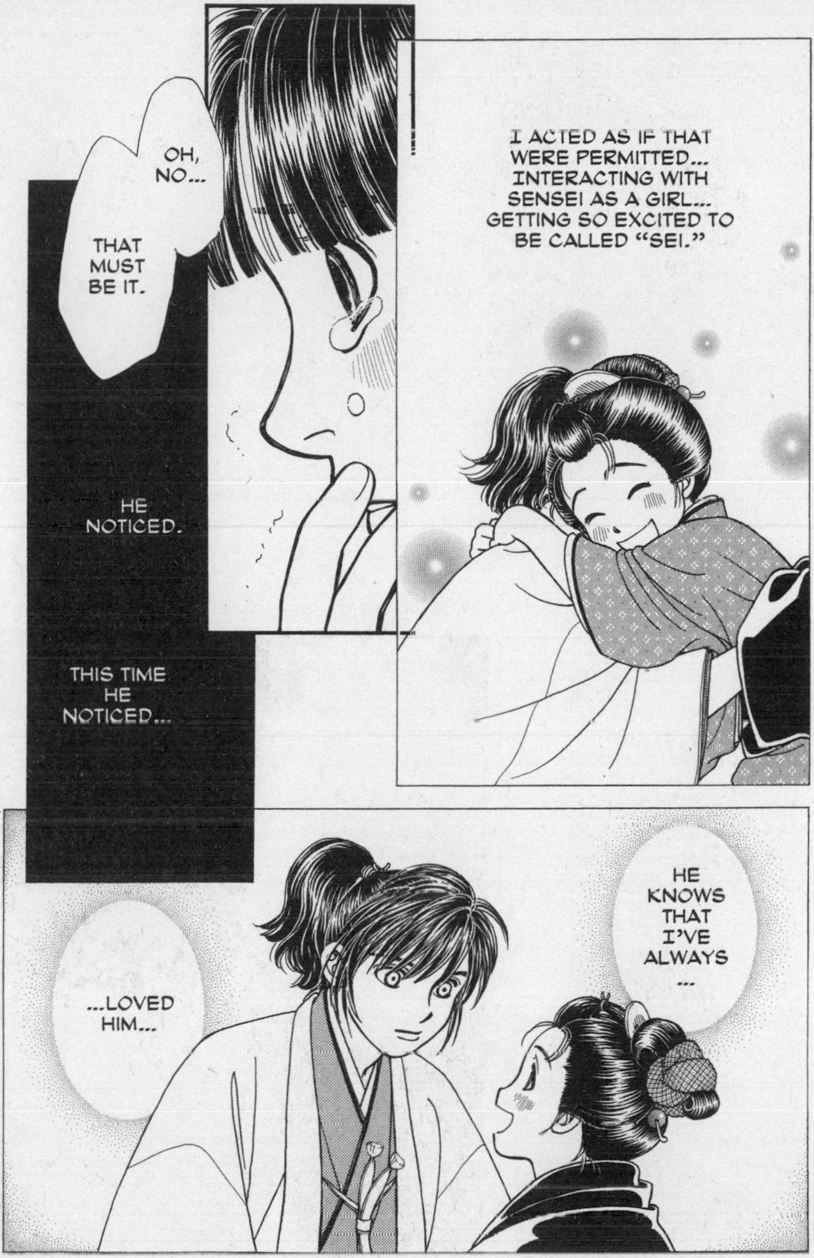
I ACTED AS IF THAT WERE PERMITTED... INTERACTING WITH SENSEI AS A GIRL... GETTING SO EXCITED TO BE CALLED "SEI."
OH, NO...
THAT MUST BE IT.
HE NOTICED.
THIS TIME HE NOTICED...
HE KNOWS THAT I'VE ALWAYS...
...LOVED HIM...

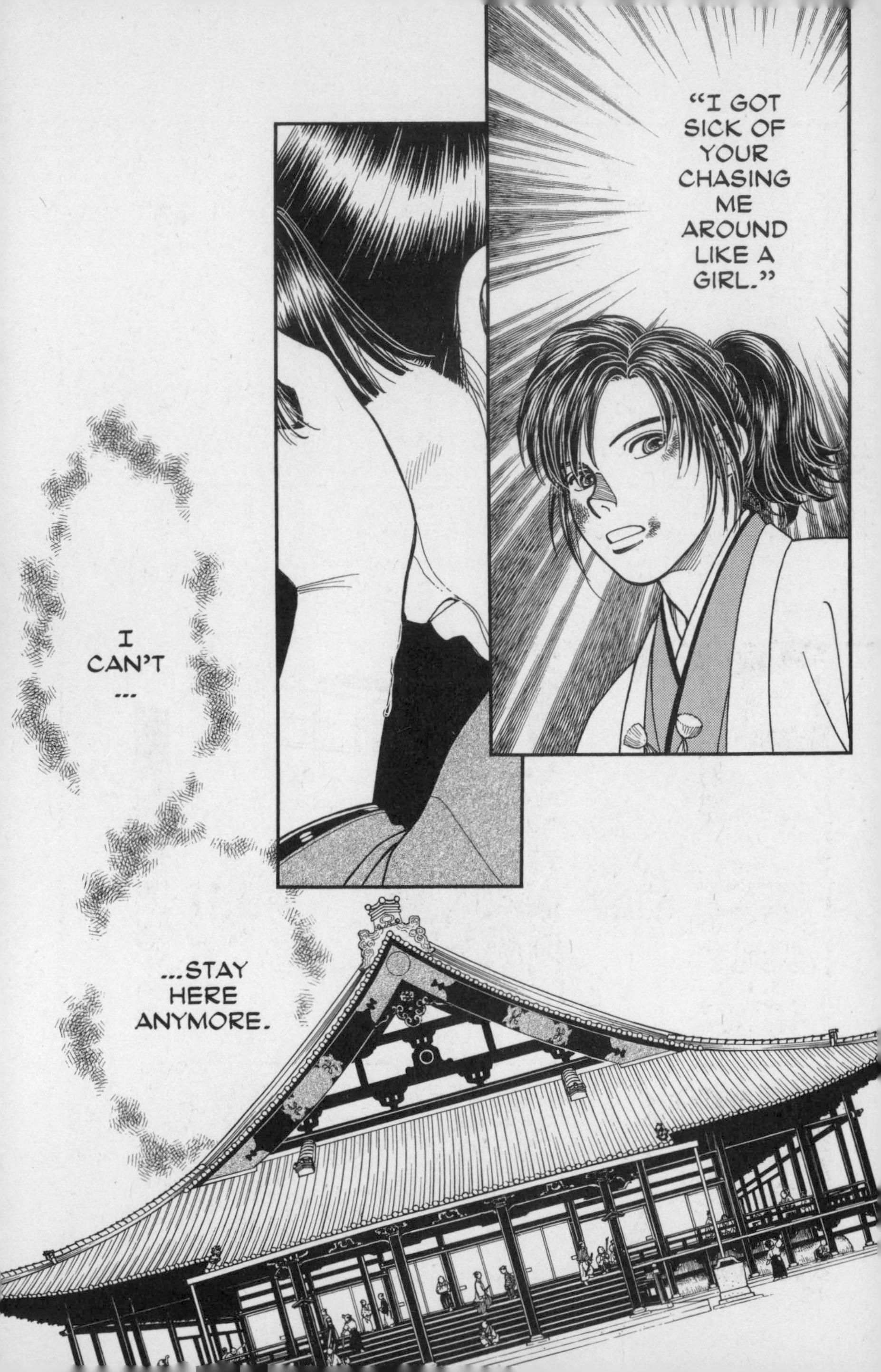
"I GOT SICK OF YOUR CHASING ME AROUND LIKE A GIRL."
I CAN'T ...
...STAY HERE ANYMORE.

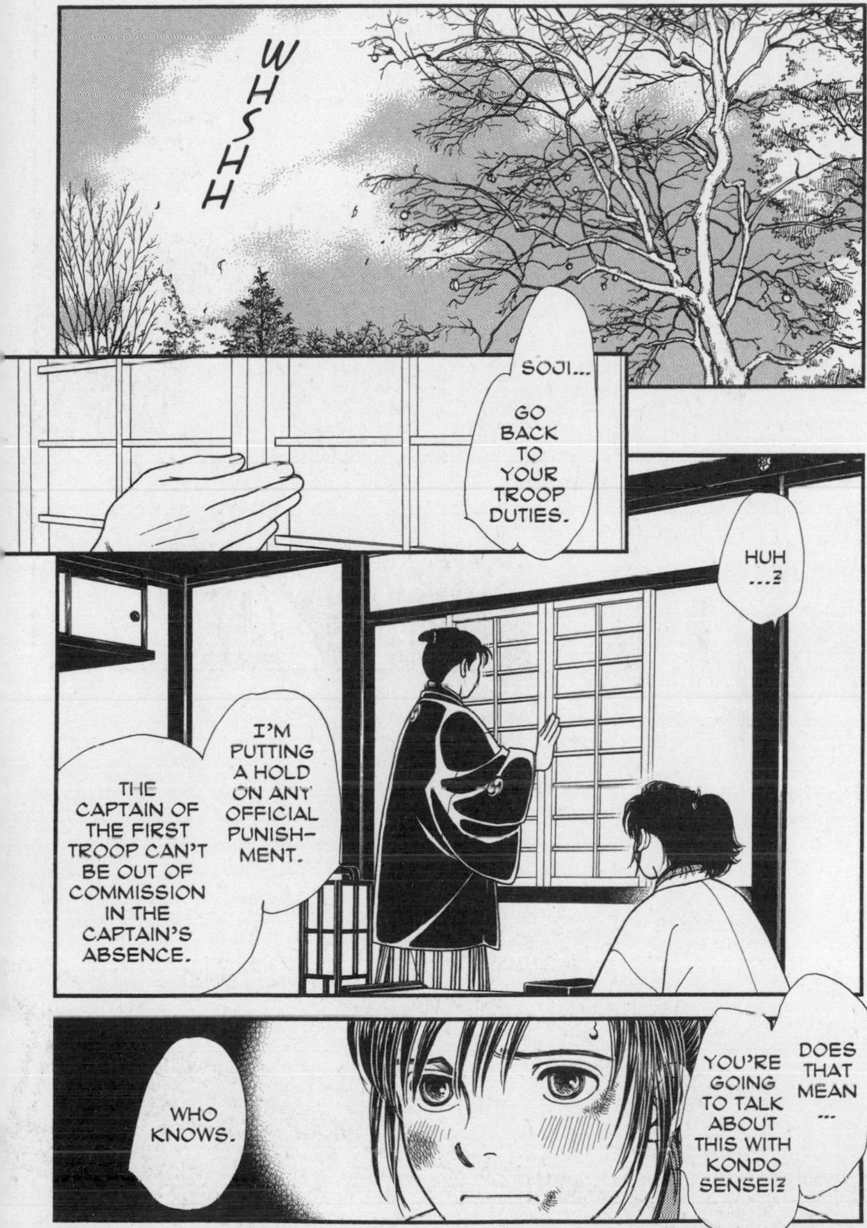
WHSHH
SOJI... GO BACK TO YOUR TROOP DUTIES.
HUH...?
I'M PUTTING A HOLD ON ANY OFFICIAL PUNISHMENT.
THE CAPTAIN OF THE FIRST TROOP CAN'T BE OUT OF COMMISSION IN THE CAPTAIN'S ABSENCE.
DOES THAT MEAN...
YOU'RE GOING TO TALK ABOUT THIS WITH KONDO SENSEI?
WHO KNOWS.

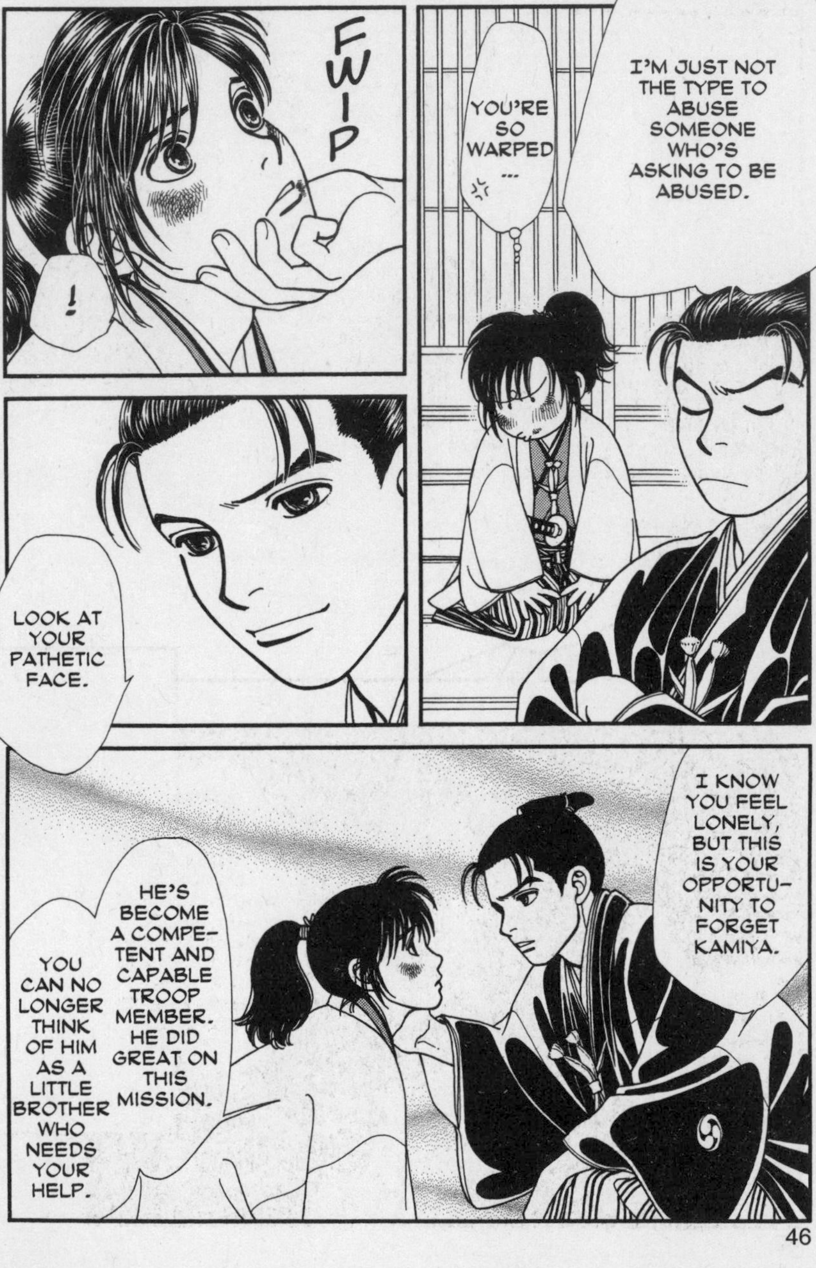
I'M JUST NOT THE TYPE TO ABUSE SOMEONE WHO'S ASKING TO BE ABUSED.
YOU'RE SO WARPED ...
FWIP
!
LOOK AT YOUR PATHETIC FACE.
I KNOW YOU FEEL LONELY, BUT THIS IS YOUR OPPORTUNITY TO FORGET KAMIYA.
HE'S BECOME A COMPETENT AND CAPABLE TROOP MEMBER. HE DID GREAT ON THIS MISSION.
YOU CAN NO LONGER THINK OF HIM AS A LITTLE BROTHER WHO NEEDS YOUR HELP.

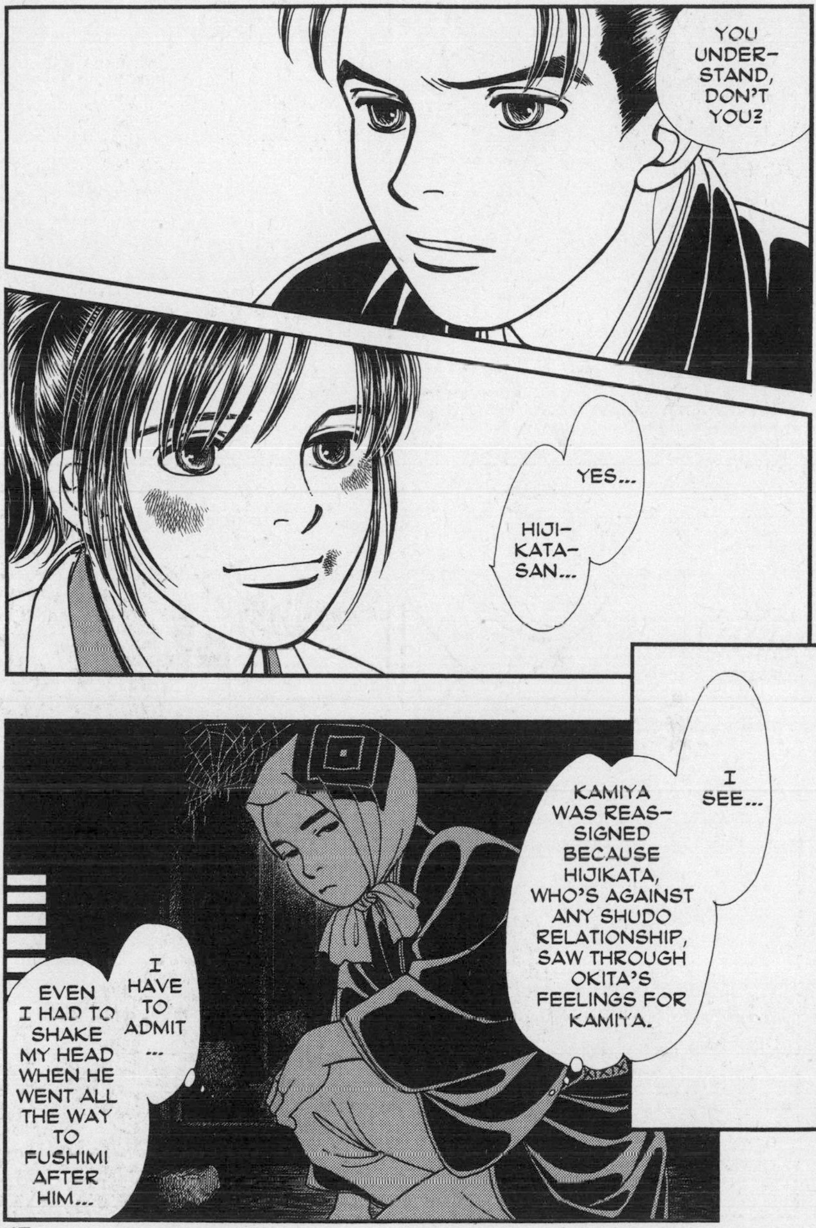
YOU UNDER-STAND, DON'T YOU?
YES...
HIJI-KATA-SAN...
I SEE...
KAMIYA WAS REAS-SIGNED BECAUSE HIJIKATA, WHO'S AGAINST ANY SHUDO RELATIONSHIP, SAW THROUGH OKITA'S FEELINGS FOR KAMIYA.
I HAVE TO ADMIT ...
EVEN I HAD TO SHAKE MY HEAD WHEN HE WENT ALL THE WAY TO FUSHIMI AFTER HIM...

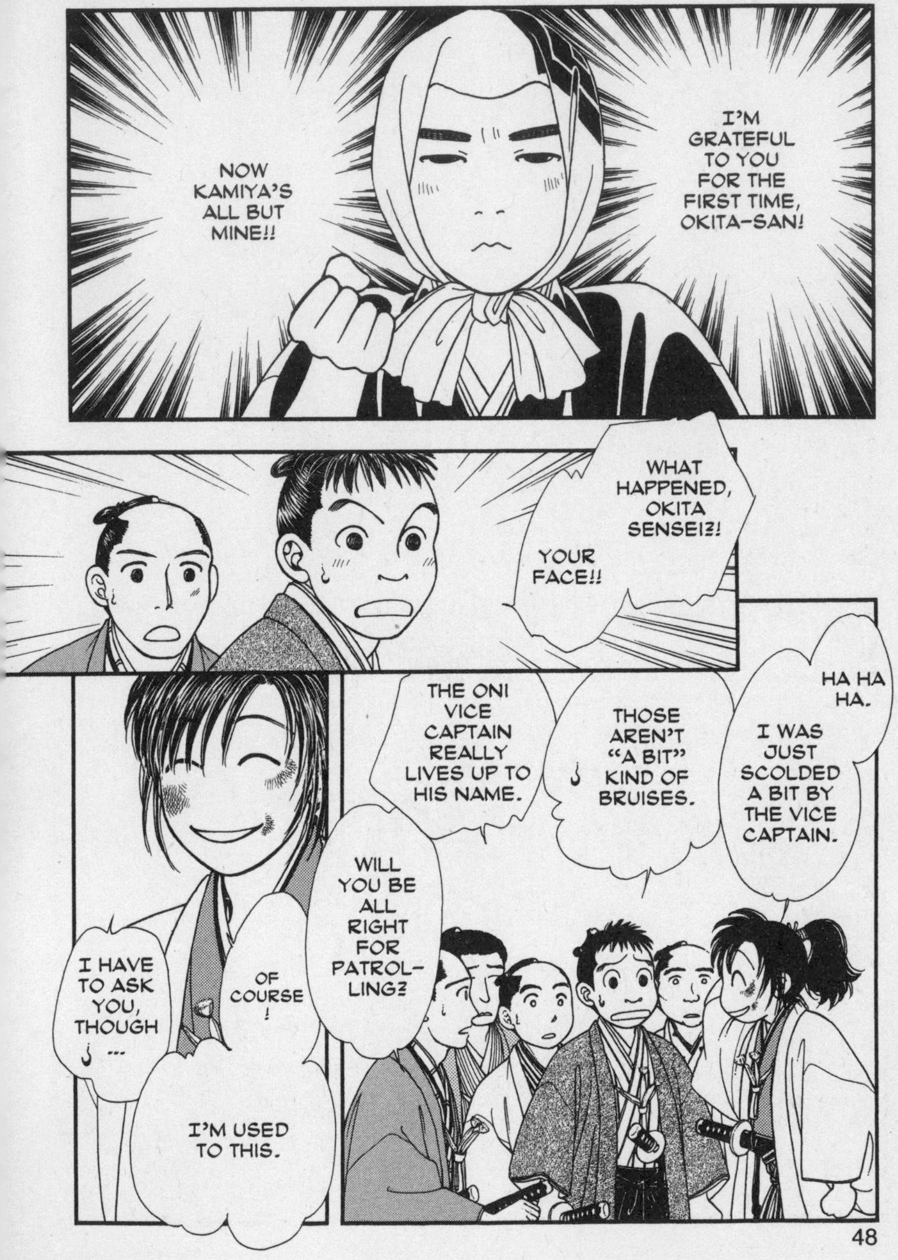
I'M GRATEFUL TO YOU FOR THE FIRST TIME, OKITA-SAN!
NOW KAMIYA'S ALL BUT MINE!!
WHAT HAPPENED, OKITA SENSEI?!
YOUR FACE!!
HA HA HA.
I WAS JUST SCOLDED A BIT BY THE VICE CAPTAIN.
THOSE AREN'T "A BIT" KIND OF BRUISES.
THE ONI VICE CAPTAIN REALLY LIVES UP TO HIS NAME.
WILL YOU BE ALL RIGHT FOR PATROL-LING?
OF COURSE!
I'M USED TO THIS.
I HAVE TO ASK YOU, THOUGH...

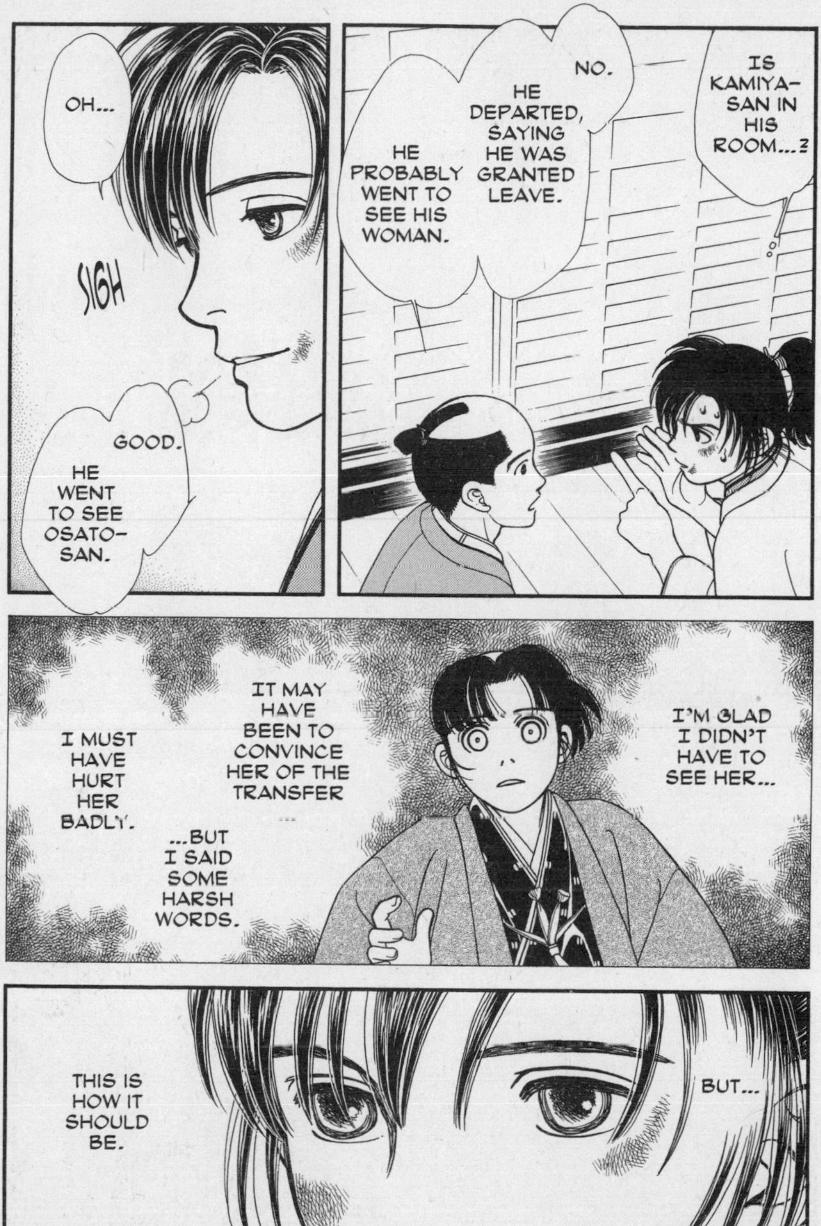
IS KAMIYA-SAN IN HIS ROOM...?
NO.
HE DEPARTED, SAYING HE WAS GRANTED LEAVE.
HE PROBABLY WENT TO SEE HIS WOMAN.
OH...
SIGH
GOOD.
HE WENT TO SEE OSATO-SAN.
I'M GLAD I DIDN'T HAVE TO SEE HER...
IT MAY HAVE BEEN TO CONVINCE HER OF THE TRANSFER ...
...BUT I SAID SOME HARSH WORDS.
I MUST HAVE HURT HER BADLY.
BUT...
THIS IS HOW IT SHOULD BE.

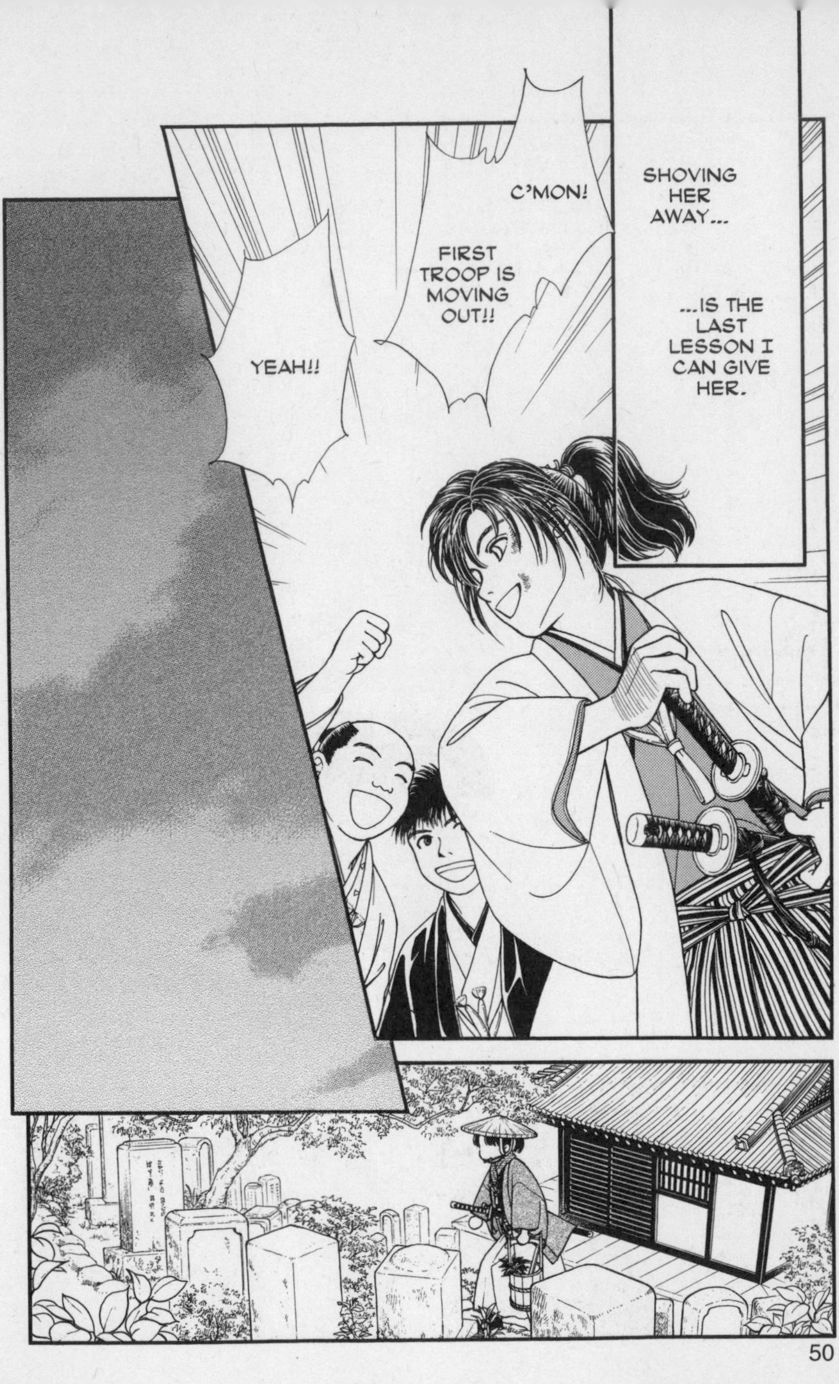
SHOVING HER AWAY...
...IS THE LAST LESSON I CAN GIVE HER.
C'MON!
FIRST TROOP IS MOVING OUT!!
YEAH!!

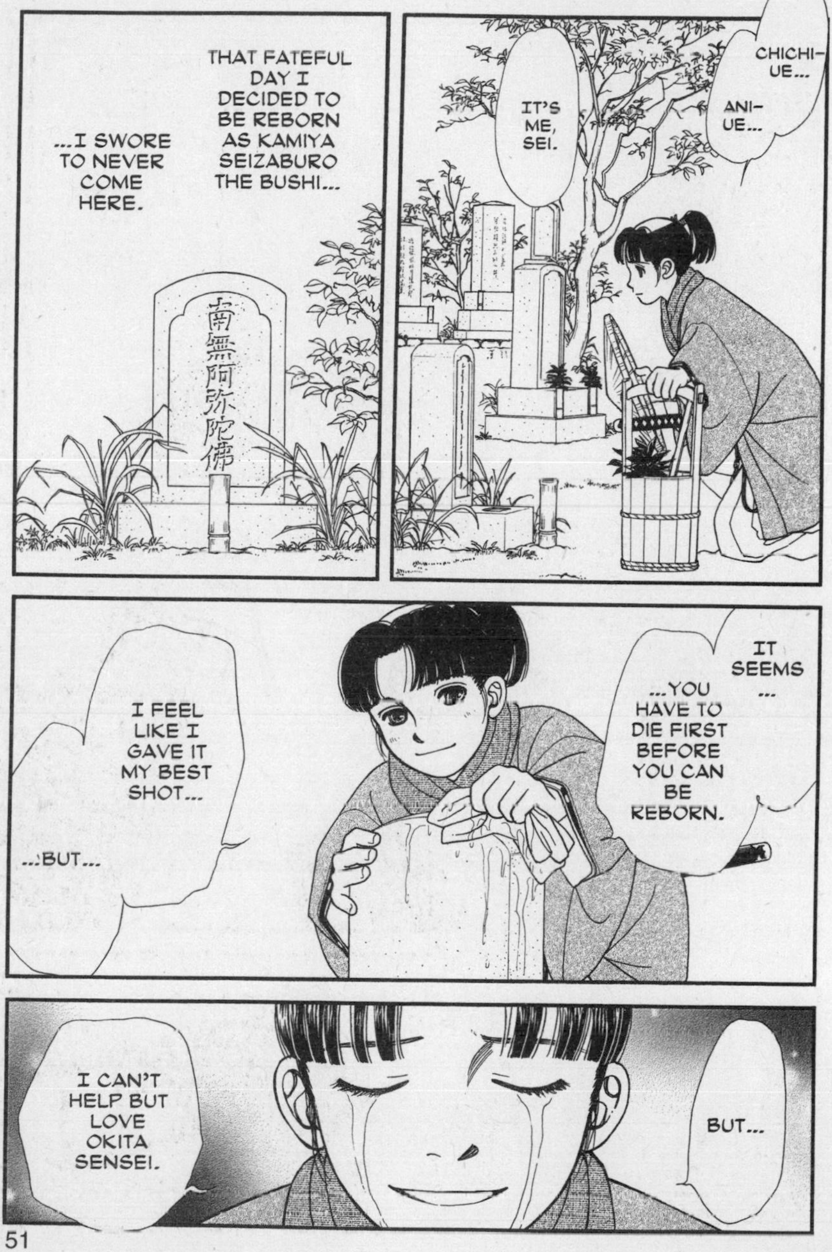
CHICHI-UE...
ANI-UE...
IT'S ME, SEI.
THAT FATEFUL DAY I DECIDED TO BE REBORN AS KAMIYA SEIZABURO THE BUSHI...
...I SWORE TO NEVER COME HERE.
南無阿弥陀佛
IT SEEMS...
...YOU HAVE TO DIE FIRST BEFORE YOU CAN BE REBORN.
I FEEL LIKE I GAVE IT MY BEST SHOT...
...BUT...
BUT...
I CAN'T HELP BUT LOVE OKITA SENSEI.

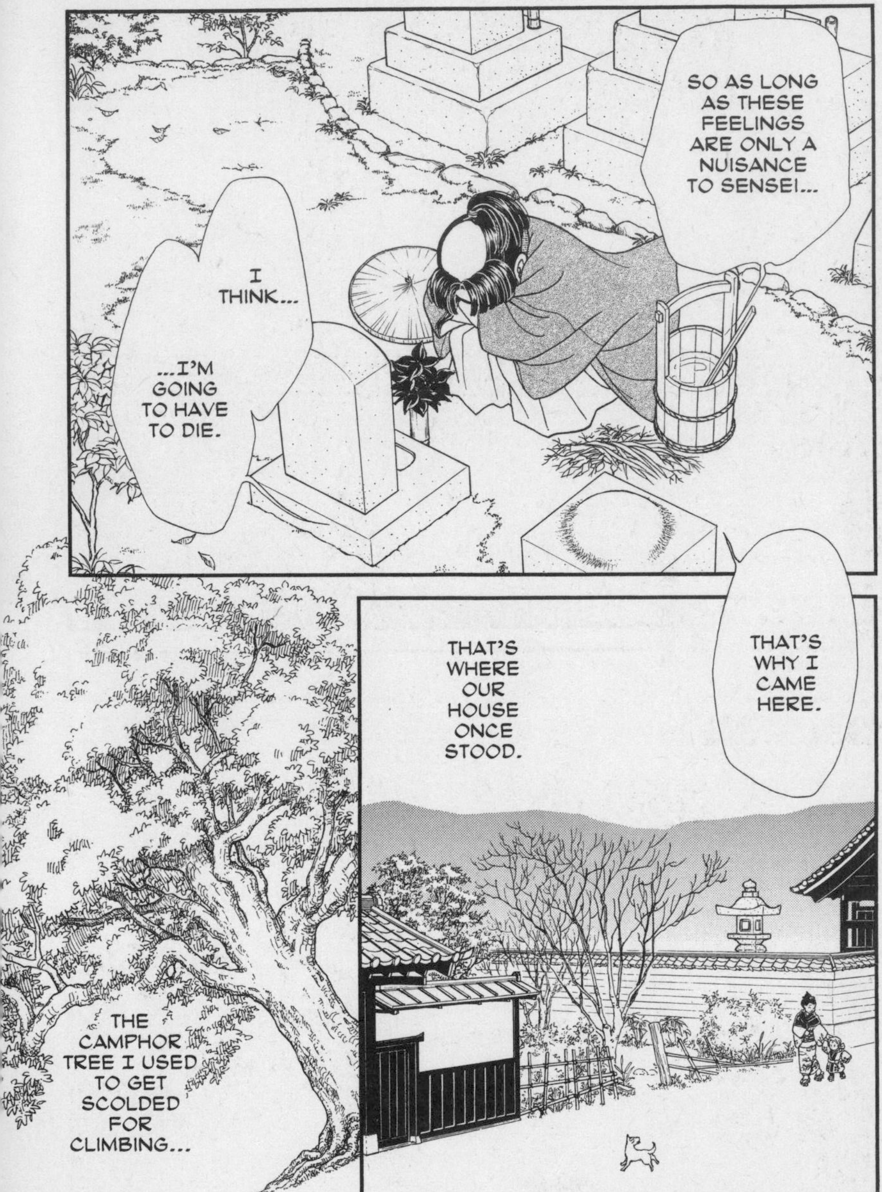
SO AS LONG AS THESE FEELINGS ARE ONLY A NUISANCE TO SENSEI...
I THINK...
...I'M GOING TO HAVE TO DIE.
THAT'S WHY I CAME HERE.
THAT'S WHERE OUR HOUSE ONCE STOOD.
THE CAMPHOR TREE I USED TO GET SCOLDED FOR CLIMBING...

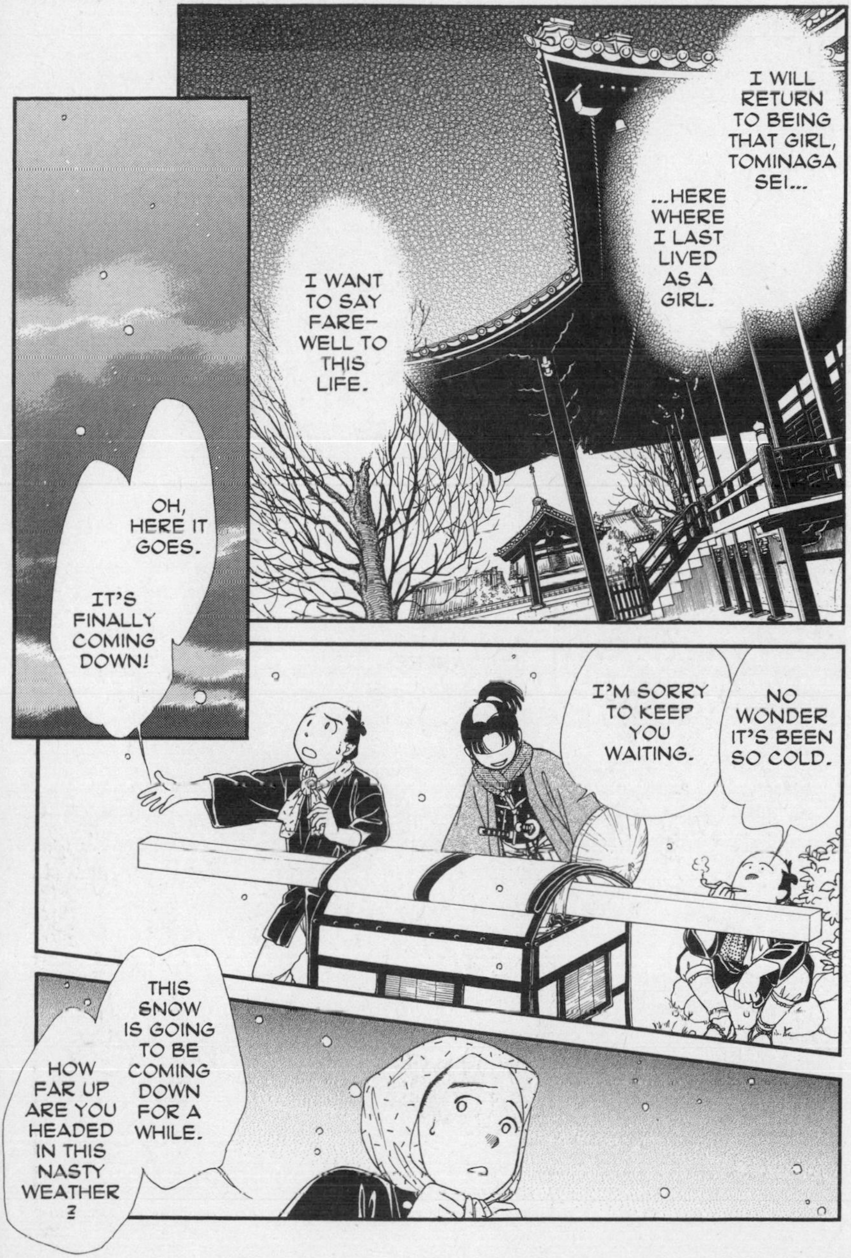
I WILL RETURN TO BEING THAT GIRL, TOMINAGA SEI...
...HERE WHERE I LAST LIVED AS A GIRL.
I WANT TO SAY FARE-WELL TO THIS LIFE.
OH, HERE IT GOES.
IT'S FINALLY COMING DOWN!
NO WONDER IT'S BEEN SO COLD.
I'M SORRY TO KEEP YOU WAITING.
THIS SNOW IS GOING TO BE COMING DOWN FOR A WHILE.
HOW FAR UP ARE YOU HEADED IN THIS NASTY WEATHER?

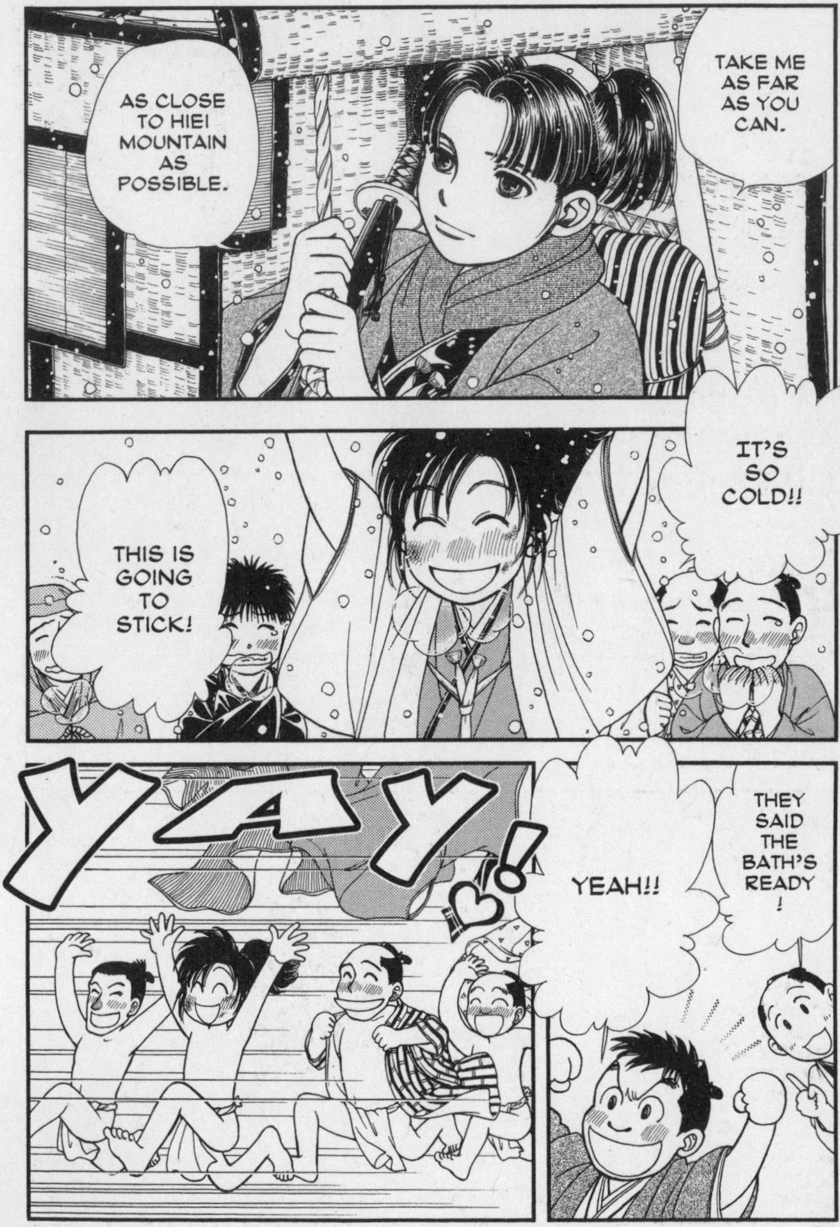
TAKE ME AS FAR AS YOU CAN.
AS CLOSE TO HIEI MOUNTAIN AS POSSIBLE.
IT'S SO COLD!!
THIS IS GOING TO STICK!
THEY SAID THE BATH'S READY!
YEAH!!
YAY!

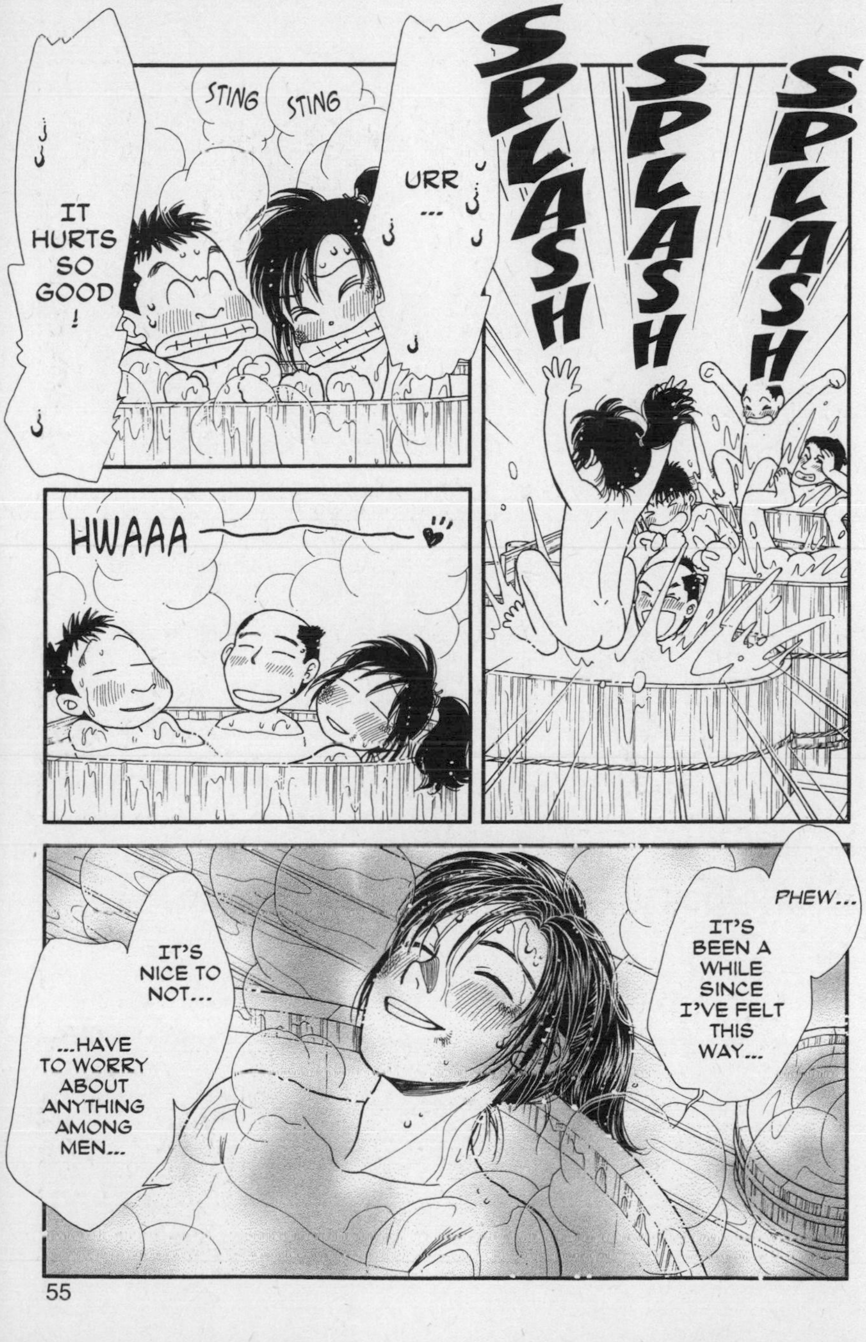
SPLASH
SPLASH
SPLASH
URR ...
STING STING
IT HURTS SO GOOD!
HWAAA
PHEW...
IT'S BEEN A WHILE SINCE I'VE FELT THIS WAY...
IT'S NICE TO NOT...
...HAVE TO WORRY ABOUT ANYTHING AMONG MEN...

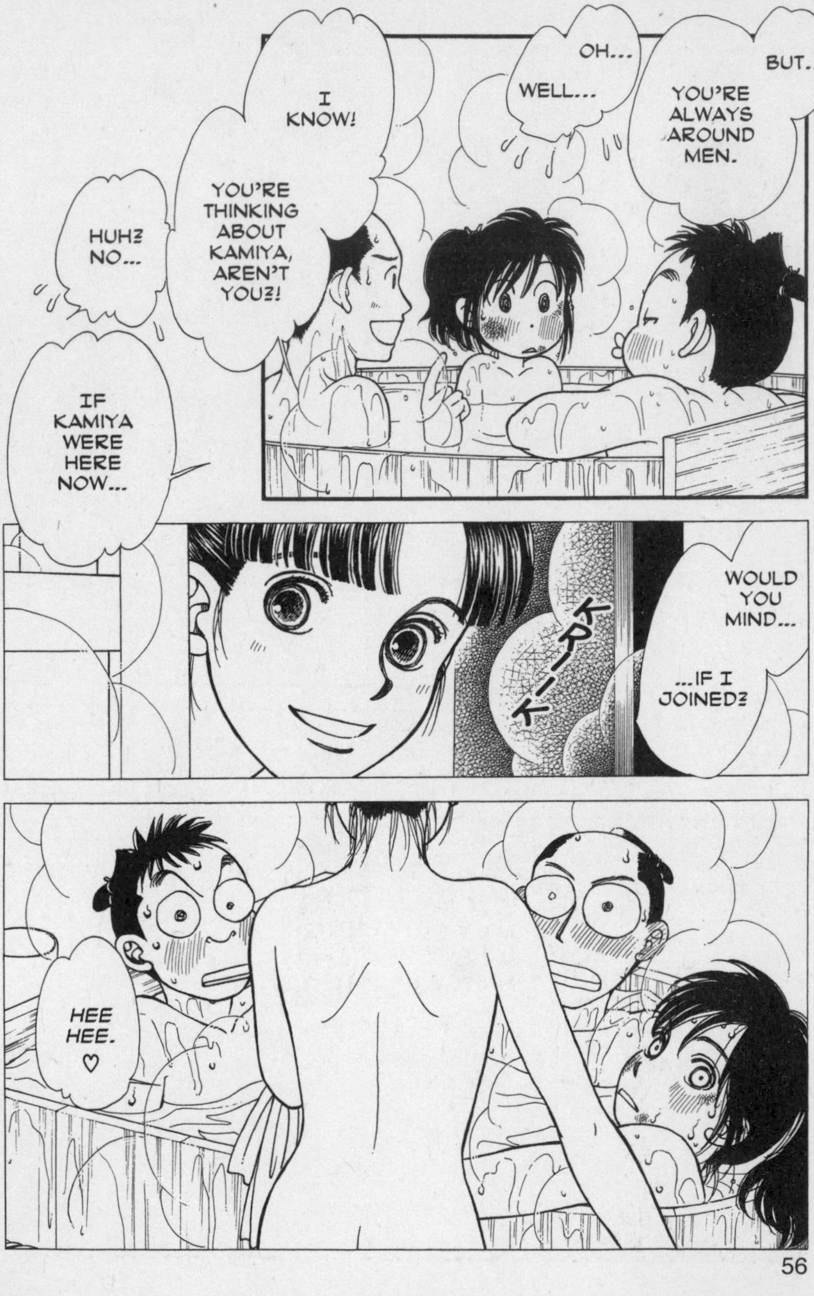
BUT... YOU'RE ALWAYS AROUND MEN.
OH... WELL...
I KNOW!
YOU'RE THINKING ABOUT KAMIYA, AREN'T YOU?!
HUH? NO...
IF KAMIYA WERE HERE NOW...
WOULD YOU MIND...
...IF I JOINED?
KRI--K
HEE HEE. ♡

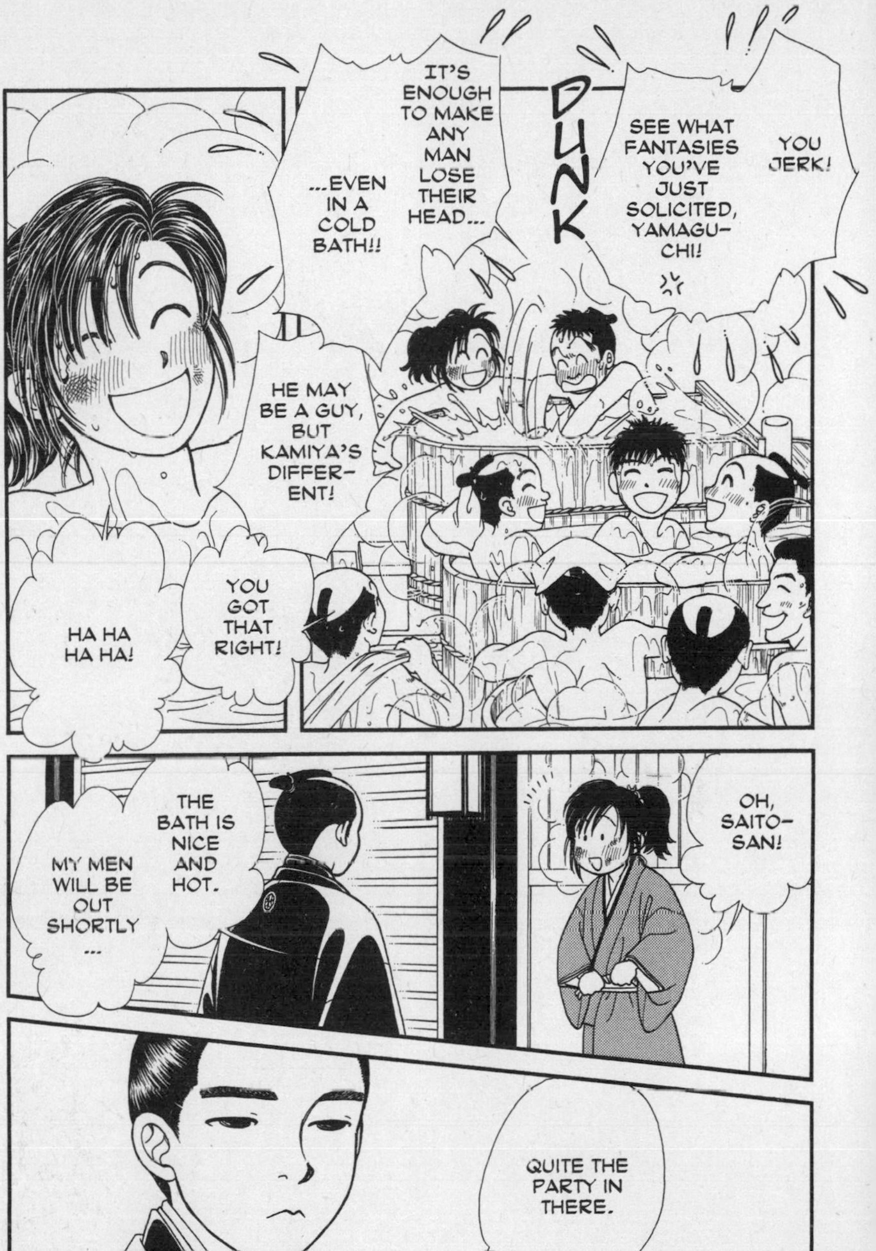
YOU JERK!
SEE WHAT FANTASIES YOU'VE JUST SOLICITED, YAMAGUCHI!
DUNK
IT'S ENOUGH TO MAKE ANY MAN LOSE THEIR HEAD...
...EVEN IN A COLD BATH!!
HE MAY BE A GUY, BUT KAMIYA'S DIFFERENT!
YOU GOT THAT RIGHT!
HA HA HA HA!
OH, SAITO-SAN!
THE BATH IS NICE AND HOT.
MY MEN WILL BE OUT SHORTLY ...
QUITE THE PARTY IN THERE.

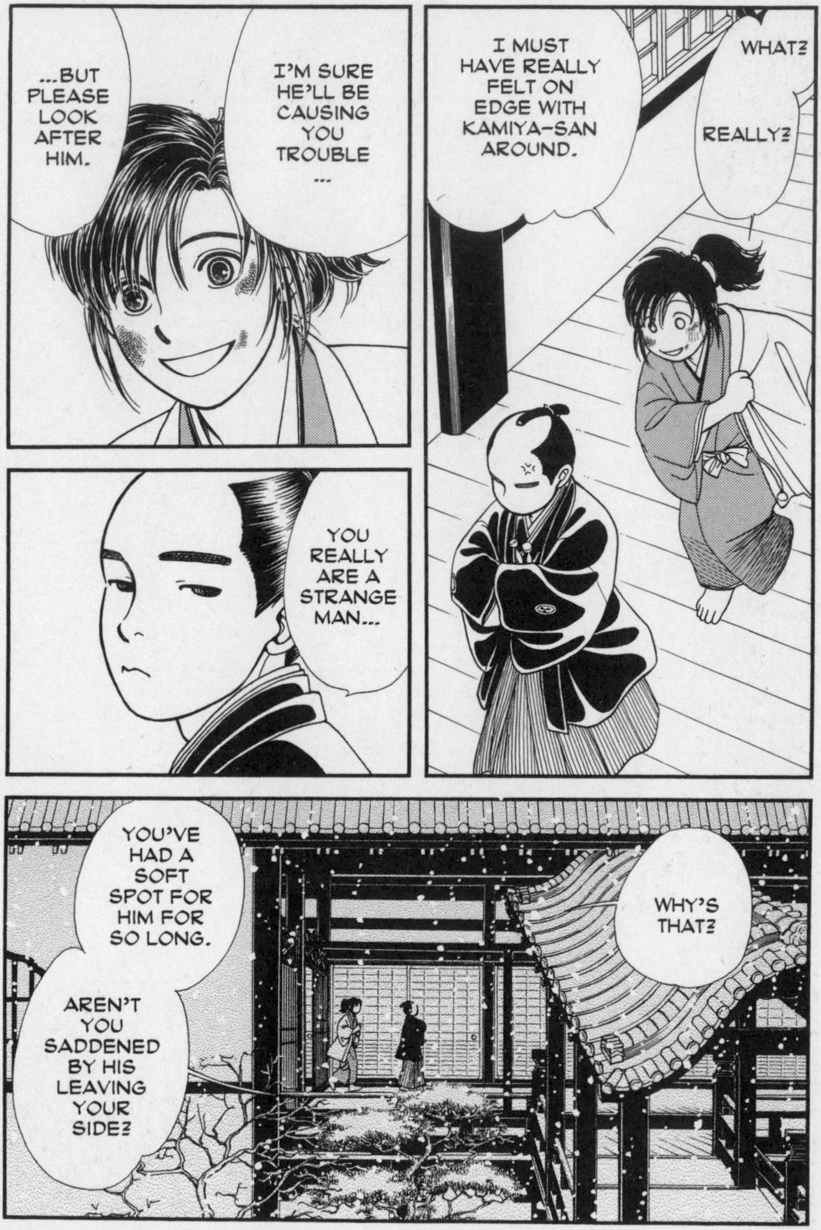
WHAT?
REALLY?
I MUST HAVE REALLY FELT ON EDGE WITH KAMIYA-SAN AROUND.
I'M SURE HE'LL BE CAUSING YOU TROUBLE ...
...BUT PLEASE LOOK AFTER HIM.
YOU REALLY ARE A STRANGE MAN...
WHY'S THAT?
YOU'VE HAD A SOFT SPOT FOR HIM FOR SO LONG.
AREN'T YOU SADDENED BY HIS LEAVING YOUR SIDE?

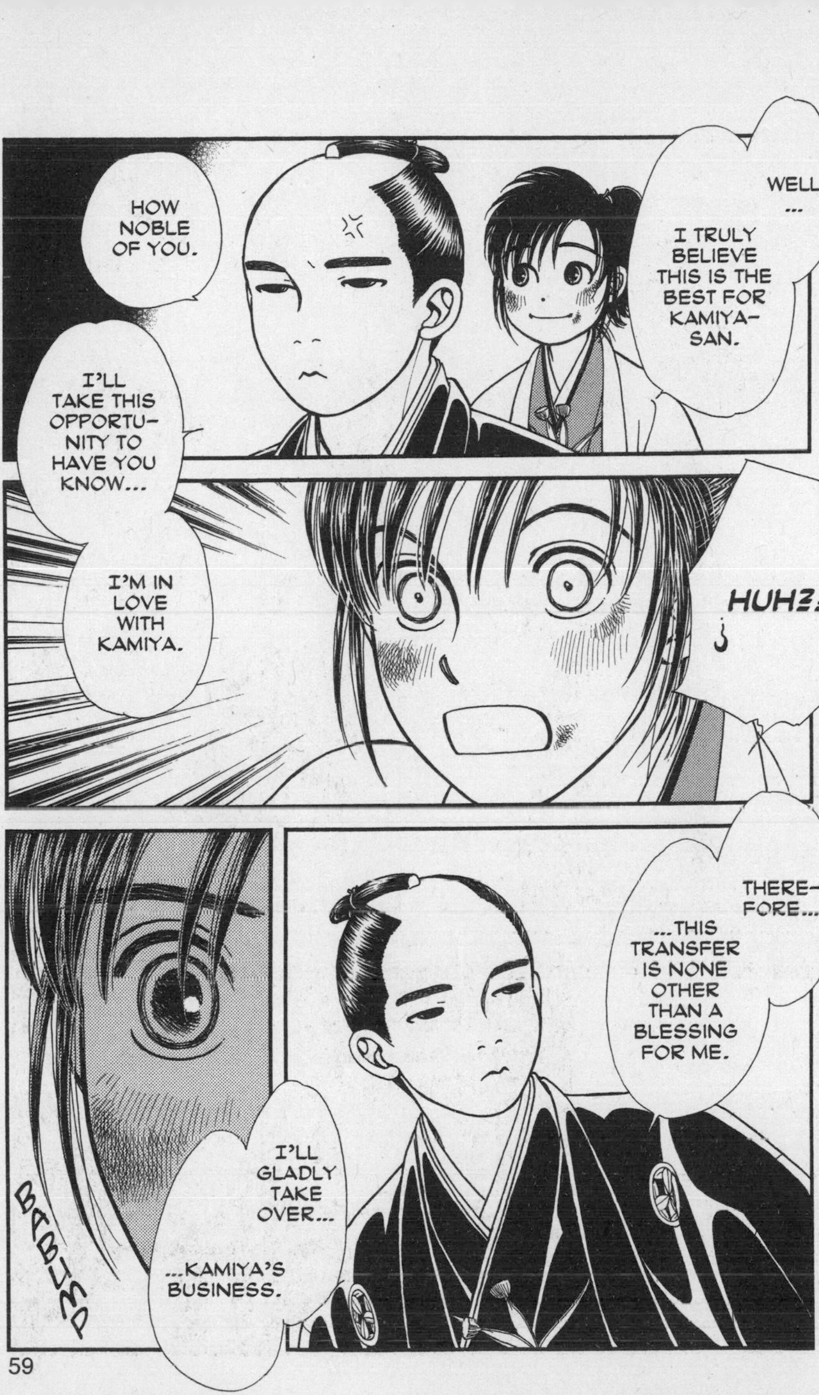
WELL ... I TRULY BELIEVE THIS IS THE BEST FOR KAMIYA-SAN.
HOW NOBLE OF YOU.
I'LL TAKE THIS OPPORTU-NITY TO HAVE YOU KNOW...
I'M IN LOVE WITH KAMIYA.
HUH?!
THERE-FORE...
...THIS TRANSFER IS NONE OTHER THAN A BLESSING FOR ME.
I'LL GLADLY TAKE OVER...
...KAMIYA'S BUSINESS.
BABUMP

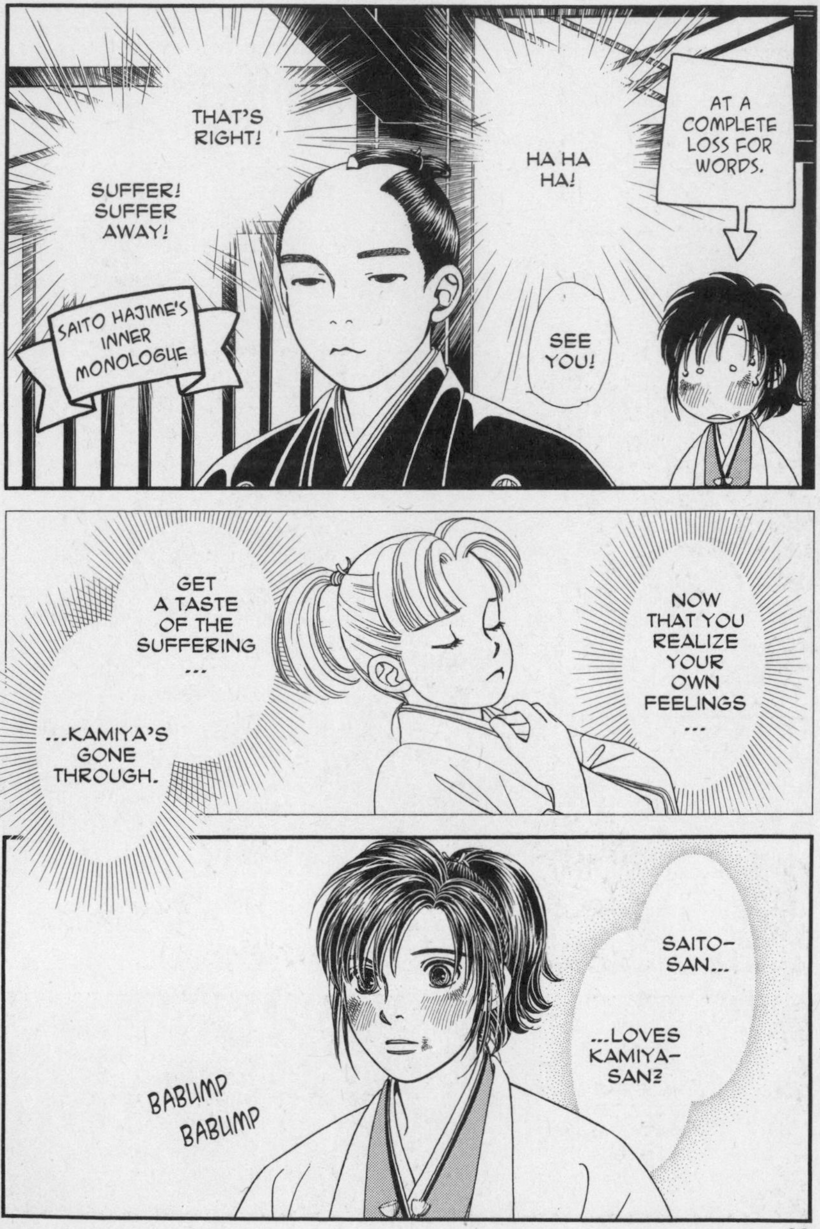
AT A COMPLETE LOSS FOR WORDS.
HA HA HA!
THAT'S RIGHT!
SEE YOU!
SUFFER! SUFFER AWAY!
SAITO HAJIME'S INNER MONOLOGUE
NOW THAT YOU REALIZE YOUR OWN FEELINGS...
GET A TASTE OF THE SUFFERING...
...KAMIYA'S GONE THROUGH.
SAITO-SAN...
...LOVES KAMIYA-SAN?
BABUMP
BABUMP

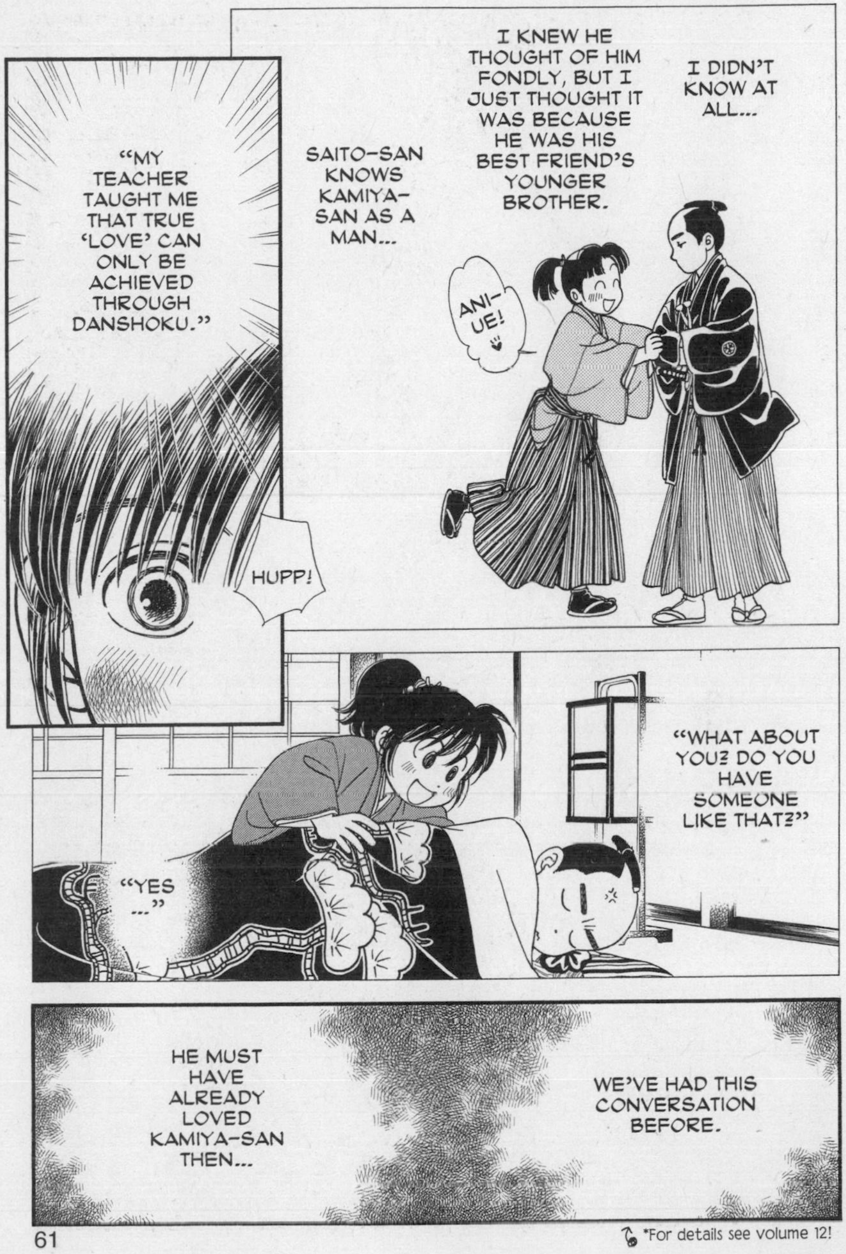
I DIDN'T KNOW AT ALL...
I KNEW HE THOUGHT OF HIM FONDLY, BUT I JUST THOUGHT IT WAS BECAUSE HE WAS HIS BEST FRIEND'S YOUNGER BROTHER.
SAITO-SAN KNOWS KAMIYA-SAN AS A MAN...
ANI-UE! ♥
"MY TEACHER TAUGHT ME THAT TRUE 'LOVE' CAN ONLY BE ACHIEVED THROUGH DANSHOKU."
HUPP!
"WHAT ABOUT YOU? DO YOU HAVE SOMEONE LIKE THAT?"
"YES ..."
WE'VE HAD THIS CONVERSATION BEFORE.
HE MUST HAVE ALREADY LOVED KAMIYA-SAN THEN...

*For details see volume 12!

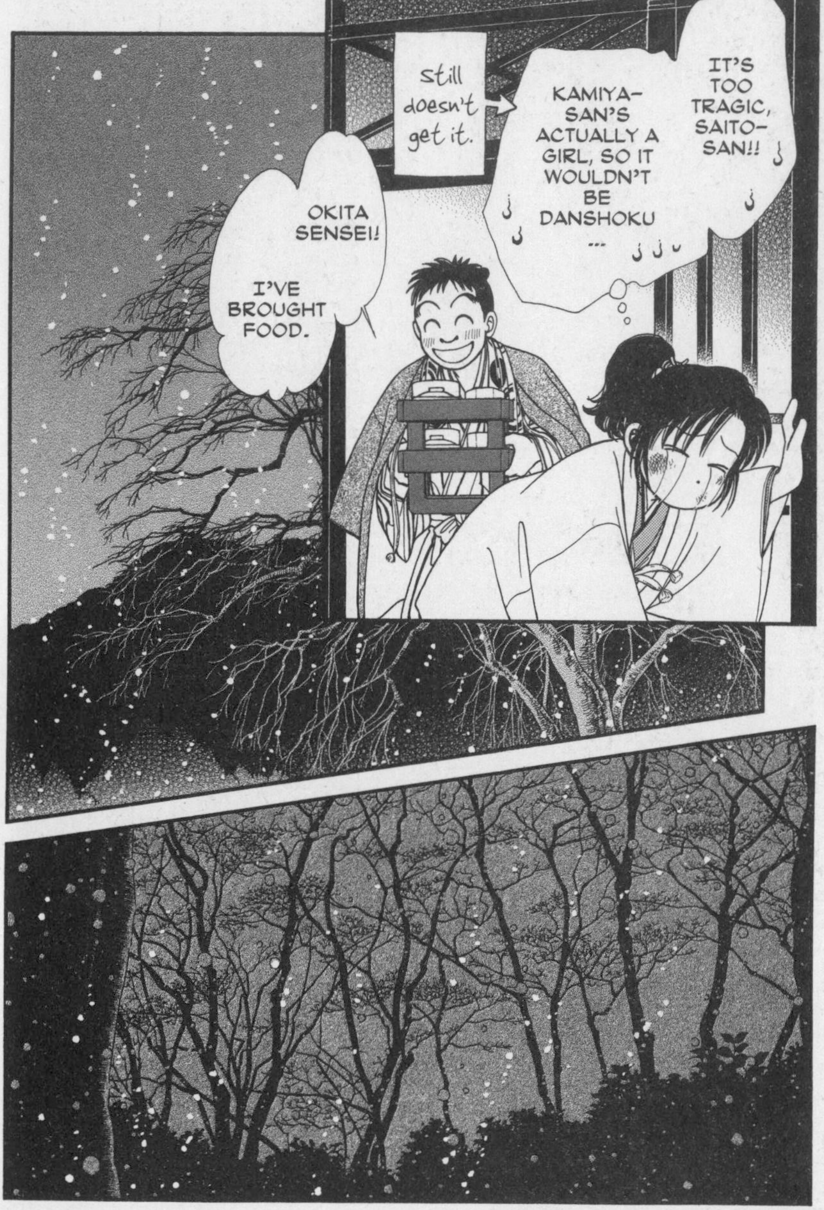
IT'S TOO TRAGIC, SAITO-SAN!!
KAMIYA-SAN'S ACTUALLY A GIRL, SO IT WOULDN'T BE DANSHOKU ...
still doesn't get it.
OKITA SENSEI!
I'VE BROUGHT FOOD.

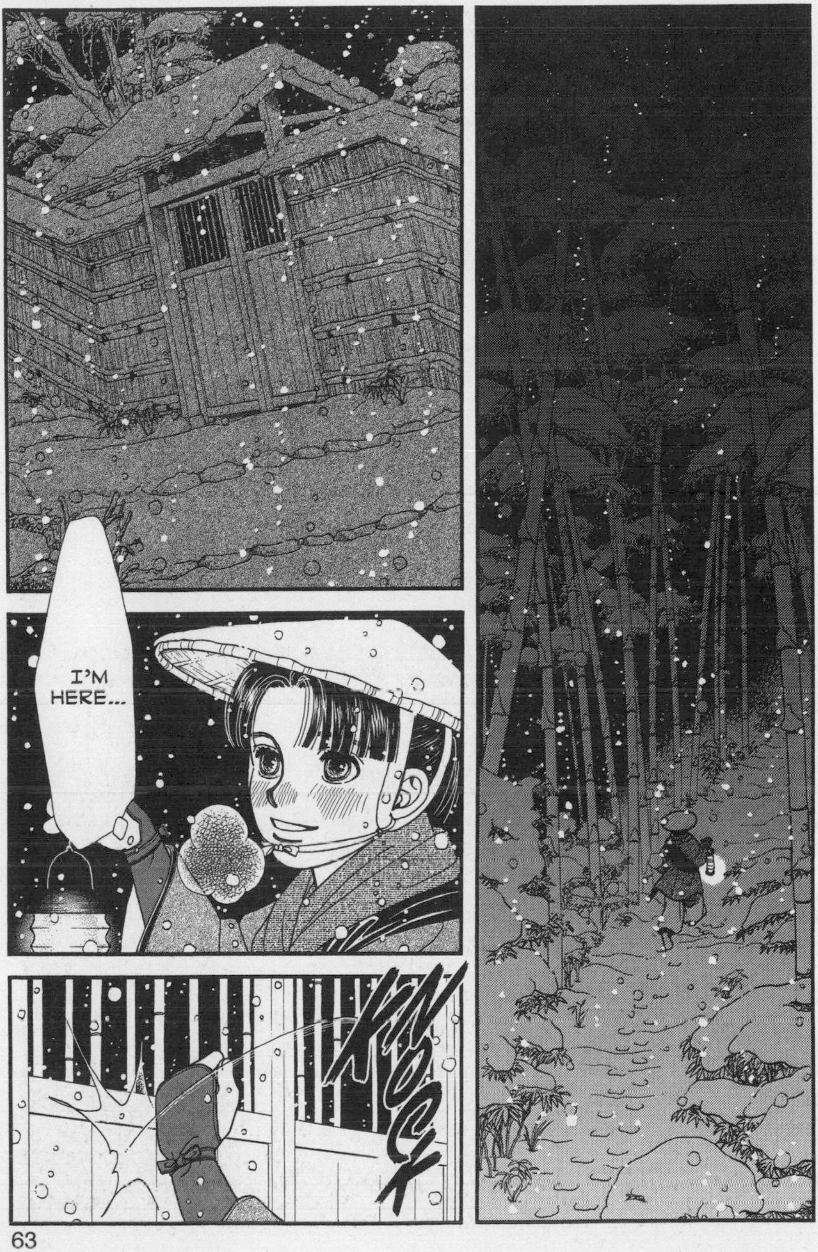
I'M HERE...
KNOCK

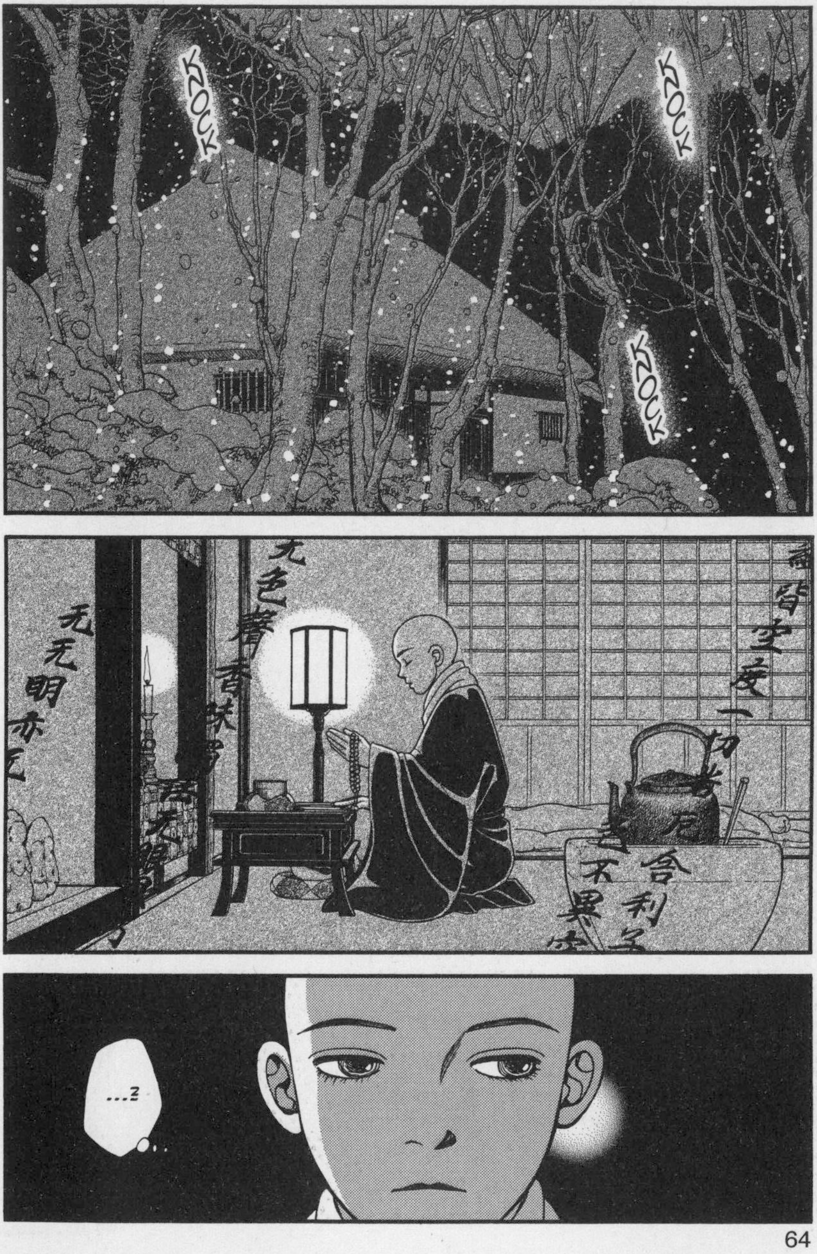
KNOCK
KNOCK
KNOCK
...?

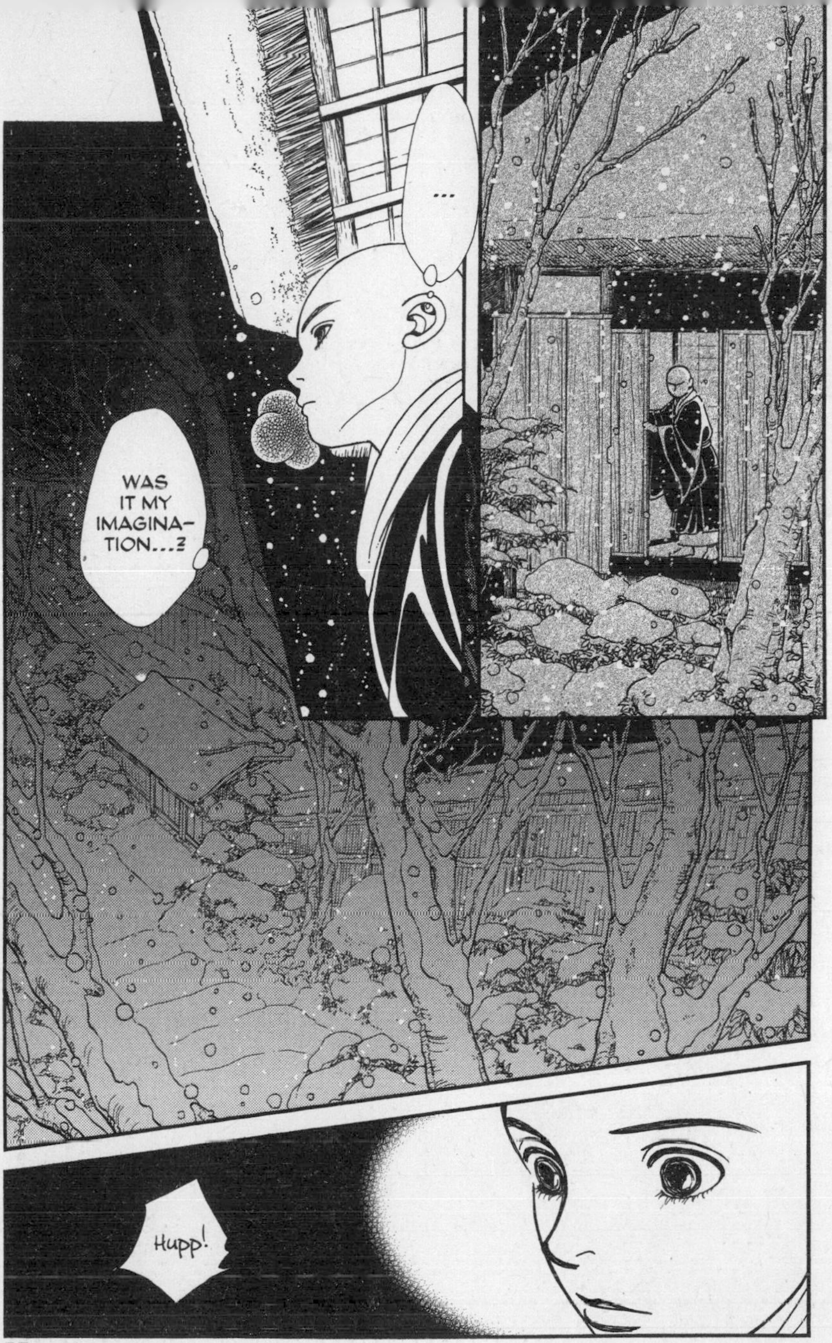
...
WAS IT MY IMAGINATION...?
Hupp!

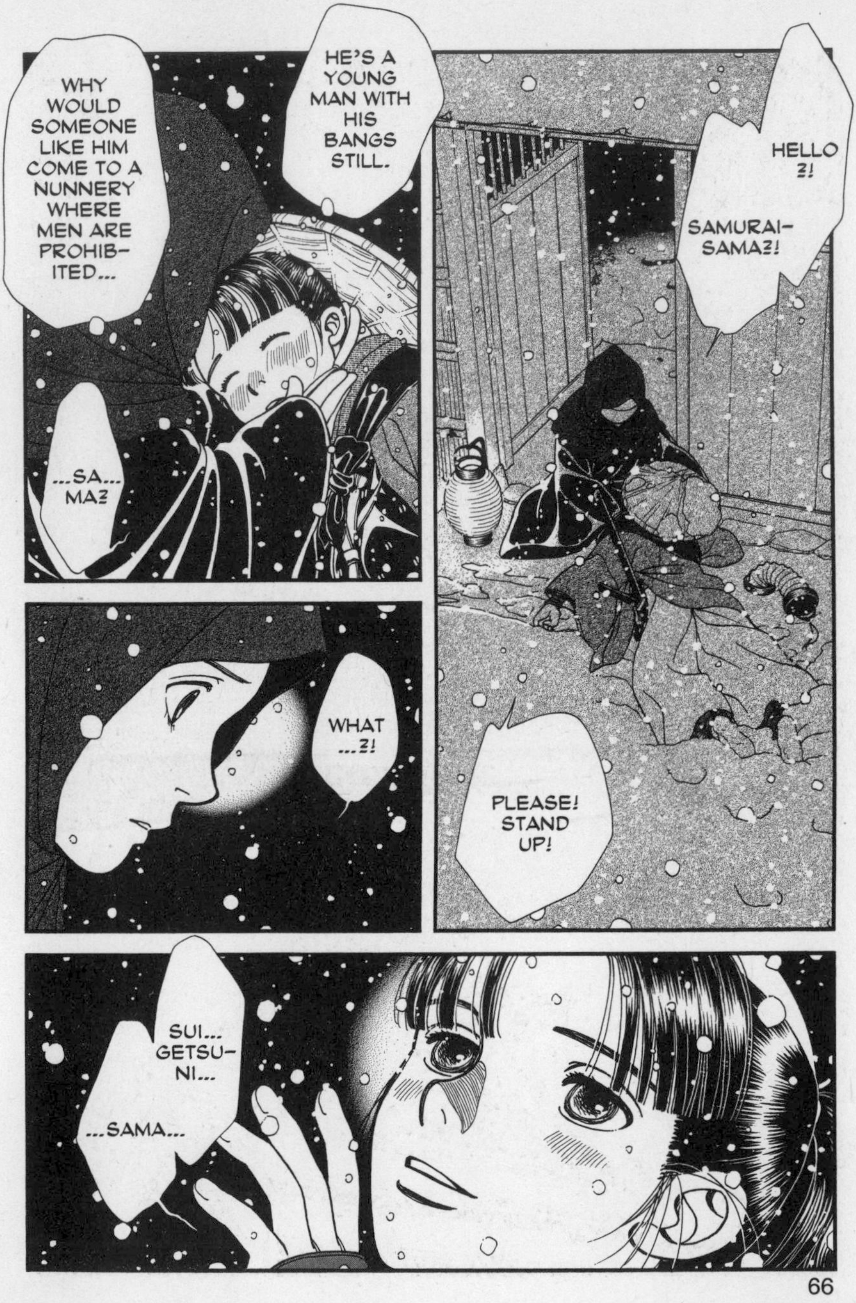
HELLO ?!
SAMURAI-SAMA?!
PLEASE! STAND UP!
HE'S A YOUNG MAN WITH HIS BANGS STILL.
WHY WOULD SOMEONE LIKE HIM COME TO A NUNNERY WHERE MEN ARE PROHIB-ITED...
...SA... MA?
WHAT ...?!
SUI... GETSU-NI...
...SAMA...

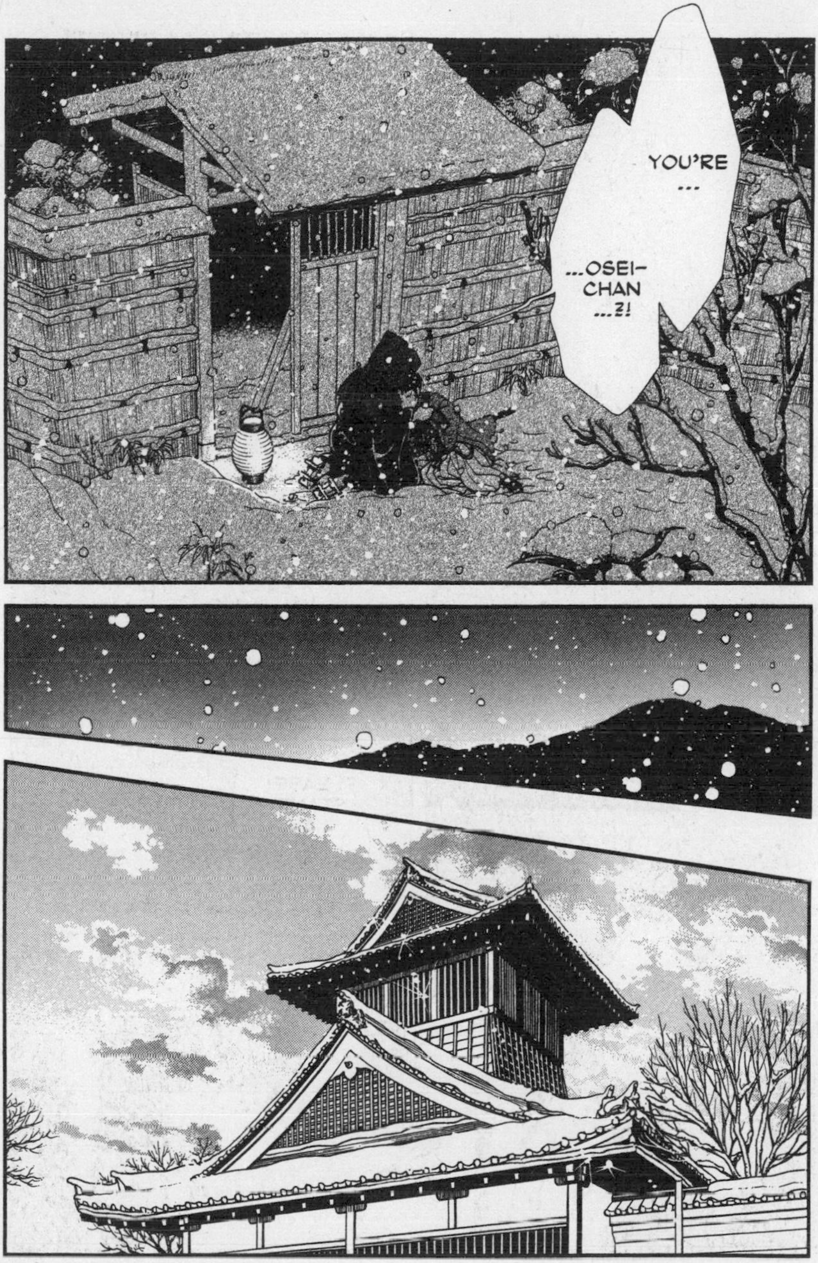
YOU'RE ... ...OSEI-CHAN ...?!

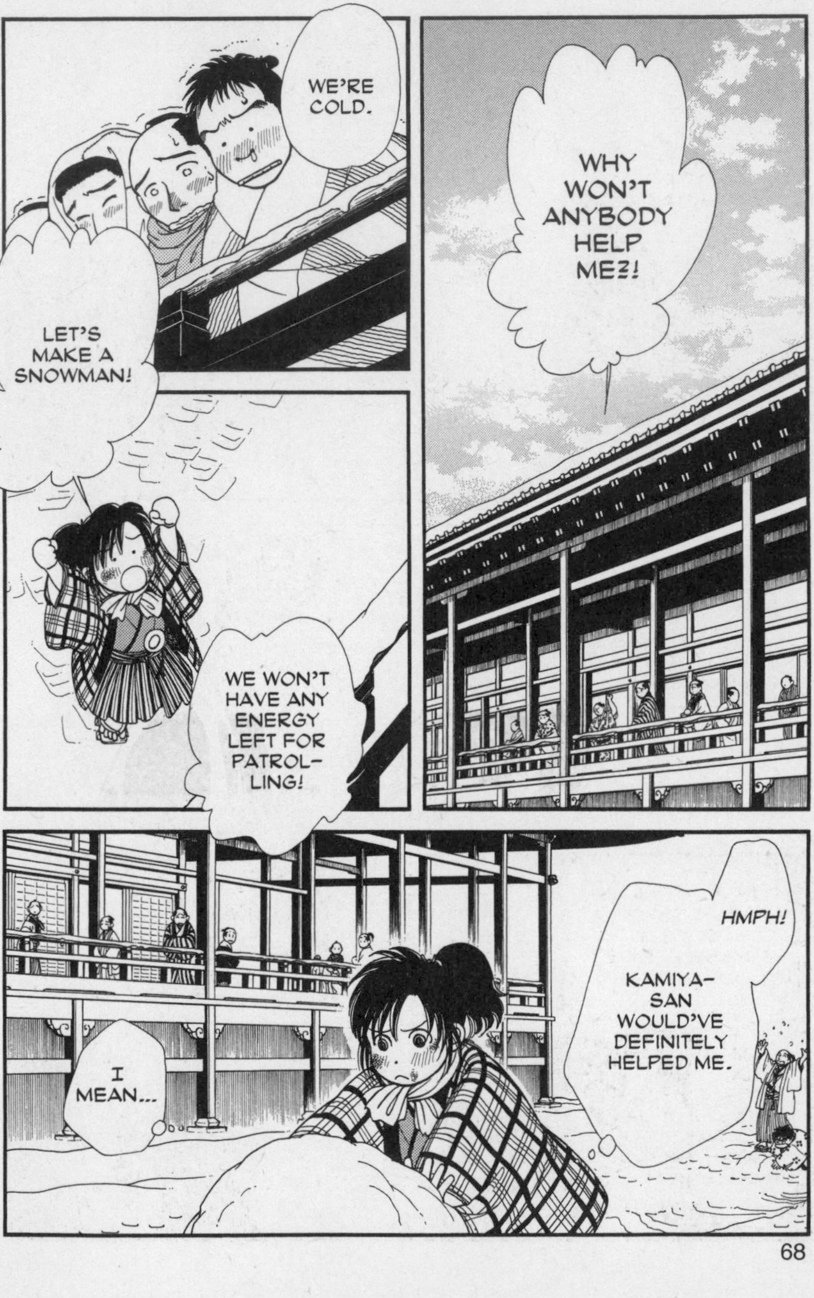
WHY WON'T ANYBODY HELP ME?!
WE'RE COLD.
LET'S MAKE A SNOWMAN!
WE WON'T HAVE ANY ENERGY LEFT FOR PATROL-LING!
HMPH!
KAMIYA-SAN WOULD'VE DEFINITELY HELPED ME.
I MEAN...

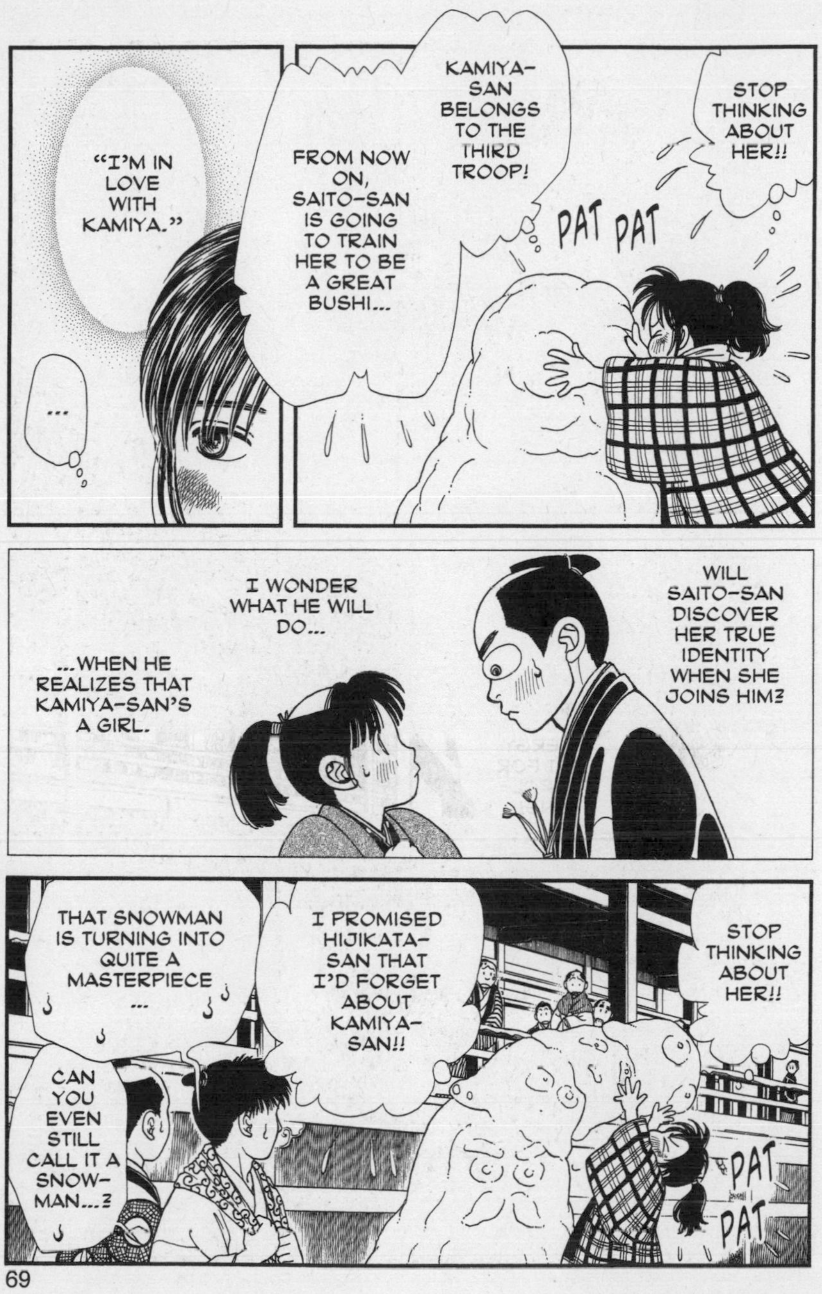
STOP THINKING ABOUT HER!!
KAMIYA-SAN BELONGS TO THE THIRD TROOP!
FROM NOW ON, SAITO-SAN IS GOING TO TRAIN HER TO BE A GREAT BUSHI...
PAT PAT
"I'M IN LOVE WITH KAMIYA."
...
WILL SAITO-SAN DISCOVER HER TRUE IDENTITY WHEN SHE JOINS HIM?
I WONDER WHAT HE WILL DO...
...WHEN HE REALIZES THAT KAMIYA-SAN'S A GIRL.
STOP THINKING ABOUT HER!!
PAT PAT
I PROMISED HIJIKATA-SAN THAT I'D FORGET ABOUT KAMIYA-SAN!!
THAT SNOWMAN IS TURNING INTO QUITE A MASTERPIECE ...
CAN YOU EVEN STILL CALL IT A SNOW-MAN...?

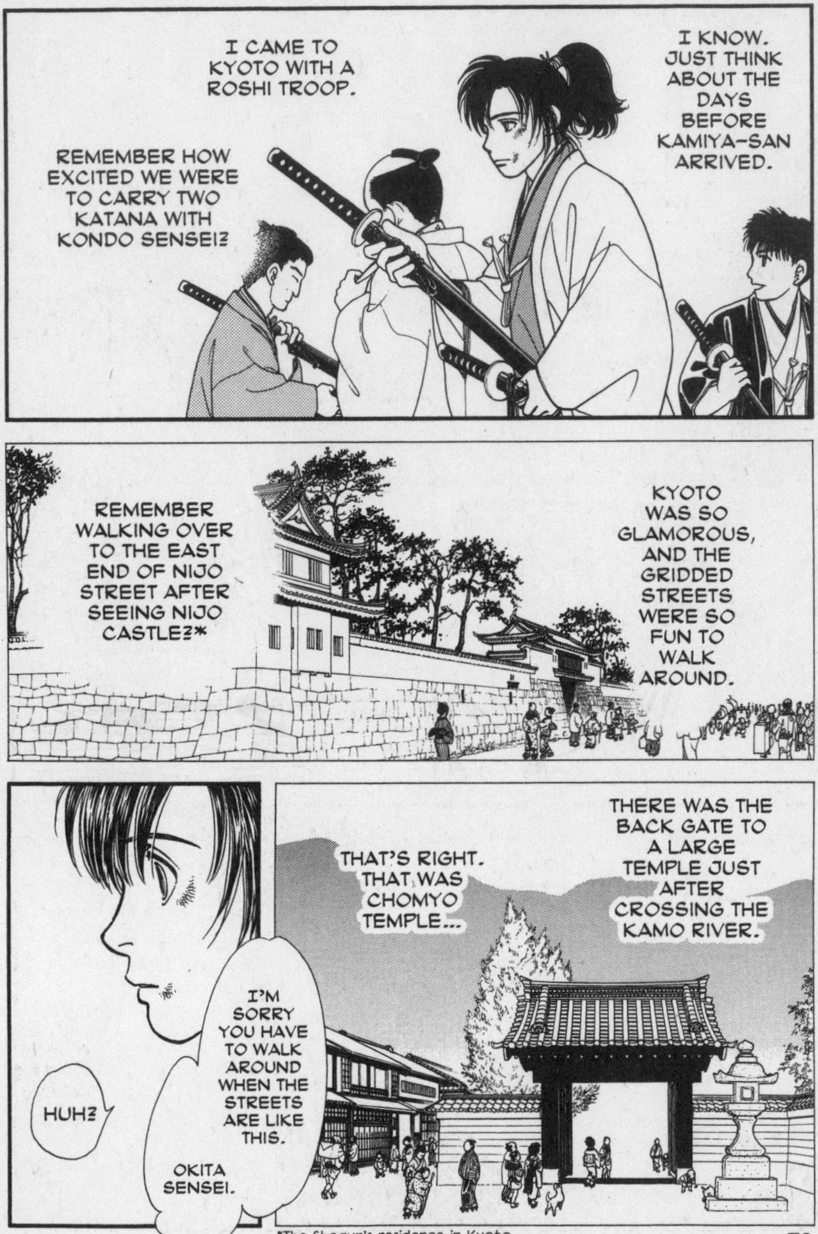
I KNOW. JUST THINK ABOUT THE DAYS BEFORE KAMIYA-SAN ARRIVED.
I CAME TO KYOTO WITH A ROSHI TROOP.
REMEMBER HOW EXCITED WE WERE TO CARRY TWO KATANA WITH KONDO SENSEI?
KYOTO WAS SO GLAMOROUS, AND THE GRIDDED STREETS WERE SO FUN TO WALK AROUND.
REMEMBER WALKING OVER TO THE EAST END OF NIJO STREET AFTER SEEING NIJO CASTLE?*
THERE WAS THE BACK GATE TO A LARGE TEMPLE JUST AFTER CROSSING THE KAMO RIVER.
THAT'S RIGHT. THAT WAS CHOMYO TEMPLE...
I'M SORRY YOU HAVE TO WALK AROUND WHEN THE STREETS ARE LIKE THIS.
OKITA SENSEI.
HUH?

*The Shogun's residence in Kyoto.

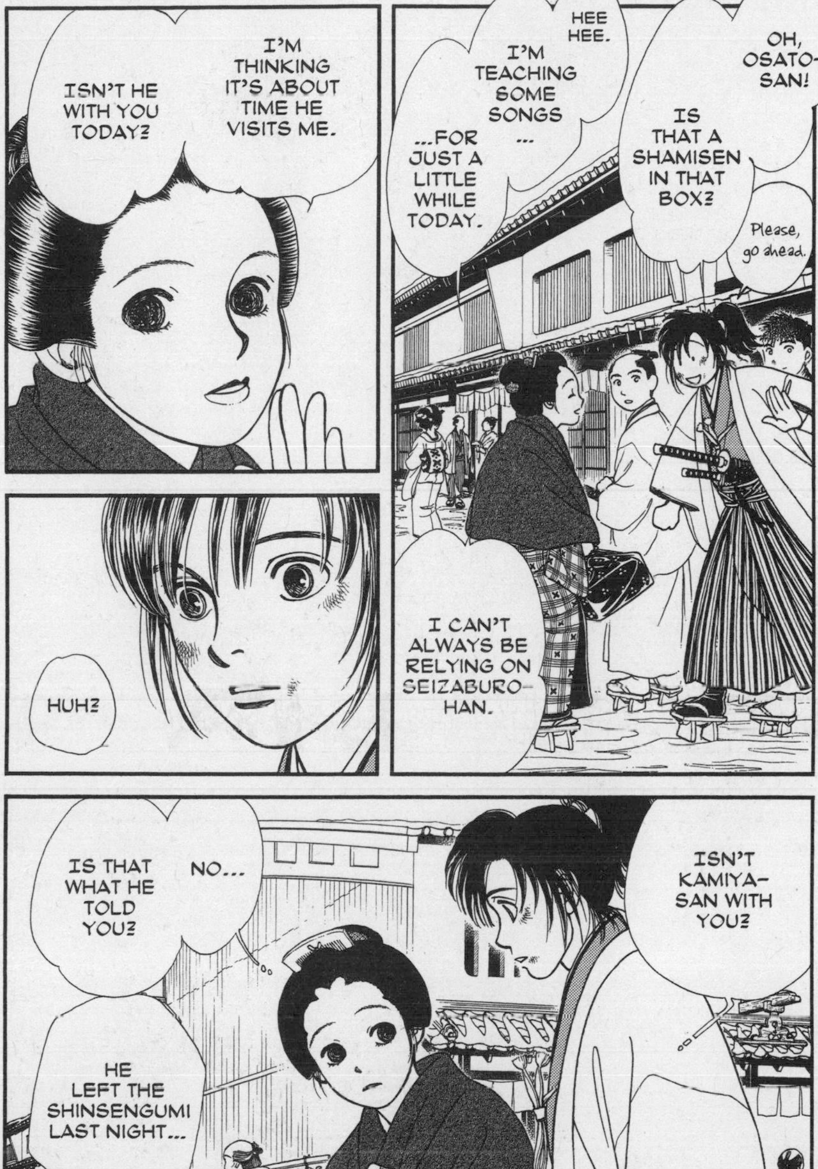
OH, OSATO-SAN!
IS THAT A SHAMISEN IN THAT BOX?
HEE HEE.
I'M TEACHING SOME SONGS ...
...FOR JUST A LITTLE WHILE TODAY.
Please, go ahead.
I CAN'T ALWAYS BE RELYING ON SEIZABURO-HAN.
I'M THINKING IT'S ABOUT TIME HE VISITS ME.
ISN'T HE WITH YOU TODAY?
HUH?
ISN'T KAMIYA-SAN WITH YOU?
NO...
IS THAT WHAT HE TOLD YOU?
HE LEFT THE SHINSENGUMI LAST NIGHT...

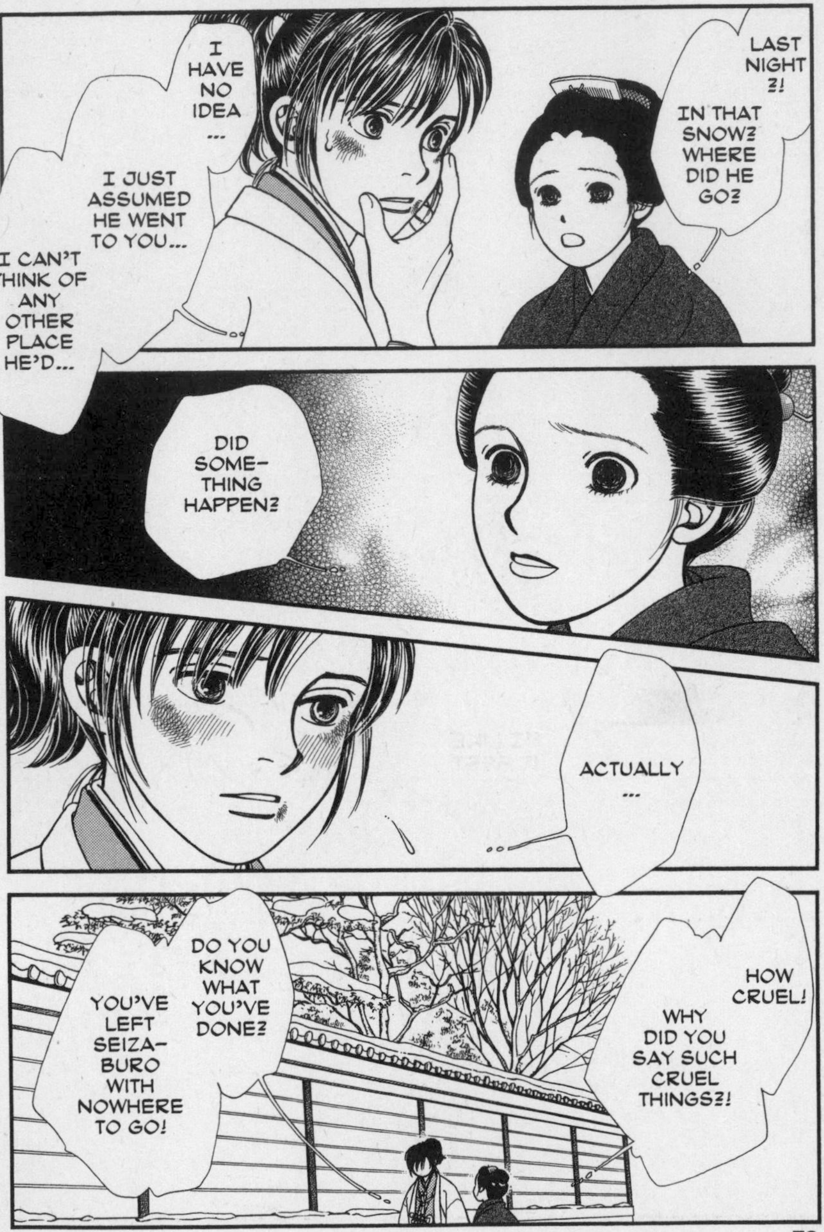
LAST NIGHT?!
IN THAT SNOW? WHERE DID HE GO?
I HAVE NO IDEA ...
I JUST ASSUMED HE WENT TO YOU...
I CAN'T THINK OF ANY OTHER PLACE HE'D...
DID SOME-THING HAPPEN?
ACTUALLY ...
HOW CRUEL!
WHY DID YOU SAY SUCH CRUEL THINGS?!
DO YOU KNOW WHAT YOU'VE DONE?
YOU'VE LEFT SEIZA-BURO WITH NOWHERE TO GO!

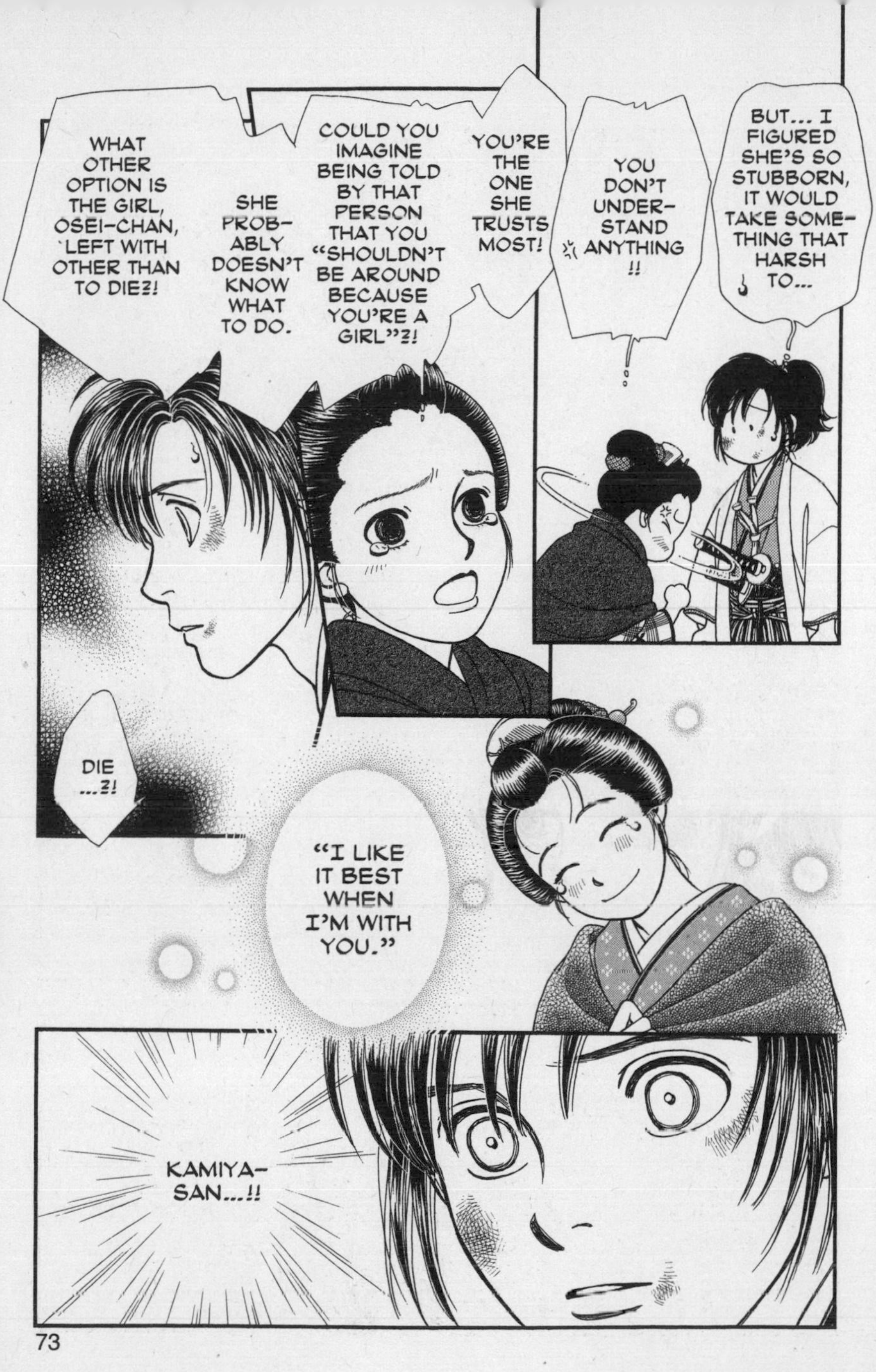
BUT... I FIGURED SHE'S SO STUBBORN, IT WOULD TAKE SOMETHING THAT HARSH TO...
YOU DON'T UNDERSTAND ANYTHING!!
YOU'RE THE ONE SHE TRUSTS MOST!
COULD YOU IMAGINE BEING TOLD BY THAT PERSON THAT YOU "SHOULDN'T BE AROUND BECAUSE YOU'RE A GIRL"?!
SHE PROBABLY DOESN'T KNOW WHAT TO DO.
WHAT OTHER OPTION IS THE GIRL, OSEI-CHAN, LEFT WITH OTHER THAN TO DIE?!
DIE...?!
"I LIKE IT BEST WHEN I'M WITH YOU."
KAMIYA-SAN...!!

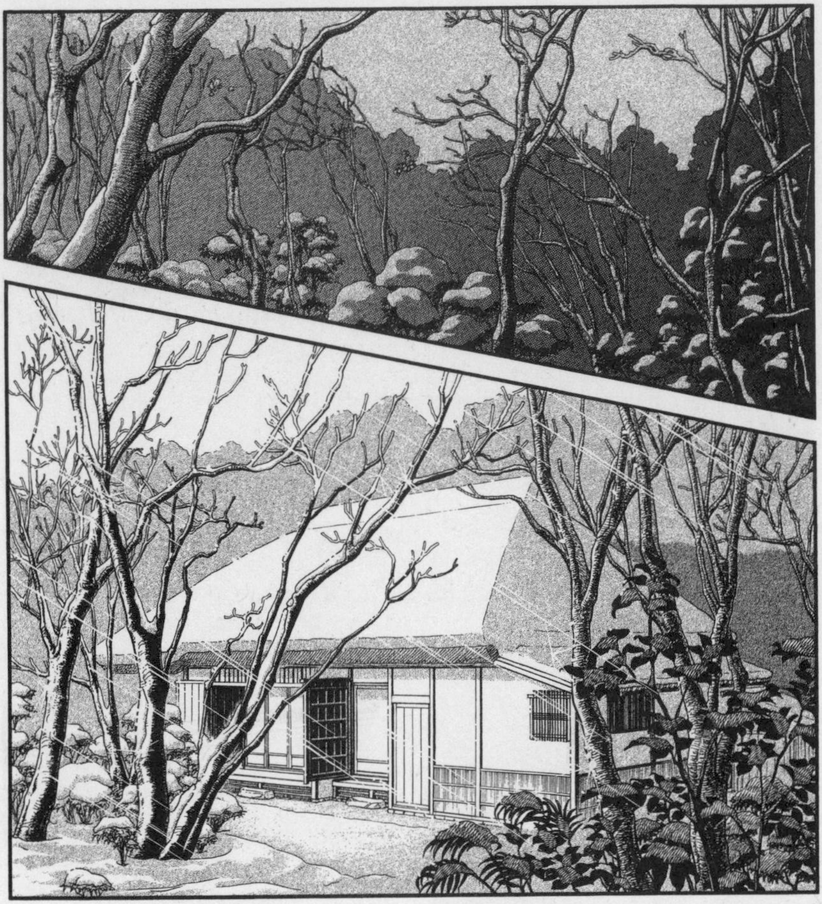

KAZE HIKARU IROHA KARUTA

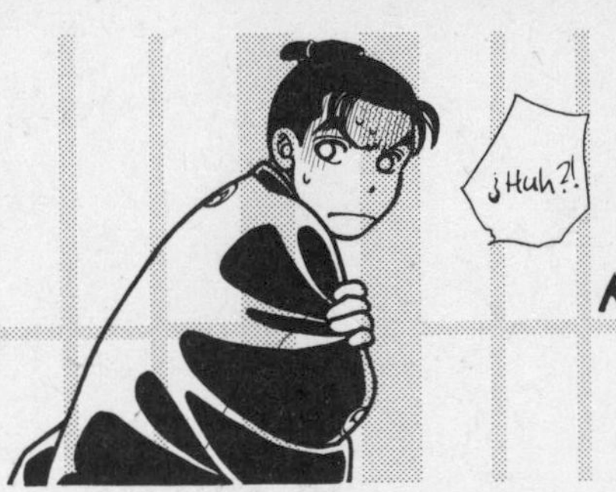
¡Huh?!

"KA" か

KASHI TAN TAN

"READY TO AMBUSH, KASHI"

by Marble-san from Nara

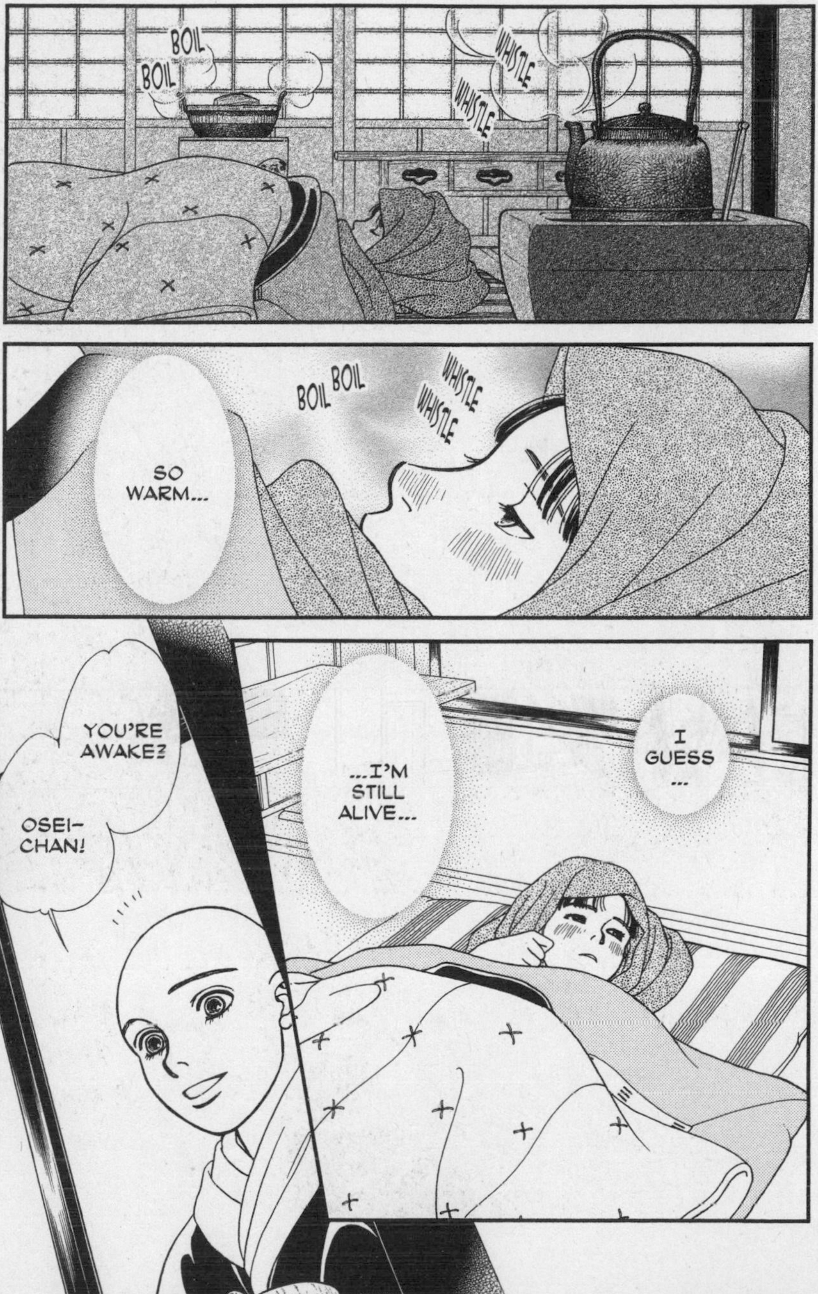
WHISTLE WHISTLE
BOIL BOIL
WHISTLE WHISTLE
BOIL BOIL
SO WARM...
I GUESS ...
...I'M STILL ALIVE...
YOU'RE AWAKE?
OSEI-CHAN!

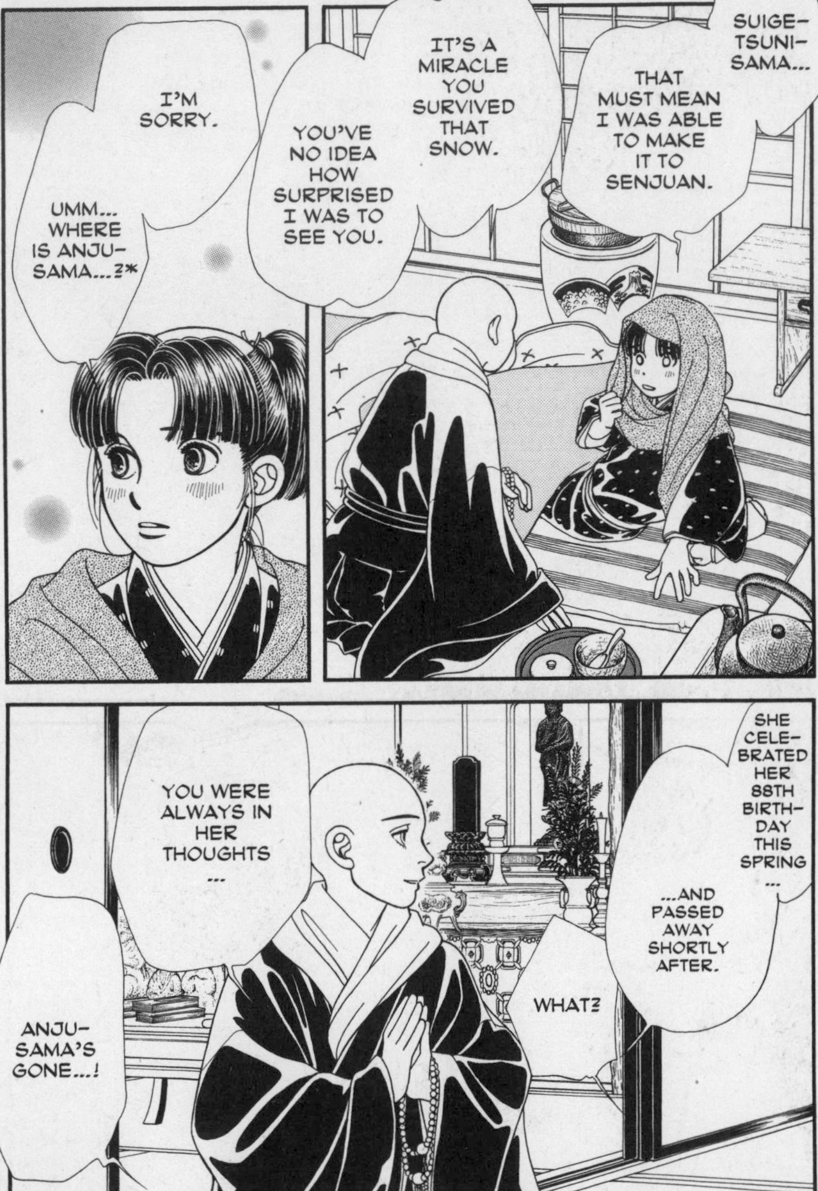
SUIGE-TSUNI-SAMA...
THAT MUST MEAN I WAS ABLE TO MAKE IT TO SENJUAN.
IT'S A MIRACLE YOU SURVIVED THAT SNOW.
YOU'VE NO IDEA HOW SURPRISED I WAS TO SEE YOU.
I'M SORRY.
UMM... WHERE IS ANJU-SAMA...?*
SHE CELEBRATED HER 88TH BIRTHDAY THIS SPRING...
...AND PASSED AWAY SHORTLY AFTER.
WHAT?
ANJU-SAMA'S GONE...!
YOU WERE ALWAYS IN HER THOUGHTS...

*A nun who runs a hermitage.

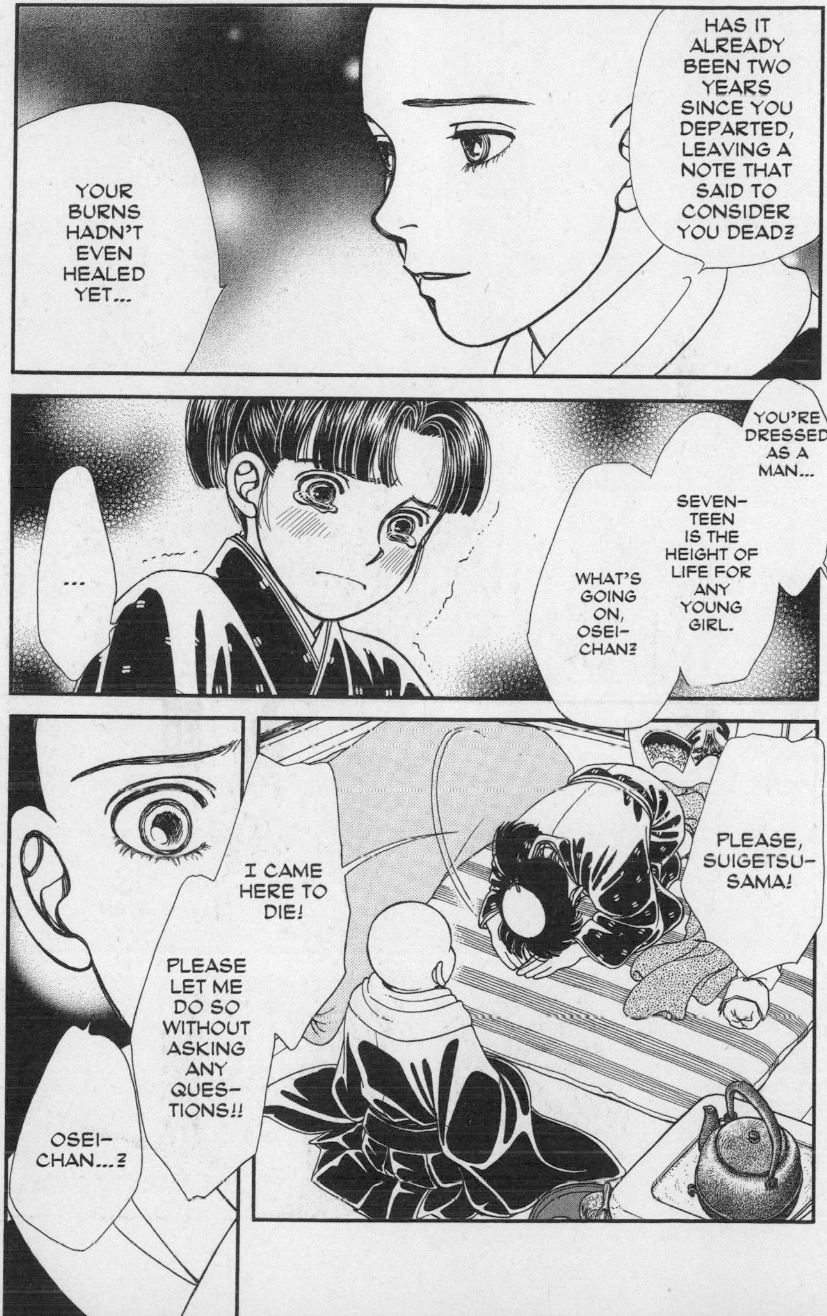
HAS IT ALREADY BEEN TWO YEARS SINCE YOU DEPARTED, LEAVING A NOTE THAT SAID TO CONSIDER YOU DEAD?
YOUR BURNS HADN'T EVEN HEALED YET...
YOU'RE DRESSED AS A MAN...
SEVENTEEN IS THE HEIGHT OF LIFE FOR ANY YOUNG GIRL.
WHAT'S GOING ON, OSEI-CHAN?
...
PLEASE, SUIGETSU-SAMA!
I CAME HERE TO DIE!
PLEASE LET ME DO SO WITHOUT ASKING ANY QUESTIONS!!
OSEI-CHAN...?

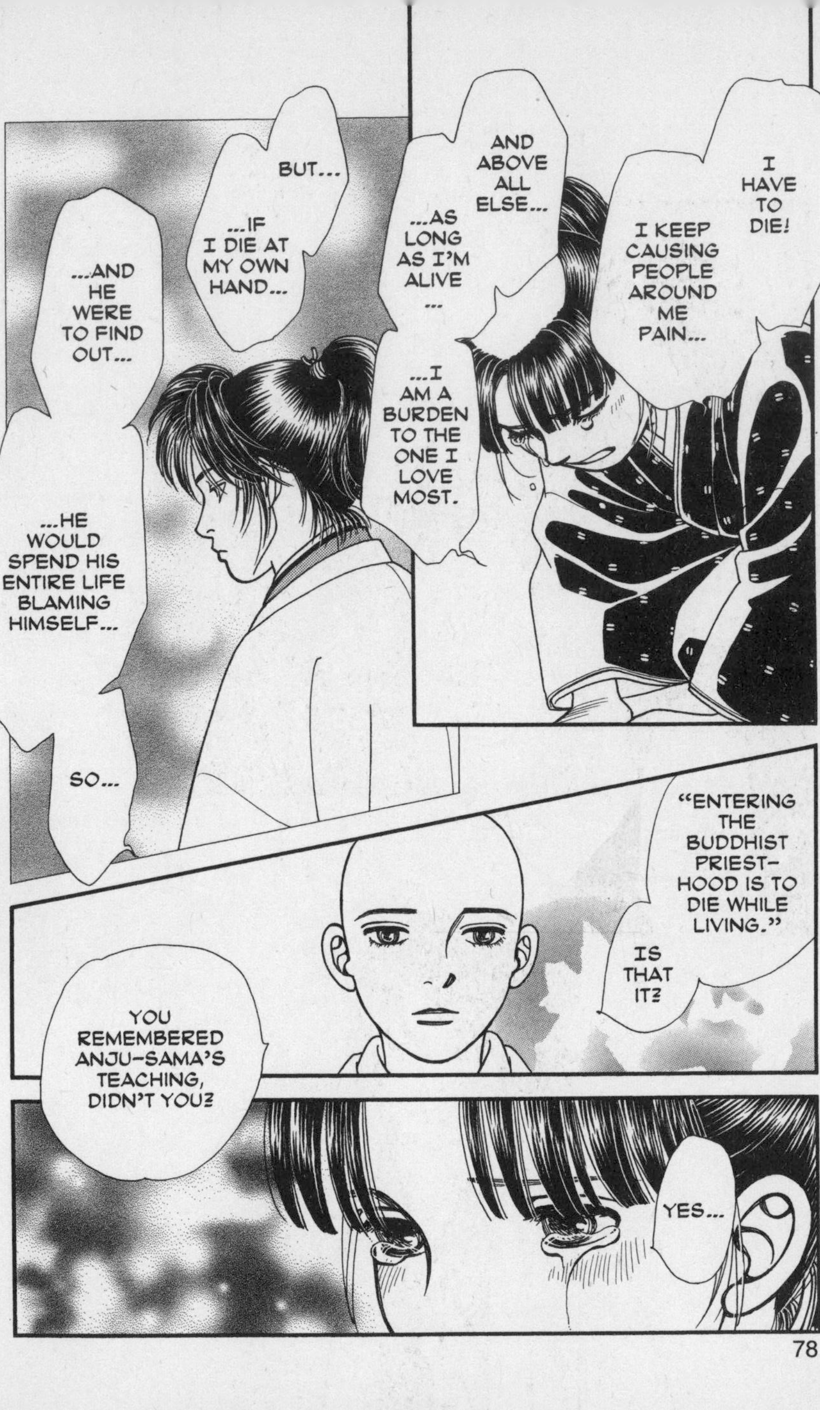
I HAVE TO DIE!
I KEEP CAUSING PEOPLE AROUND ME PAIN...
AND ABOVE ALL ELSE...
...AS LONG AS I'M ALIVE ...
...I AM A BURDEN TO THE ONE I LOVE MOST.
BUT...
...IF I DIE AT MY OWN HAND...
...AND HE WERE TO FIND OUT...
...HE WOULD SPEND HIS ENTIRE LIFE BLAMING HIMSELF...
SO...
"ENTERING THE BUDDHIST PRIEST-HOOD IS TO DIE WHILE LIVING."
IS THAT IT?
YOU REMEMBERED ANJU-SAMA'S TEACHING, DIDN'T YOU?
YES...

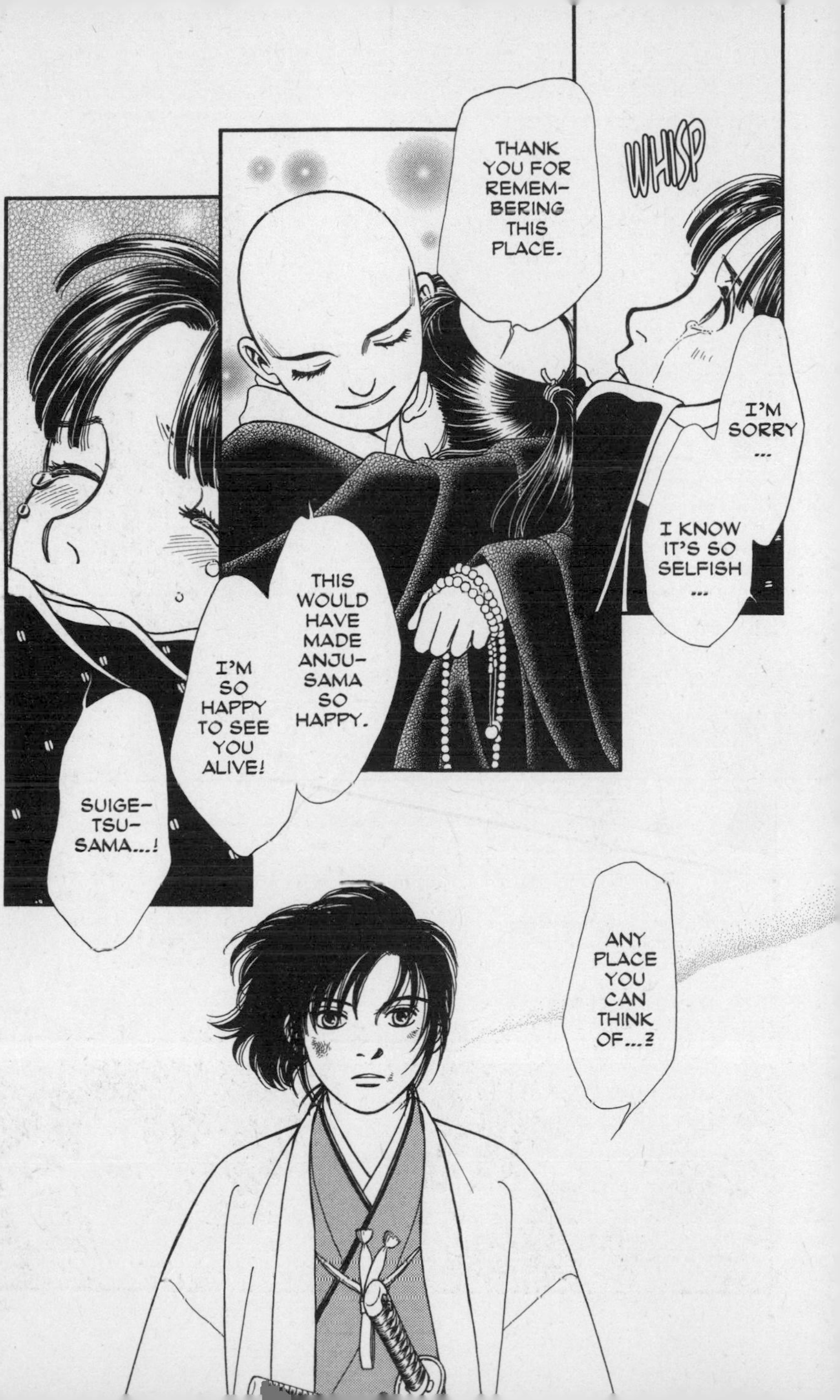
WHISP
I'M SORRY...
I KNOW IT'S SO SELFISH...
THANK YOU FOR REMEMBERING THIS PLACE.
THIS WOULD HAVE MADE ANJU-SAMA SO HAPPY.
I'M SO HAPPY TO SEE YOU ALIVE!
SUIGETSU-SAMA...!
ANY PLACE YOU CAN THINK OF...?

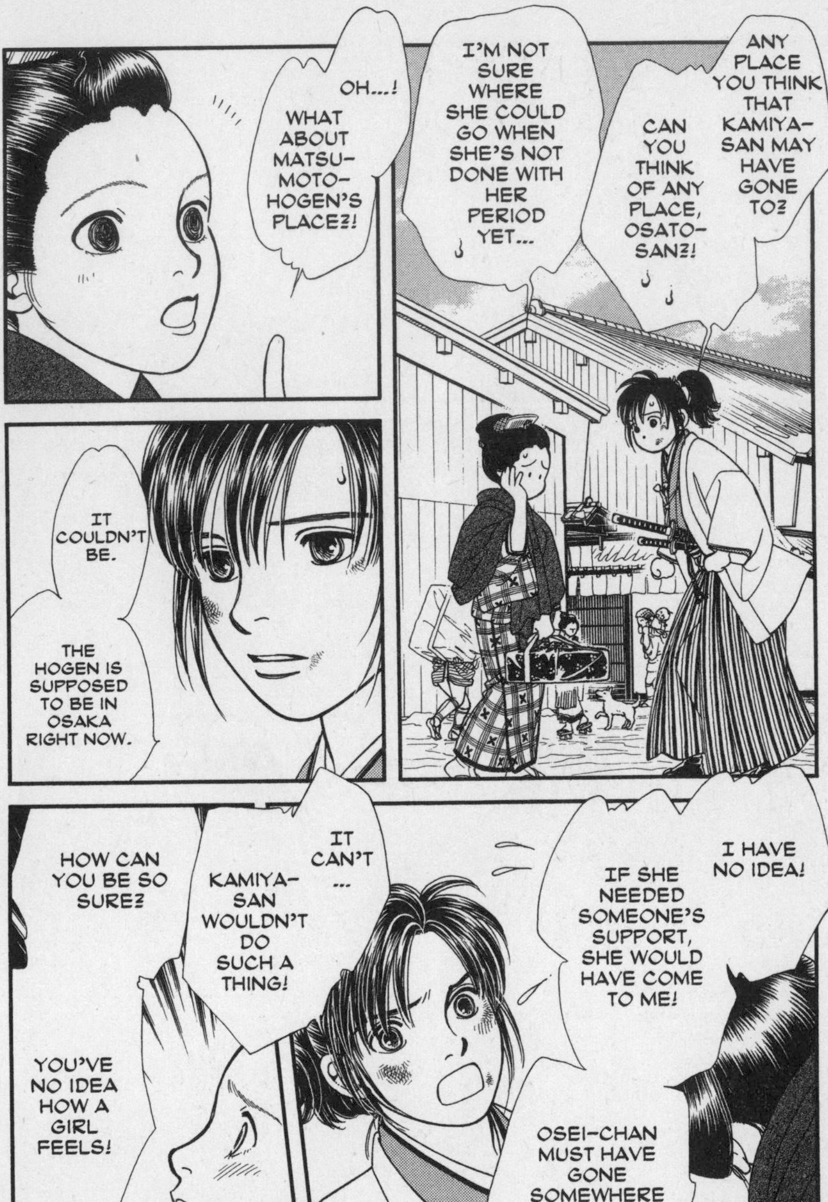
ANY PLACE YOU THINK THAT KAMIYA-SAN MAY HAVE GONE TO?
CAN YOU THINK OF ANY PLACE, OSATO-SAN?!
I'M NOT SURE WHERE SHE COULD GO WHEN SHE'S NOT DONE WITH HER PERIOD YET...
OH...!
WHAT ABOUT MATSU-MOTO-HOGEN'S PLACE?!
IT COULDN'T BE.
THE HOGEN IS SUPPOSED TO BE IN OSAKA RIGHT NOW.
I HAVE NO IDEA!
IF SHE NEEDED SOMEONE'S SUPPORT, SHE WOULD HAVE COME TO ME!
OSEI-CHAN MUST HAVE GONE SOMEWHERE TO DIE!
IT CAN'T ...
KAMIYA-SAN WOULDN'T DO SUCH A THING!
HOW CAN YOU BE SO SURE?
YOU'VE NO IDEA HOW A GIRL FEELS!

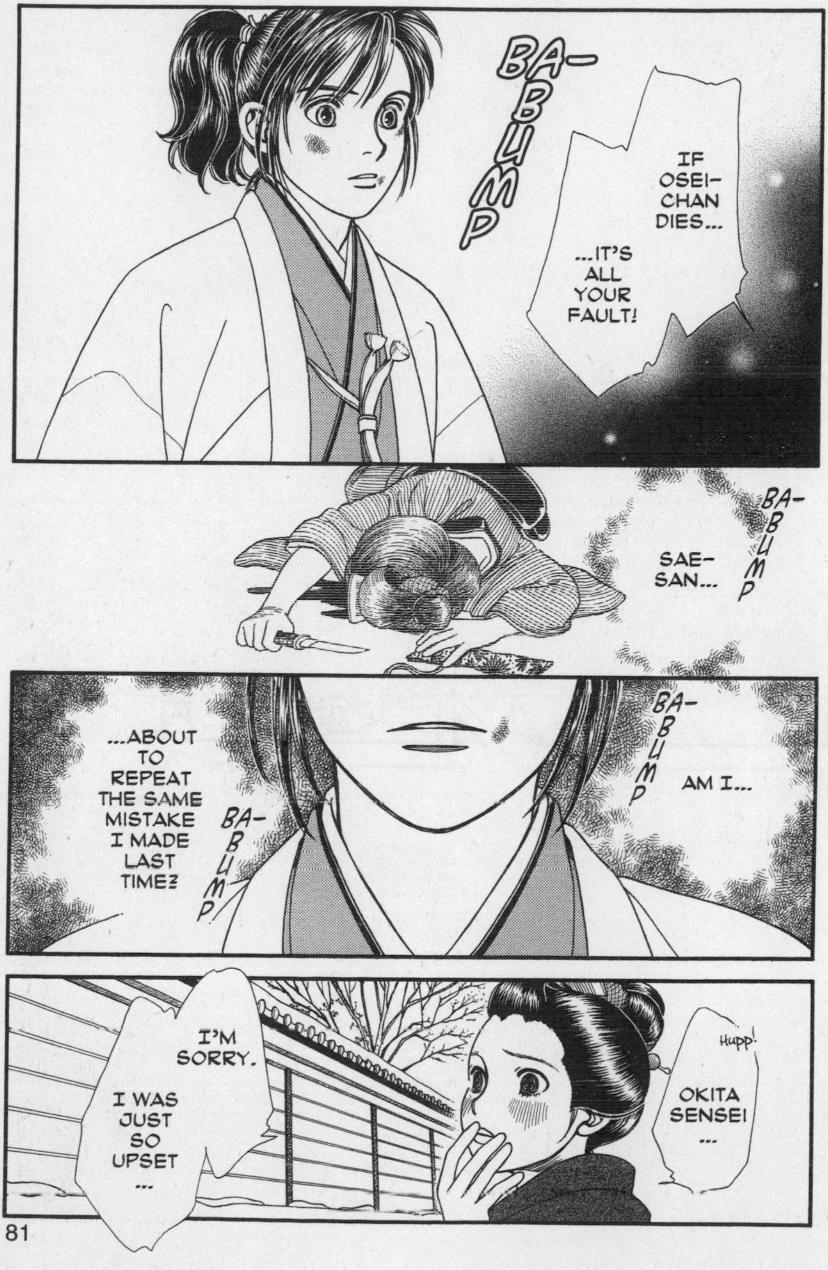
IF OSEI-CHAN DIES...
...IT'S ALL YOUR FAULT!
BA-BUMP
BA-BUMP
SAE-SAN...
BA-BUMP
AM I...
...ABOUT TO REPEAT THE SAME MISTAKE I MADE LAST TIME?
BA-BUMP
Hupp!
OKITA SENSEI...
I'M SORRY.
I WAS JUST SO UPSET...

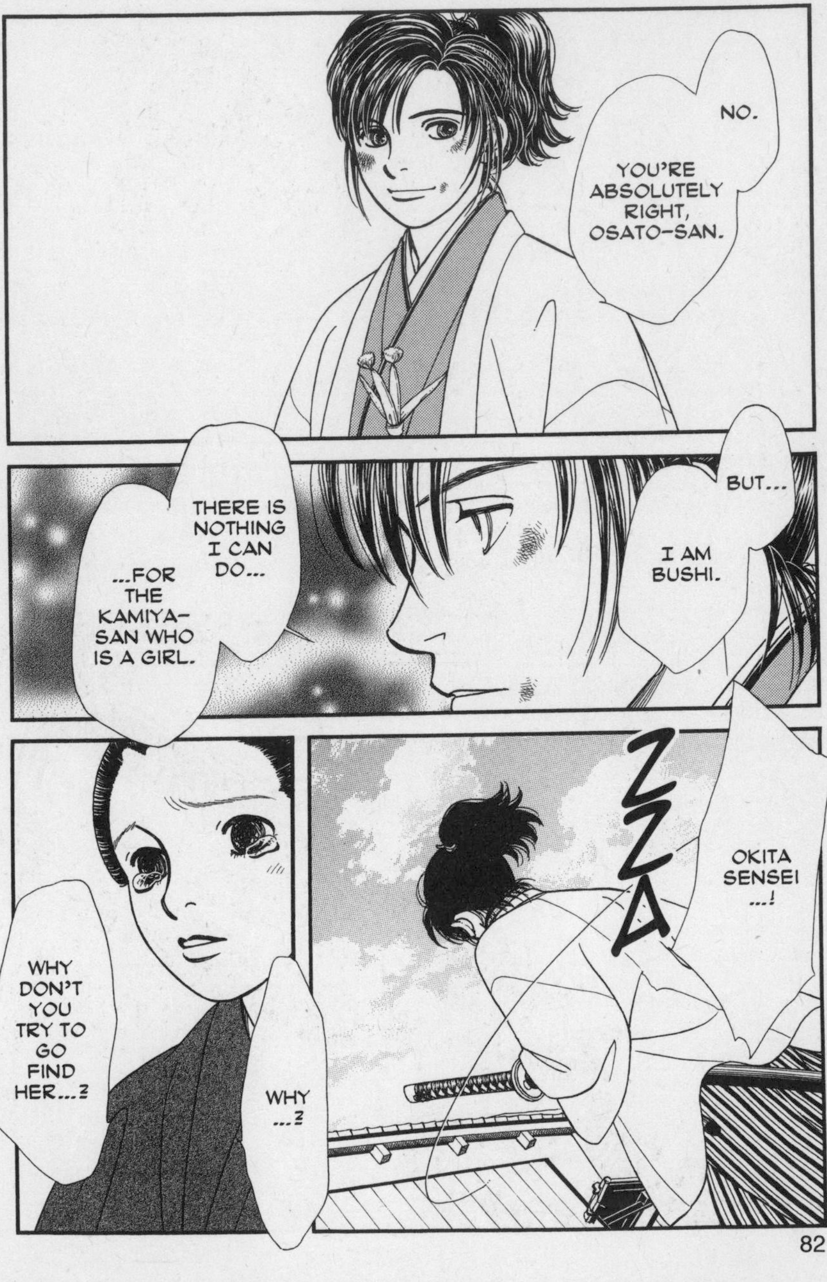
NO.
YOU'RE ABSOLUTELY RIGHT, OSATO-SAN.
BUT...
I AM BUSHI.
THERE IS NOTHING I CAN DO...
...FOR THE KAMIYA-SAN WHO IS A GIRL.
ZZA
OKITA SENSEI ...!
WHY ...?
WHY DON'T YOU TRY TO GO FIND HER...?

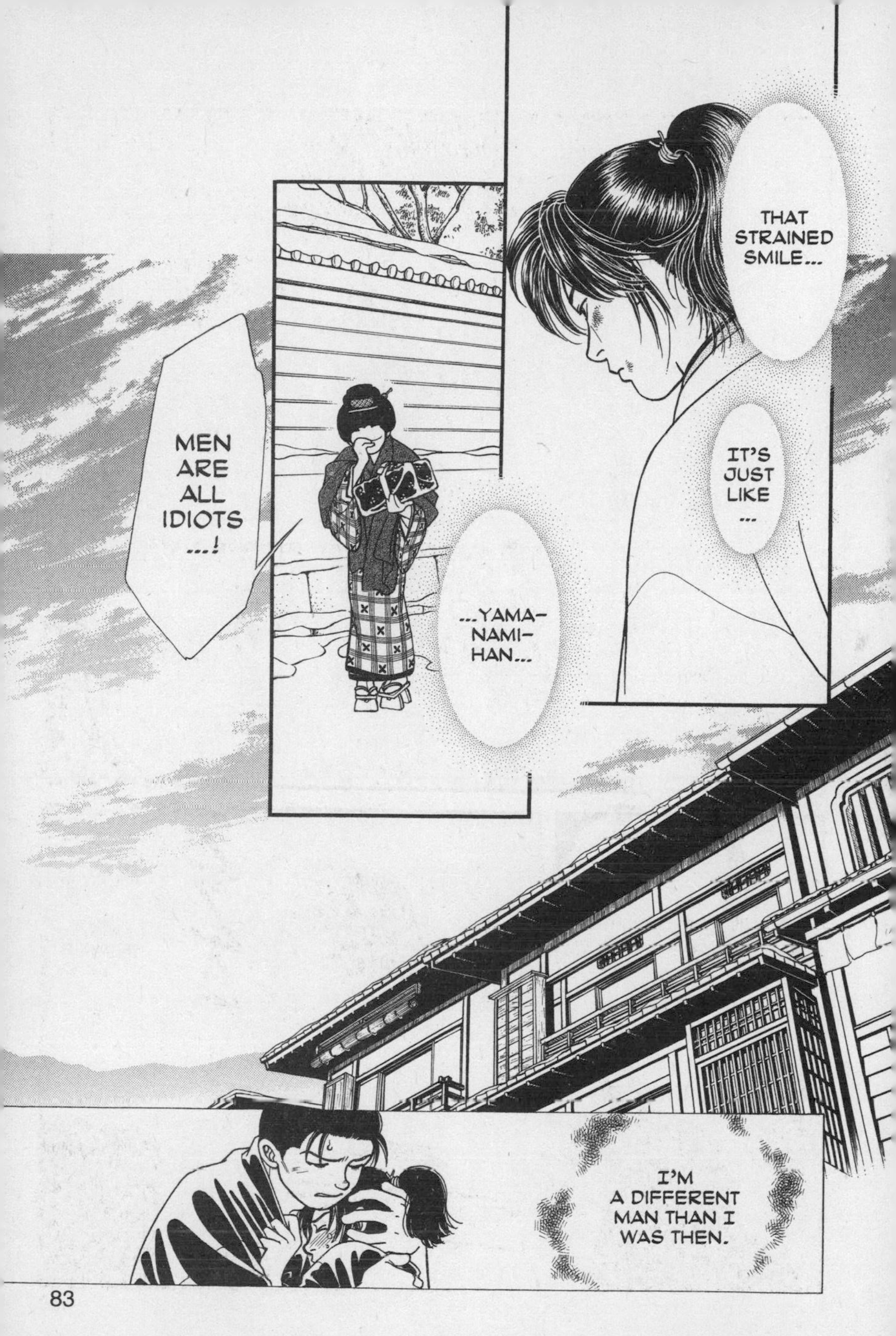
THAT STRAINED SMILE...
IT'S JUST LIKE ...
...YAMA-NAMI-HAN...
MEN ARE ALL IDIOTS ...!
I'M A DIFFERENT MAN THAN I WAS THEN.

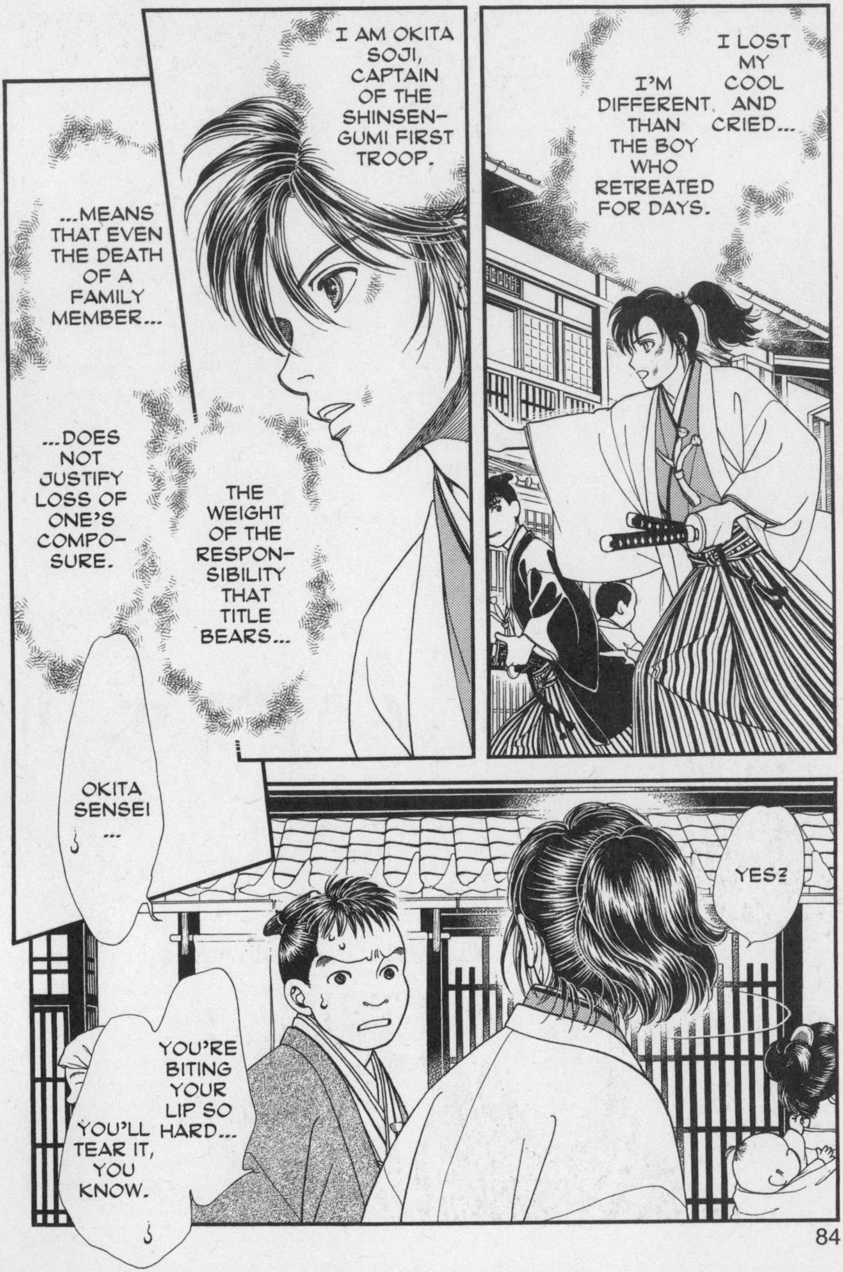
I LOST MY COOL AND CRIED...
I'M DIFFERENT THAN THE BOY WHO RETREATED FOR DAYS.
I AM OKITA SOJI, CAPTAIN OF THE SHINSEN-GUMI FIRST TROOP.
THE WEIGHT OF THE RESPON-SIBILITY THAT TITLE BEARS...
...MEANS THAT EVEN THE DEATH OF A FAMILY MEMBER...
...DOES NOT JUSTIFY LOSS OF ONE'S COMPO-SURE.
OKITA SENSEI ...
YES?
YOU'RE BITING YOUR LIP SO HARD...
YOU'LL TEAR IT, YOU KNOW.

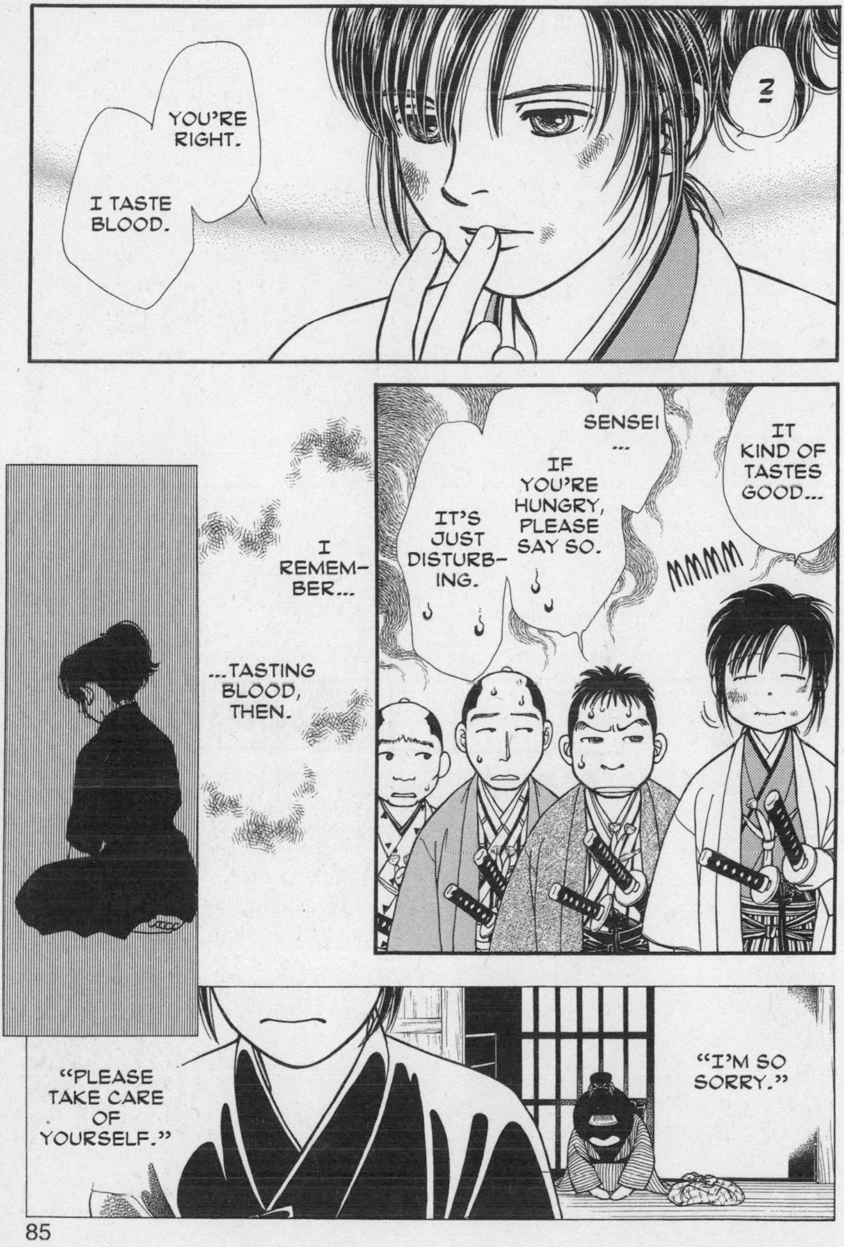
?
YOU'RE RIGHT.
I TASTE BLOOD.
IT KIND OF TASTES GOOD...
MMMMM
SENSEI ...
IF YOU'RE HUNGRY, PLEASE SAY SO.
IT'S JUST DISTURBING.
I REMEMBER...
...TASTING BLOOD, THEN.
"I'M SO SORRY."
"PLEASE TAKE CARE OF YOURSELF."

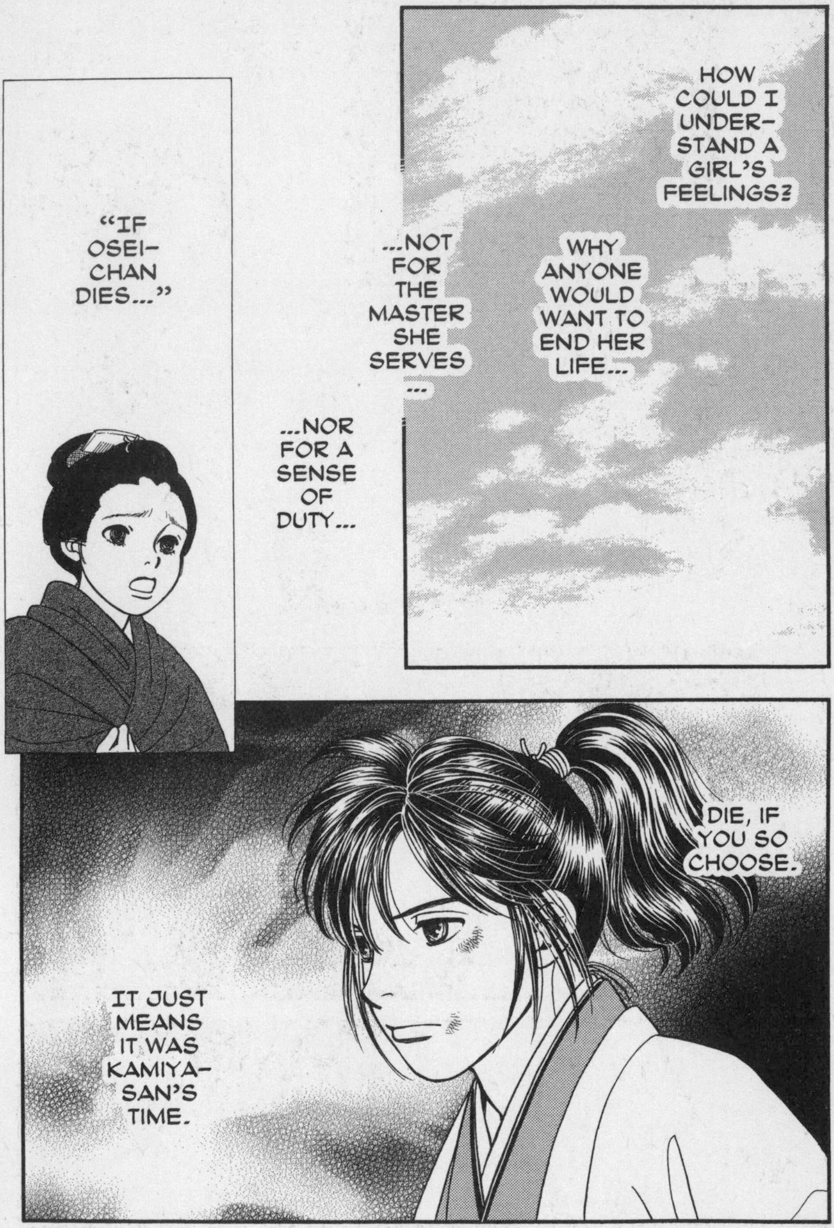
HOW COULD I UNDER-STAND A GIRL'S FEELINGS?
WHY ANYONE WOULD WANT TO END HER LIFE...
...NOT FOR THE MASTER SHE SERVES...
...NOR FOR A SENSE OF DUTY...
"IF OSEI-CHAN DIES..."
DIE, IF YOU SO CHOOSE.
IT JUST MEANS IT WAS KAMIYA-SAN'S TIME.

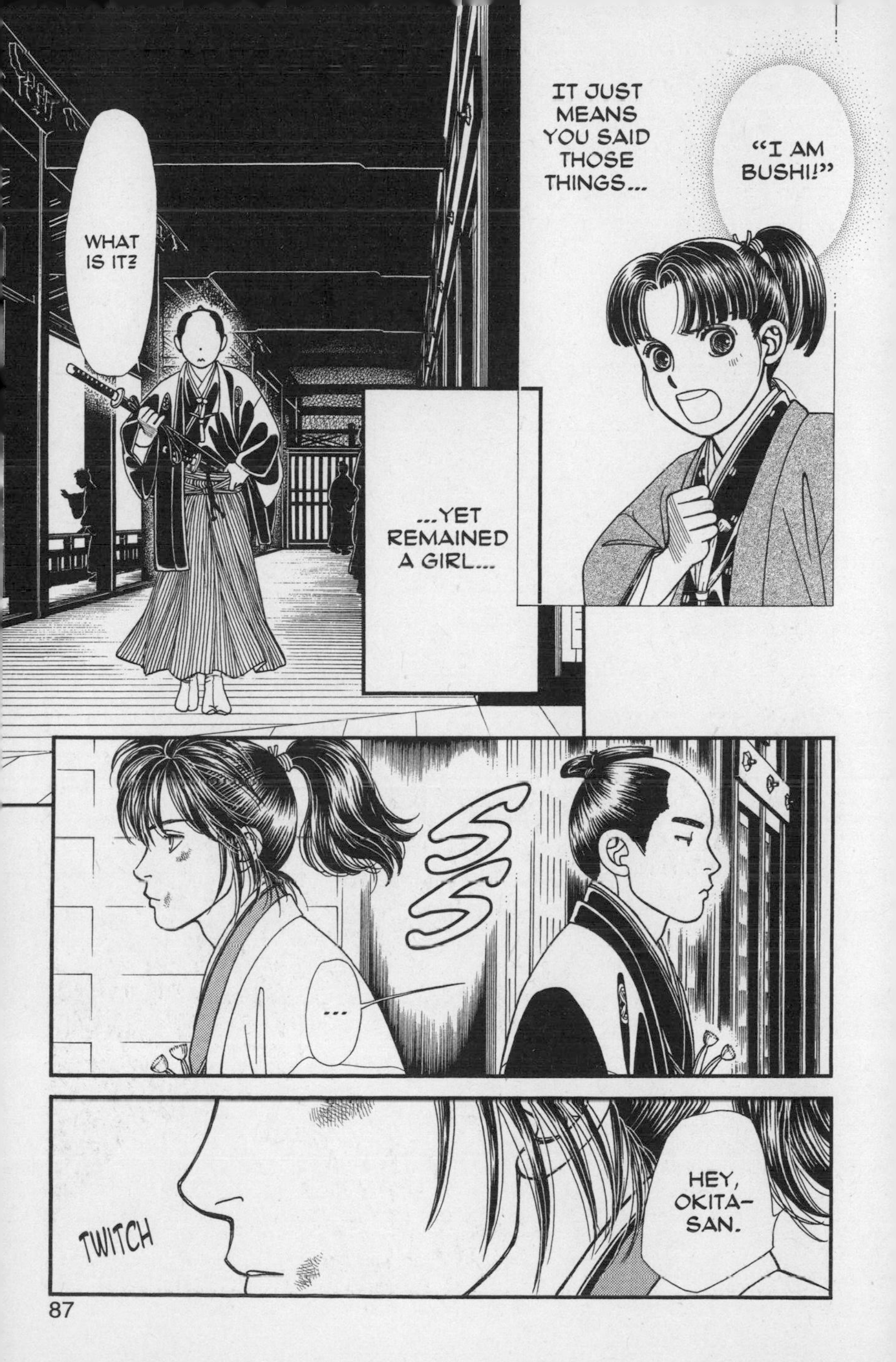
"I AM BUSHI!"
IT JUST MEANS YOU SAID THOSE THINGS...
...YET REMAINED A GIRL...
WHAT IS IT?
...
HEY, OKITA-SAN.
TWITCH

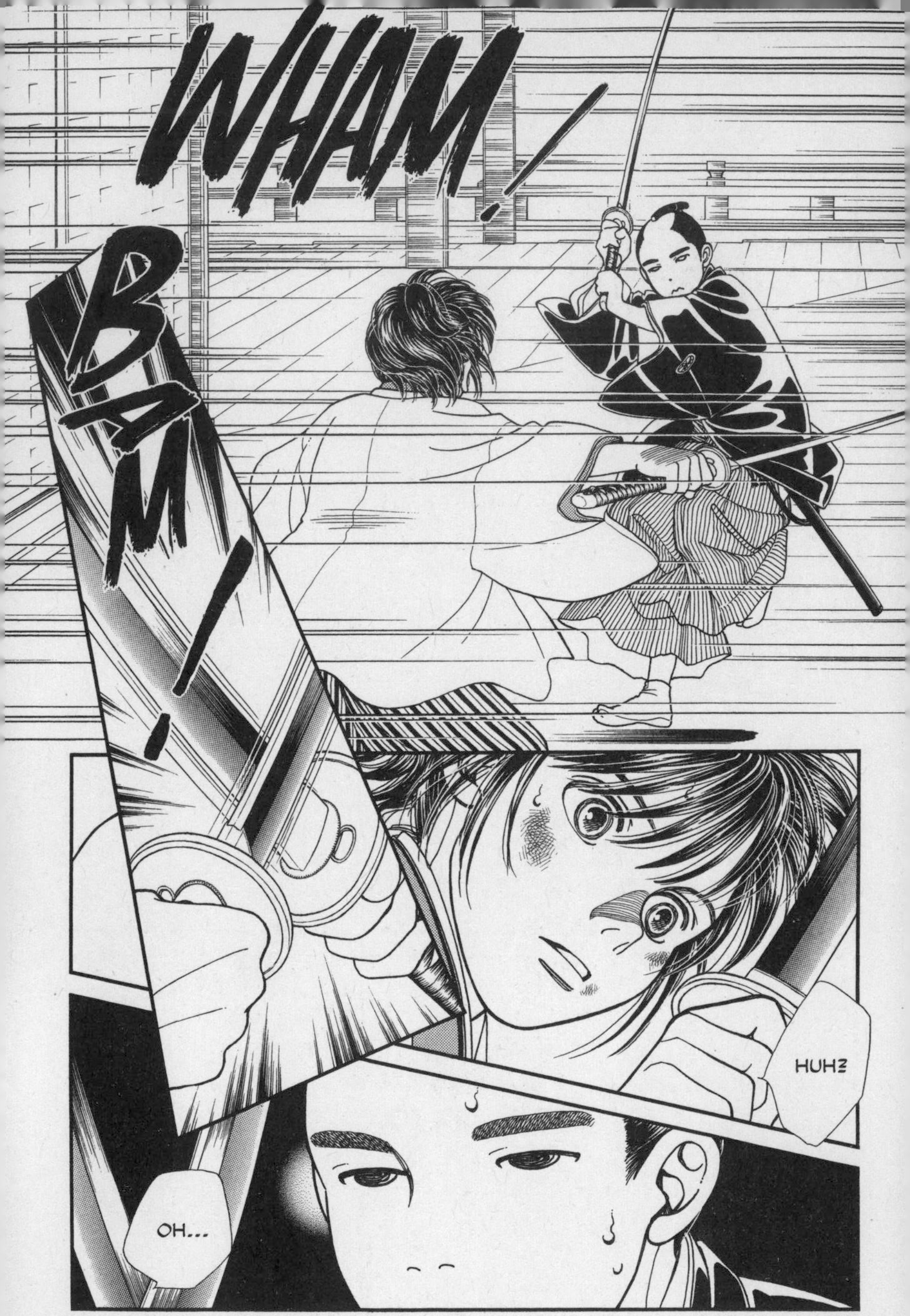
WHAM!
BAM!
HUH?
OH...

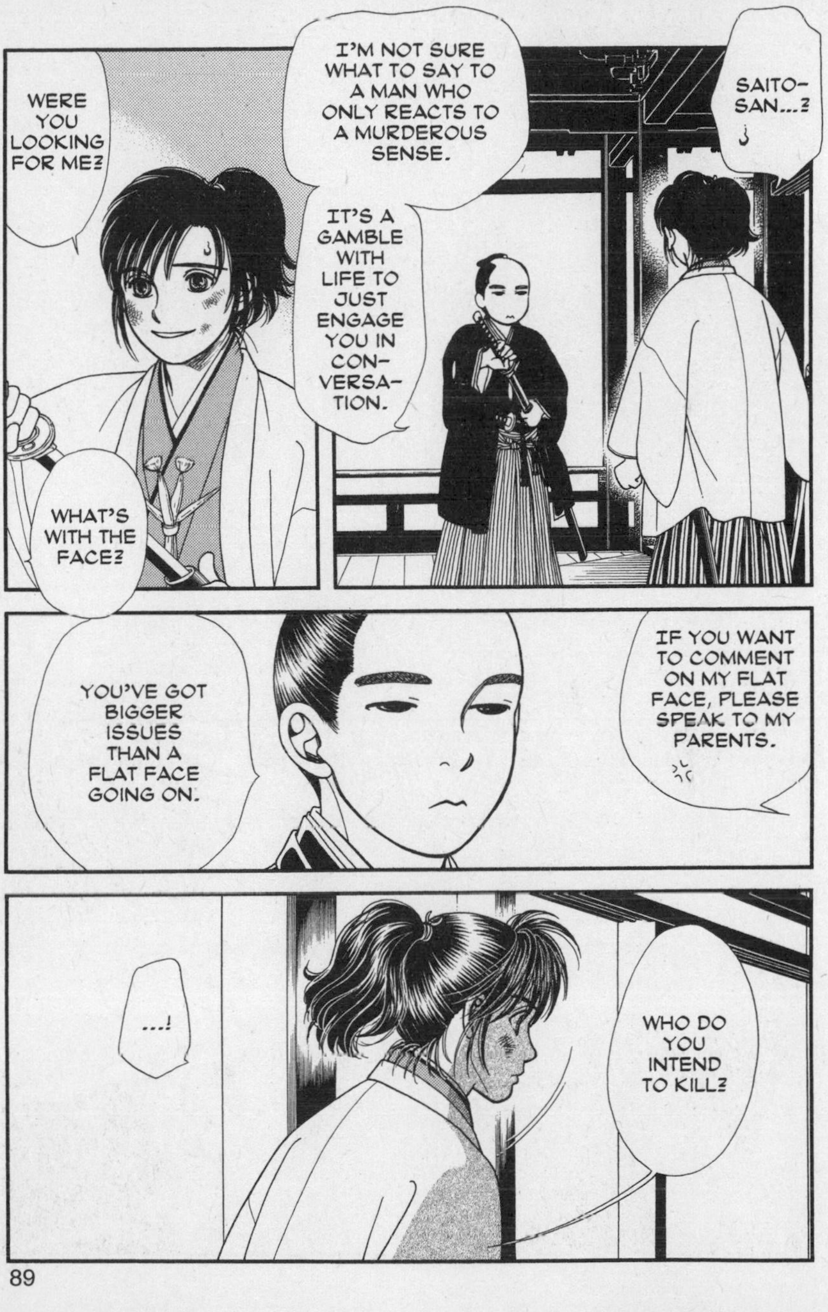
SAITO-SAN...?
I'M NOT SURE WHAT TO SAY TO A MAN WHO ONLY REACTS TO A MURDEROUS SENSE.
IT'S A GAMBLE WITH LIFE TO JUST ENGAGE YOU IN CON-VERSA-TION.
WERE YOU LOOKING FOR ME?
WHAT'S WITH THE FACE?
IF YOU WANT TO COMMENT ON MY FLAT FACE, PLEASE SPEAK TO MY PARENTS.
YOU'VE GOT BIGGER ISSUES THAN A FLAT FACE GOING ON.
WHO DO YOU INTEND TO KILL?
...!

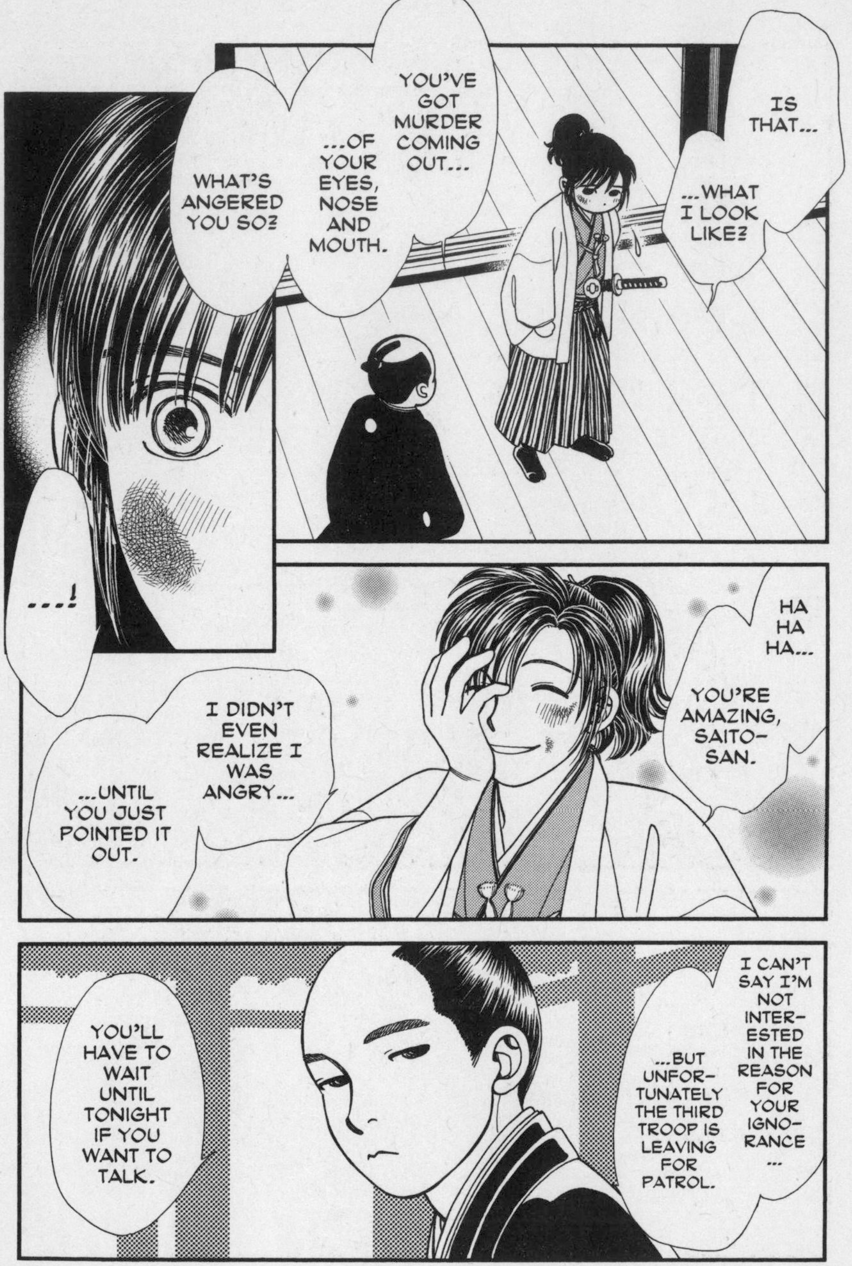
IS THAT...
...WHAT I LOOK LIKE?
YOU'VE GOT MURDER COMING OUT...
...OF YOUR EYES, NOSE AND MOUTH.
WHAT'S ANGERED YOU SO?
...!
HA HA HA...
YOU'RE AMAZING, SAITO-SAN.
I DIDN'T EVEN REALIZE I WAS ANGRY...
...UNTIL YOU JUST POINTED IT OUT.
I CAN'T SAY I'M NOT INTER-ESTED IN THE REASON FOR YOUR IGNO-RANCE...
...BUT UNFOR-TUNATELY THE THIRD TROOP IS LEAVING FOR PATROL.
YOU'LL HAVE TO WAIT UNTIL TONIGHT IF YOU WANT TO TALK.

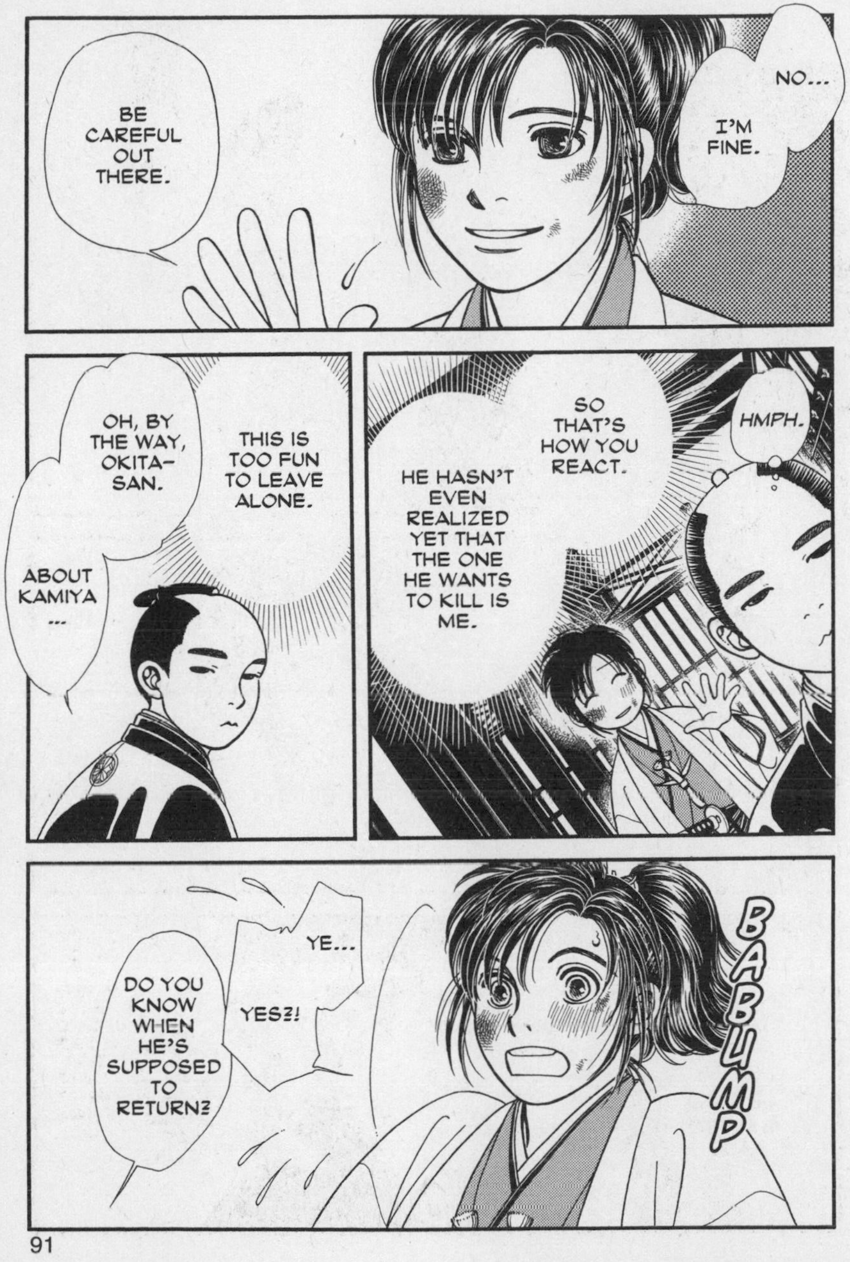
NO... I'M FINE.
BE CAREFUL OUT THERE.
HMPH.
SO THAT'S HOW YOU REACT.
HE HASN'T EVEN REALIZED YET THAT THE ONE HE WANTS TO KILL IS ME.
THIS IS TOO FUN TO LEAVE ALONE.
OH, BY THE WAY, OKITA-SAN.
ABOUT KAMIYA ...
BABUMP
YE... YES?!
DO YOU KNOW WHEN HE'S SUPPOSED TO RETURN?

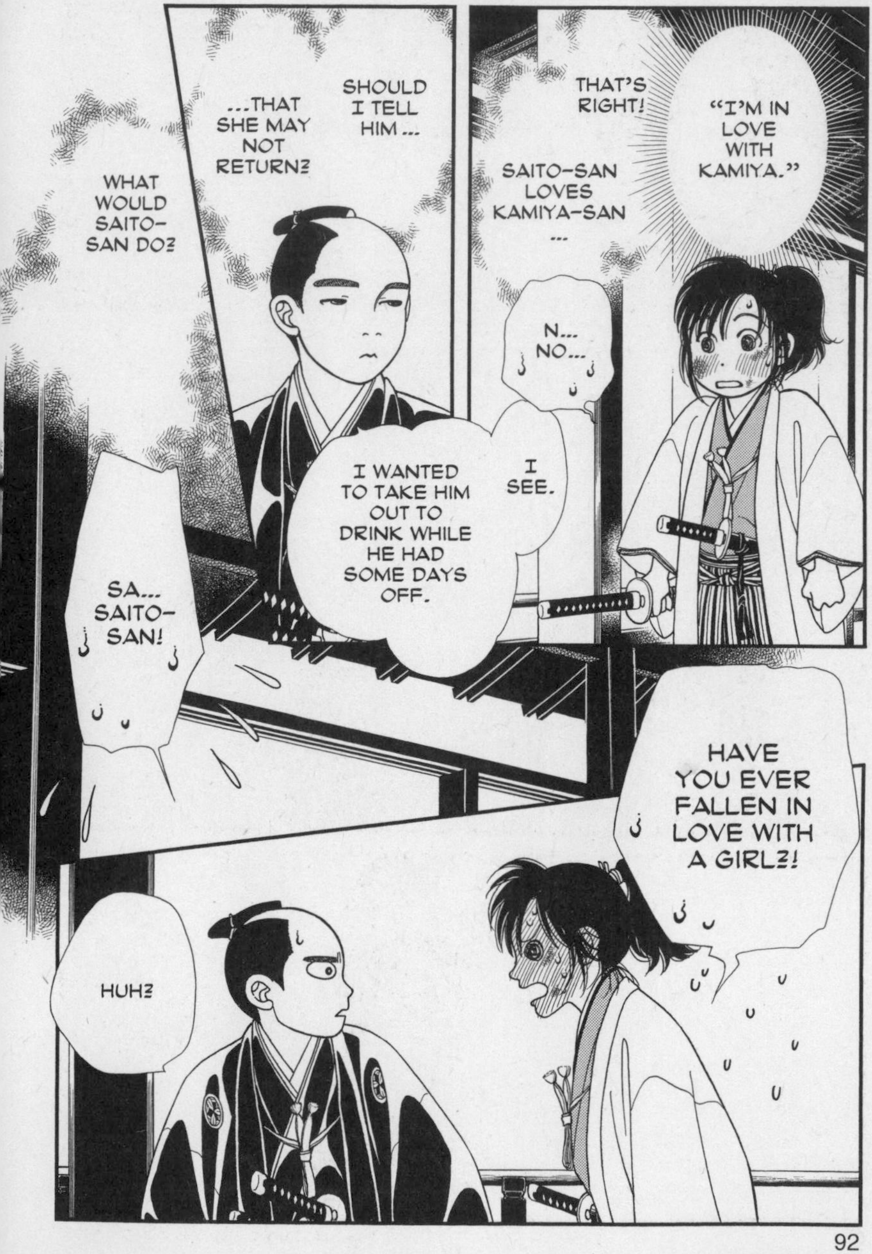
"I'M IN LOVE WITH KAMIYA."
THAT'S RIGHT!
SAITO-SAN LOVES KAMIYA-SAN ...
N... NO...
SHOULD I TELL HIM ...
...THAT SHE MAY NOT RETURN?
WHAT WOULD SAITO-SAN DO?
I SEE.
I WANTED TO TAKE HIM OUT TO DRINK WHILE HE HAD SOME DAYS OFF.
SA... SAITO-SAN!
HAVE YOU EVER FALLEN IN LOVE WITH A GIRL?!
HUH?

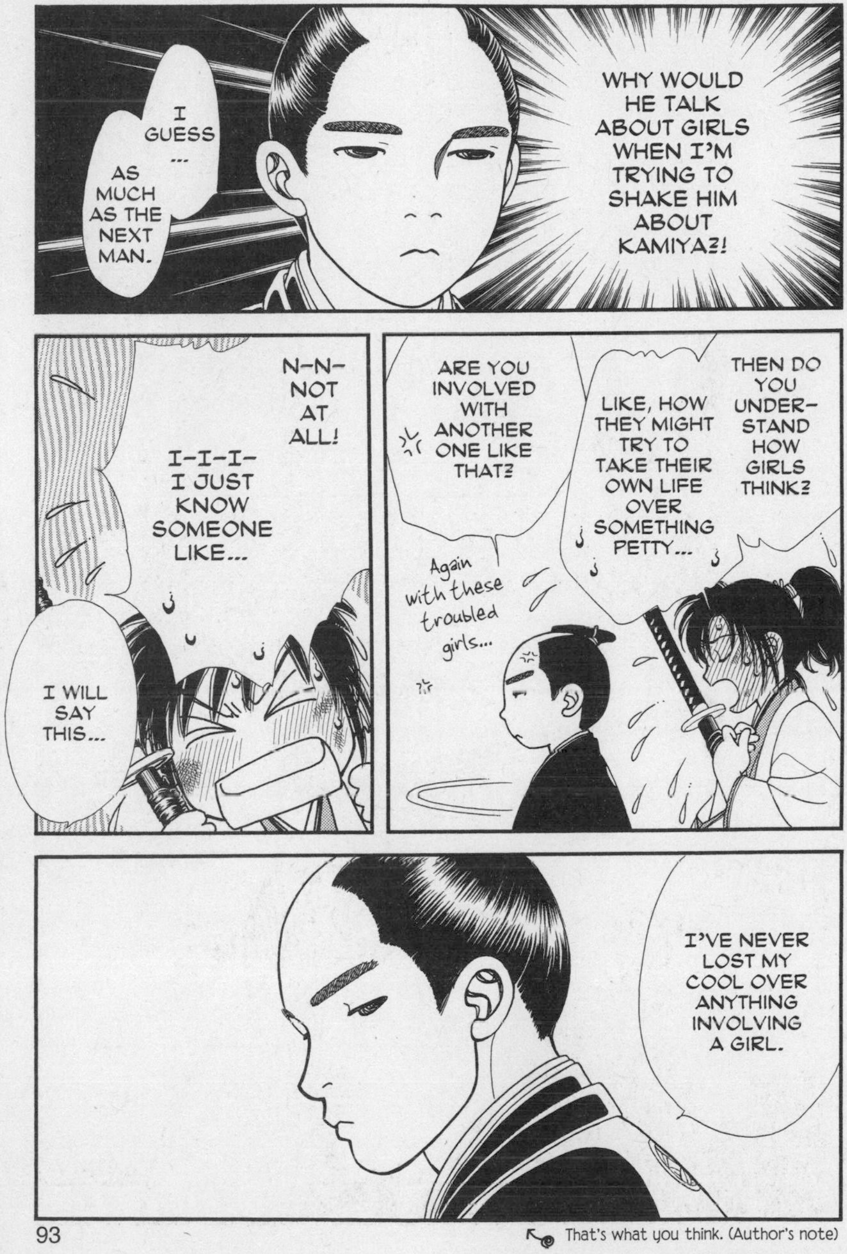
I GUESS ... AS MUCH AS THE NEXT MAN.
WHY WOULD HE TALK ABOUT GIRLS WHEN I'M TRYING TO SHAKE HIM ABOUT KAMIYA?!
THEN DO YOU UNDERSTAND HOW GIRLS THINK?
LIKE, HOW THEY MIGHT TRY TO TAKE THEIR OWN LIFE OVER SOMETHING PETTY...
ARE YOU INVOLVED WITH ANOTHER ONE LIKE THAT?
Again with these troubled girls...
N-N-NOT AT ALL!
I-I-I-I JUST KNOW SOMEONE LIKE...
I WILL SAY THIS...
I'VE NEVER LOST MY COOL OVER ANYTHING INVOLVING A GIRL.

That's what you think. (Author's note)

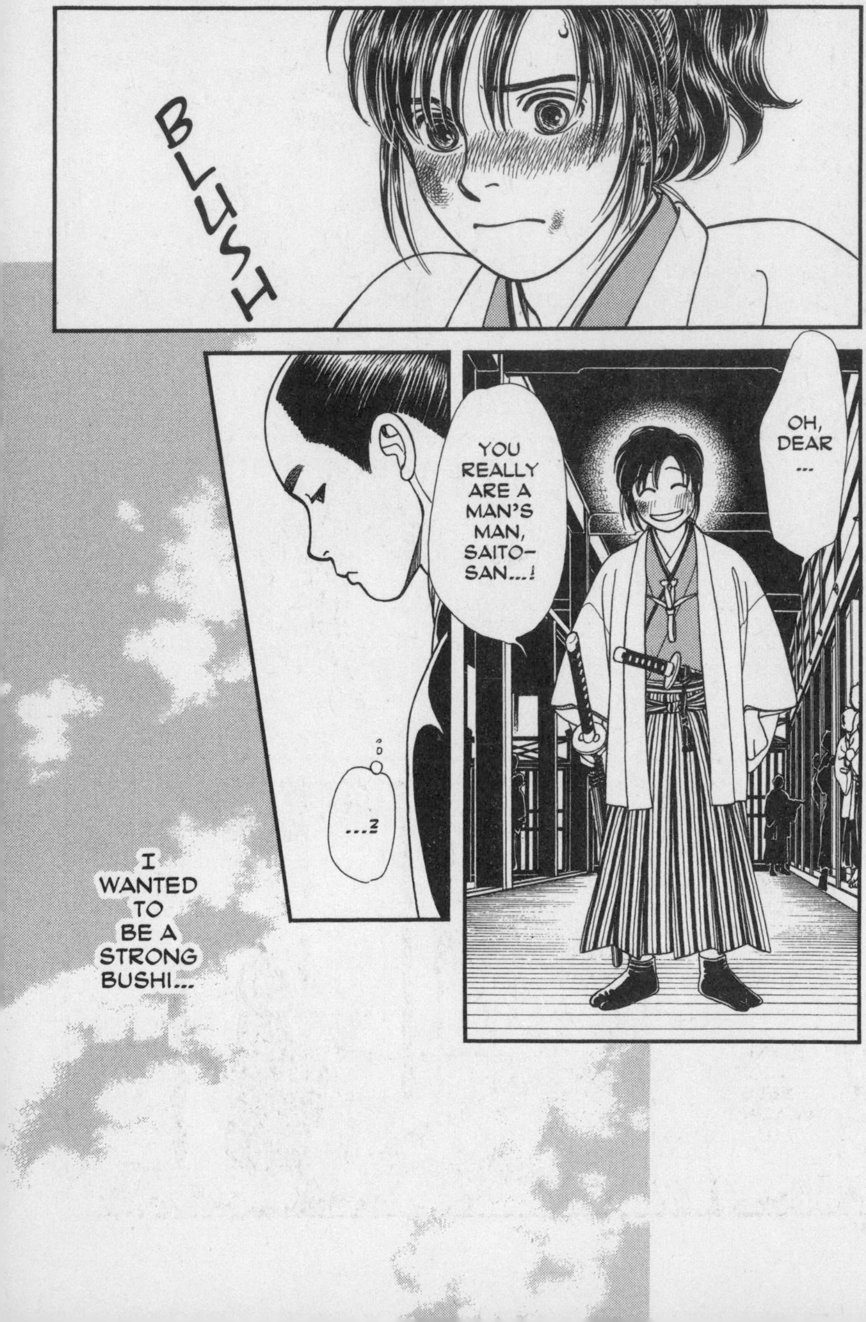
BLUSH
OH, DEAR ...
YOU REALLY ARE A MAN'S MAN, SAITO-SAN...!
...?
I WANTED TO BE A STRONG BUSHI...

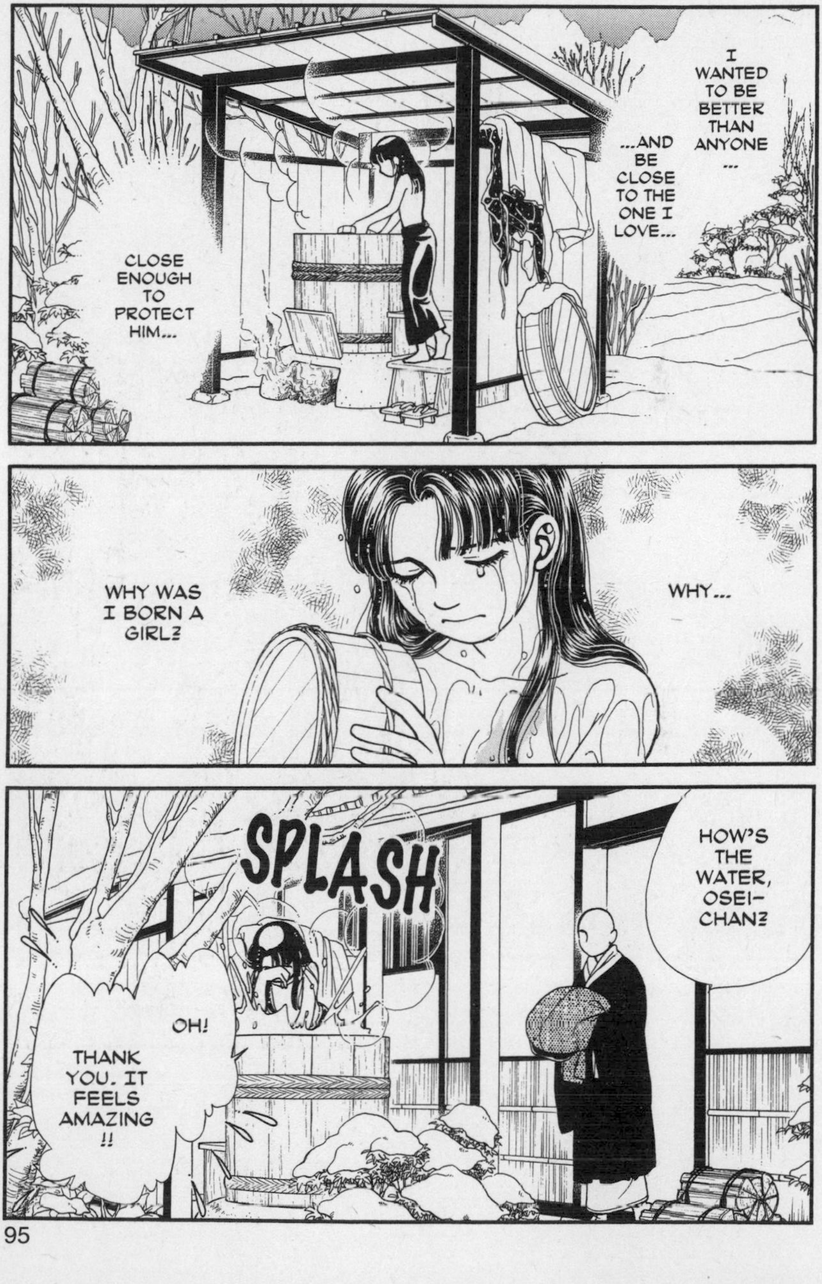
I WANTED TO BE BETTER THAN ANYONE...
...AND BE CLOSE TO THE ONE I LOVE...
CLOSE ENOUGH TO PROTECT HIM...
WHY...
WHY WAS I BORN A GIRL?
HOW'S THE WATER, OSEI-CHAN?
SPLASH
OH!
THANK YOU. IT FEELS AMAZING!!

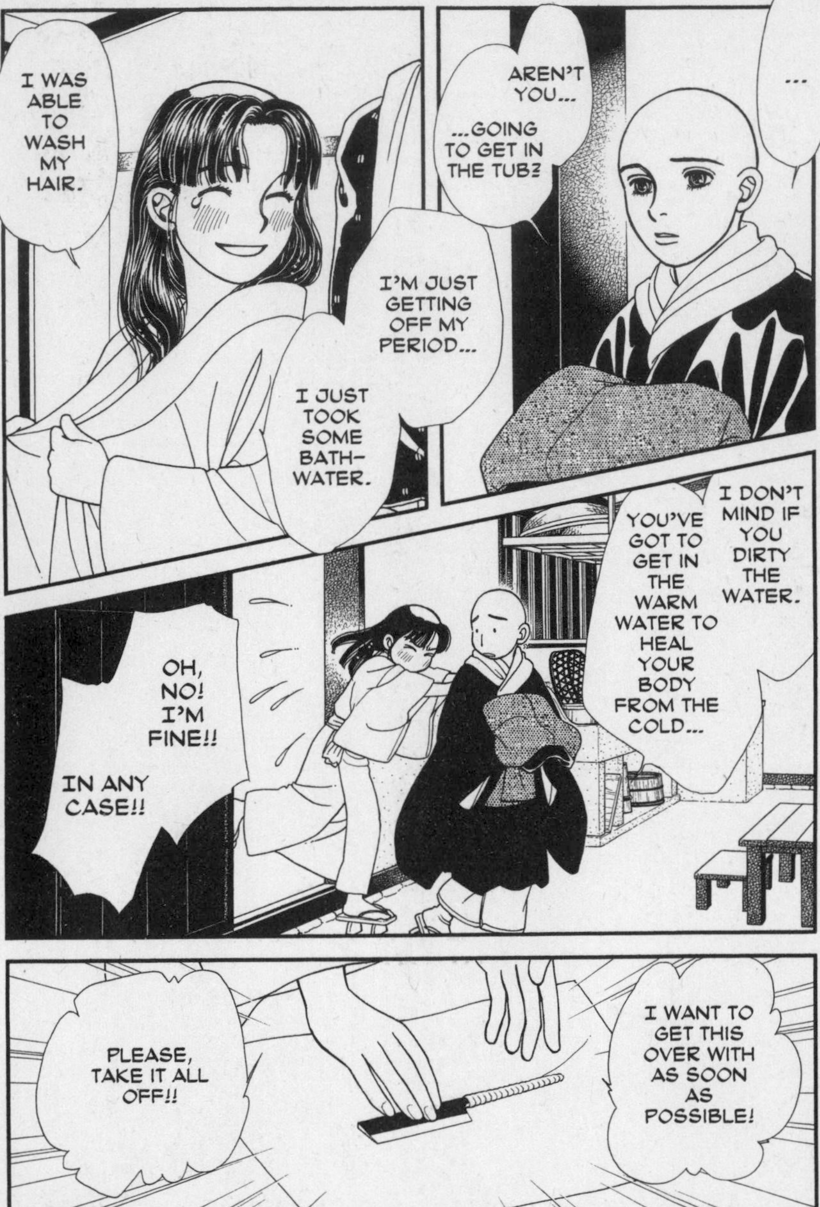
...
AREN'T YOU...
...GOING TO GET IN THE TUB?
I WAS ABLE TO WASH MY HAIR.
I'M JUST GETTING OFF MY PERIOD...
I JUST TOOK SOME BATH-WATER.
I DON'T MIND IF YOU DIRTY THE WATER.
YOU'VE GOT TO GET IN THE WARM WATER TO HEAL YOUR BODY FROM THE COLD...
OH, NO! I'M FINE!!
IN ANY CASE!!
I WANT TO GET THIS OVER WITH AS SOON AS POSSIBLE!
PLEASE, TAKE IT ALL OFF!!

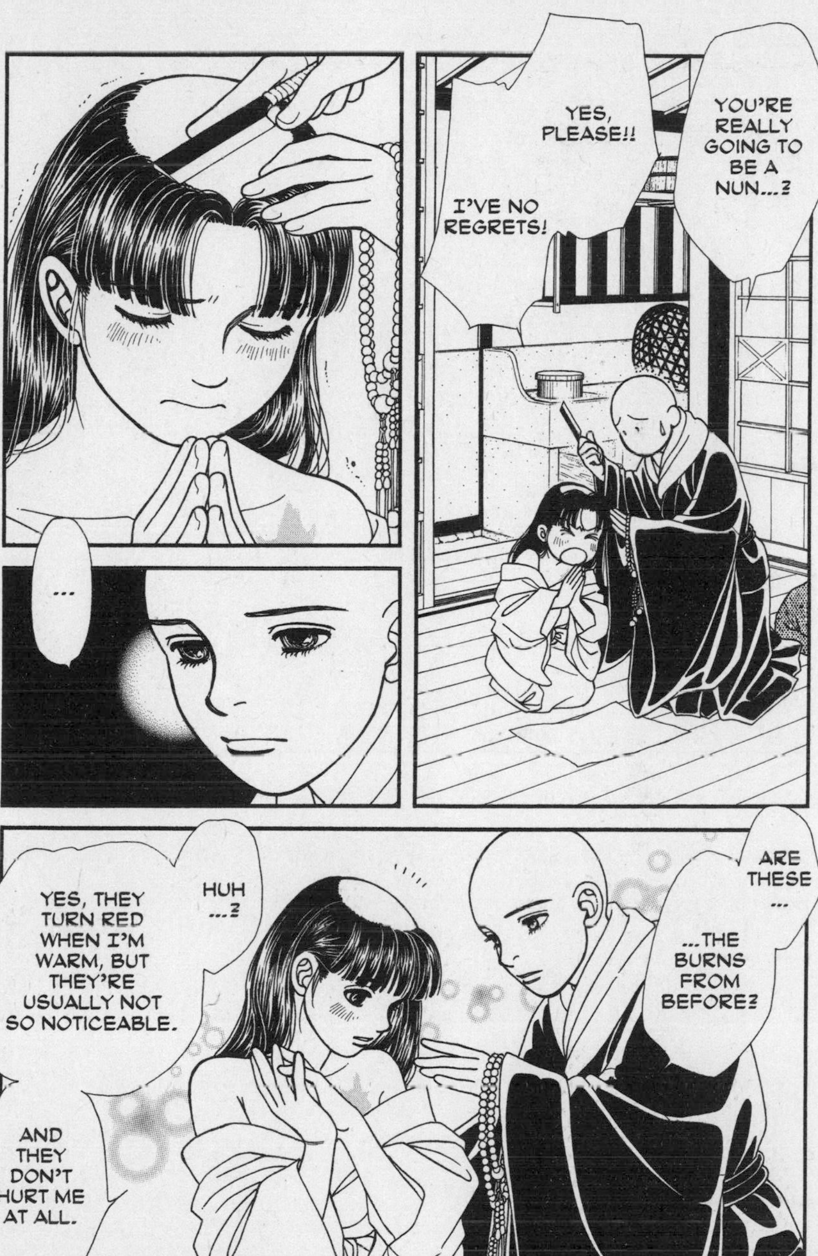
YOU'RE REALLY GOING TO BE A NUN...?
YES, PLEASE!!
I'VE NO REGRETS!
...
ARE THESE ...
...THE BURNS FROM BEFORE?
HUH ...?
YES, THEY TURN RED WHEN I'M WARM, BUT THEY'RE USUALLY NOT SO NOTICEABLE.
AND THEY DON'T HURT ME AT ALL.

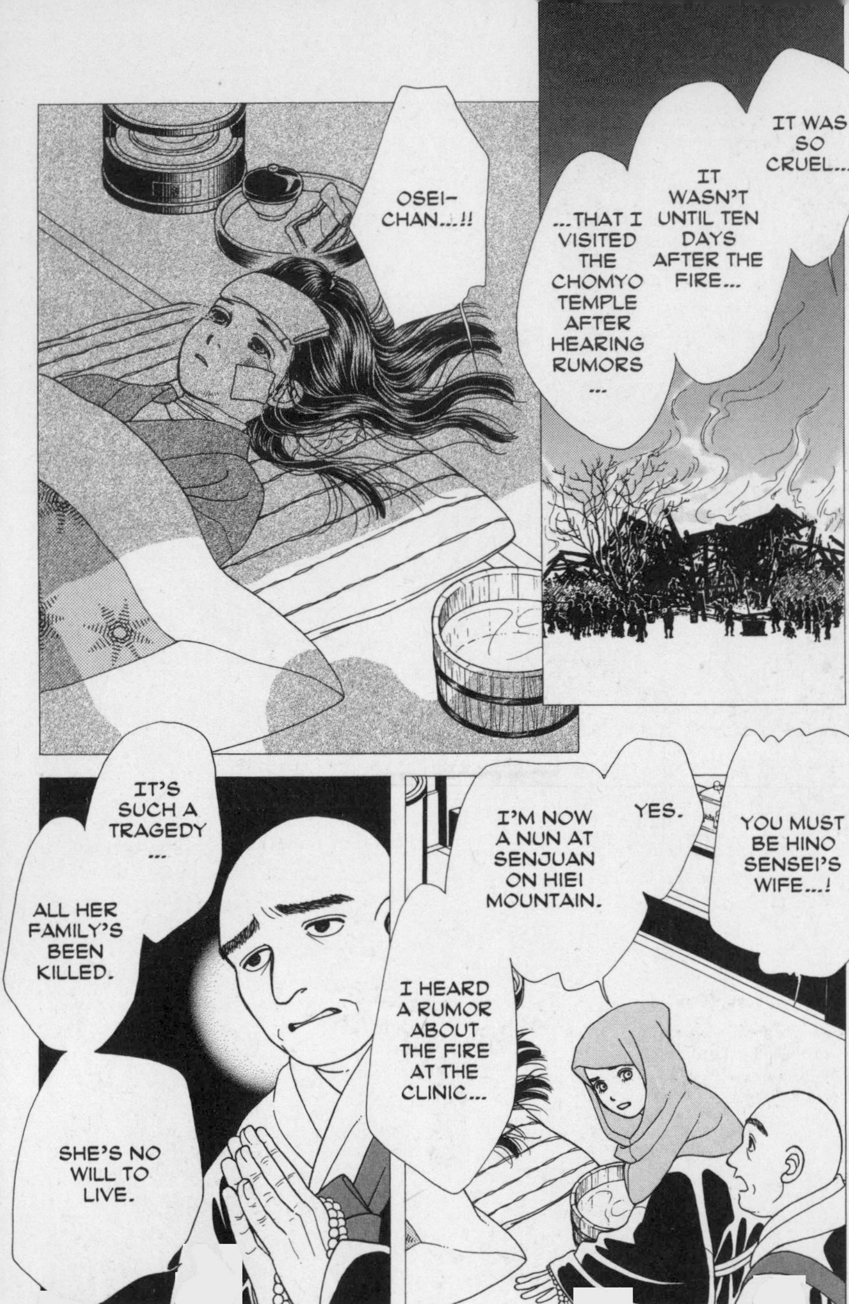
IT WAS SO CRUEL...
IT WASN'T UNTIL TEN DAYS AFTER THE FIRE...
...THAT I VISITED THE CHOMYO TEMPLE AFTER HEARING RUMORS...
OSEI-CHAN...!!
YOU MUST BE HINO SENSEI'S WIFE...!
YES.
I'M NOW A NUN AT SENJUAN ON HIEI MOUNTAIN.
I HEARD A RUMOR ABOUT THE FIRE AT THE CLINIC...
IT'S SUCH A TRAGEDY...
ALL HER FAMILY'S BEEN KILLED.
SHE'S NO WILL TO LIVE.

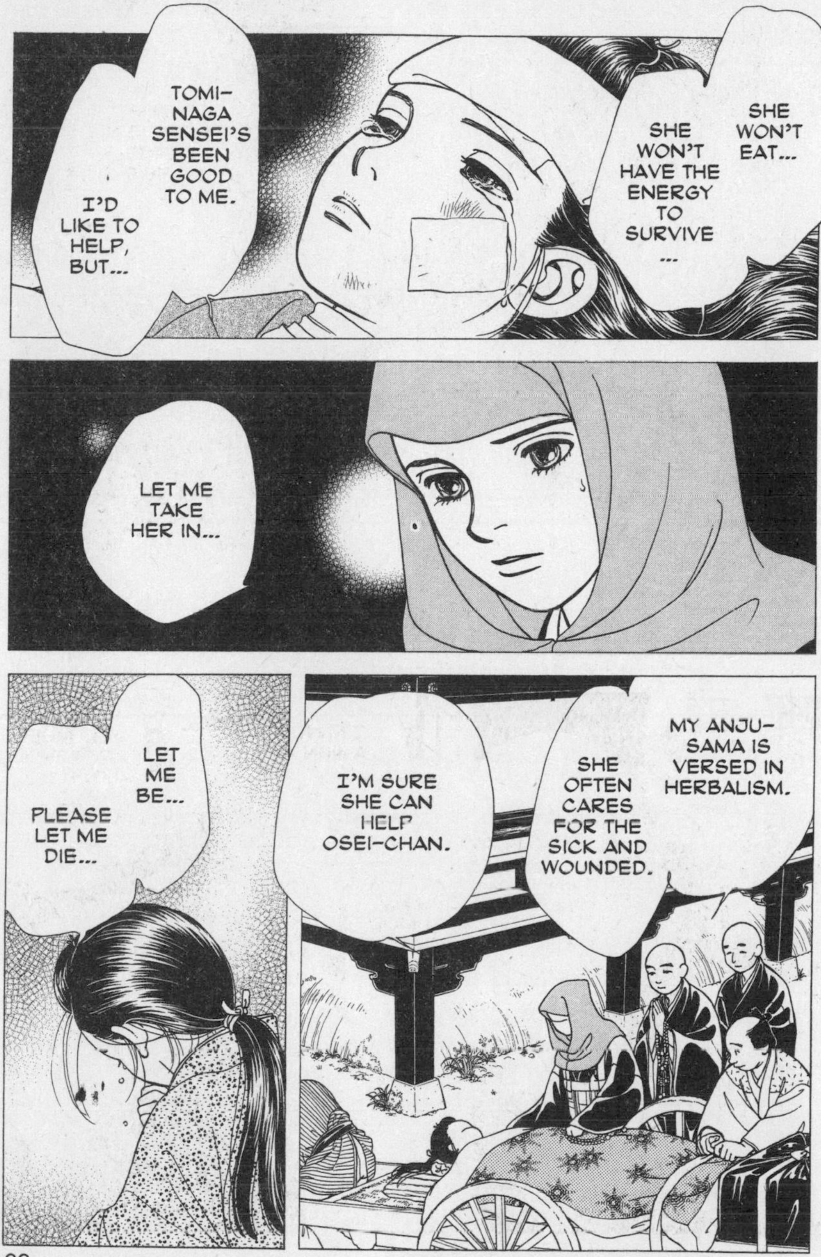
SHE WON'T EAT...
SHE WON'T HAVE THE ENERGY TO SURVIVE ...
TOMI-NAGA SENSEI'S BEEN GOOD TO ME.
I'D LIKE TO HELP, BUT...
LET ME TAKE HER IN...
MY ANJU-SAMA IS VERSED IN HERBALISM.
SHE OFTEN CARES FOR THE SICK AND WOUNDED.
I'M SURE SHE CAN HELP OSEI-CHAN.
LET ME BE...
PLEASE LET ME DIE...

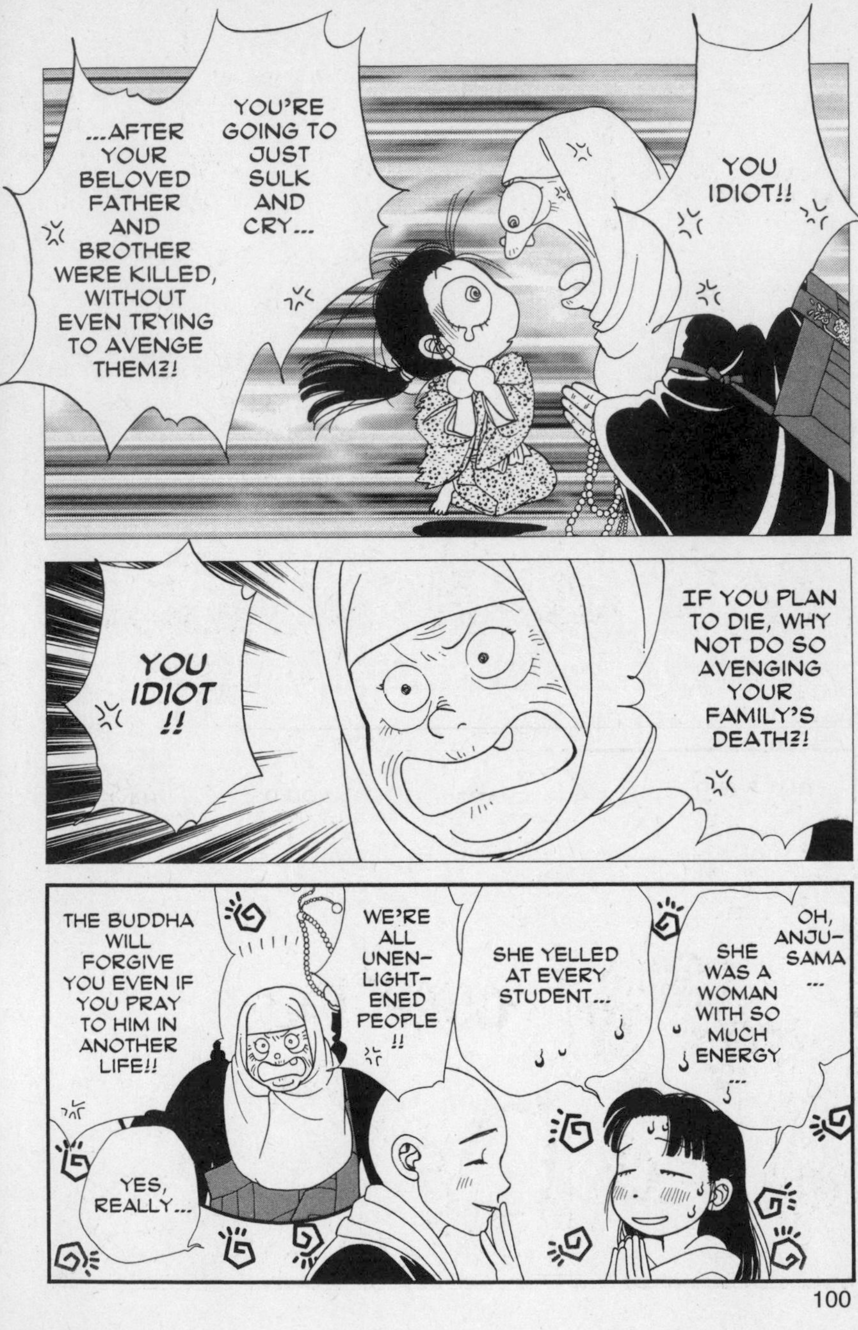
YOU IDIOT!!
YOU'RE GOING TO JUST SULK AND CRY...
...AFTER YOUR BELOVED FATHER AND BROTHER WERE KILLED, WITHOUT EVEN TRYING TO AVENGE THEM?!
IF YOU PLAN TO DIE, WHY NOT DO SO AVENGING YOUR FAMILY'S DEATH?!
YOU IDIOT!!
OH, ANJU-SAMA...
SHE WAS A WOMAN WITH SO MUCH ENERGY...
SHE YELLED AT EVERY STUDENT...
WE'RE ALL UNENLIGHTENED PEOPLE!!
THE BUDDHA WILL FORGIVE YOU EVEN IF YOU PRAY TO HIM IN ANOTHER LIFE!!
YES, REALLY...

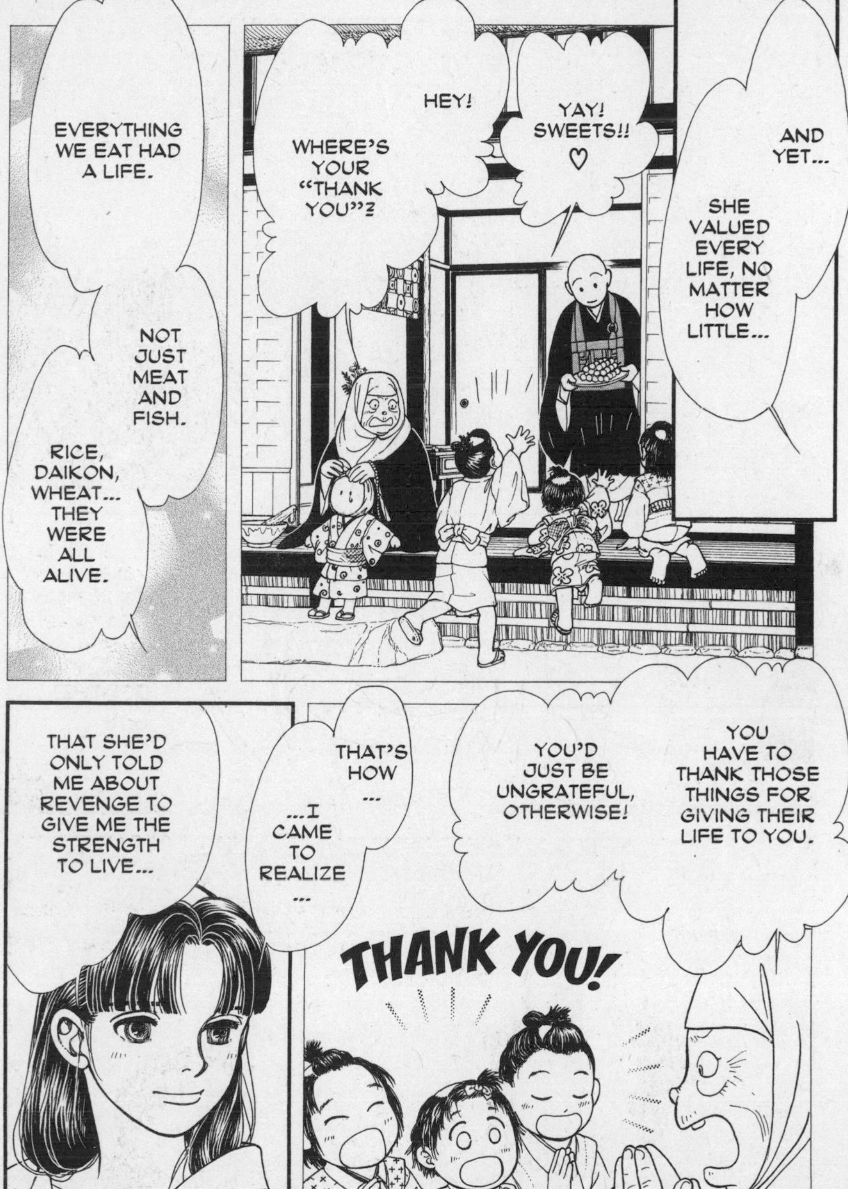
AND YET...
SHE VALUED EVERY LIFE, NO MATTER HOW LITTLE...
YAY! SWEETS!! ♡
HEY!
WHERE'S YOUR "THANK YOU"?
EVERYTHING WE EAT HAD A LIFE.
NOT JUST MEAT AND FISH.
RICE, DAIKON, WHEAT... THEY WERE ALL ALIVE.
YOU HAVE TO THANK THOSE THINGS FOR GIVING THEIR LIFE TO YOU.
YOU'D JUST BE UNGRATEFUL, OTHERWISE!
THANK YOU!
THAT'S HOW...
...I CAME TO REALIZE...
THAT SHE'D ONLY TOLD ME ABOUT REVENGE TO GIVE ME THE STRENGTH TO LIVE...

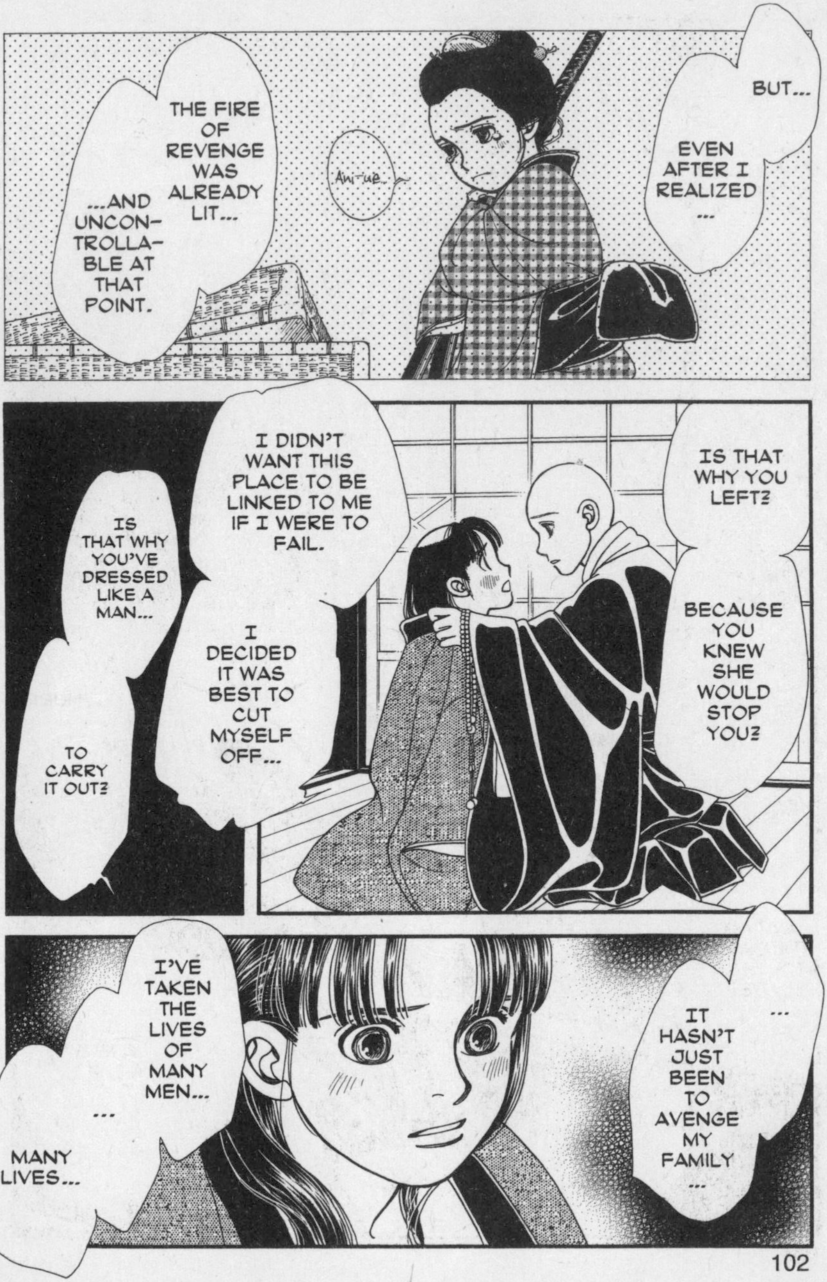
BUT...
EVEN AFTER I REALIZED ...
Ani-ue..
THE FIRE OF REVENGE WAS ALREADY LIT...
...AND UNCON-TROLLA-BLE AT THAT POINT.
IS THAT WHY YOU LEFT?
BECAUSE YOU KNEW SHE WOULD STOP YOU?
I DIDN'T WANT THIS PLACE TO BE LINKED TO ME IF I WERE TO FAIL.
I DECIDED IT WAS BEST TO CUT MYSELF OFF...
IS THAT WHY YOU'VE DRESSED LIKE A MAN...
TO CARRY IT OUT?
...
IT HASN'T JUST BEEN TO AVENGE MY FAMILY ...
I'VE TAKEN THE LIVES OF MANY MEN...
...
MANY LIVES...

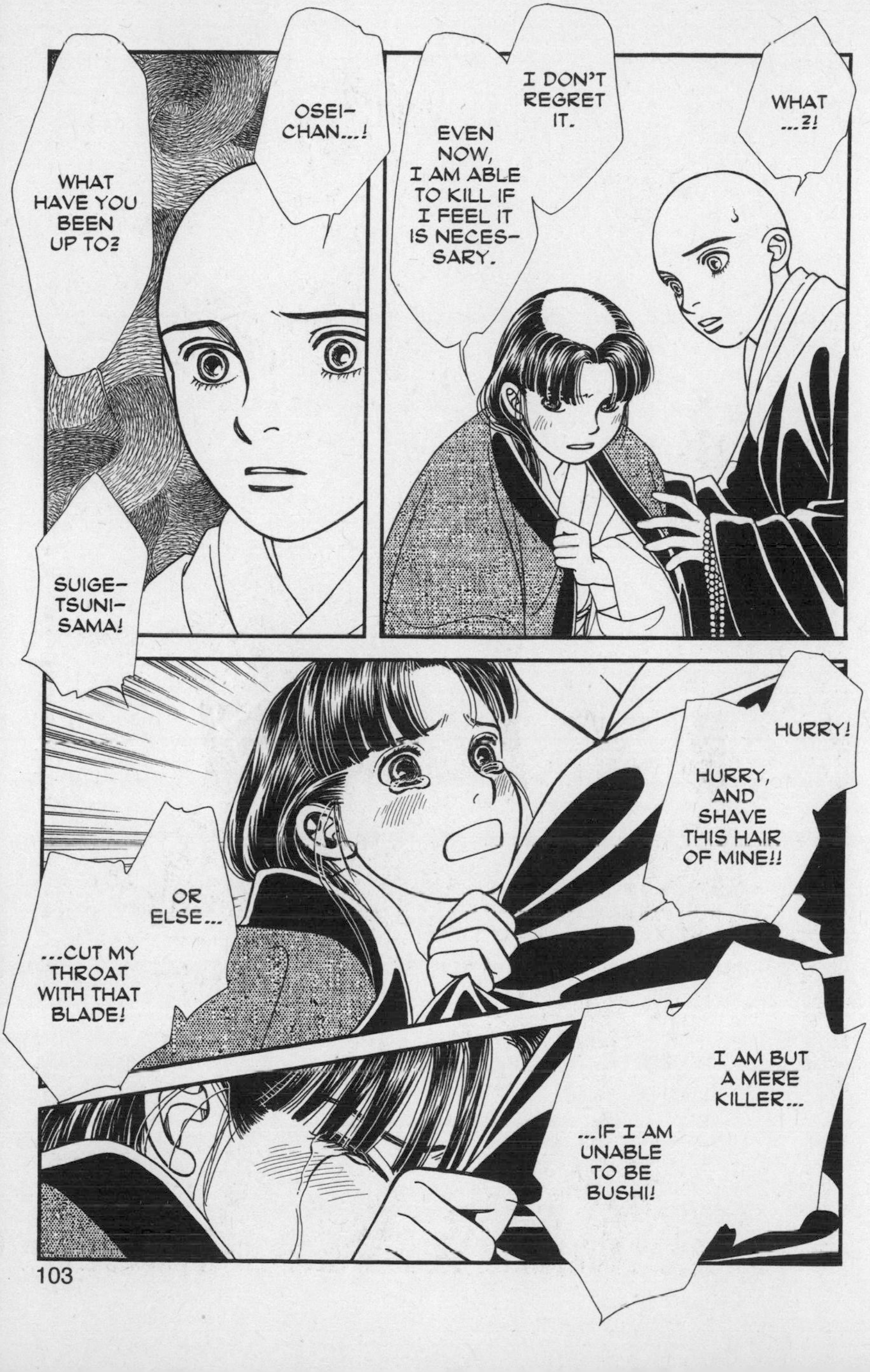
WHAT ...?!
I DON'T REGRET IT.
EVEN NOW, I AM ABLE TO KILL IF I FEEL IT IS NECESSARY.
OSEI-CHAN...!
WHAT HAVE YOU BEEN UP TO?
SUIGETSUNI-SAMA!
HURRY!
HURRY, AND SHAVE THIS HAIR OF MINE!!
OR ELSE...
...CUT MY THROAT WITH THAT BLADE!
I AM BUT A MERE KILLER...
...IF I AM UNABLE TO BE BUSHI!

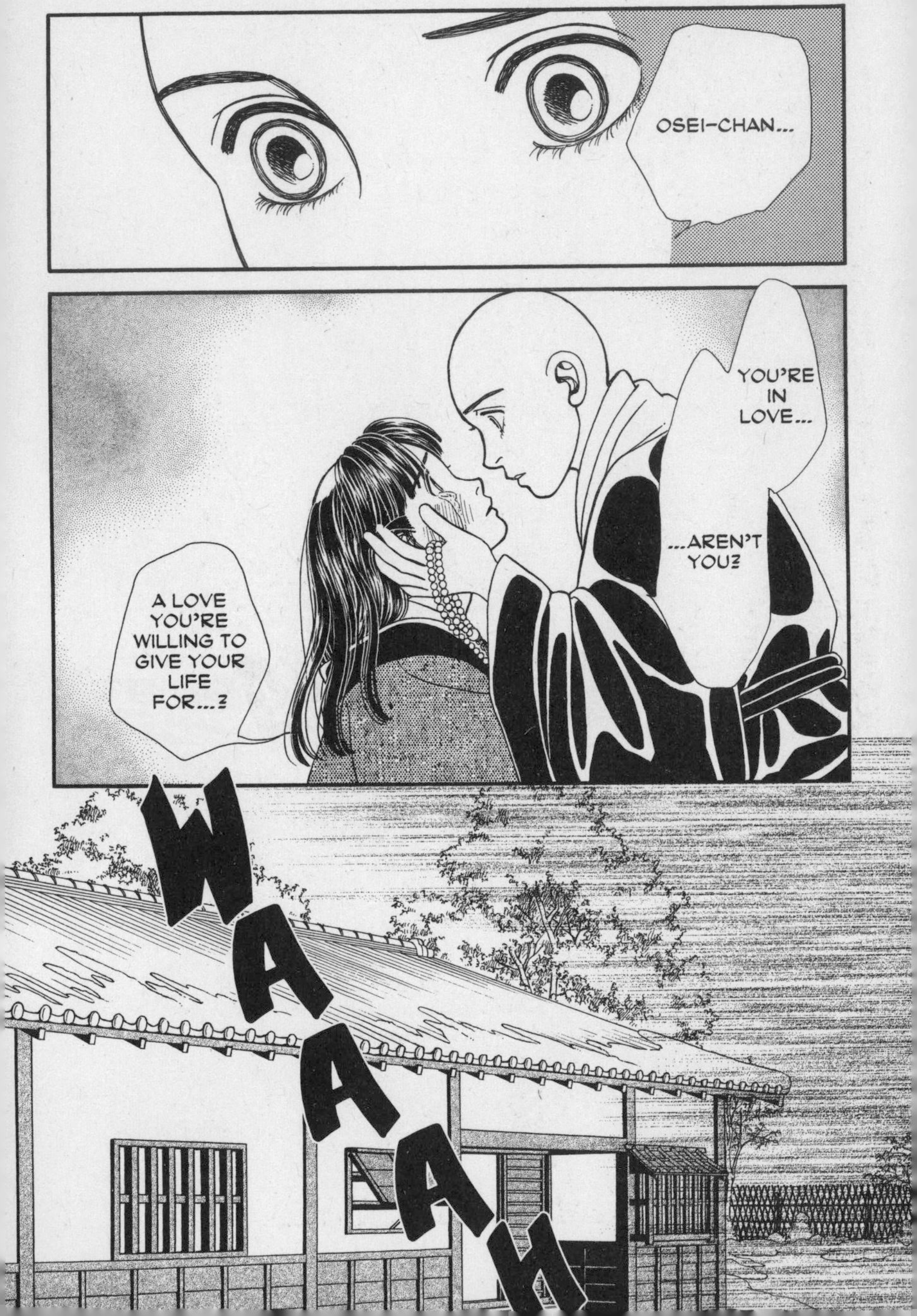
OSEI-CHAN...
YOU'RE IN LOVE...
...AREN'T YOU?
A LOVE YOU'RE WILLING TO GIVE YOUR LIFE FOR...?
WAAAAH

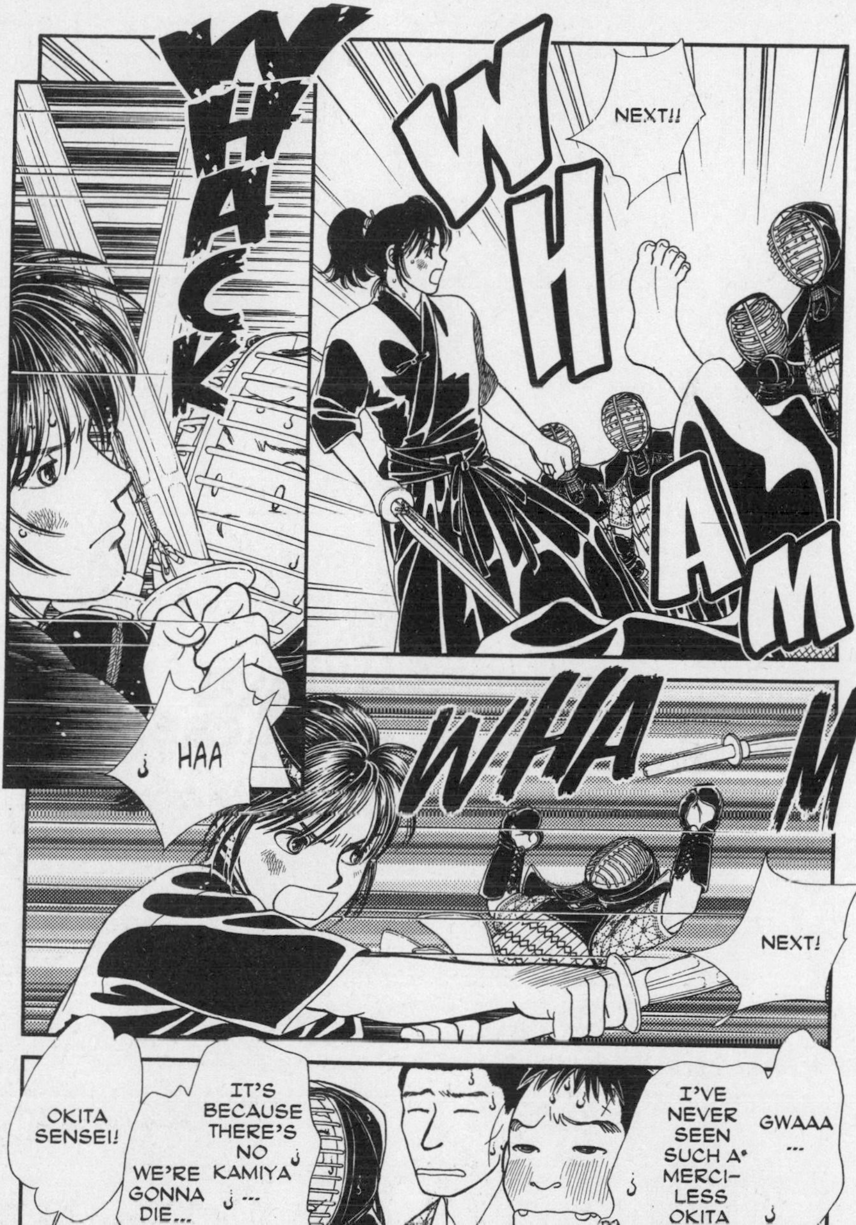
WHAM
NEXT!!
WHACK
HAA
WHAM
NEXT!
GWAAA...
I'VE NEVER SEEN SUCH A MERCILESS OKITA SENSEI.
IT'S BECAUSE THERE'S NO KAMIYA...
WE'RE GONNA DIE...
OKITA SENSEI!

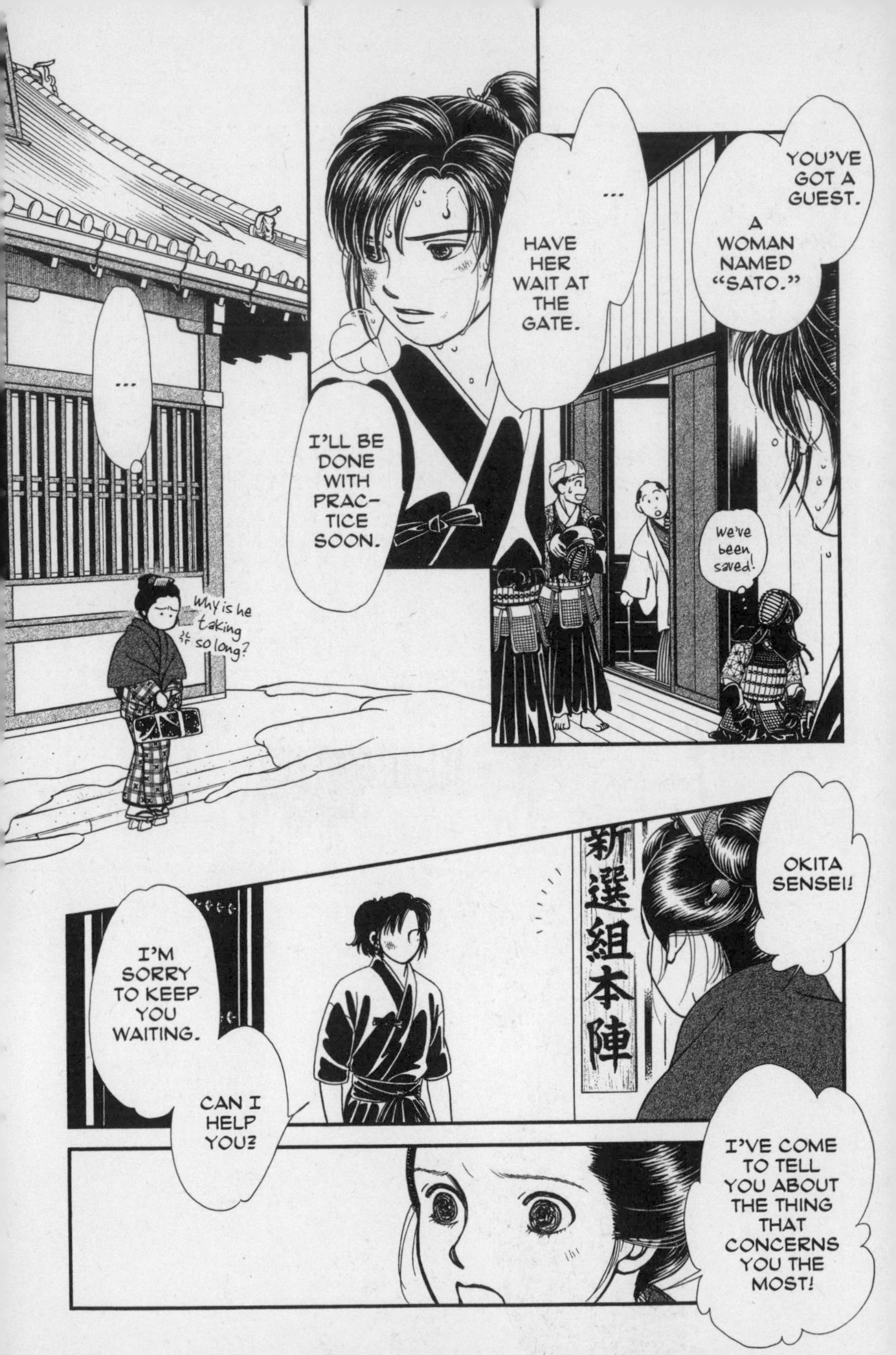
YOU'VE GOT A GUEST.
A WOMAN NAMED "SATO."
We've been saved!
...
HAVE HER WAIT AT THE GATE.
I'LL BE DONE WITH PRAC-TICE SOON.
...
Why is he taking so long?
OKITA SENSEI!
新選組本陣
I'M SORRY TO KEEP YOU WAITING.
CAN I HELP YOU?
I'VE COME TO TELL YOU ABOUT THE THING THAT CONCERNS YOU THE MOST!

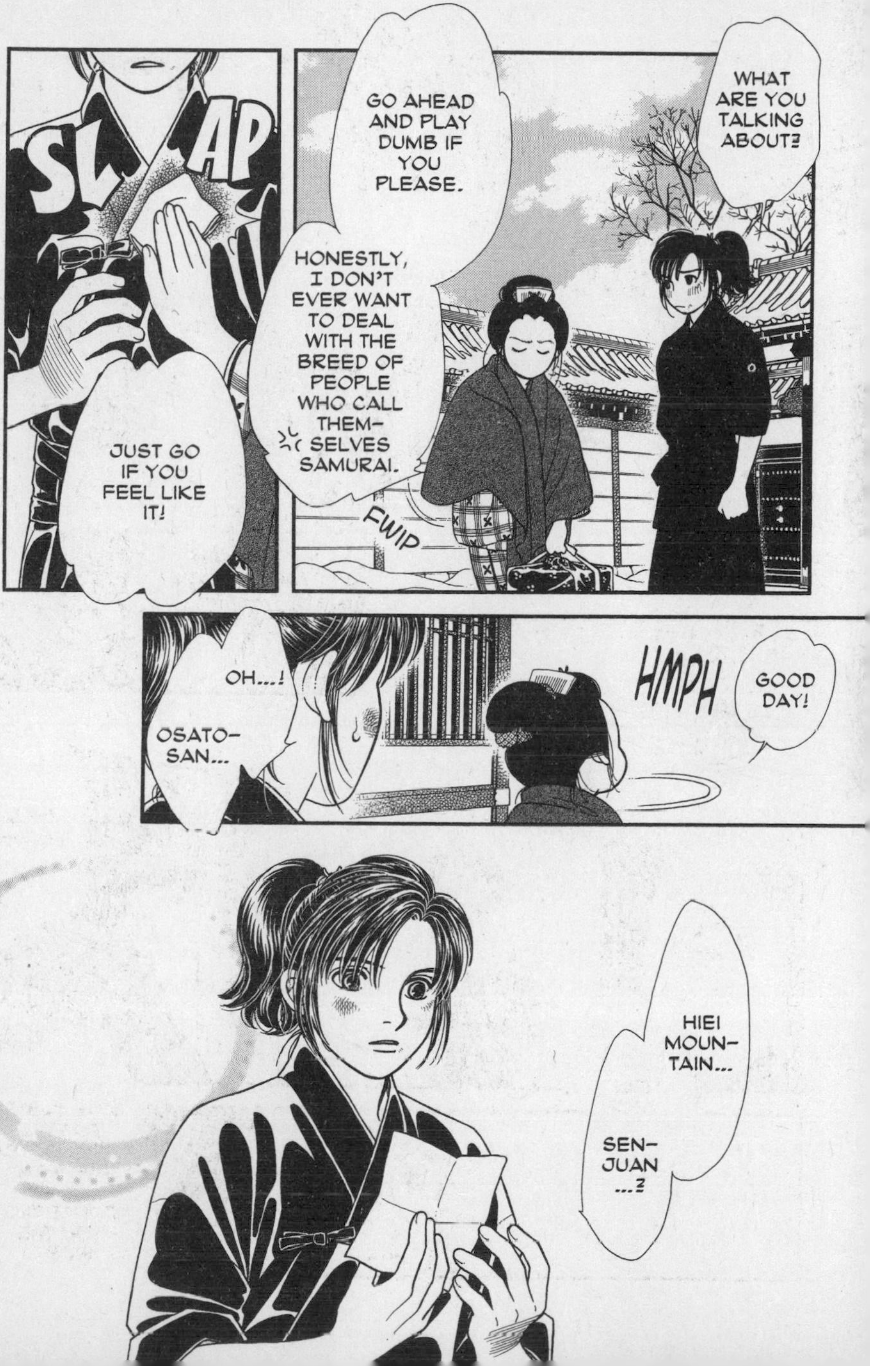
WHAT ARE YOU TALKING ABOUT?
GO AHEAD AND PLAY DUMB IF YOU PLEASE.
HONESTLY, I DON'T EVER WANT TO DEAL WITH THE BREED OF PEOPLE WHO CALL THEM-SELVES SAMURAI.
FWIP
SLAP
JUST GO IF YOU FEEL LIKE IT!
GOOD DAY!
HMPH
OH...!
OSATO-SAN...
HIEI MOUN-TAIN...
SEN-JUAN...?

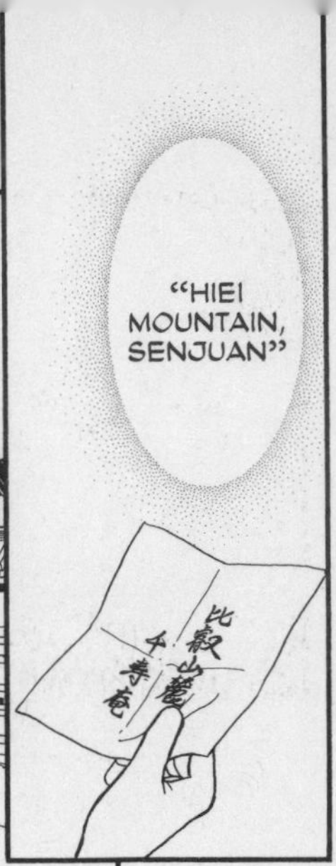
"HIEI MOUNTAIN, SENJUAN"
比叡山麓
千寿庵

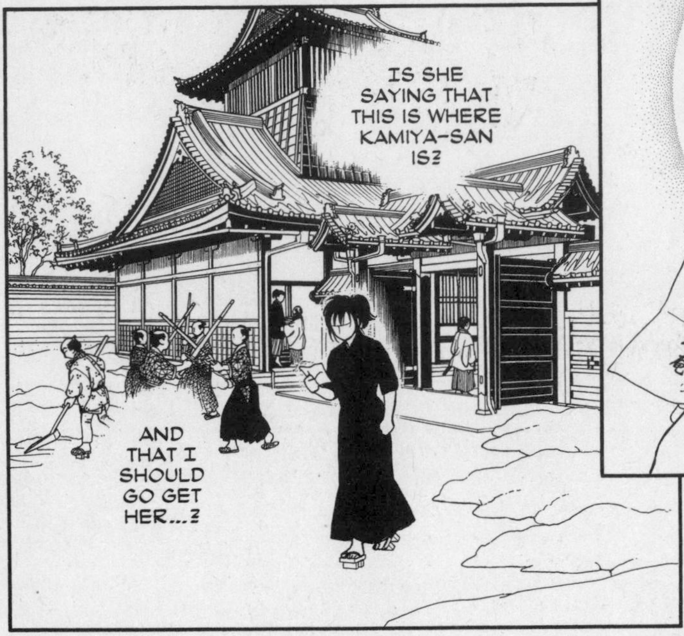
IS SHE SAYING THAT THIS IS WHERE KAMIYA-SAN IS?
AND THAT I SHOULD GO GET HER...?

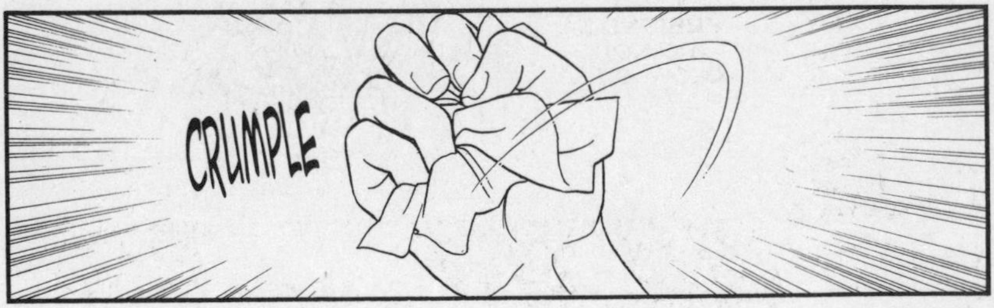
CRUMPLE

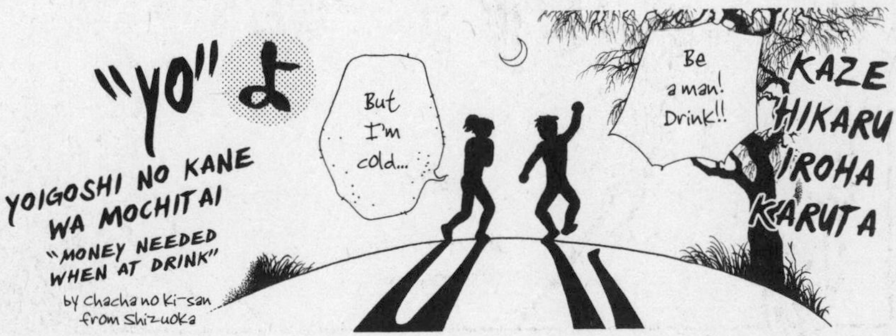
KAZE HIKARU IROHA KARUTA
Be a man! Drink!!
But I'm cold...
"YO" よ
YOIGOSHI NO KANE WA MOCHITAI
"MONEY NEEDED WHEN AT DRINK"
by Chacha no Ki-san from Shizuoka

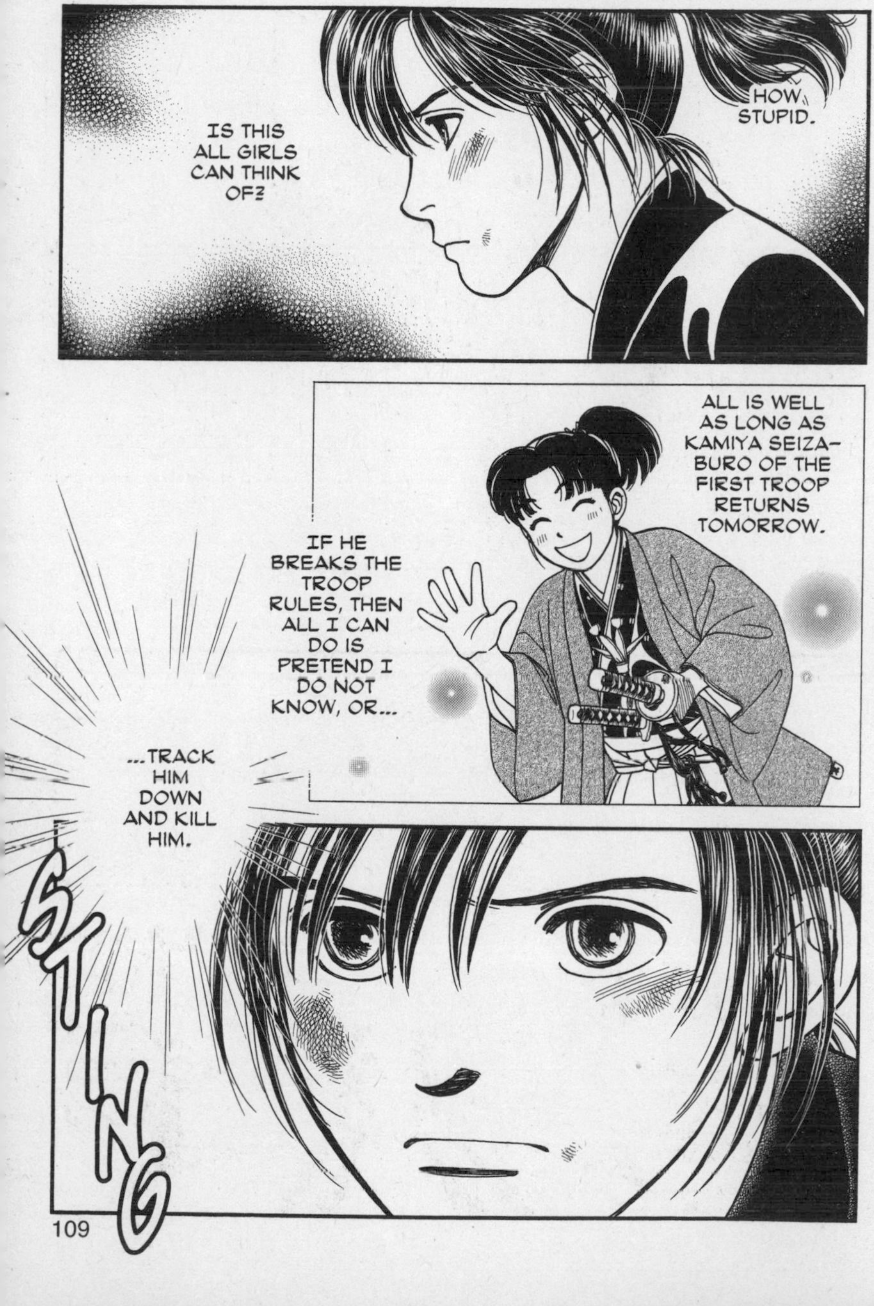
HOW STUPID.
IS THIS ALL GIRLS CAN THINK OF?
ALL IS WELL AS LONG AS KAMIYA SEIZA-BURO OF THE FIRST TROOP RETURNS TOMORROW.
IF HE BREAKS THE TROOP RULES, THEN ALL I CAN DO IS PRETEND I DO NOT KNOW, OR...
...TRACK HIM DOWN AND KILL HIM.
STING

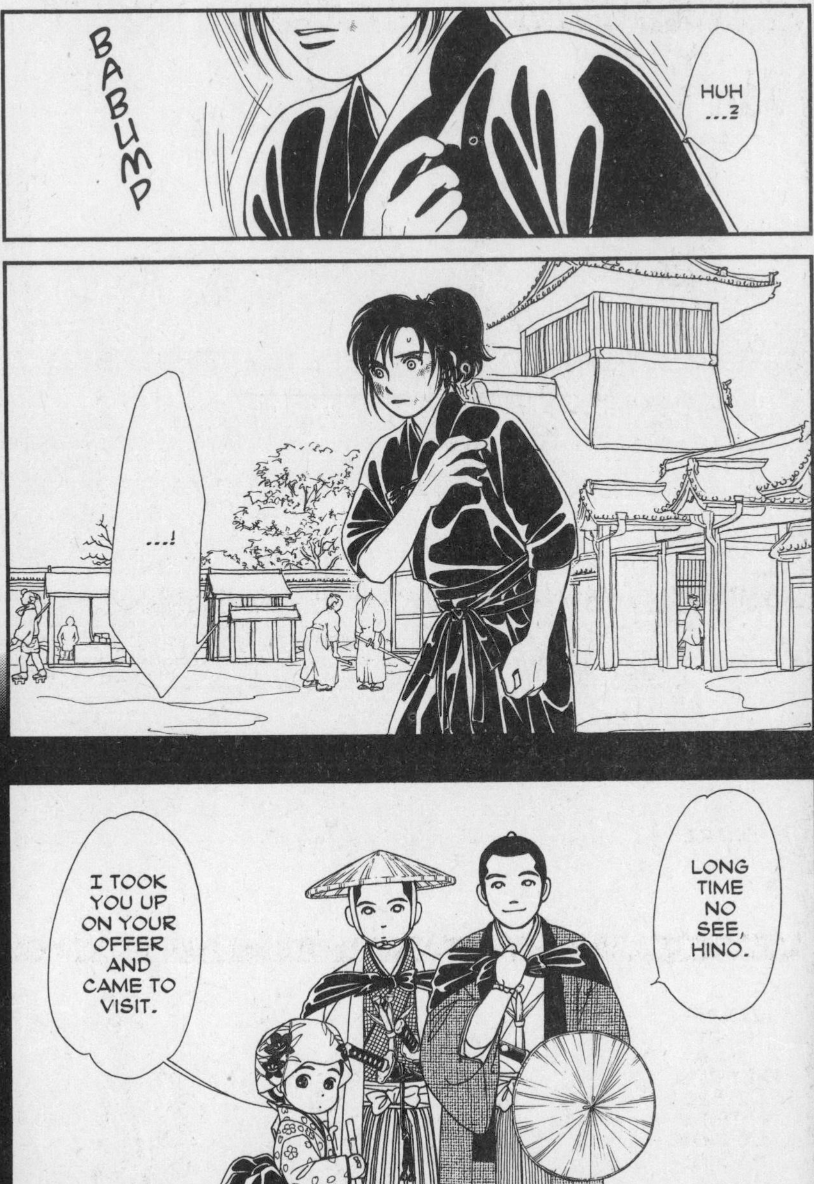
HUH ...?
BABUMP
...!
LONG TIME NO SEE, HINO.
I TOOK YOU UP ON YOUR OFFER AND CAME TO VISIT.

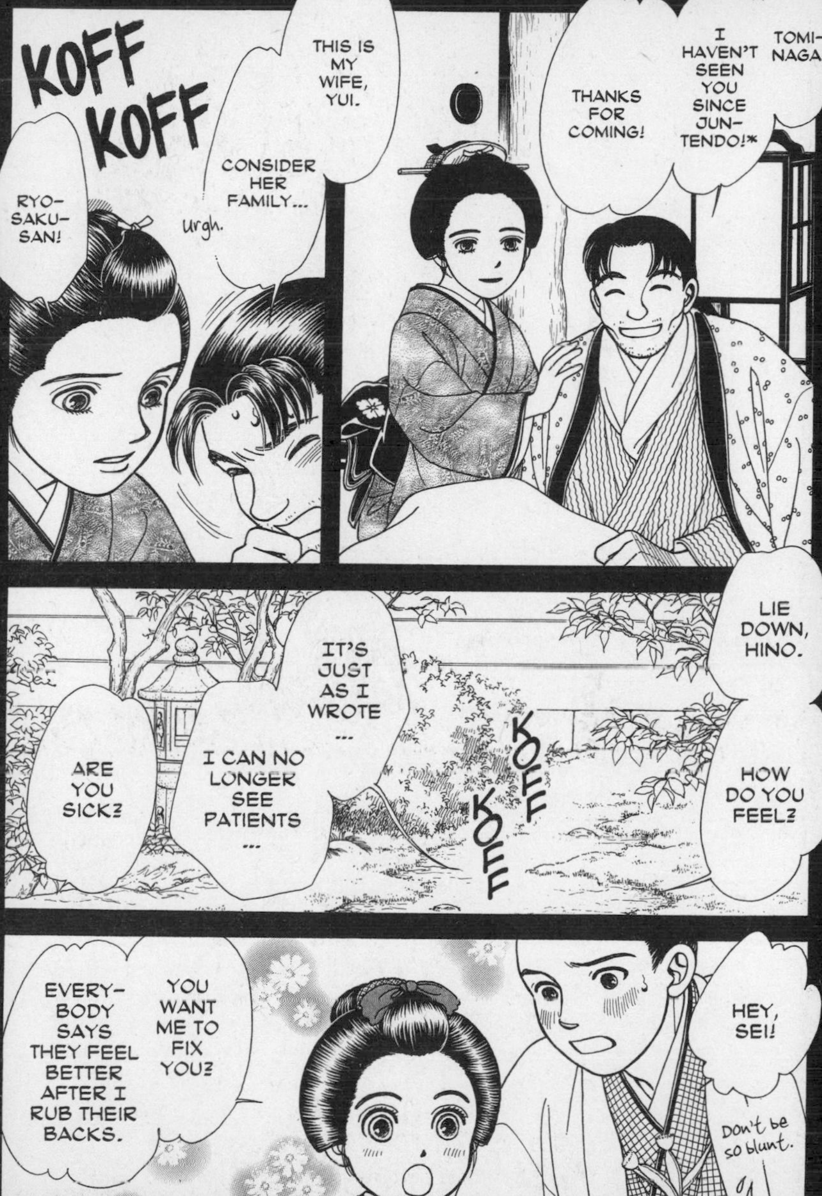
TOMI-NAGA!
I HAVEN'T SEEN YOU SINCE JUN-TENDO!*
THANKS FOR COMING!
THIS IS MY WIFE, YUI.
CONSIDER HER FAMILY...
KOFF KOFF
Urgh.
RYO-SAKU-SAN!
LIE DOWN, HINO.
HOW DO YOU FEEL?
KOFF KOFF
IT'S JUST AS I WROTE...
I CAN NO LONGER SEE PATIENTS...
ARE YOU SICK?
HEY, SEI!
Don't be so blunt.
YOU WANT ME TO FIX YOU?
EVERY-BODY SAYS THEY FEEL BETTER AFTER I RUB THEIR BACKS.

*The Western medicine school in Sakura (Chiba prefecture) where Sei's father studied for many years.

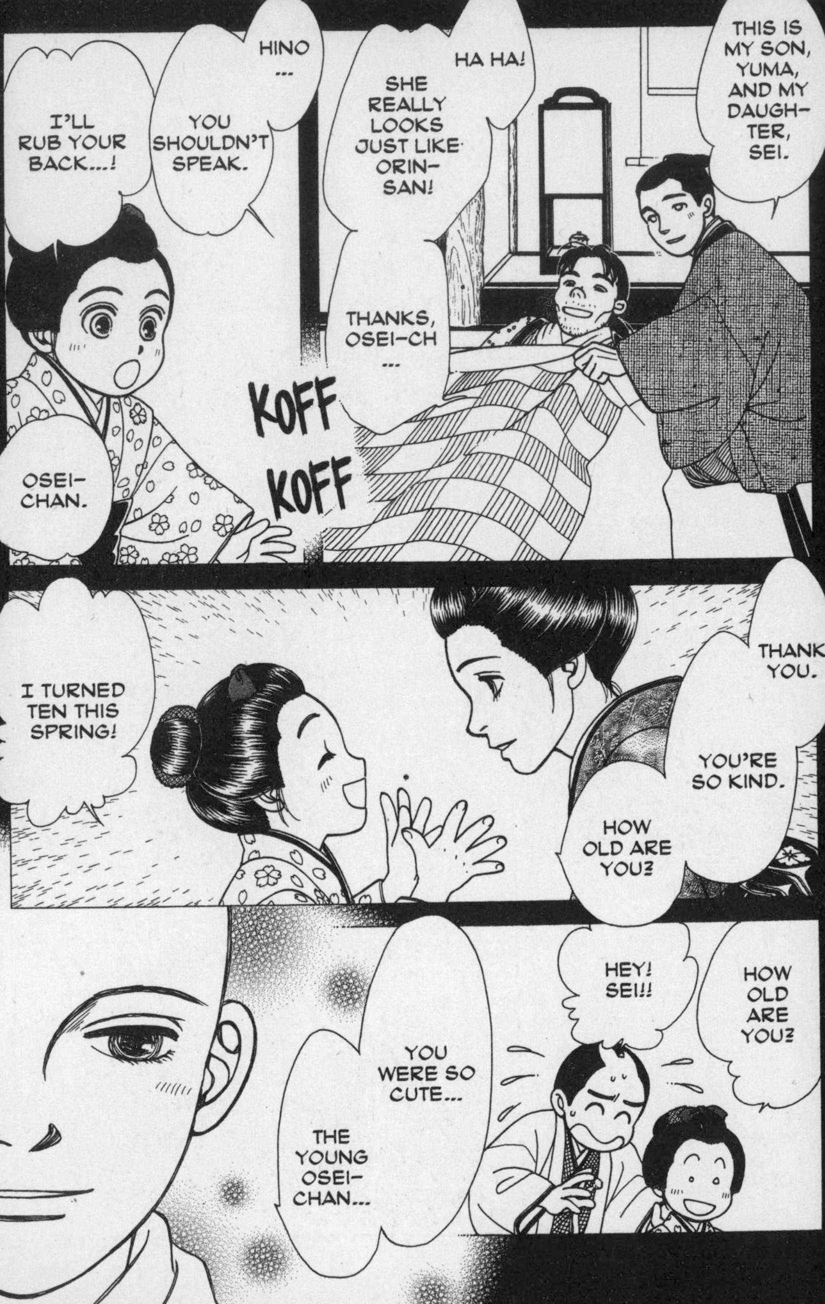
THIS IS MY SON, YUMA, AND MY DAUGHTER, SEI.
HA HA!
SHE REALLY LOOKS JUST LIKE ORIN-SAN!
HINO ...
YOU SHOULDN'T SPEAK.
I'LL RUB YOUR BACK...!
THANKS, OSEI-CH ...
KOFF KOFF
OSEI-CHAN.
THANK YOU.
YOU'RE SO KIND.
HOW OLD ARE YOU?
I TURNED TEN THIS SPRING!
HOW OLD ARE YOU?
HEY! SEI!!
YOU WERE SO CUTE...
THE YOUNG OSEI-CHAN...

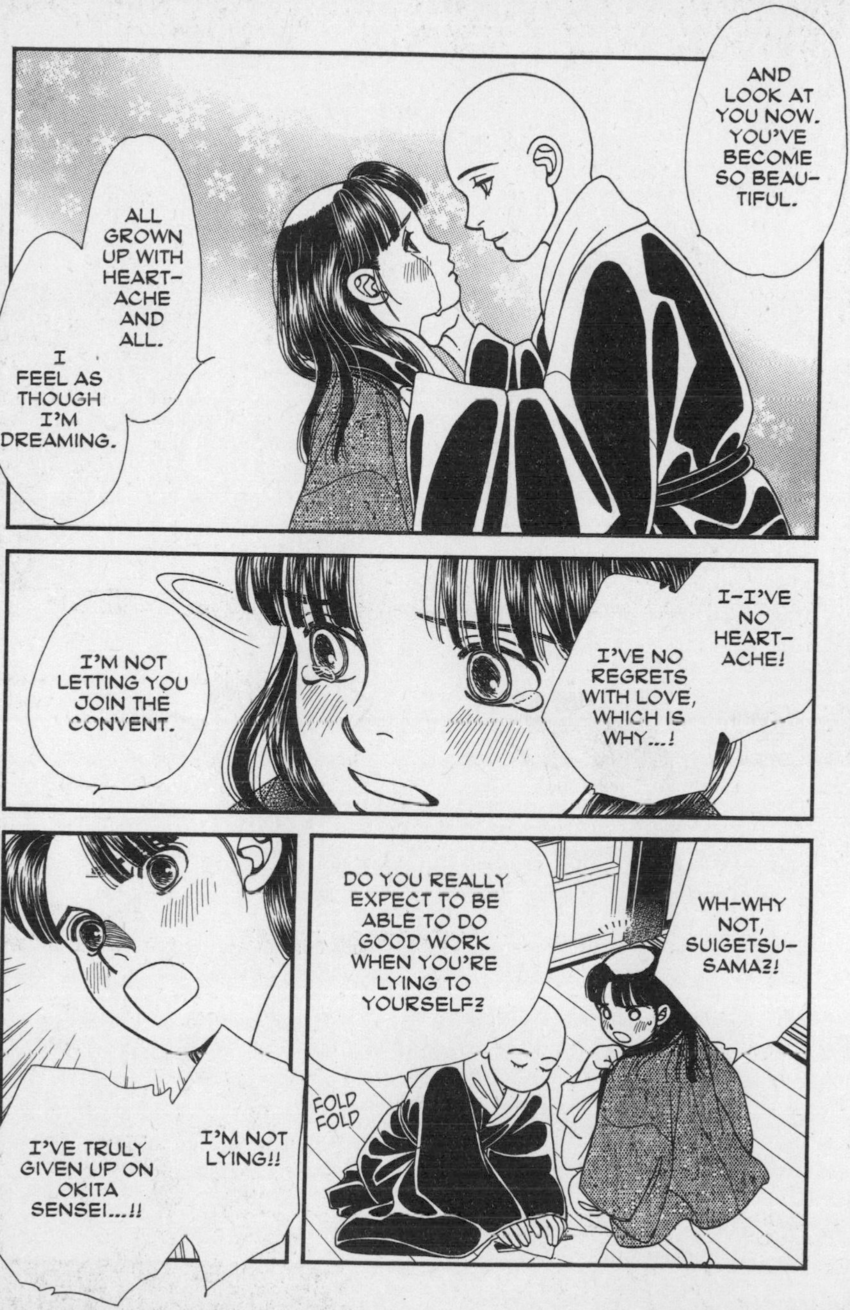
AND LOOK AT YOU NOW. YOU'VE BECOME SO BEAU-TIFUL.
ALL GROWN UP WITH HEART-ACHE AND ALL.
I FEEL AS THOUGH I'M DREAMING.
I-I'VE NO HEART-ACHE!
I'VE NO REGRETS WITH LOVE, WHICH IS WHY...!
I'M NOT LETTING YOU JOIN THE CONVENT.
WH-WHY NOT, SUIGETSU-SAMA?!
DO YOU REALLY EXPECT TO BE ABLE TO DO GOOD WORK WHEN YOU'RE LYING TO YOURSELF?
FOLD FOLD
I'M NOT LYING!!
I'VE TRULY GIVEN UP ON OKITA SENSEI...!!

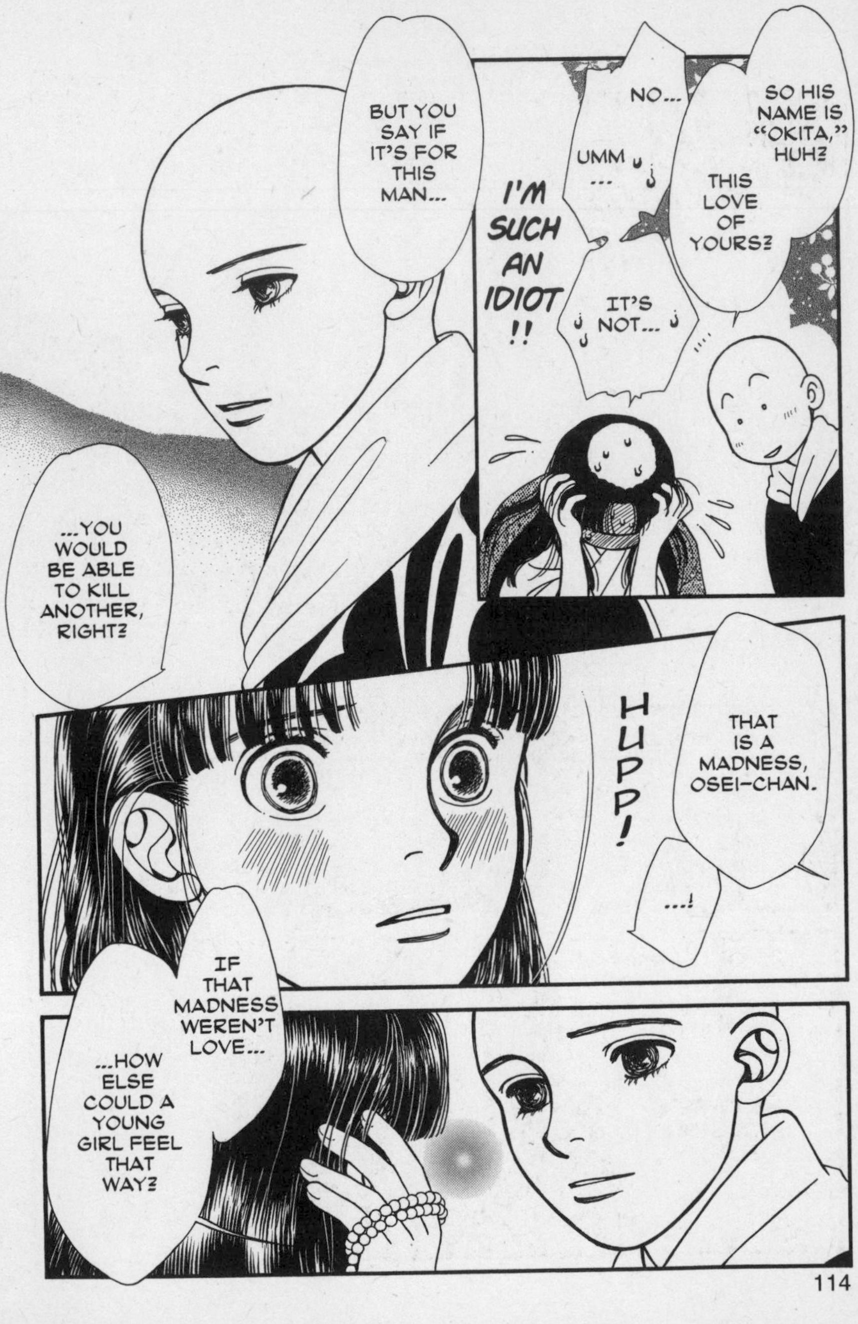
SO HIS NAME IS "OKITA," HUH?
THIS LOVE OF YOURS?
NO...
UMM...
IT'S NOT...
I'M SUCH AN IDIOT!!
BUT YOU SAY IF IT'S FOR THIS MAN...
...YOU WOULD BE ABLE TO KILL ANOTHER, RIGHT?
THAT IS A MADNESS, OSEI-CHAN.
HUPP!
...!
IF THAT MADNESS WEREN'T LOVE...
...HOW ELSE COULD A YOUNG GIRL FEEL THAT WAY?

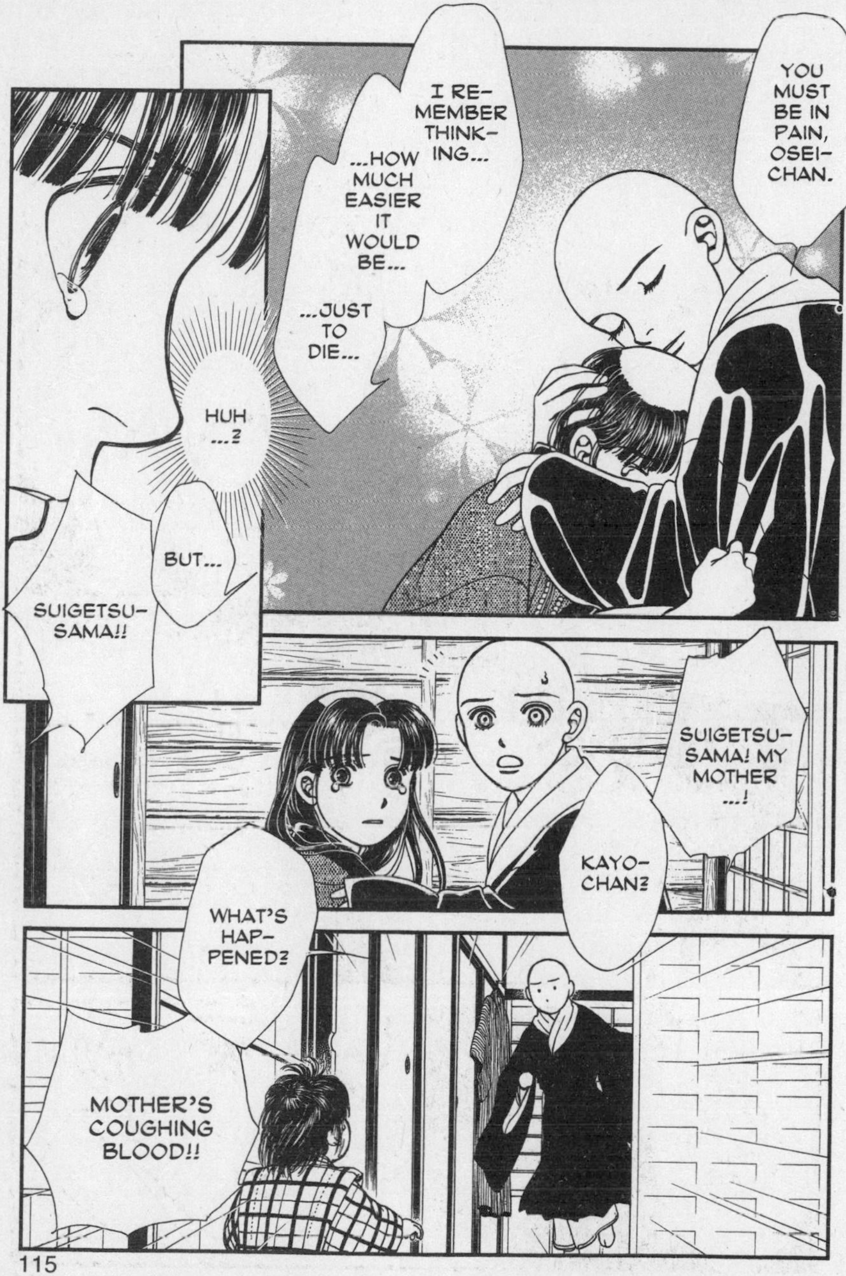
YOU MUST BE IN PAIN, OSEI-CHAN.
I RE-MEMBER THINK-ING...
...HOW MUCH EASIER IT WOULD BE...
...JUST TO DIE...
HUH ...?
BUT...
SUIGETSU-SAMA!!
SUIGETSU-SAMA! MY MOTHER ...!
KAYO-CHAN?
WHAT'S HAP-PENED?
MOTHER'S COUGHING BLOOD!!

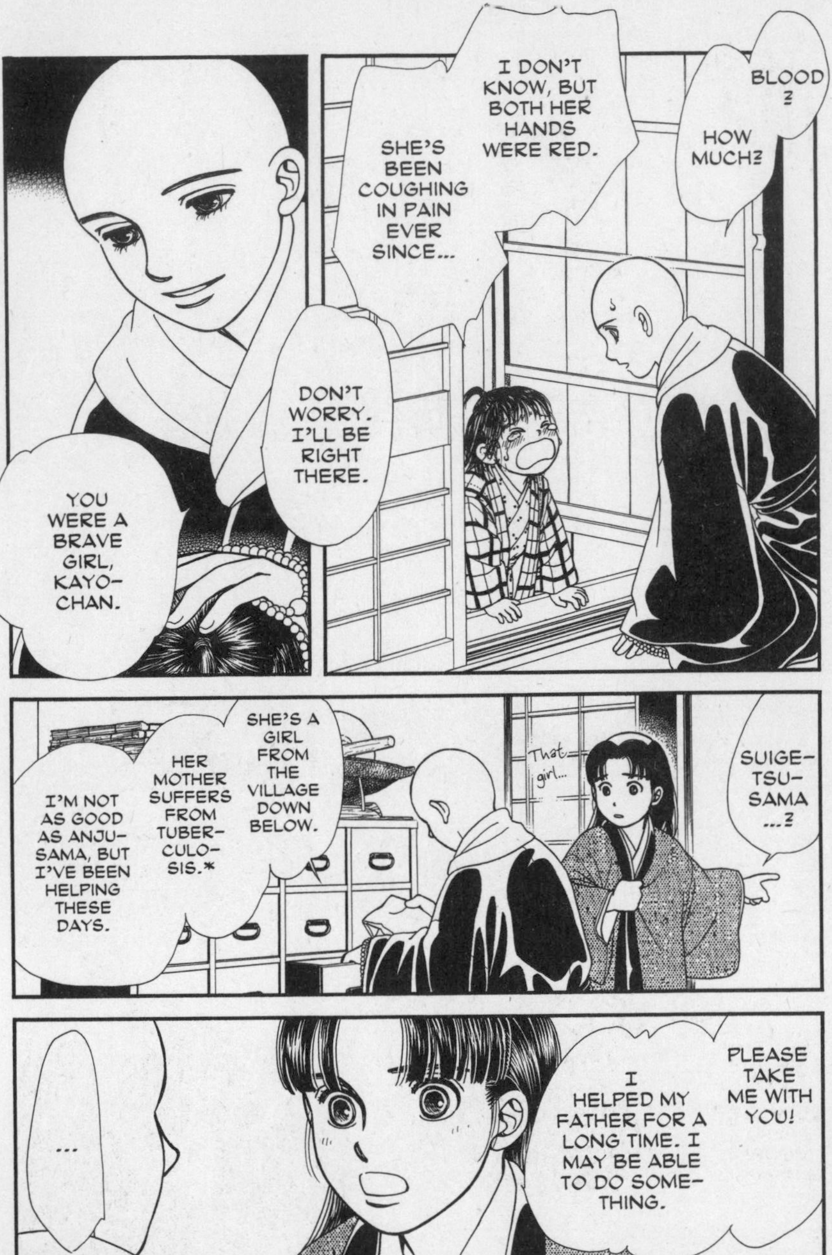
BLOOD? HOW MUCH?
I DON'T KNOW, BUT BOTH HER HANDS WERE RED.
SHE'S BEEN COUGHING IN PAIN EVER SINCE...
DON'T WORRY. I'LL BE RIGHT THERE.
YOU WERE A BRAVE GIRL, KAYO-CHAN.
SUIGE-TSU-SAMA...?
That girl...
SHE'S A GIRL FROM THE VILLAGE DOWN BELOW.
HER MOTHER SUFFERS FROM TUBER-CULO-SIS.*
I'M NOT AS GOOD AS ANJU-SAMA, BUT I'VE BEEN HELPING THESE DAYS.
PLEASE TAKE ME WITH YOU!
I HELPED MY FATHER FOR A LONG TIME. I MAY BE ABLE TO DO SOME-THING.
...

*Death from tuberculosis was extremely common, and people feared catching the disease though they did not know how it was spread.

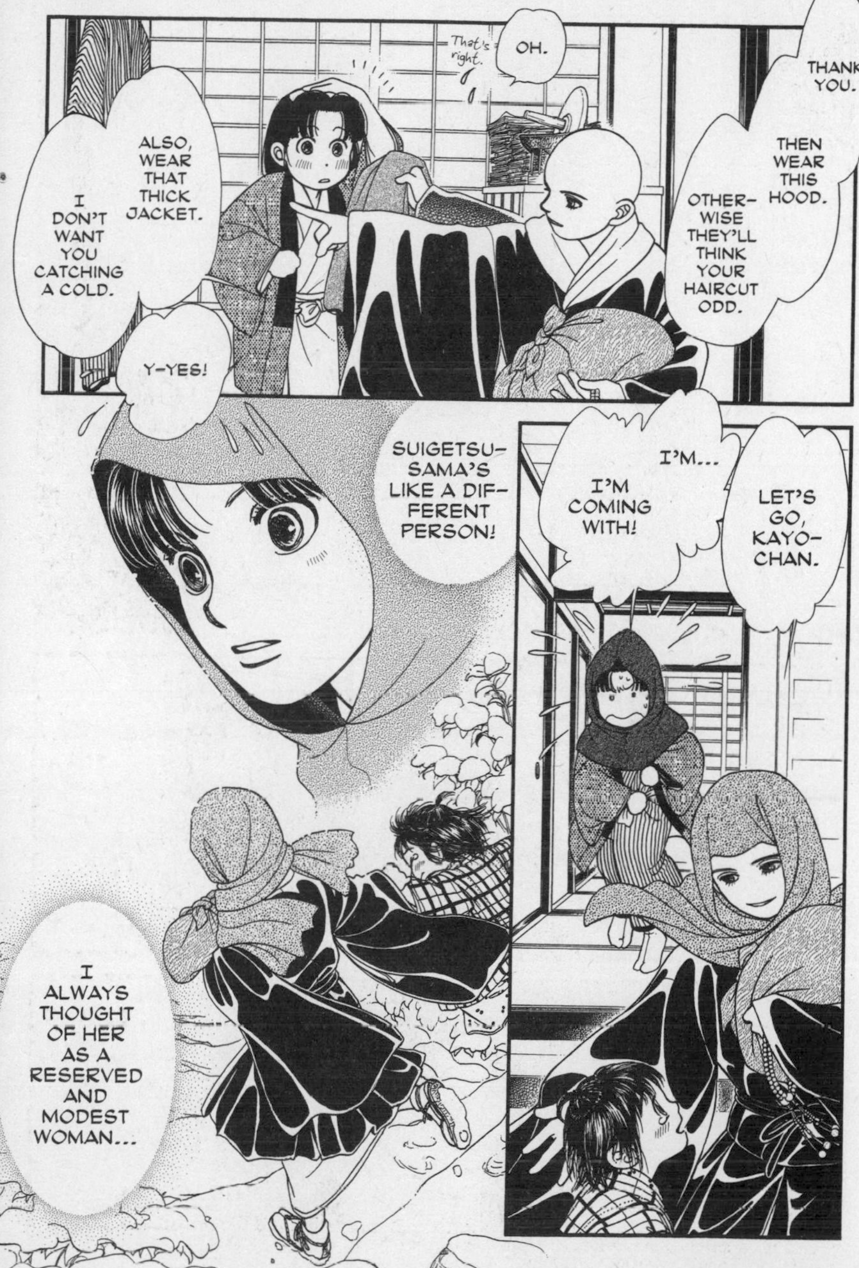
THANK YOU.
THEN WEAR THIS HOOD.
OTHER-WISE THEY'LL THINK YOUR HAIRCUT ODD.
OH.
That's right.
ALSO, WEAR THAT THICK JACKET.
I DON'T WANT YOU CATCHING A COLD.
Y-YES!
LET'S GO, KAYO-CHAN.
I'M...
I'M COMING WITH!
SUIGETSU-SAMA'S LIKE A DIF-FERENT PERSON!
I ALWAYS THOUGHT OF HER AS A RESERVED AND MODEST WOMAN...

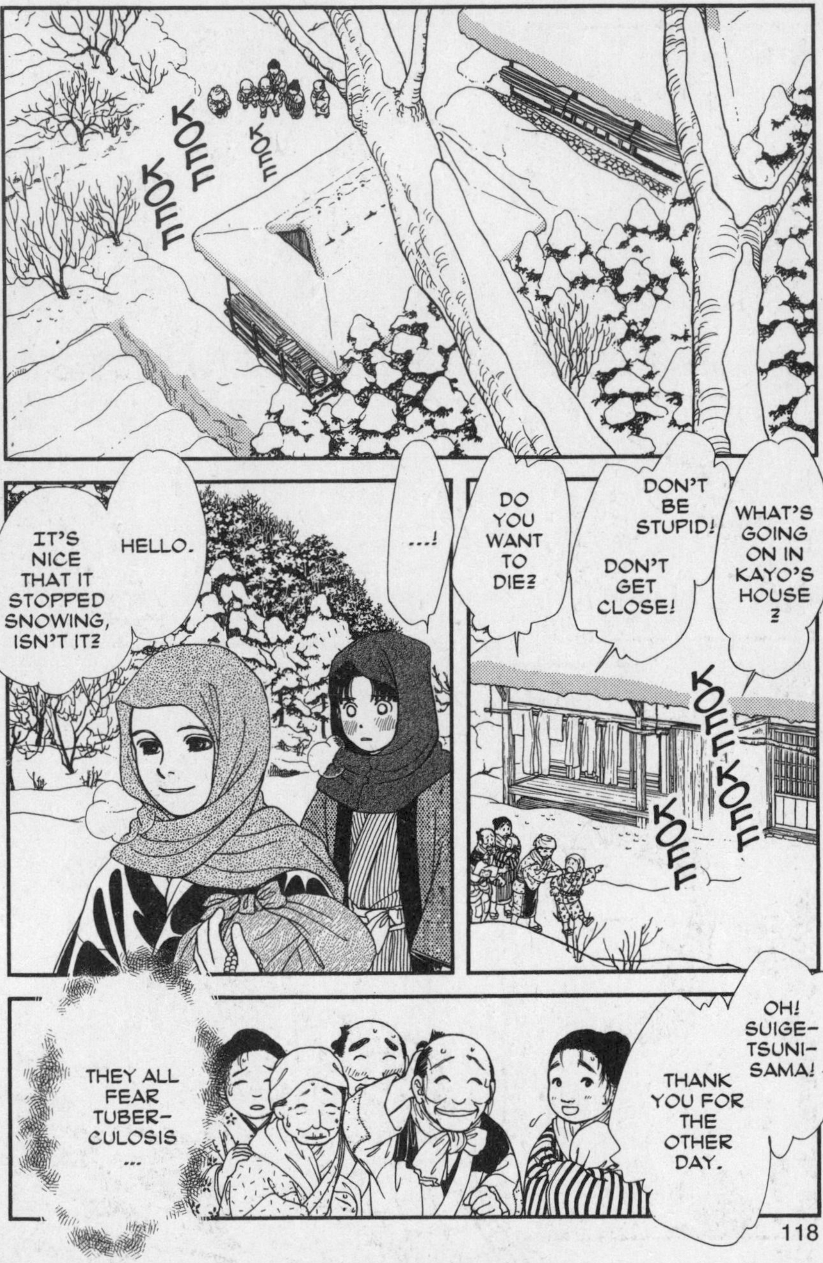
KOFF
KOFF KOFF
WHAT'S GOING ON IN KAYO'S HOUSE?
DON'T BE STUPID!
DON'T GET CLOSE!
DO YOU WANT TO DIE?
KOFF KOFF KOFF
...!
HELLO.
IT'S NICE THAT IT STOPPED SNOWING, ISN'T IT?
OH! SUIGETSUNI-SAMA!
THANK YOU FOR THE OTHER DAY.
THEY ALL FEAR TUBERCULOSIS...

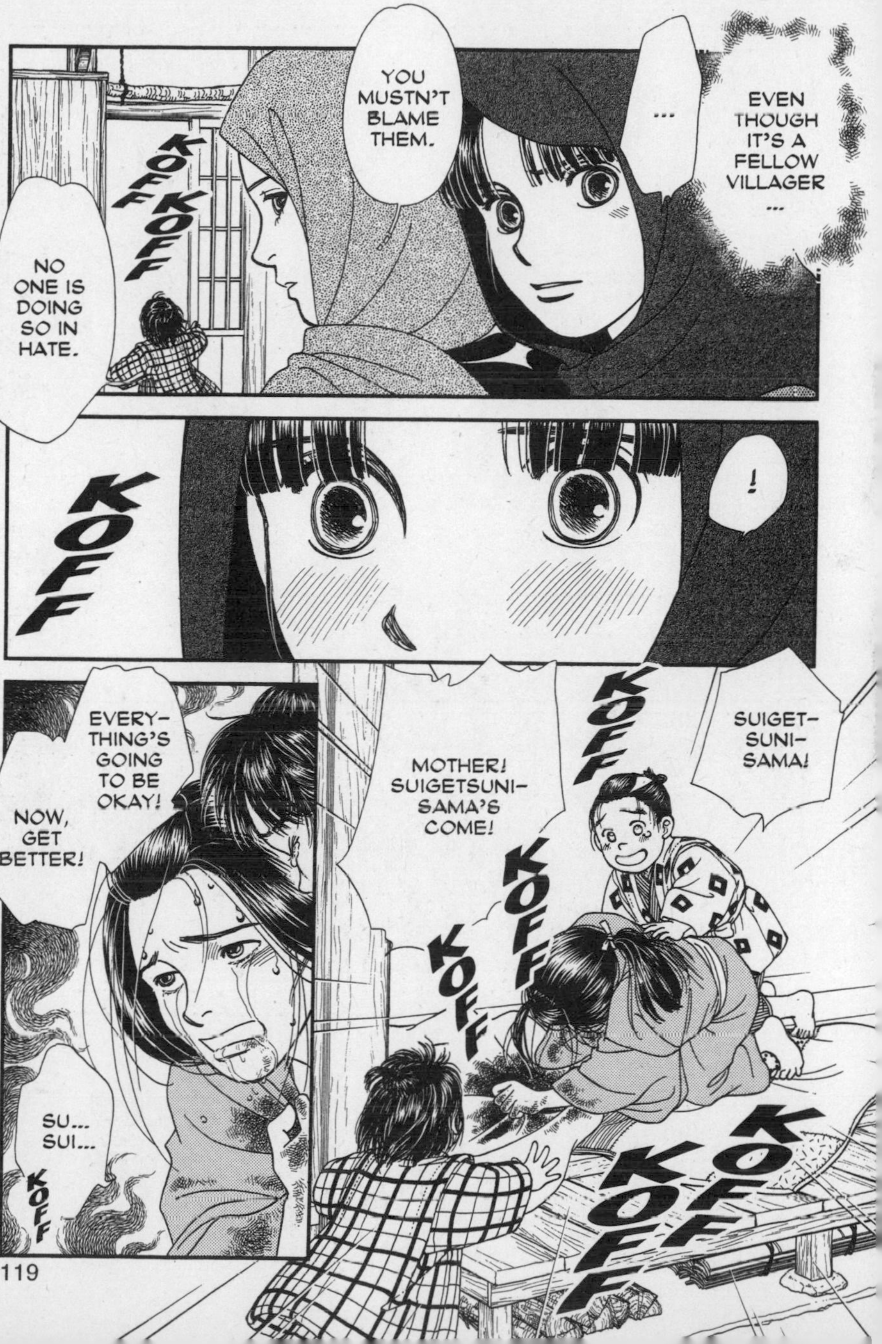
EVEN THOUGH IT'S A FELLOW VILLAGER ...
...
YOU MUSTN'T BLAME THEM.
KOFF KOFF
NO ONE IS DOING SO IN HATE.
!
KOFF
SUIGETSUNI-SAMA!
KOFF
MOTHER! SUIGETSUNI-SAMA'S COME!
KOFF
KOFF
KOFF KOFF
EVERYTHING'S GOING TO BE OKAY!
NOW, GET BETTER!
SU... SUI...
KOFF

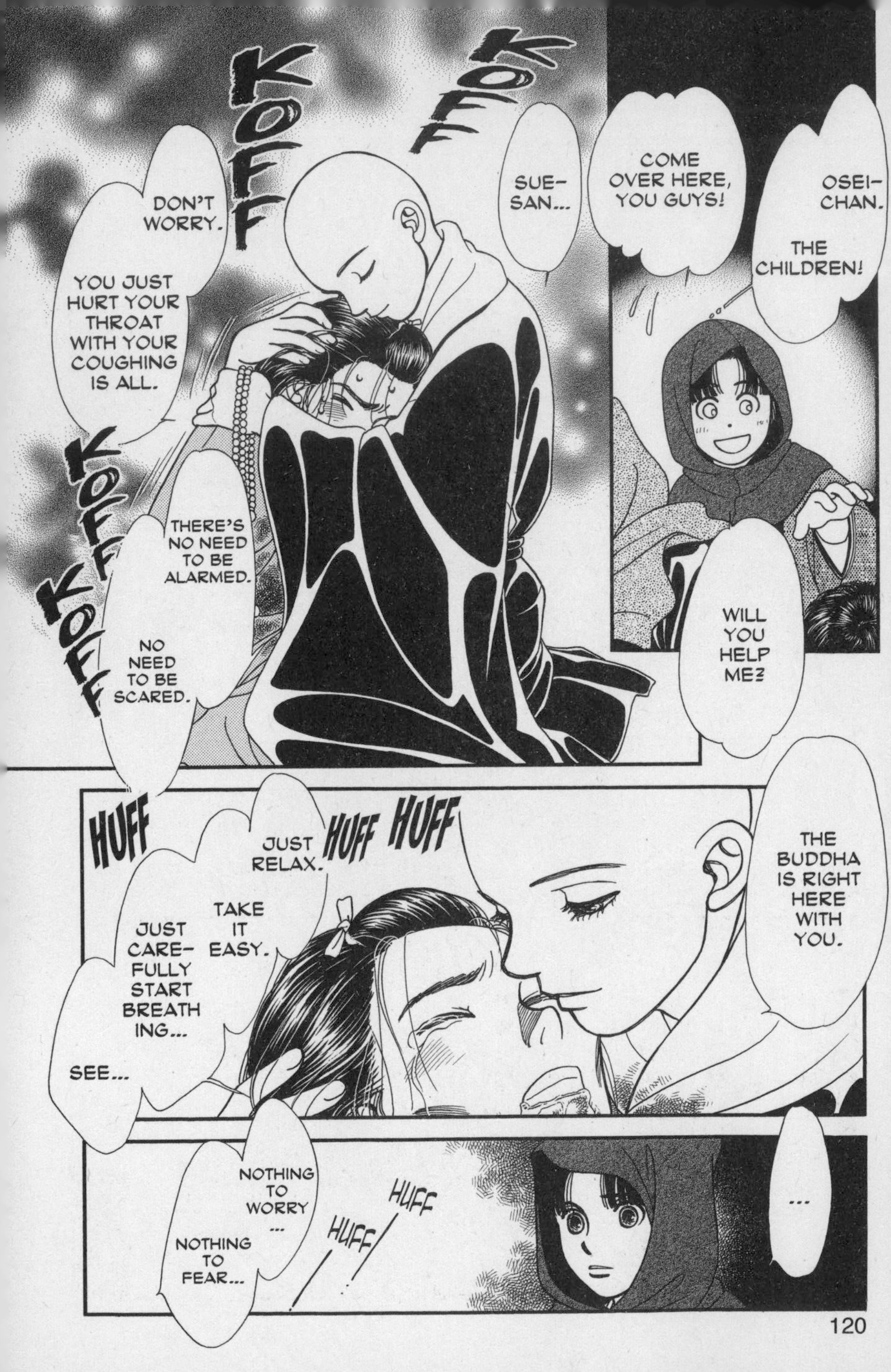

OSEI-CHAN.
THE CHILDREN!
COME OVER HERE, YOU GUYS!
SUE-SAN...
WILL YOU HELP ME?
KOFF KOFF
DON'T WORRY.
YOU JUST HURT YOUR THROAT WITH YOUR COUGHING IS ALL.
KOFF KOFF KOFF KOFF
THERE'S NO NEED TO BE ALARMED.
NO NEED TO BE SCARED.
THE BUDDHA IS RIGHT HERE WITH YOU.
HUFF HUFF
JUST RELAX.
TAKE IT EASY.
HUFF
JUST CARE-FULLY START BREATH ING...
SEE...
...
HUFF HUFF
NOTHING TO WORRY ...
NOTHING TO FEAR...

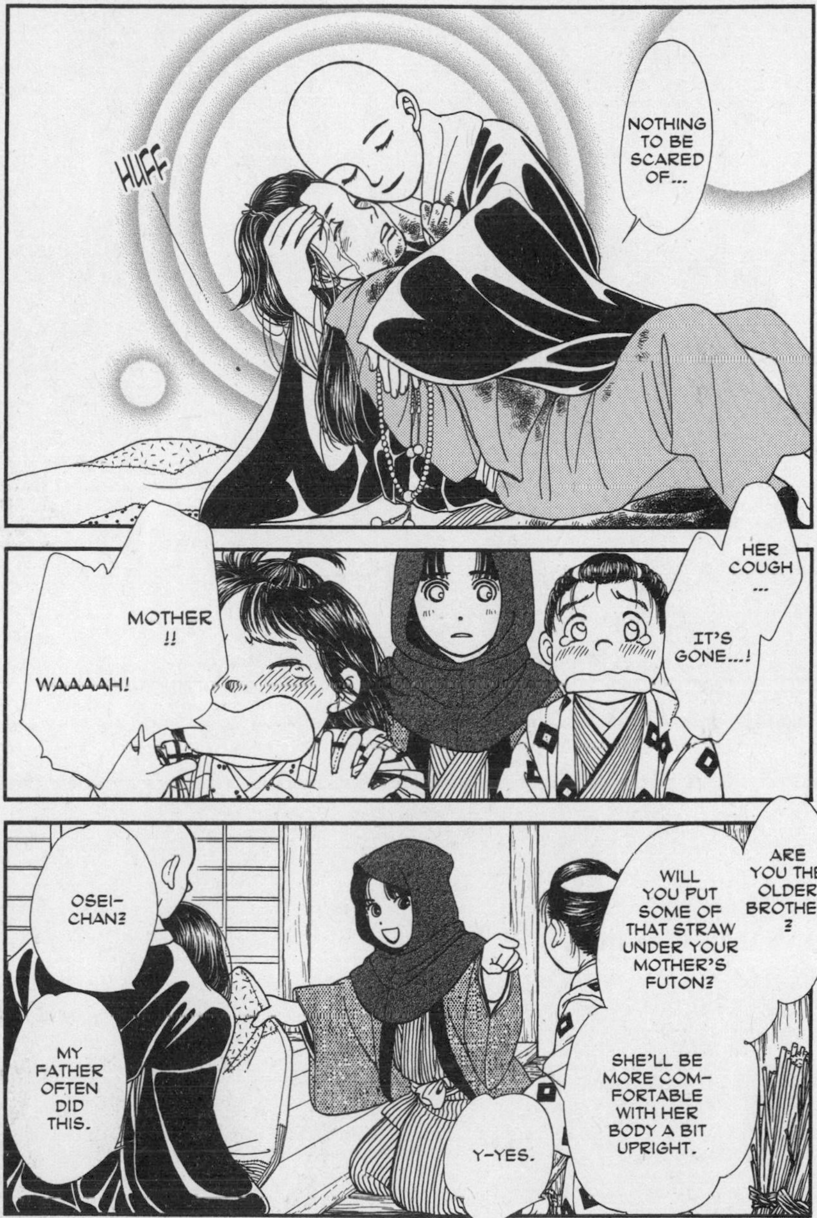
NOTHING TO BE SCARED OF...
HUFF
HER COUGH ...
IT'S GONE...!
MOTHER !!
WAAAAH!
ARE YOU THE OLDER BROTHER ?
WILL YOU PUT SOME OF THAT STRAW UNDER YOUR MOTHER'S FUTON?
SHE'LL BE MORE COM-FORTABLE WITH HER BODY A BIT UPRIGHT.
Y-YES.
OSEI-CHAN?
MY FATHER OFTEN DID THIS.

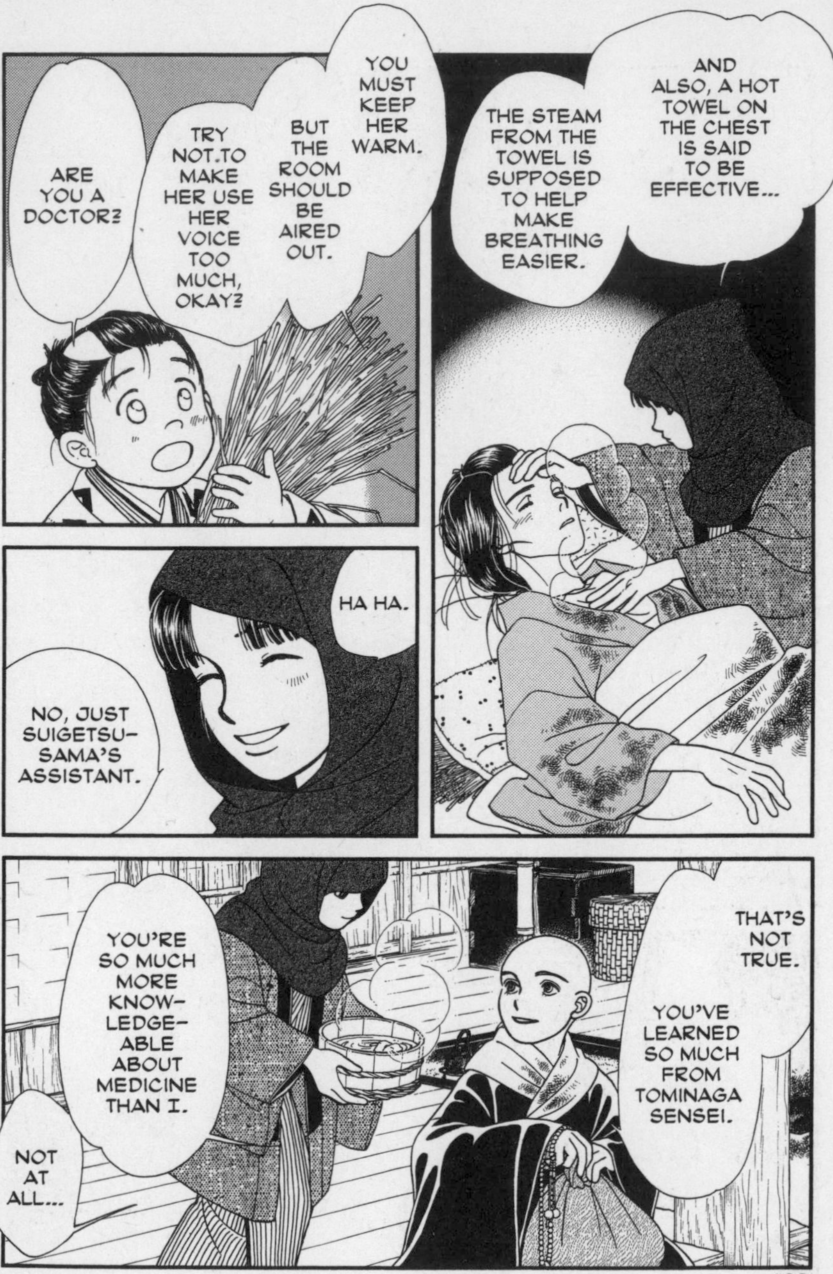
AND ALSO, A HOT TOWEL ON THE CHEST IS SAID TO BE EFFECTIVE...
THE STEAM FROM THE TOWEL IS SUPPOSED TO HELP MAKE BREATHING EASIER.
YOU MUST KEEP HER WARM.
BUT THE ROOM SHOULD BE AIRED OUT.
TRY NOT TO MAKE HER USE HER VOICE TOO MUCH, OKAY?
ARE YOU A DOCTOR?
HA HA.
NO, JUST SUIGETSU-SAMA'S ASSISTANT.
THAT'S NOT TRUE.
YOU'VE LEARNED SO MUCH FROM TOMINAGA SENSEI.
YOU'RE SO MUCH MORE KNOW-LEDGE-ABLE ABOUT MEDICINE THAN I.
NOT AT ALL...

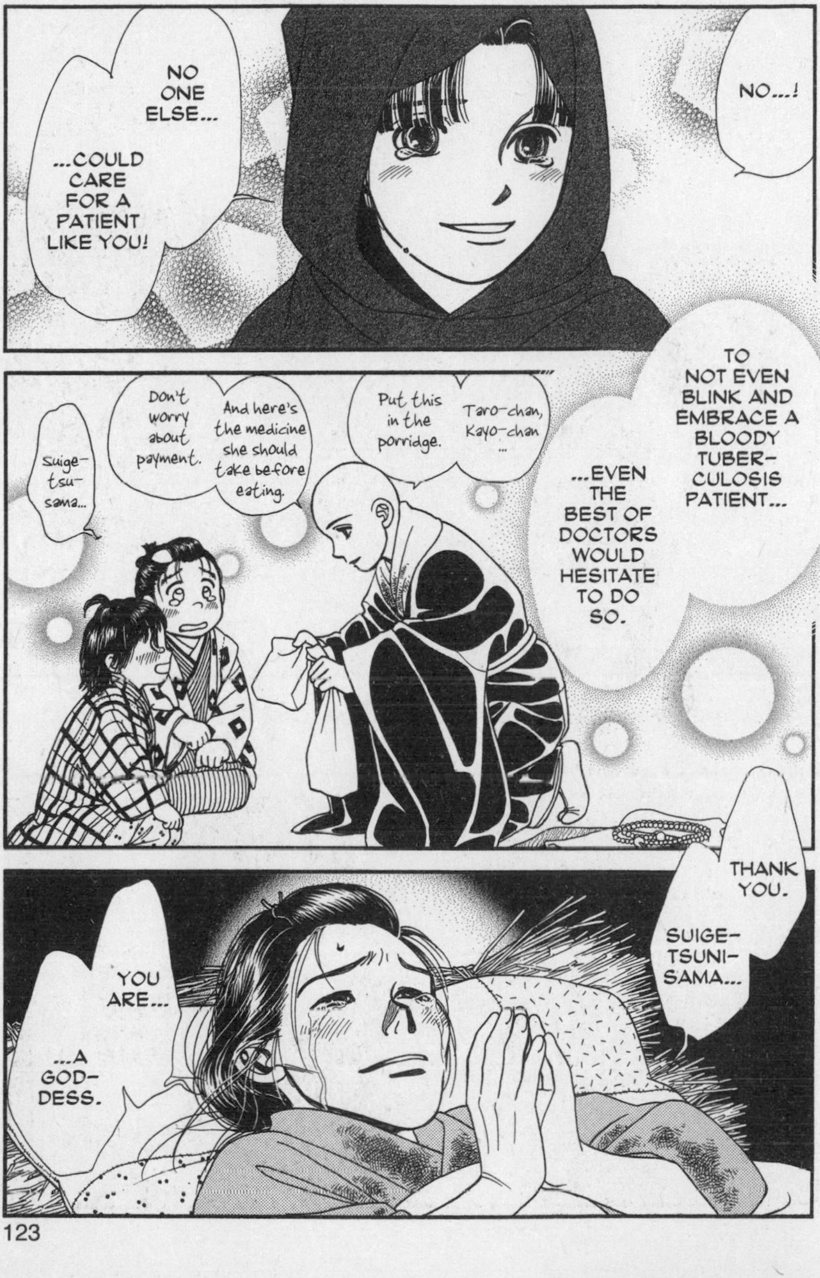
NO...!
NO ONE ELSE...
...COULD CARE FOR A PATIENT LIKE YOU!
TO NOT EVEN BLINK AND EMBRACE A BLOODY TUBER-CULOSIS PATIENT...
...EVEN THE BEST OF DOCTORS WOULD HESITATE TO DO SO.
Taro-chan, Kayo-chan...
Put this in the porridge.
And here's the medicine she should take before eating.
Don't worry about payment.
Suige-tsu-sama...
THANK YOU.
SUIGE-TSUNI-SAMA...
YOU ARE...
...A GOD-DESS.

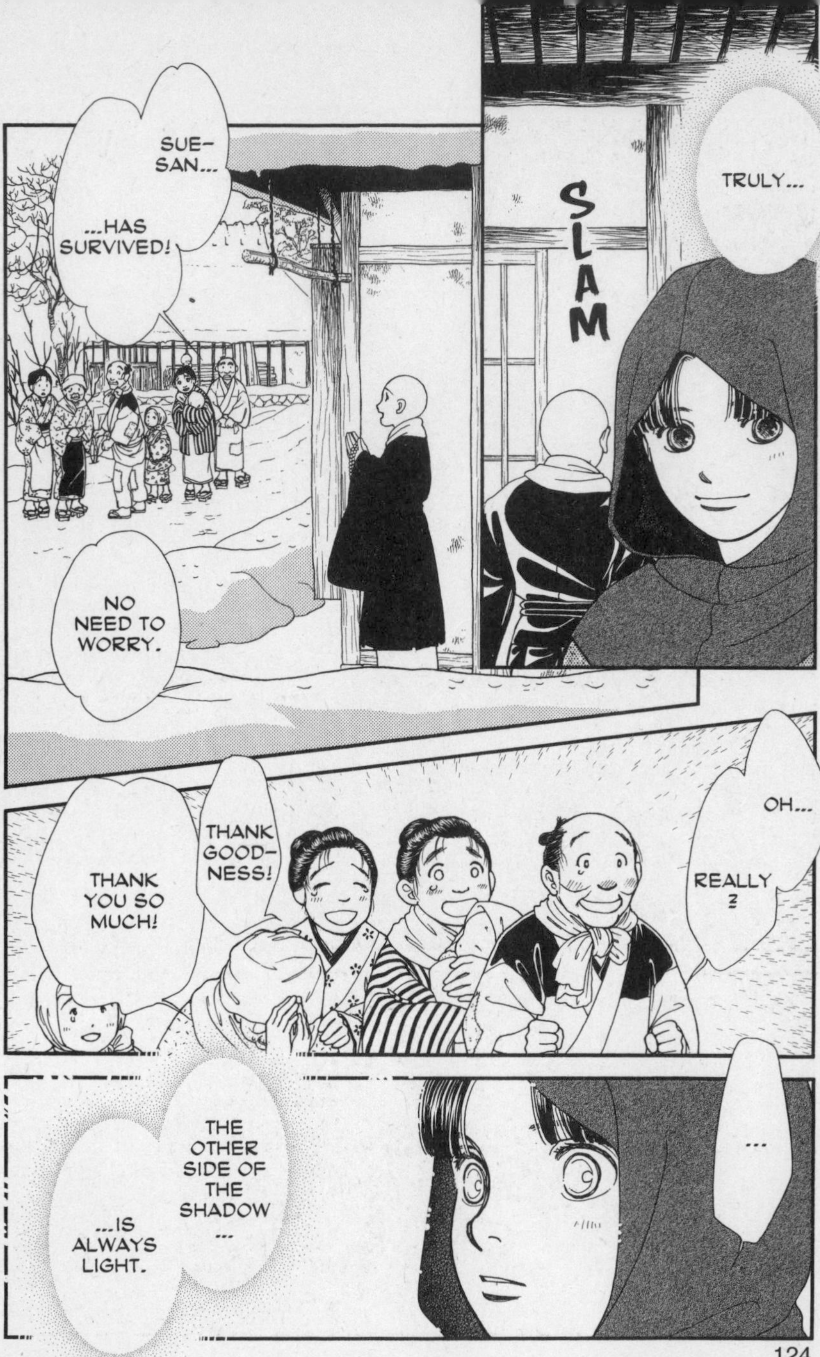
TRULY...
SLAM
SUE-SAN...
...HAS SURVIVED!
NO NEED TO WORRY.
OH...
REALLY?
THANK GOODNESS!
THANK YOU SO MUCH!
...
THE OTHER SIDE OF THE SHADOW...
...IS ALWAYS LIGHT.

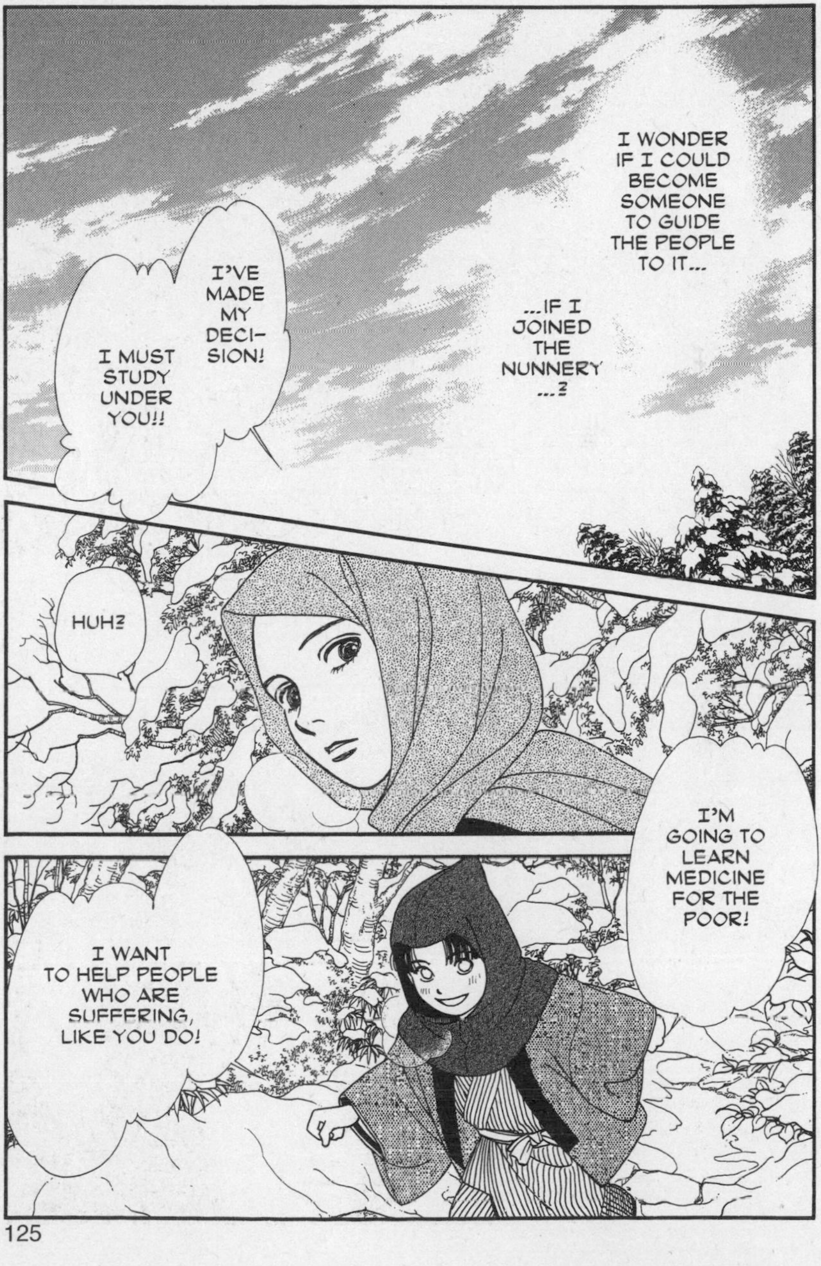
I WONDER IF I COULD BECOME SOMEONE TO GUIDE THE PEOPLE TO IT...
...IF I JOINED THE NUNNERY ...?
I'VE MADE MY DECISION!
I MUST STUDY UNDER YOU!!
HUH?
I'M GOING TO LEARN MEDICINE FOR THE POOR!
I WANT TO HELP PEOPLE WHO ARE SUFFERING, LIKE YOU DO!

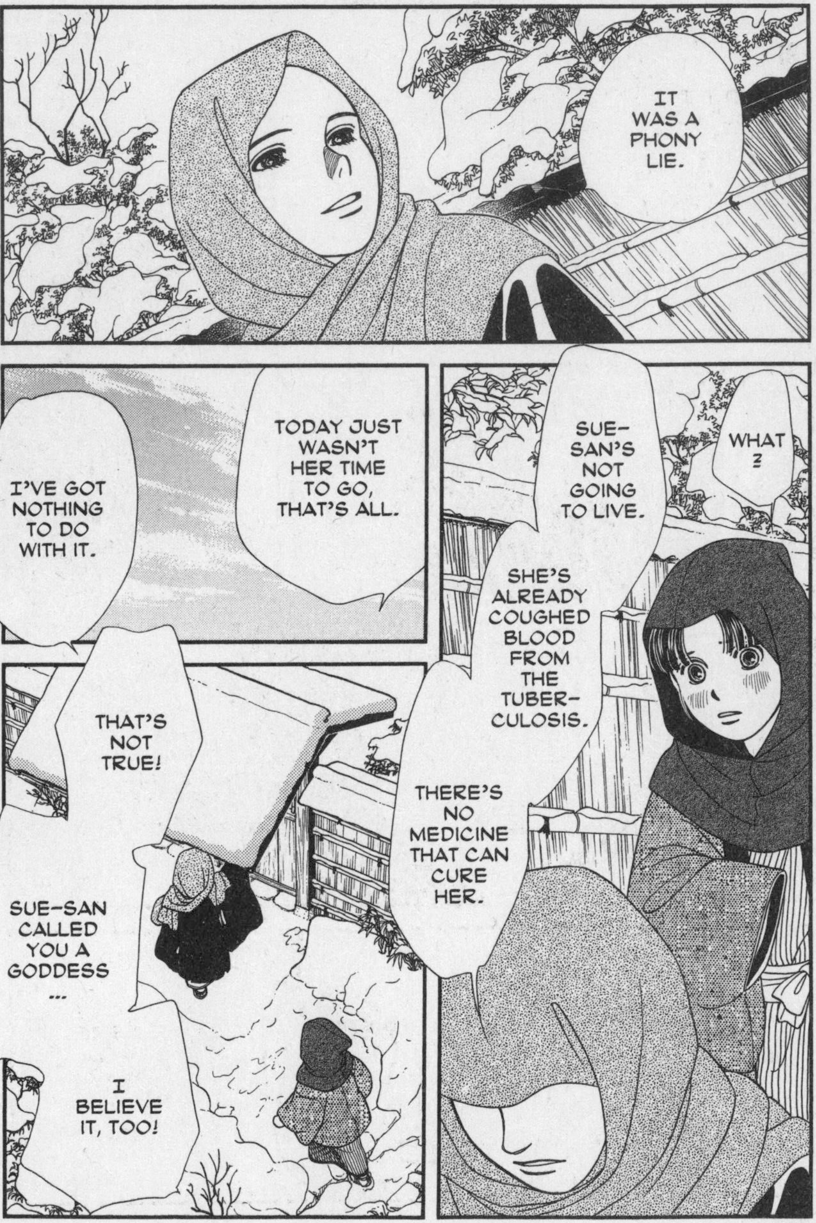
IT WAS A PHONY LIE.
WHAT?
SUE-SAN'S NOT GOING TO LIVE.
SHE'S ALREADY COUGHED BLOOD FROM THE TUBERCULOSIS.
THERE'S NO MEDICINE THAT CAN CURE HER.
TODAY JUST WASN'T HER TIME TO GO, THAT'S ALL.
I'VE GOT NOTHING TO DO WITH IT.
THAT'S NOT TRUE!
SUE-SAN CALLED YOU A GODDESS...
I BELIEVE IT, TOO!

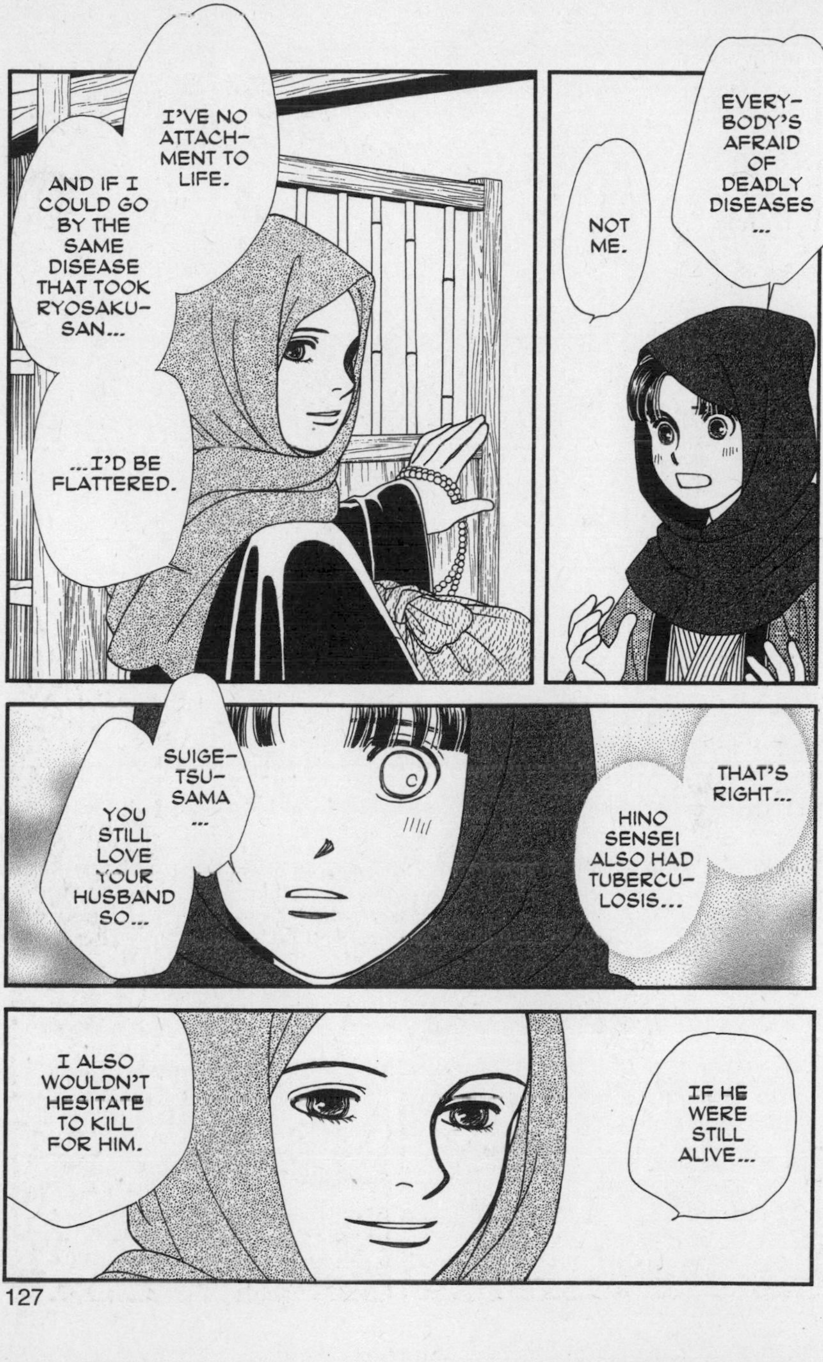
EVERY-BODY'S AFRAID OF DEADLY DISEASES...
NOT ME.
I'VE NO ATTACH-MENT TO LIFE.
AND IF I COULD GO BY THE SAME DISEASE THAT TOOK RYOSAKU-SAN...
...I'D BE FLATTERED.
THAT'S RIGHT...
HINO SENSEI ALSO HAD TUBERCU-LOSIS...
SUIGE-TSU-SAMA...
YOU STILL LOVE YOUR HUSBAND SO...
IF HE WERE STILL ALIVE...
I ALSO WOULDN'T HESITATE TO KILL FOR HIM.

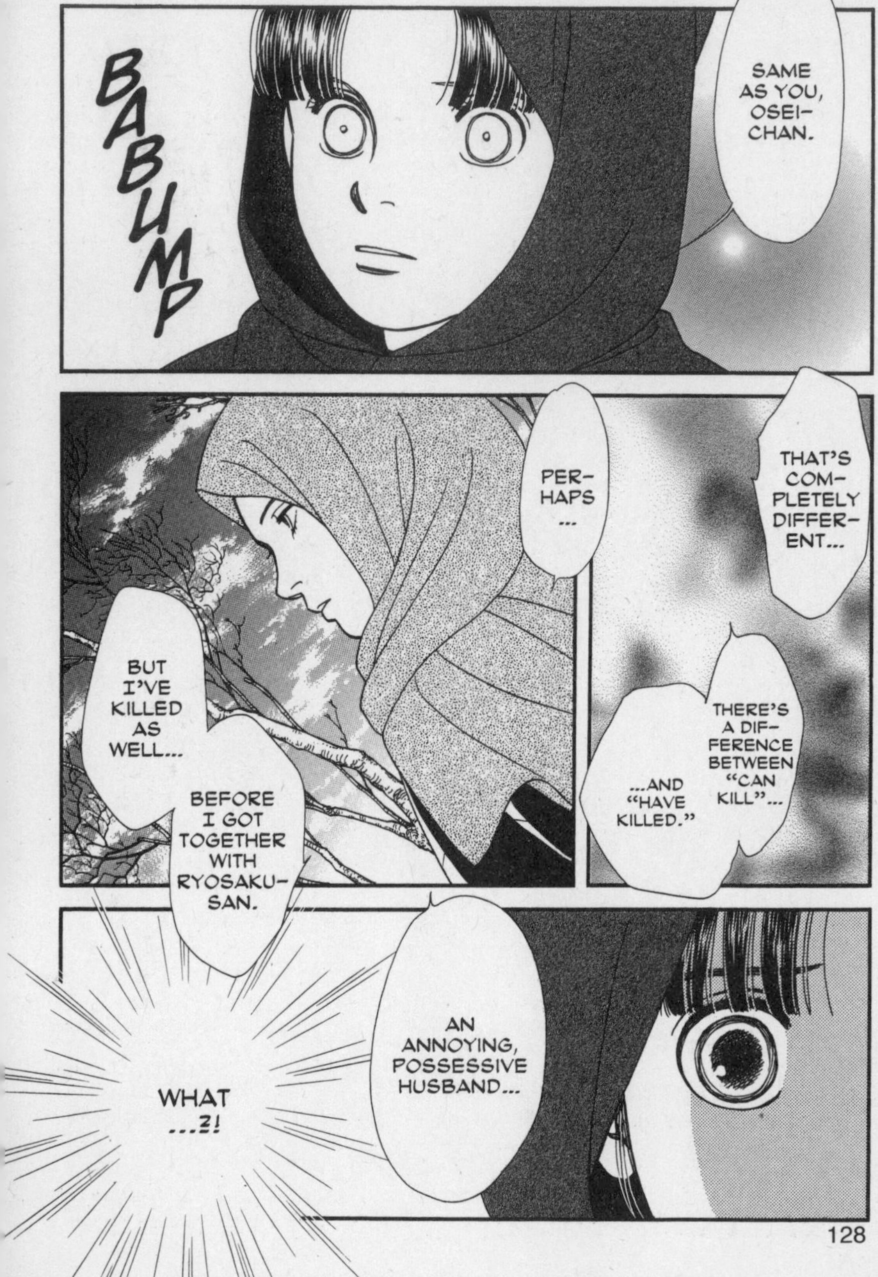
SAME AS YOU, OSEI-CHAN.
BABUMP
THAT'S COM-PLETELY DIFFER-ENT...
THERE'S A DIF-FERENCE BETWEEN "CAN KILL"...
...AND "HAVE KILLED."
PER-HAPS...
BUT I'VE KILLED AS WELL...
BEFORE I GOT TOGETHER WITH RYOSAKU-SAN.
AN ANNOYING, POSSESSIVE HUSBAND...
WHAT ...?!

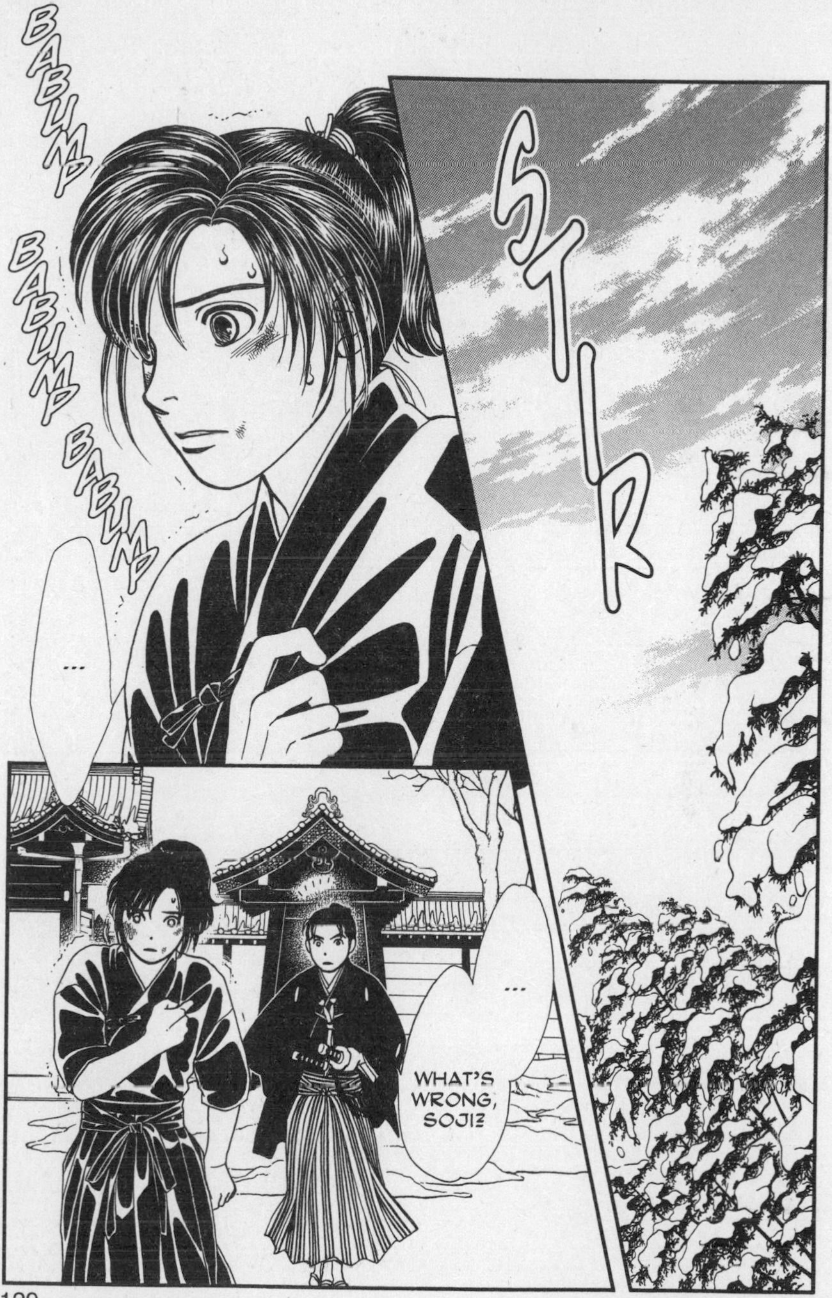
STIR
BABUMP BABUMP BABUMP BABUMP
...
...
WHAT'S WRONG, SOJI?

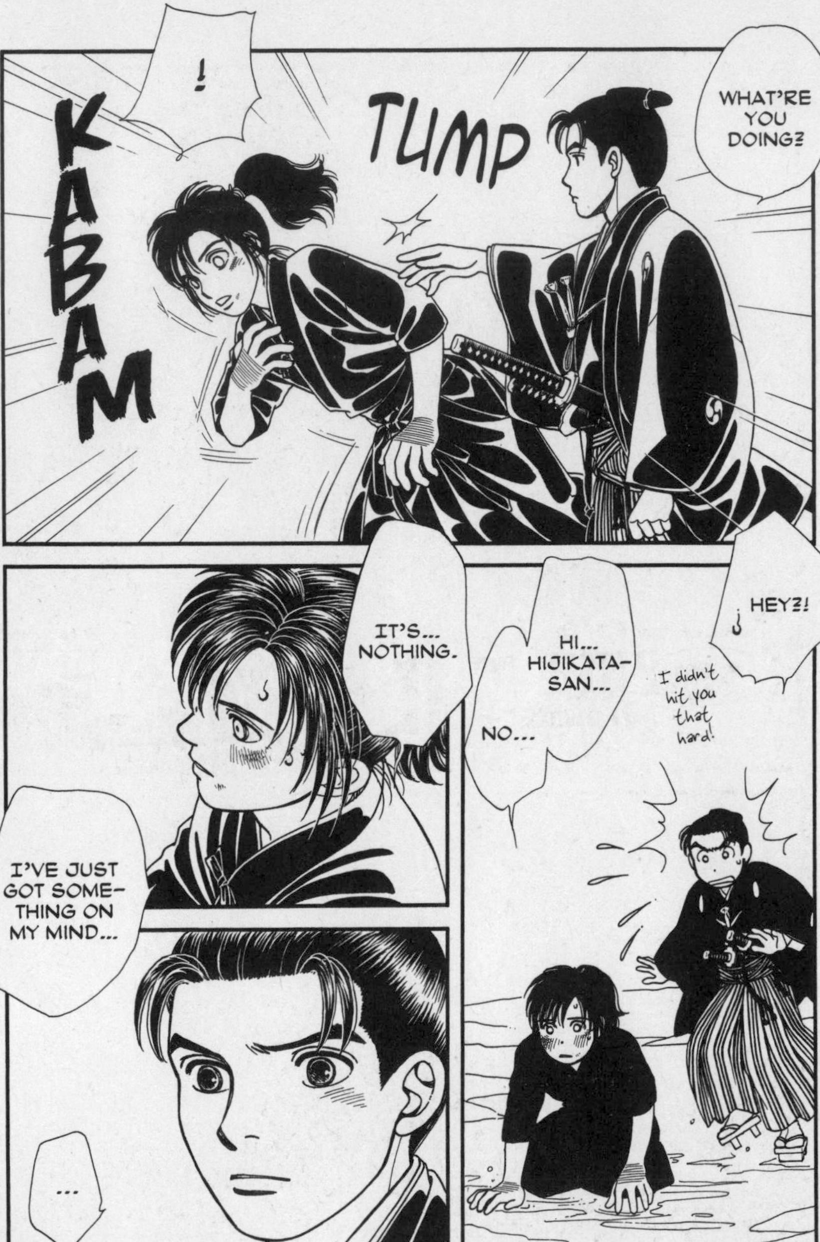
WHAT'RE YOU DOING?
TUMP
!
KABAM
HEY?!
I didn't hit you that hard!
HI... HIJIKATA-SAN...
NO...
IT'S... NOTHING.
I'VE JUST GOT SOME-THING ON MY MIND...
...

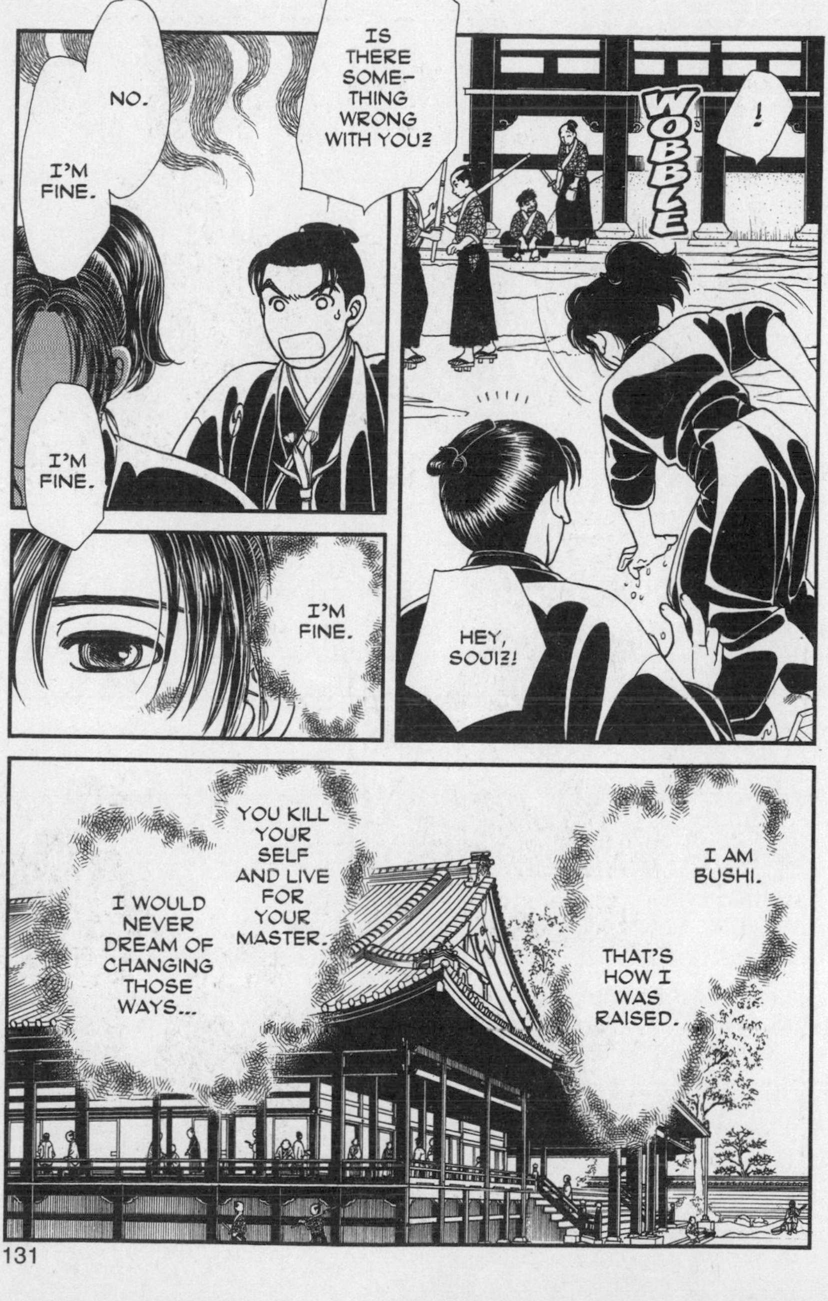
!
WOBBLE
HEY, SOJI?!
IS THERE SOMETHING WRONG WITH YOU?
NO. I'M FINE.
I'M FINE.
I'M FINE.
I AM BUSHI.
THAT'S HOW I WAS RAISED.
YOU KILL YOUR SELF AND LIVE FOR YOUR MASTER.
I WOULD NEVER DREAM OF CHANGING THOSE WAYS...

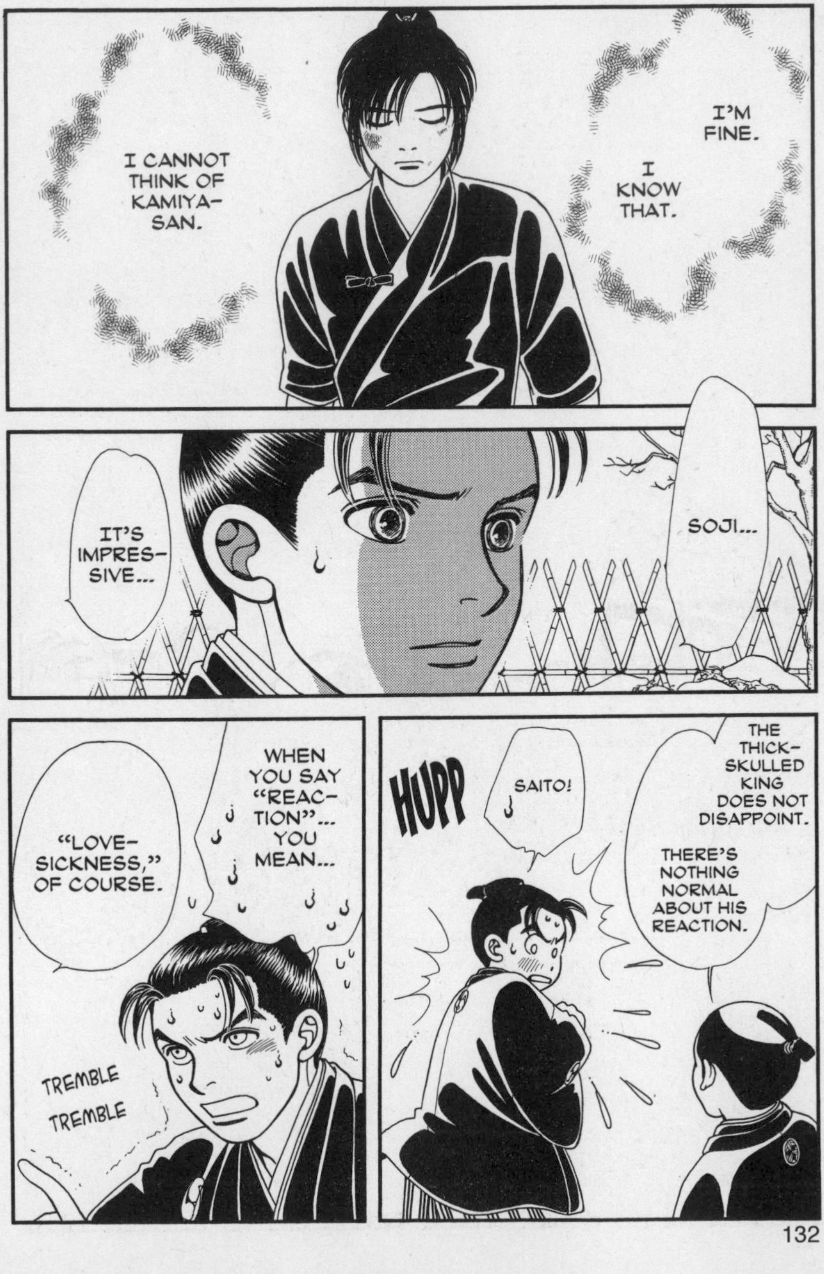
I'M FINE.
I KNOW THAT.
I CANNOT THINK OF KAMIYA-SAN.
SOJI...
IT'S IMPRESSIVE...
THE THICK-SKULLED KING DOES NOT DISAPPOINT.
THERE'S NOTHING NORMAL ABOUT HIS REACTION.
SAITO!
HUPP
WHEN YOU SAY "REACTION"... YOU MEAN...
"LOVE-SICKNESS," OF COURSE.
TREMBLE
TREMBLE

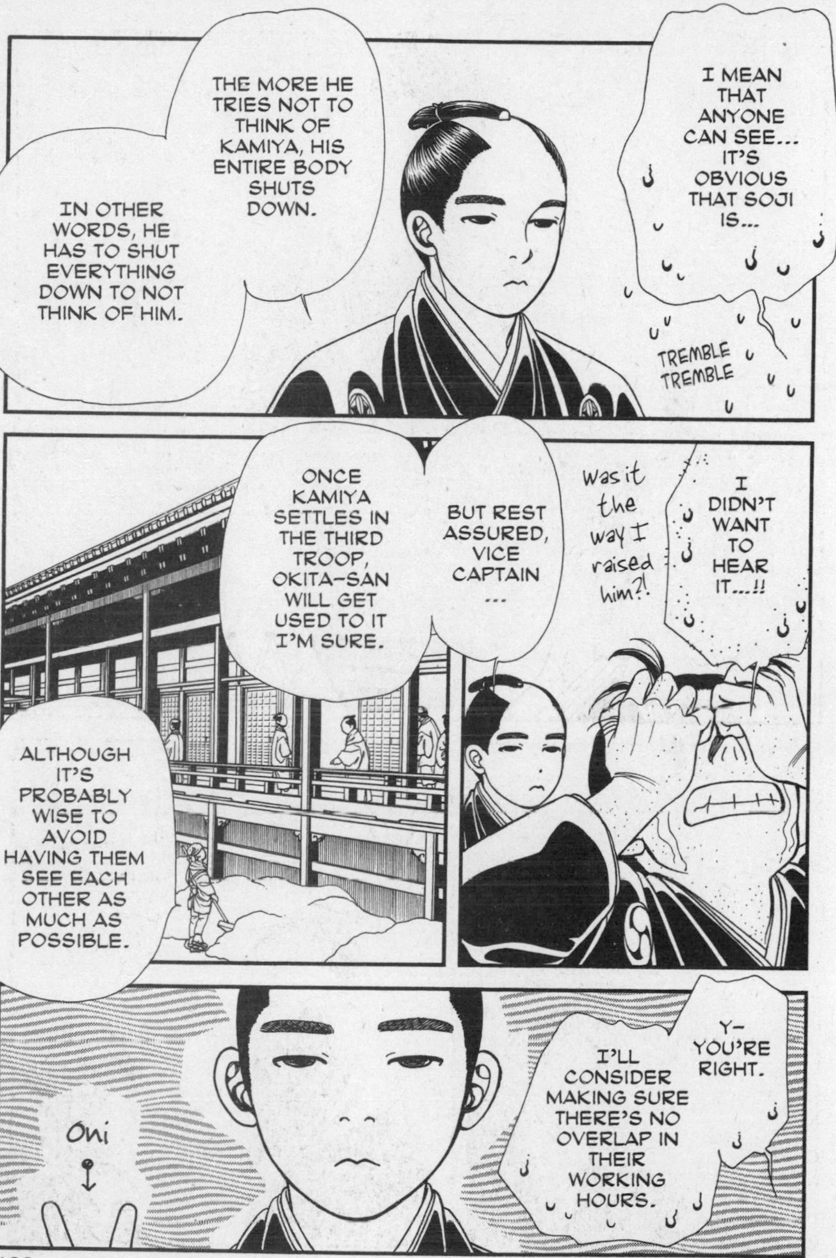
I MEAN THAT ANYONE CAN SEE... IT'S OBVIOUS THAT SOJI IS...
TREMBLE TREMBLE
THE MORE HE TRIES NOT TO THINK OF KAMIYA, HIS ENTIRE BODY SHUTS DOWN.
IN OTHER WORDS, HE HAS TO SHUT EVERYTHING DOWN TO NOT THINK OF HIM.
I DIDN'T WANT TO HEAR IT...!!
Was it the way I raised him?!
BUT REST ASSURED, VICE CAPTAIN ...
ONCE KAMIYA SETTLES IN THE THIRD TROOP, OKITA-SAN WILL GET USED TO IT I'M SURE.
ALTHOUGH IT'S PROBABLY WISE TO AVOID HAVING THEM SEE EACH OTHER AS MUCH AS POSSIBLE.
Y-YOU'RE RIGHT.
I'LL CONSIDER MAKING SURE THERE'S NO OVERLAP IN THEIR WORKING HOURS.
Oni

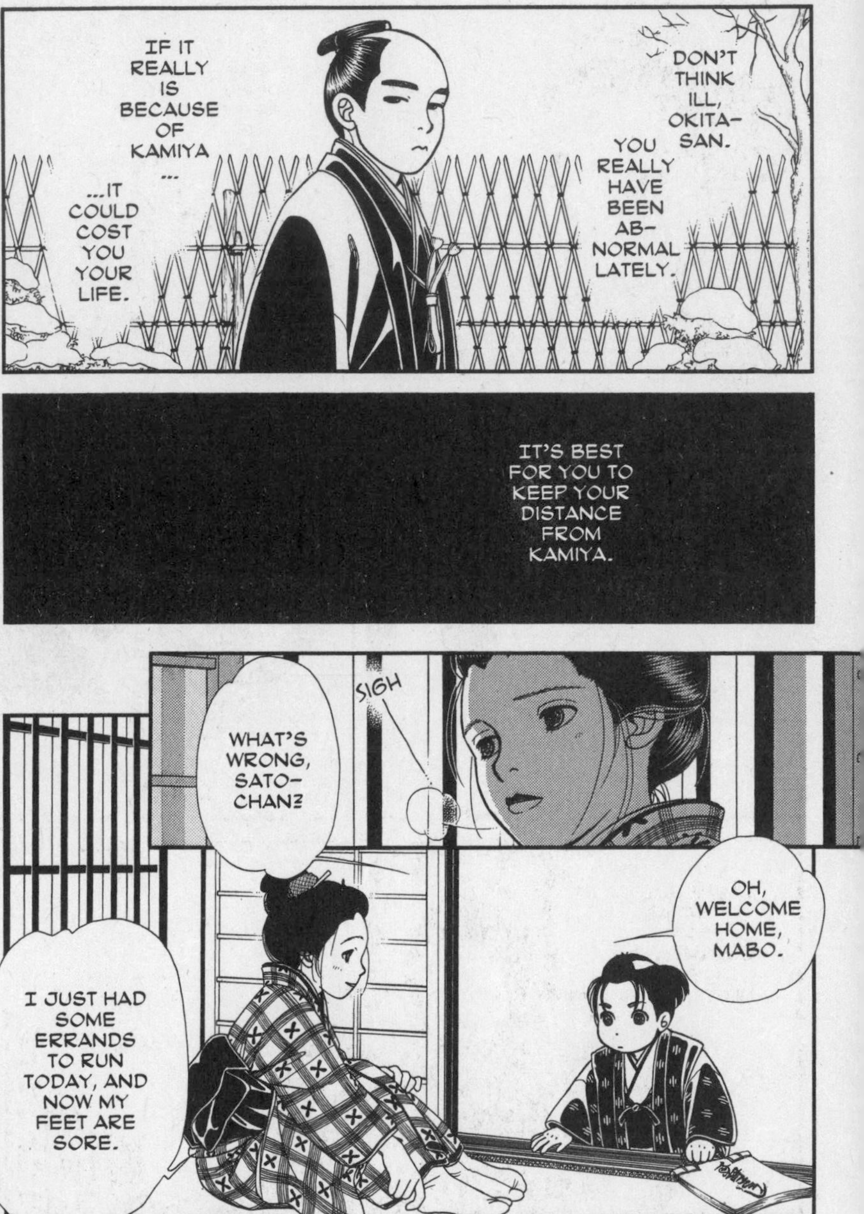
DON'T THINK ILL, OKITA-SAN.
YOU REALLY HAVE BEEN AB-NORMAL LATELY.
IF IT REALLY IS BECAUSE OF KAMIYA...
...IT COULD COST YOU YOUR LIFE.
IT'S BEST FOR YOU TO KEEP YOUR DISTANCE FROM KAMIYA.
SIGH
WHAT'S WRONG, SATO-CHAN?
OH, WELCOME HOME, MABO.
I JUST HAD SOME ERRANDS TO RUN TODAY, AND NOW MY FEET ARE SORE.

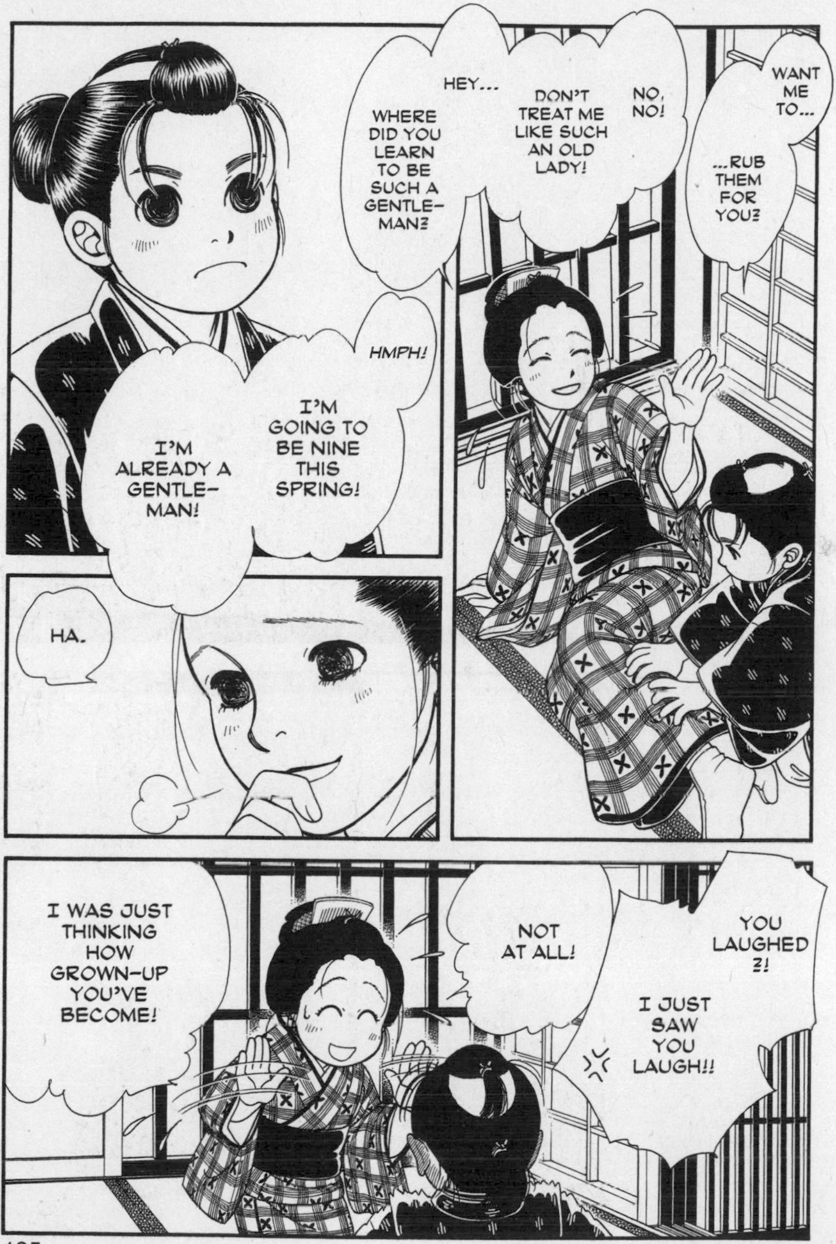
WANT ME TO...
...RUB THEM FOR YOU?
NO, NO!
DON'T TREAT ME LIKE SUCH AN OLD LADY!
HEY...
WHERE DID YOU LEARN TO BE SUCH A GENTLE-MAN?
HMPH!
I'M GOING TO BE NINE THIS SPRING!
I'M ALREADY A GENTLE-MAN!
HA.
YOU LAUGHED?!
I JUST SAW YOU LAUGH!!
NOT AT ALL!
I WAS JUST THINKING HOW GROWN-UP YOU'VE BECOME!

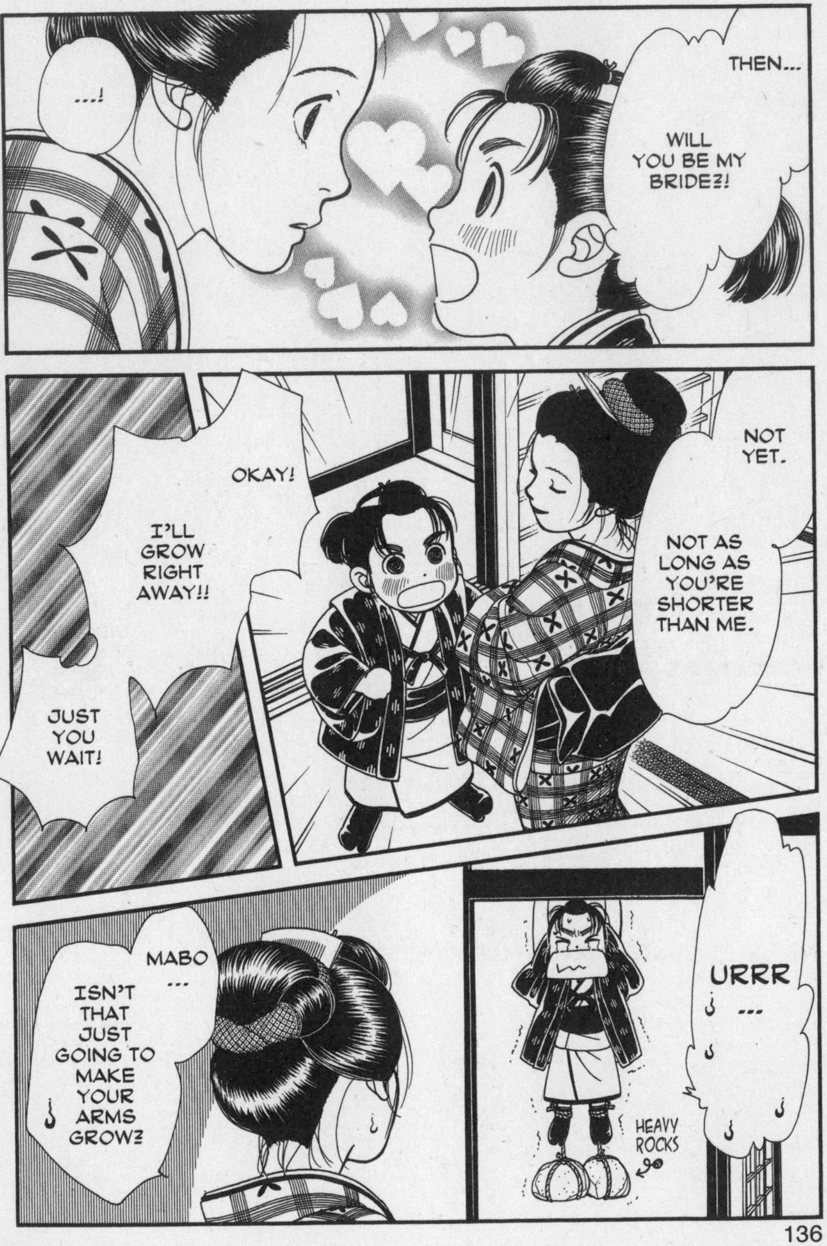
THEN...
WILL YOU BE MY BRIDE?!
...!
NOT YET.
NOT AS LONG AS YOU'RE SHORTER THAN ME.
OKAY!
I'LL GROW RIGHT AWAY!!
JUST YOU WAIT!
URRR ...
HEAVY ROCKS
MABO ...
ISN'T THAT JUST GOING TO MAKE YOUR ARMS GROW?

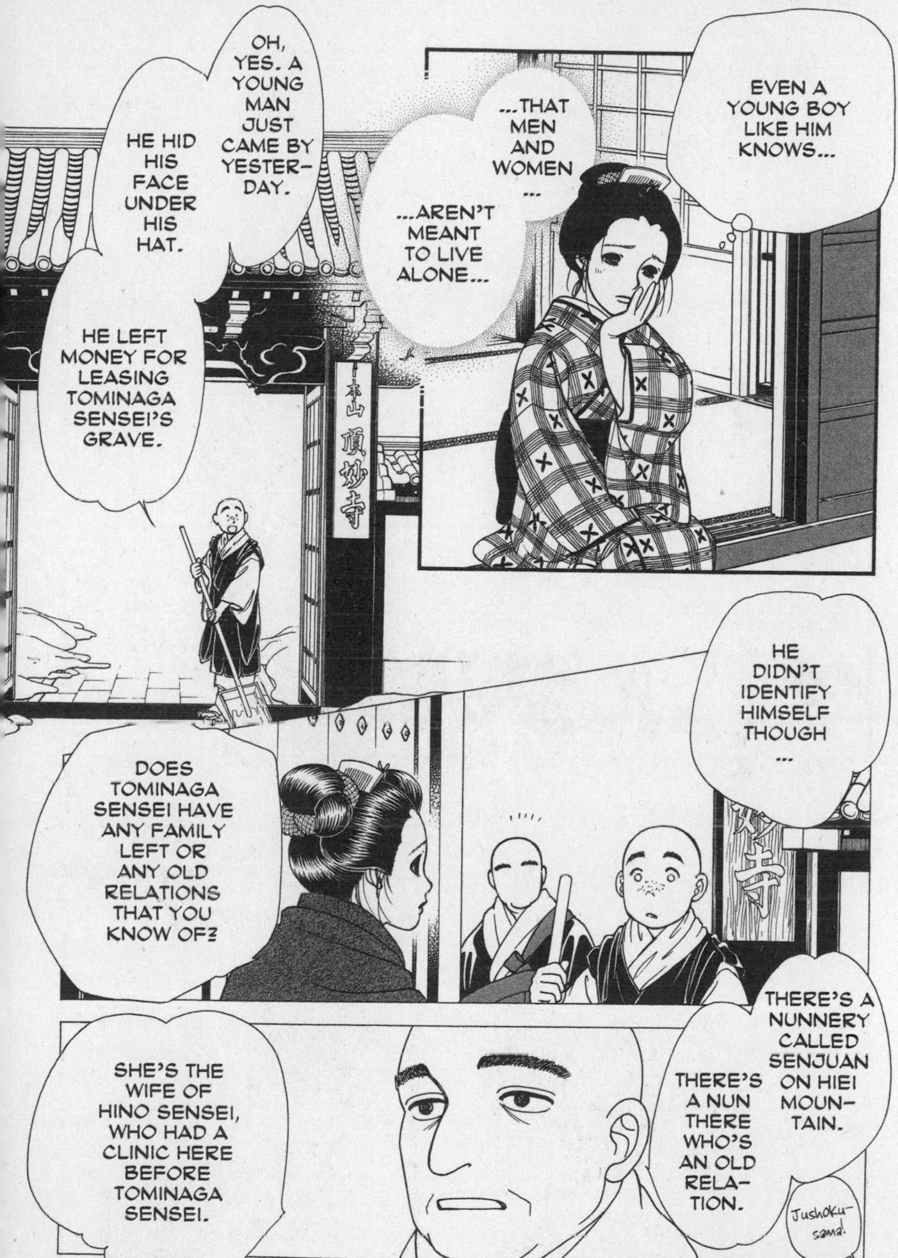
EVEN A YOUNG BOY LIKE HIM KNOWS...
...THAT MEN AND WOMEN ...
...AREN'T MEANT TO LIVE ALONE...
OH, YES. A YOUNG MAN JUST CAME BY YESTER-DAY.
HE HID HIS FACE UNDER HIS HAT.
本山 頂妙寺
HE LEFT MONEY FOR LEASING TOMINAGA SENSEI'S GRAVE.
HE DIDN'T IDENTIFY HIMSELF THOUGH ...
DOES TOMINAGA SENSEI HAVE ANY FAMILY LEFT OR ANY OLD RELATIONS THAT YOU KNOW OF?
Jushoku-sama!
THERE'S A NUNNERY CALLED SENJUAN ON HIEI MOUN-TAIN.
THERE'S A NUN THERE WHO'S AN OLD RELA-TION.
SHE'S THE WIFE OF HINO SENSEI, WHO HAD A CLINIC HERE BEFORE TOMINAGA SENSEI.

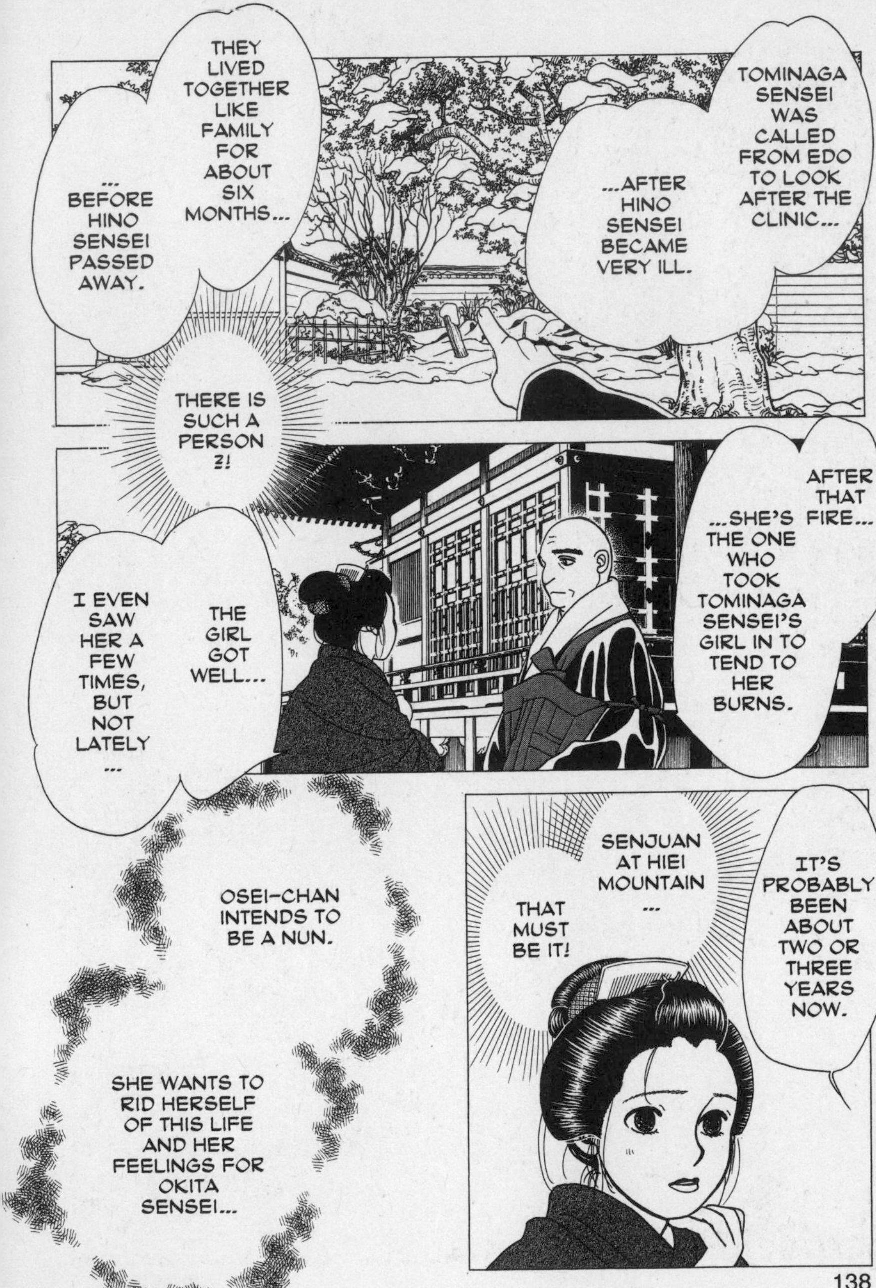
TOMINAGA SENSEI WAS CALLED FROM EDO TO LOOK AFTER THE CLINIC...
...AFTER HINO SENSEI BECAME VERY ILL.
THEY LIVED TOGETHER LIKE FAMILY FOR ABOUT SIX MONTHS...
... BEFORE HINO SENSEI PASSED AWAY.
THERE IS SUCH A PERSON ?!
AFTER THAT FIRE...
...SHE'S THE ONE WHO TOOK TOMINAGA SENSEI'S GIRL IN TO TEND TO HER BURNS.
THE GIRL GOT WELL...
I EVEN SAW HER A FEW TIMES, BUT NOT LATELY ...
IT'S PROBABLY BEEN ABOUT TWO OR THREE YEARS NOW.
SENJUAN AT HIEI MOUNTAIN ...
THAT MUST BE IT!
OSEI-CHAN INTENDS TO BE A NUN.
SHE WANTS TO RID HERSELF OF THIS LIFE AND HER FEELINGS FOR OKITA SENSEI...

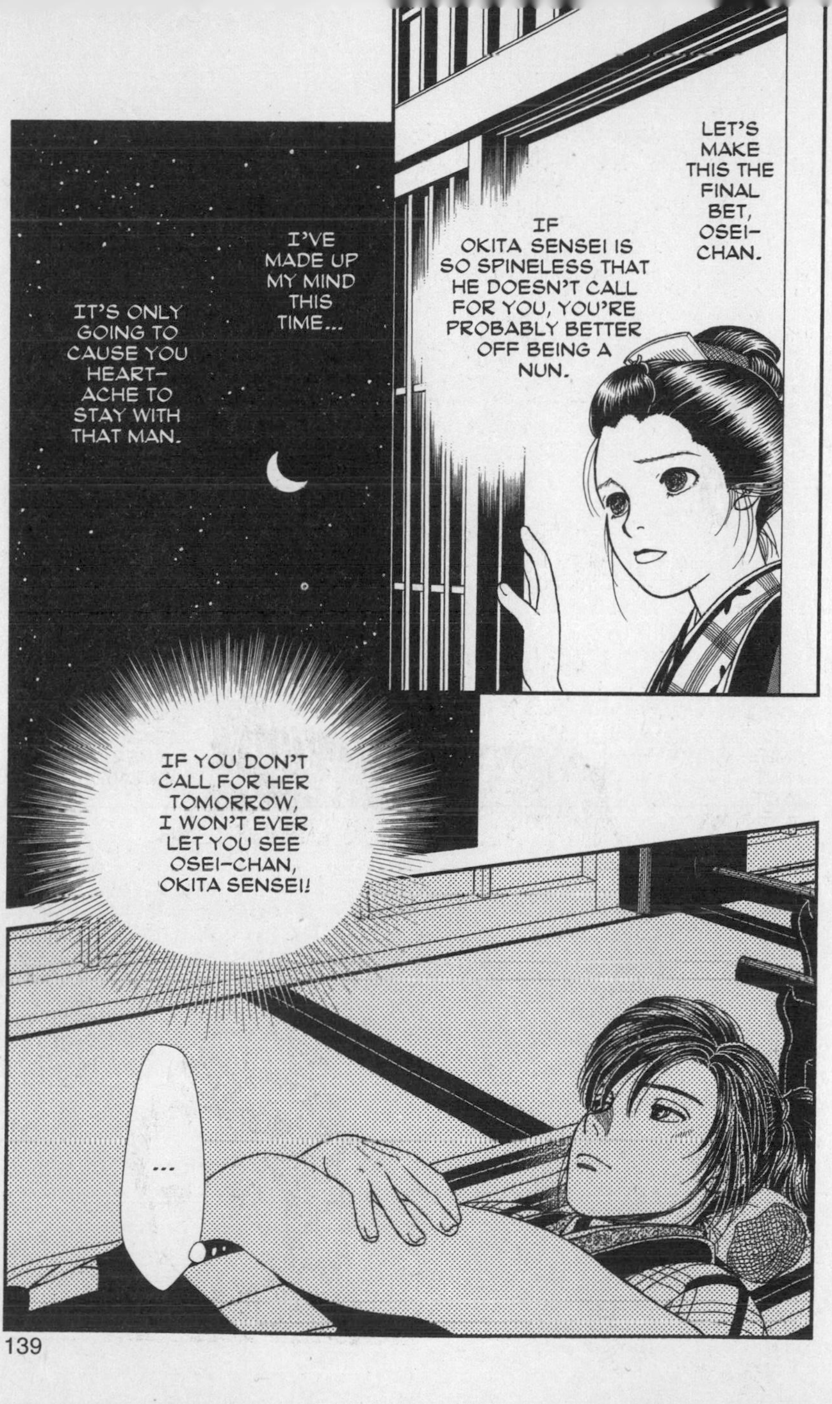
LET'S MAKE THIS THE FINAL BET, OSEI-CHAN.
IF OKITA SENSEI IS SO SPINELESS THAT HE DOESN'T CALL FOR YOU, YOU'RE PROBABLY BETTER OFF BEING A NUN.
I'VE MADE UP MY MIND THIS TIME...
IT'S ONLY GOING TO CAUSE YOU HEART-ACHE TO STAY WITH THAT MAN.
IF YOU DON'T CALL FOR HER TOMORROW, I WON'T EVER LET YOU SEE OSEI-CHAN, OKITA SENSEI!
...

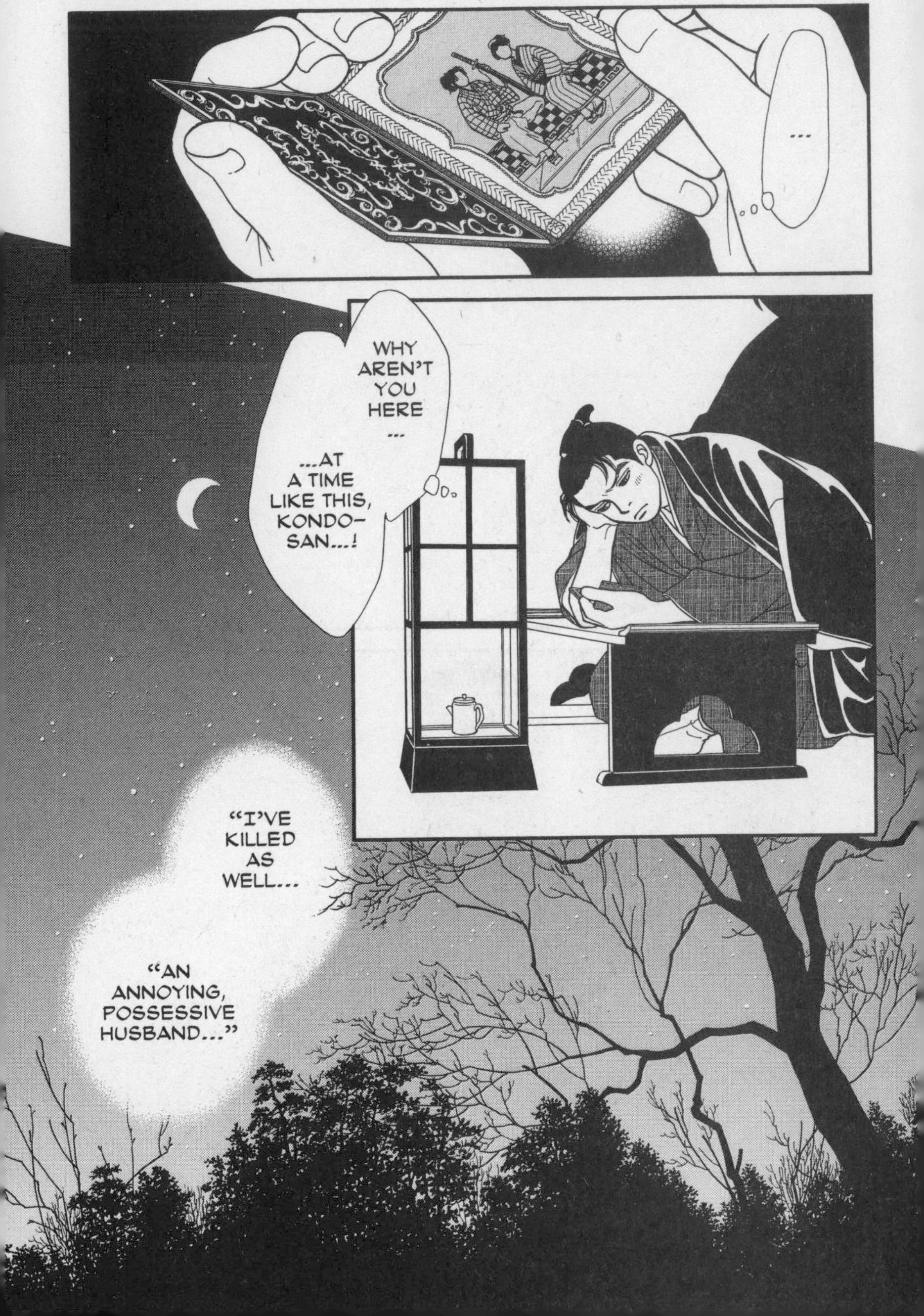
...
WHY AREN'T YOU HERE ...
...AT A TIME LIKE THIS, KONDO-SAN...!
"I'VE KILLED AS WELL...
"AN ANNOYING, POSSESSIVE HUSBAND..."

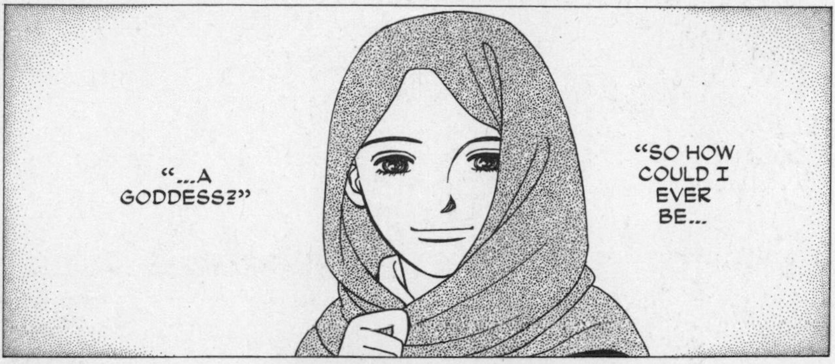
"SO HOW COULD I EVER BE...
"...A GODDESS?"
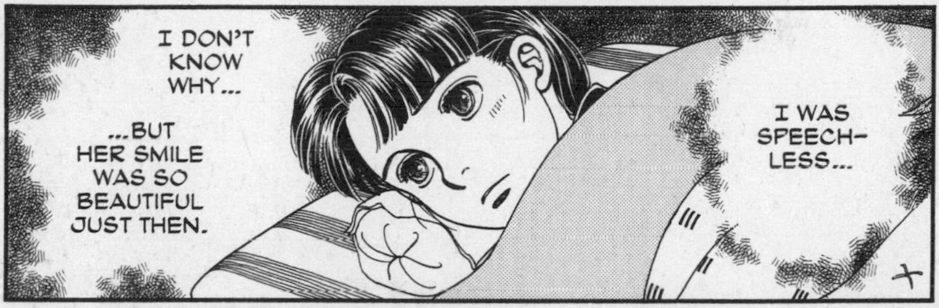
I WAS SPEECHLESS...
I DON'T KNOW WHY...
...BUT HER SMILE WAS SO BEAUTIFUL JUST THEN.
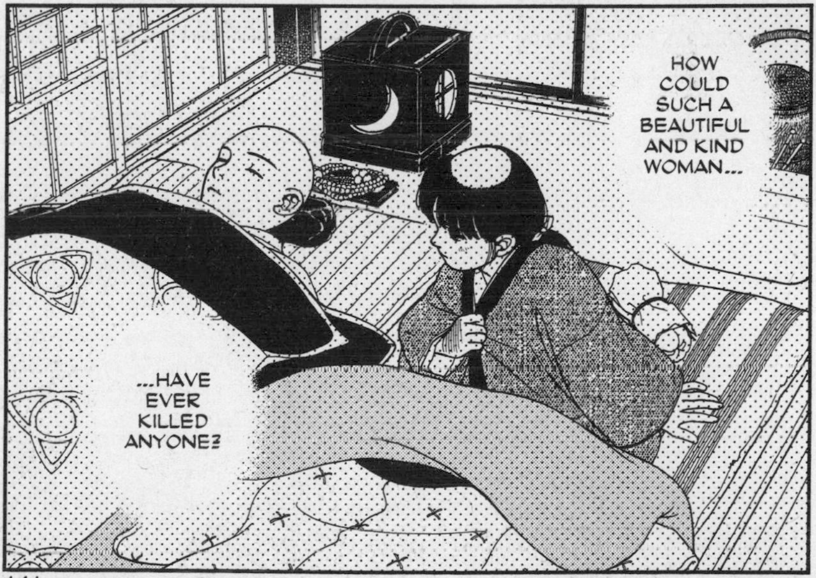
HOW COULD SUCH A BEAUTIFUL AND KIND WOMAN...
...HAVE EVER KILLED ANYONE?

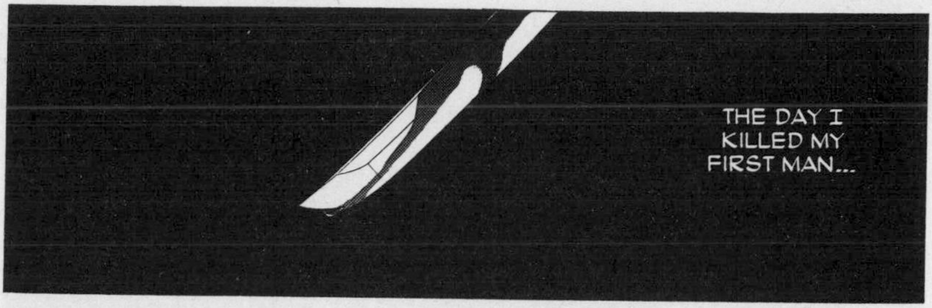
THE DAY I KILLED MY FIRST MAN...

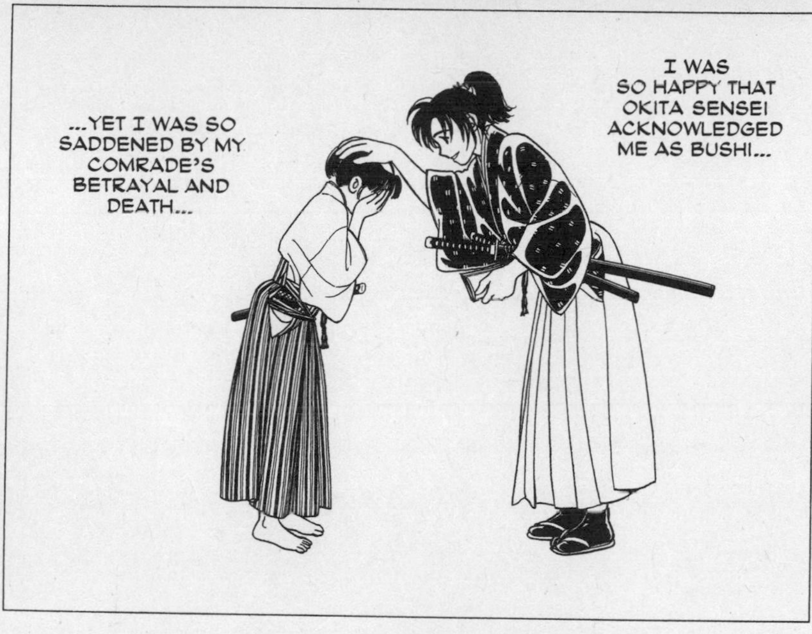
I WAS SO HAPPY THAT OKITA SENSEI ACKNOWLEDGED ME AS BUSHI...
...YET I WAS SO SADDENED BY MY COMRADE'S BETRAYAL AND DEATH...

KAZE HIKARU IROHA KARUTA

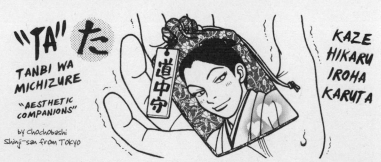

"TA" た

TANBI WA MICHIZURE

"AESTHETIC COMPANIONS"

by Chochobashi Shinji-san from Tokyo

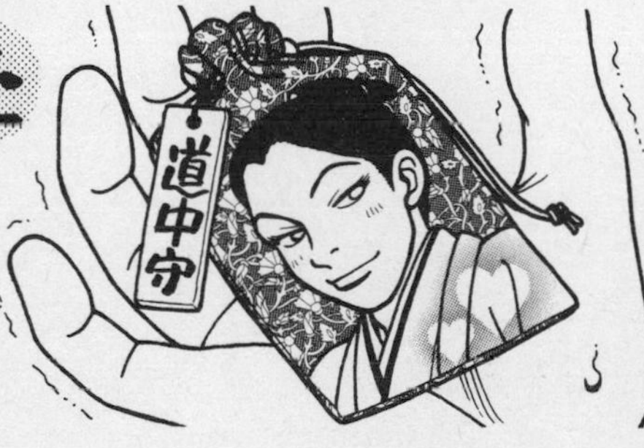
道中守

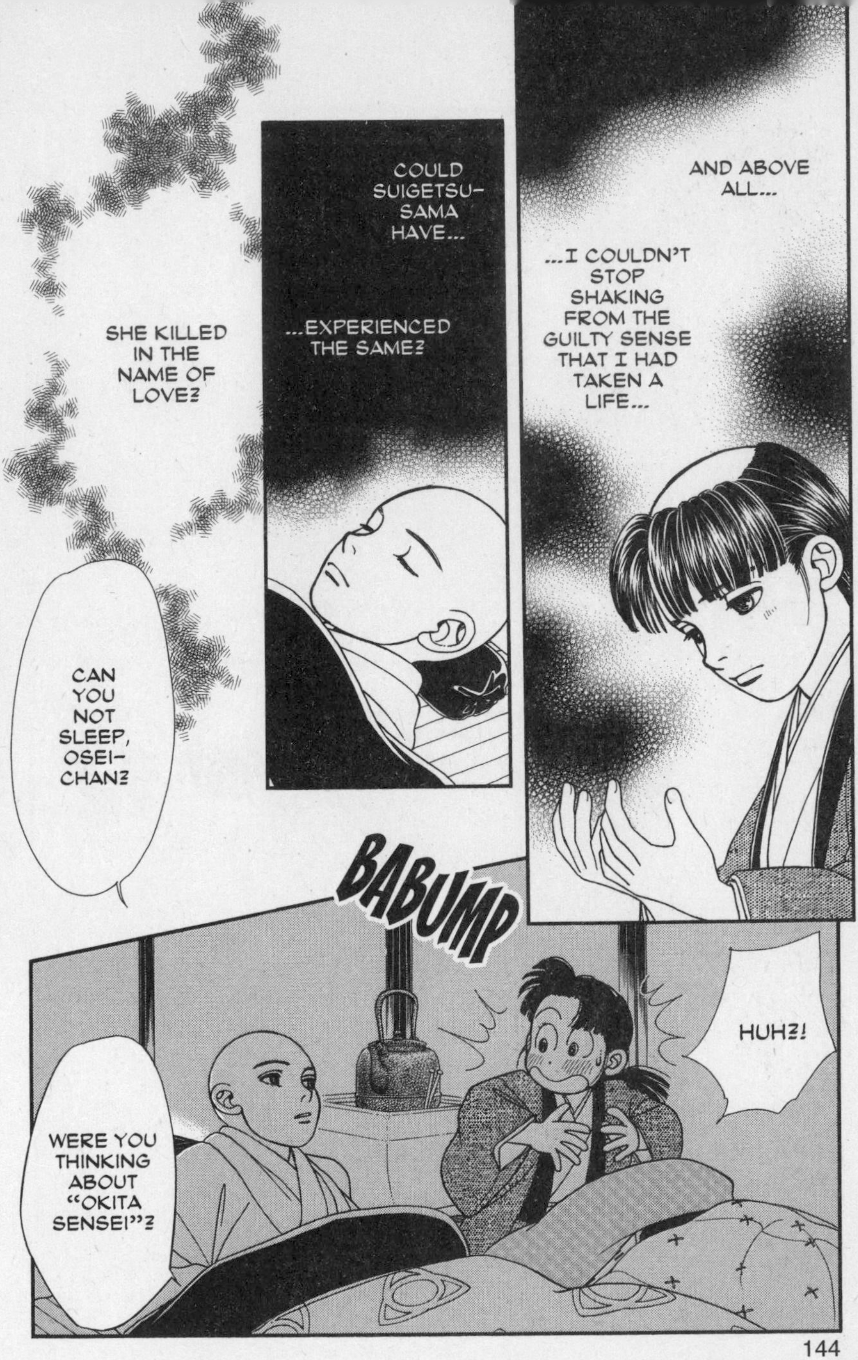
AND ABOVE ALL...
...I COULDN'T STOP SHAKING FROM THE GUILTY SENSE THAT I HAD TAKEN A LIFE...
COULD SUIGETSU-SAMA HAVE...
...EXPERIENCED THE SAME?
SHE KILLED IN THE NAME OF LOVE?
CAN YOU NOT SLEEP, OSEI-CHAN?
BABUMP
HUH?!
WERE YOU THINKING ABOUT "OKITA SENSEI"?

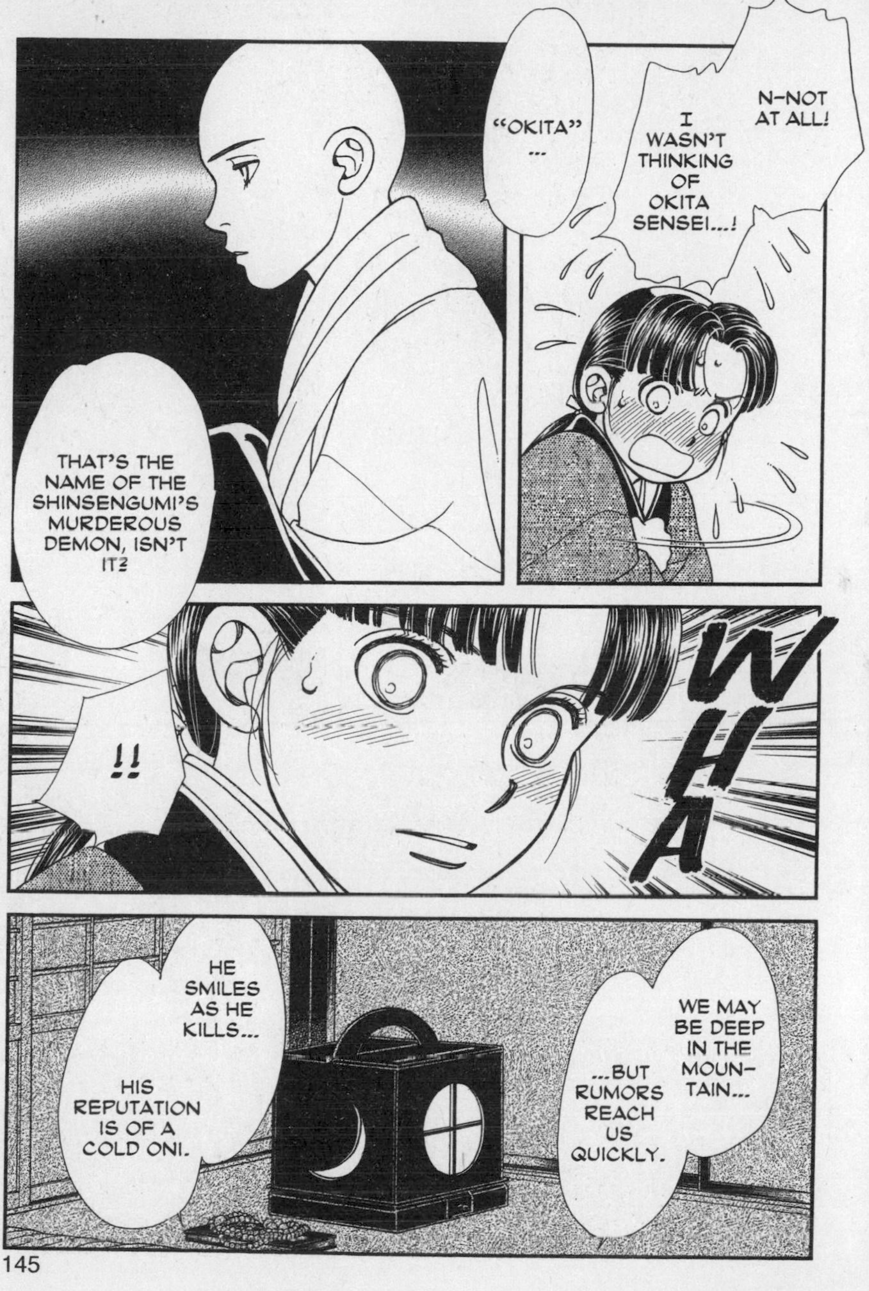
N-NOT AT ALL!
I WASN'T THINKING OF OKITA SENSEI...!
"OKITA" ...
THAT'S THE NAME OF THE SHINSENGUMI'S MURDEROUS DEMON, ISN'T IT?
WHA
!!
WE MAY BE DEEP IN THE MOUNTAIN...
...BUT RUMORS REACH US QUICKLY.
HE SMILES AS HE KILLS...
HIS REPUTATION IS OF A COLD ONI.

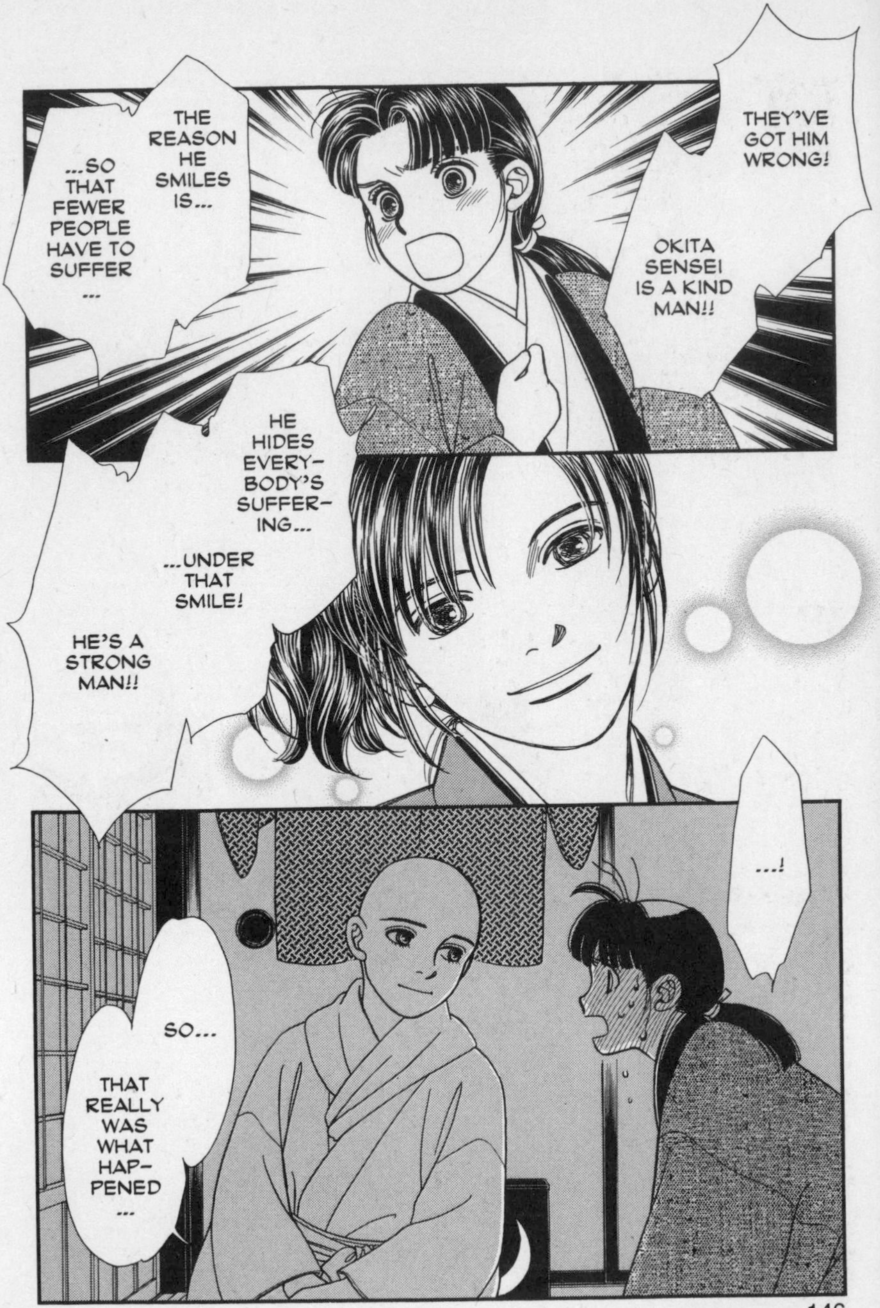
THEY'VE GOT HIM WRONG!
OKITA SENSEI IS A KIND MAN!!
THE REASON HE SMILES IS...
...SO THAT FEWER PEOPLE HAVE TO SUFFER...
HE HIDES EVERYBODY'S SUFFERING...
...UNDER THAT SMILE!
HE'S A STRONG MAN!!
...!
SO...
THAT REALLY WAS WHAT HAPPENED...

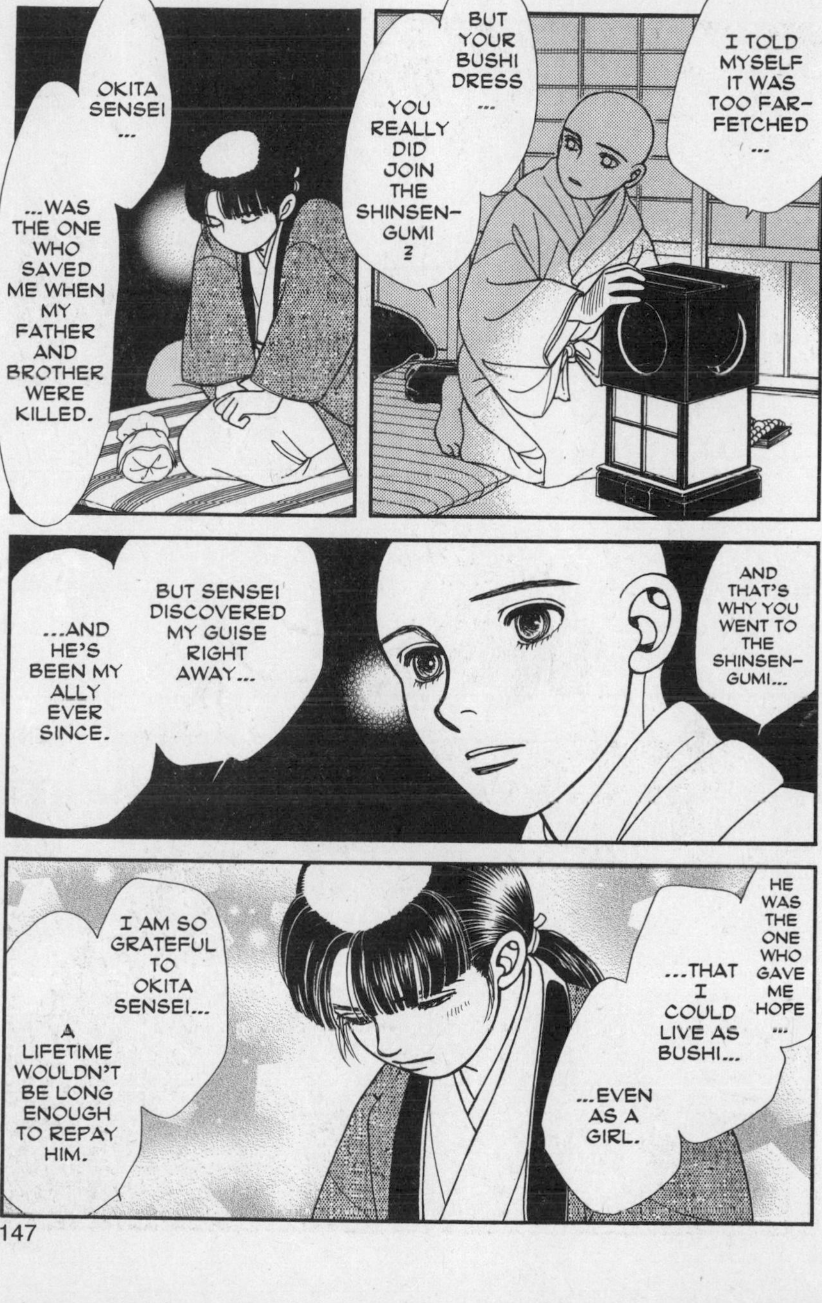
I TOLD MYSELF IT WAS TOO FAR-FETCHED ...
BUT YOUR BUSHI DRESS ...
YOU REALLY DID JOIN THE SHINSEN-GUMI?
OKITA SENSEI ...
...WAS THE ONE WHO SAVED ME WHEN MY FATHER AND BROTHER WERE KILLED.
AND THAT'S WHY YOU WENT TO THE SHINSEN-GUMI...
BUT SENSEI DISCOVERED MY GUISE RIGHT AWAY...
...AND HE'S BEEN MY ALLY EVER SINCE.
HE WAS THE ONE WHO GAVE ME HOPE ...
...THAT I COULD LIVE AS BUSHI...
...EVEN AS A GIRL.
I AM SO GRATEFUL TO OKITA SENSEI...
A LIFETIME WOULDN'T BE LONG ENOUGH TO REPAY HIM.

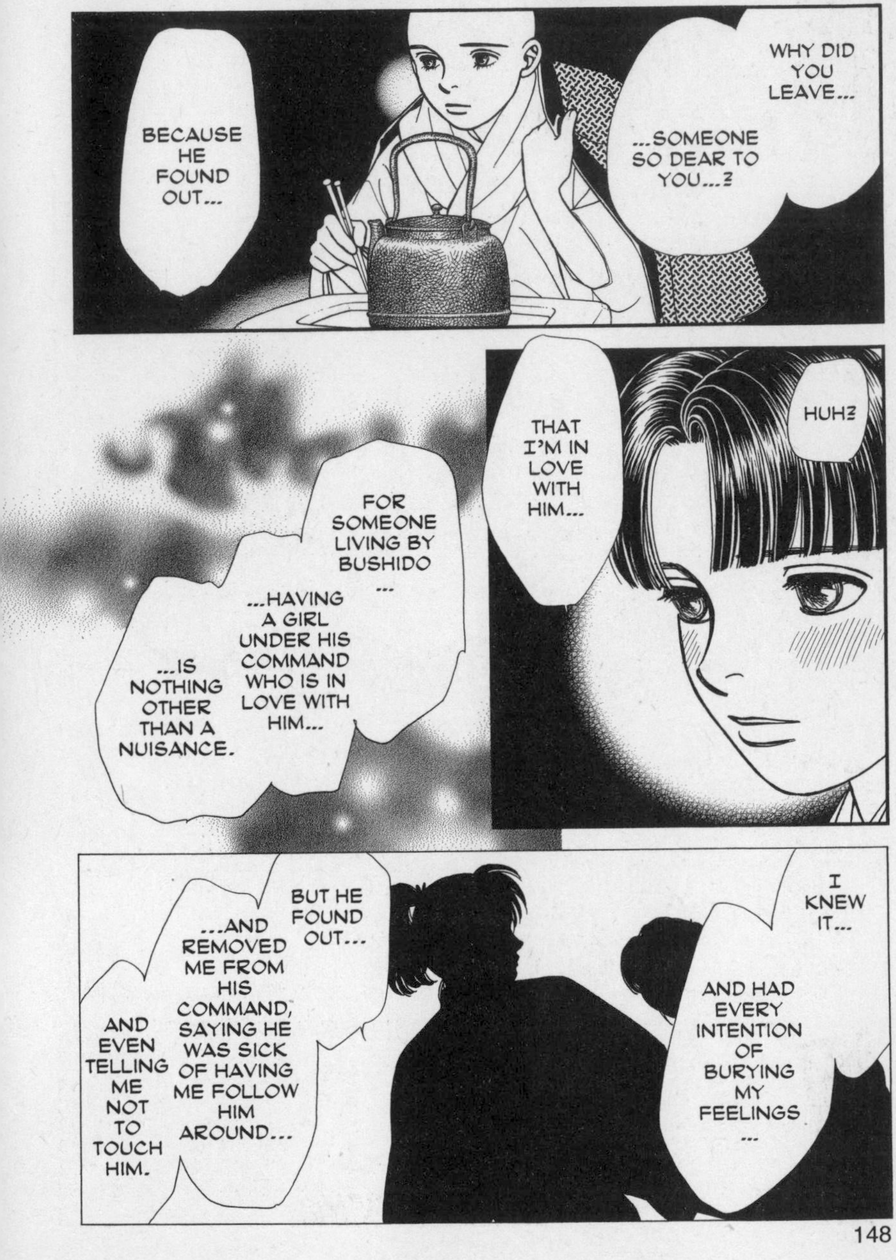
WHY DID YOU LEAVE...
...SOMEONE SO DEAR TO YOU...?
BECAUSE HE FOUND OUT...
HUH?
THAT I'M IN LOVE WITH HIM...
FOR SOMEONE LIVING BY BUSHIDO...
...HAVING A GIRL UNDER HIS COMMAND WHO IS IN LOVE WITH HIM...
...IS NOTHING OTHER THAN A NUISANCE.
I KNEW IT...
AND HAD EVERY INTENTION OF BURYING MY FEELINGS...
BUT HE FOUND OUT...
...AND REMOVED ME FROM HIS COMMAND, SAYING HE WAS SICK OF HAVING ME FOLLOW HIM AROUND...
AND EVEN TELLING ME NOT TO TOUCH HIM.

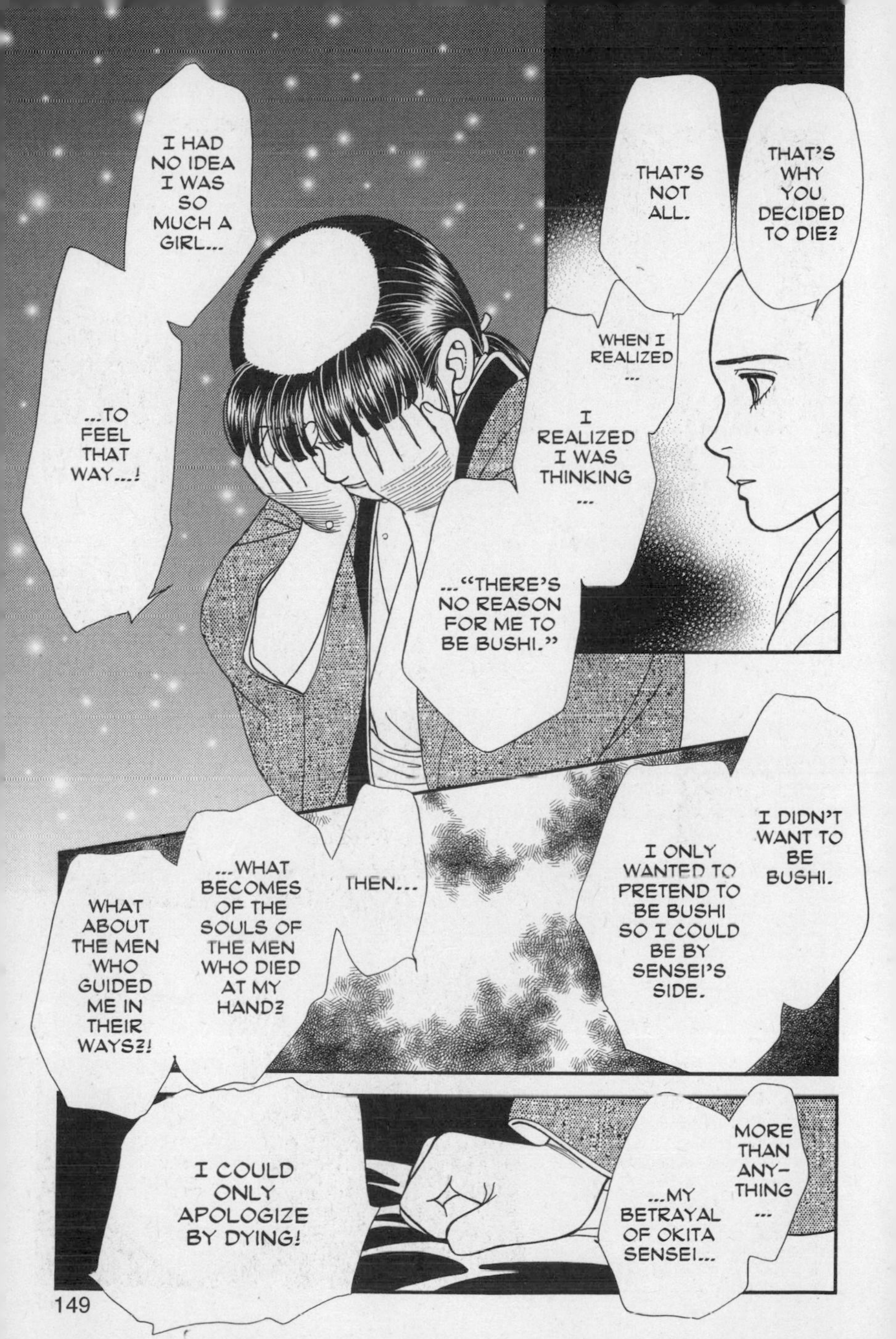
THAT'S WHY YOU DECIDED TO DIE?
THAT'S NOT ALL.
WHEN I REALIZED ...
I REALIZED I WAS THINKING ...
..."THERE'S NO REASON FOR ME TO BE BUSHI."
I HAD NO IDEA I WAS SO MUCH A GIRL...
...TO FEEL THAT WAY...!
I DIDN'T WANT TO BE BUSHI.
I ONLY WANTED TO PRETEND TO BE BUSHI SO I COULD BE BY SENSEI'S SIDE.
THEN...
...WHAT BECOMES OF THE SOULS OF THE MEN WHO DIED AT MY HAND?
WHAT ABOUT THE MEN WHO GUIDED ME IN THEIR WAYS?!
MORE THAN ANY-THING ...
...MY BETRAYAL OF OKITA SENSEI...
I COULD ONLY APOLOGIZE BY DYING!

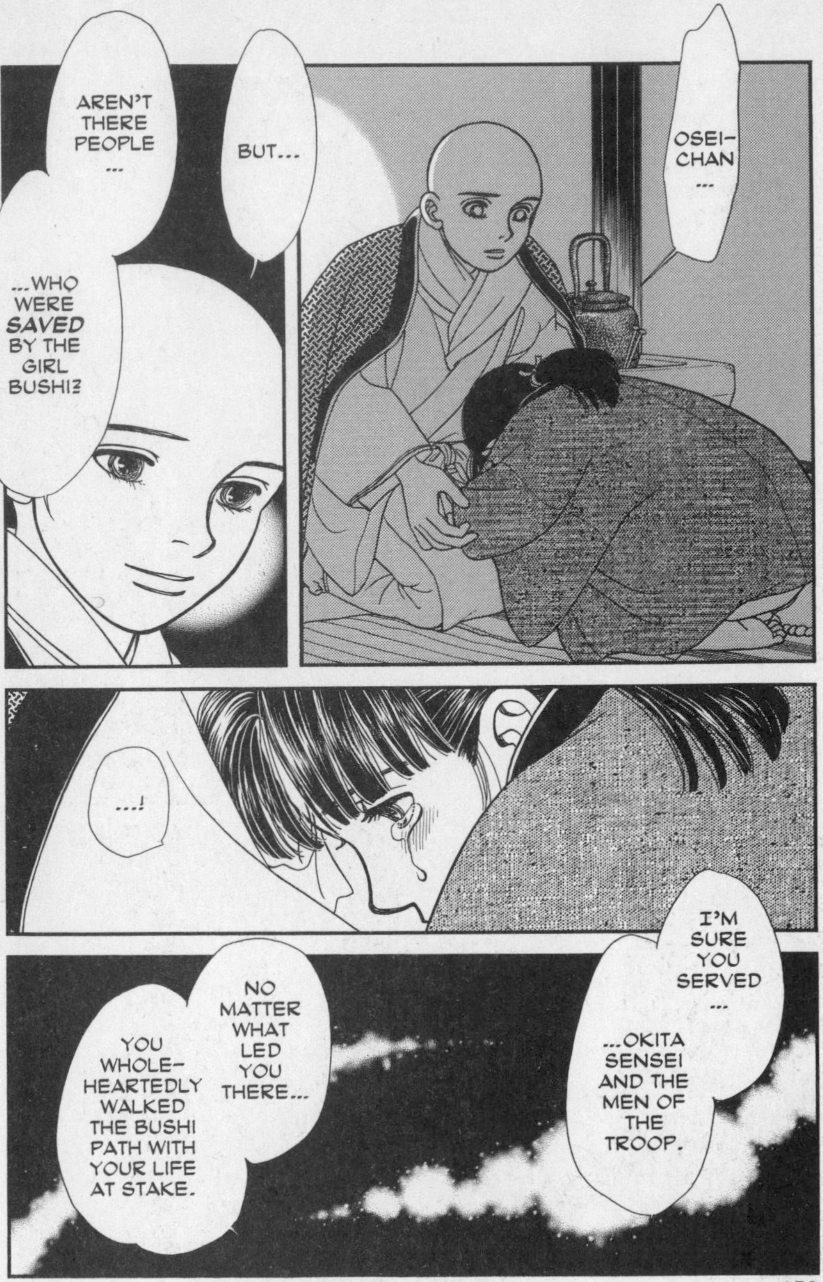
OSEI-CHAN...
BUT...
AREN'T THERE PEOPLE...
...WHO WERE *SAVED* BY THE GIRL BUSHI?
...!
I'M SURE YOU SERVED...
...OKITA SENSEI AND THE MEN OF THE TROOP.
NO MATTER WHAT LED YOU THERE...
YOU WHOLE-HEARTEDLY WALKED THE BUSHI PATH WITH YOUR LIFE AT STAKE.

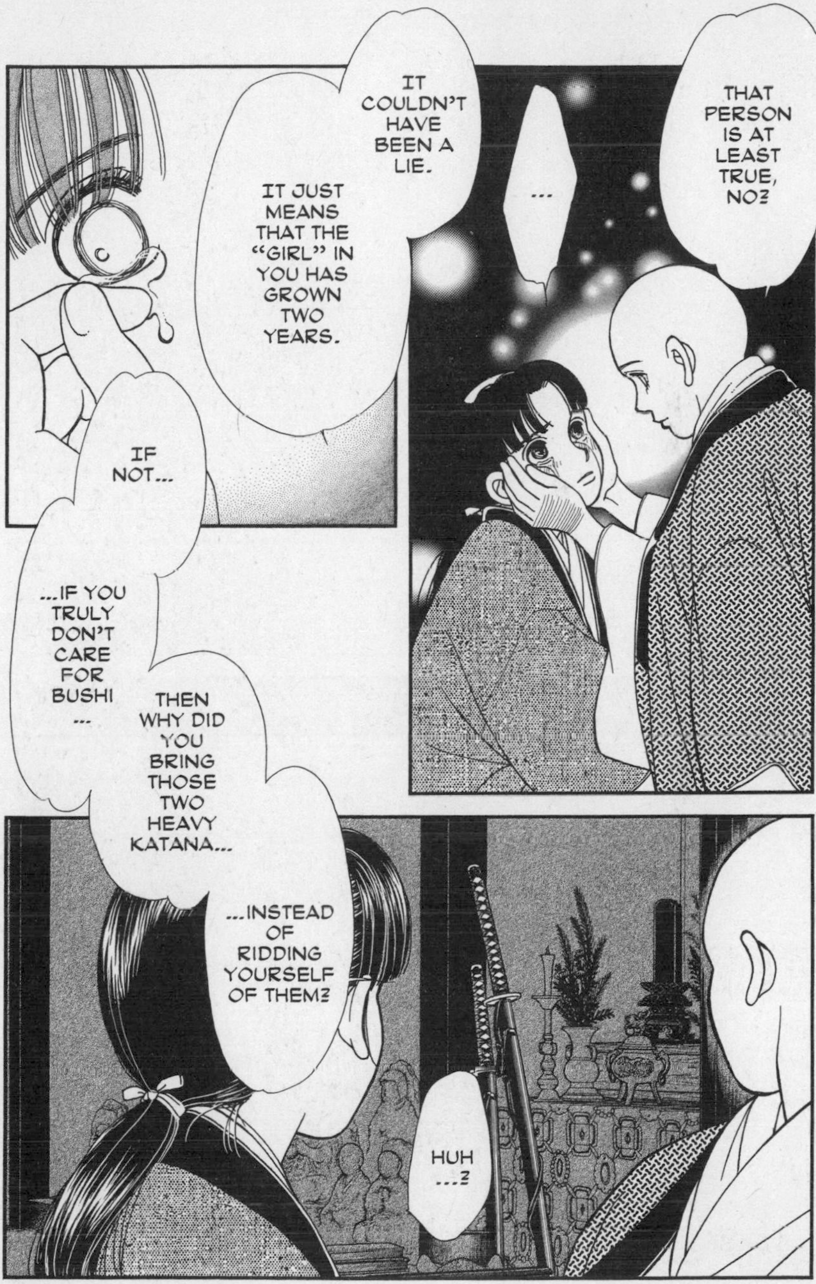
THAT PERSON IS AT LEAST TRUE, NO?
...
IT COULDN'T HAVE BEEN A LIE.
IT JUST MEANS THAT THE "GIRL" IN YOU HAS GROWN TWO YEARS.
IF NOT...
...IF YOU TRULY DON'T CARE FOR BUSHI ...
THEN WHY DID YOU BRING THOSE TWO HEAVY KATANA...
...INSTEAD OF RIDDING YOURSELF OF THEM?
HUH ...?

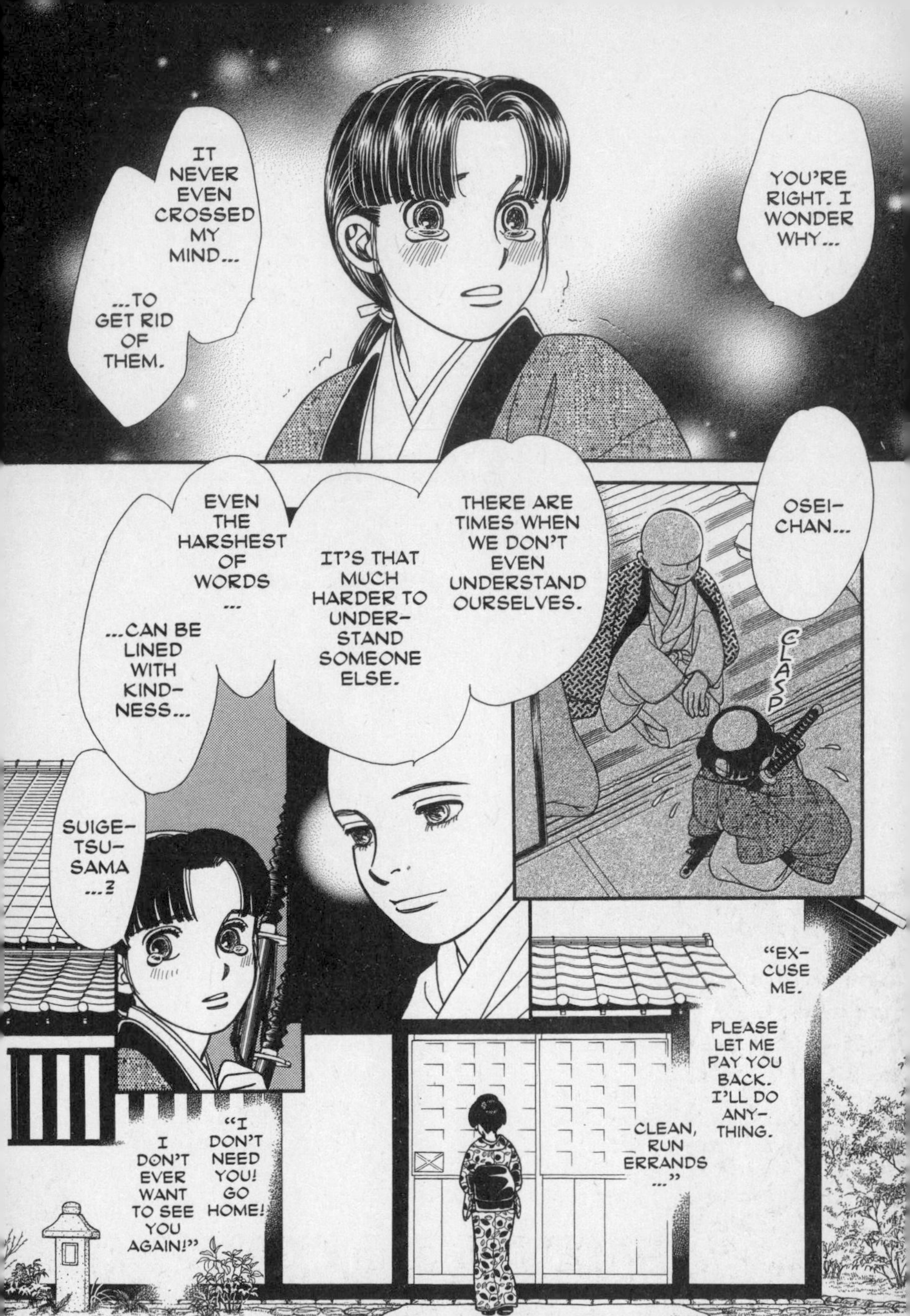
YOU'RE RIGHT. I WONDER WHY...
IT NEVER EVEN CROSSED MY MIND...
...TO GET RID OF THEM.
OSEI-CHAN...
CLASP
THERE ARE TIMES WHEN WE DON'T EVEN UNDERSTAND OURSELVES.
IT'S THAT MUCH HARDER TO UNDER-STAND SOMEONE ELSE.
EVEN THE HARSHEST OF WORDS...
...CAN BE LINED WITH KIND-NESS...
SUIGE-TSU-SAMA...?
"EX-CUSE ME.
PLEASE LET ME PAY YOU BACK. I'LL DO ANY-THING.
CLEAN, RUN ERRANDS..."
"I DON'T NEED YOU! GO HOME!
I DON'T EVER WANT TO SEE YOU AGAIN!"

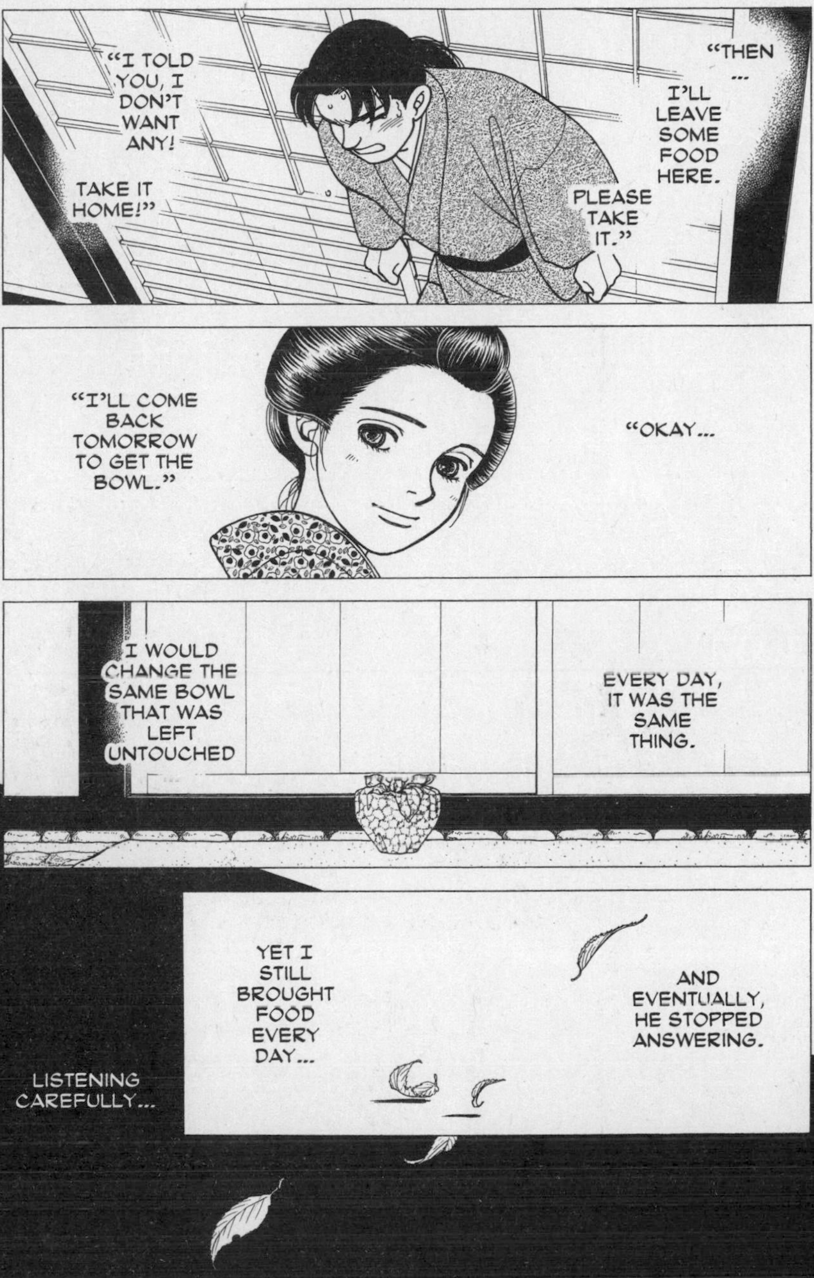
"THEN ... I'LL LEAVE SOME FOOD HERE.
PLEASE TAKE IT."
"I TOLD YOU, I DON'T WANT ANY!
TAKE IT HOME!"
"OKAY...
"I'LL COME BACK TOMORROW TO GET THE BOWL."
EVERY DAY, IT WAS THE SAME THING.
I WOULD CHANGE THE SAME BOWL THAT WAS LEFT UNTOUCHED
AND EVENTUALLY, HE STOPPED ANSWERING.
YET I STILL BROUGHT FOOD EVERY DAY...
LISTENING CAREFULLY...

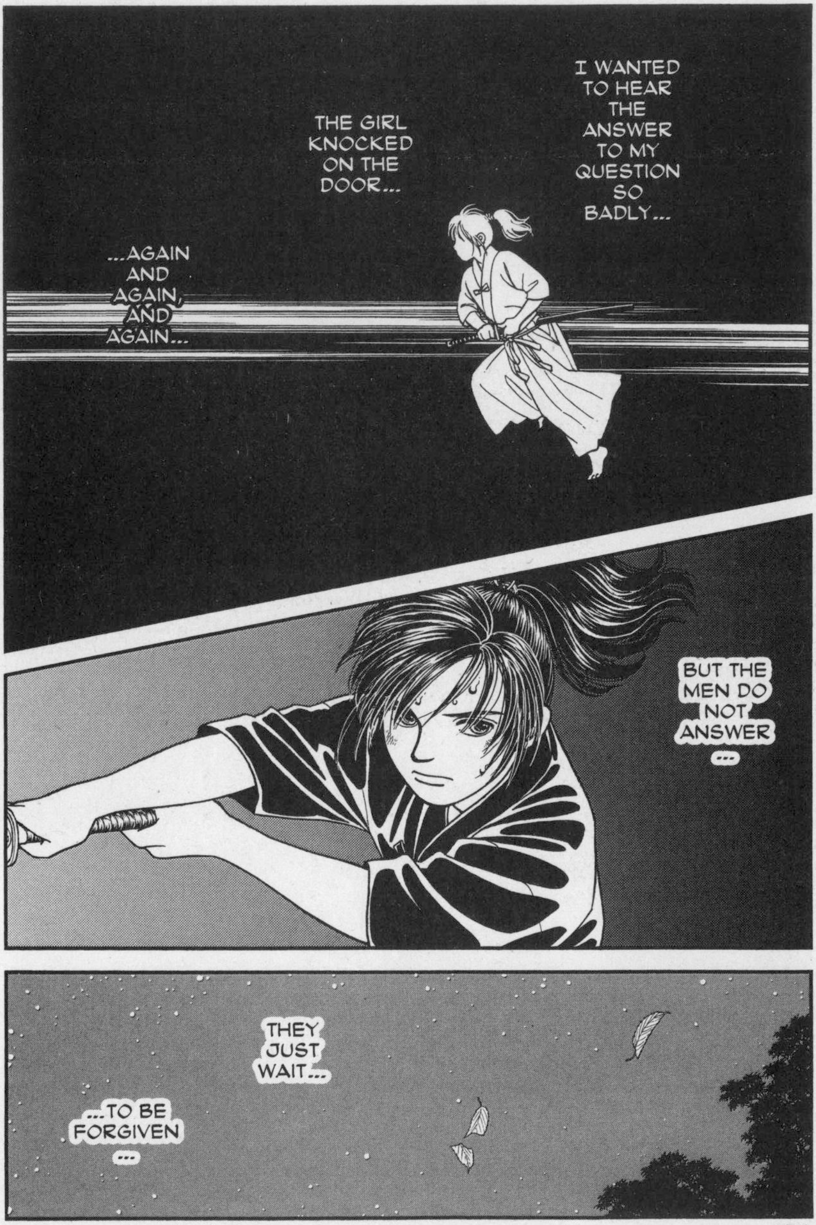
I WANTED TO HEAR THE ANSWER TO MY QUESTION SO BADLY...
THE GIRL KNOCKED ON THE DOOR...
...AGAIN AND AGAIN, AND AGAIN...
BUT THE MEN DO NOT ANSWER ...
THEY JUST WAIT...
...TO BE FORGIVEN ...

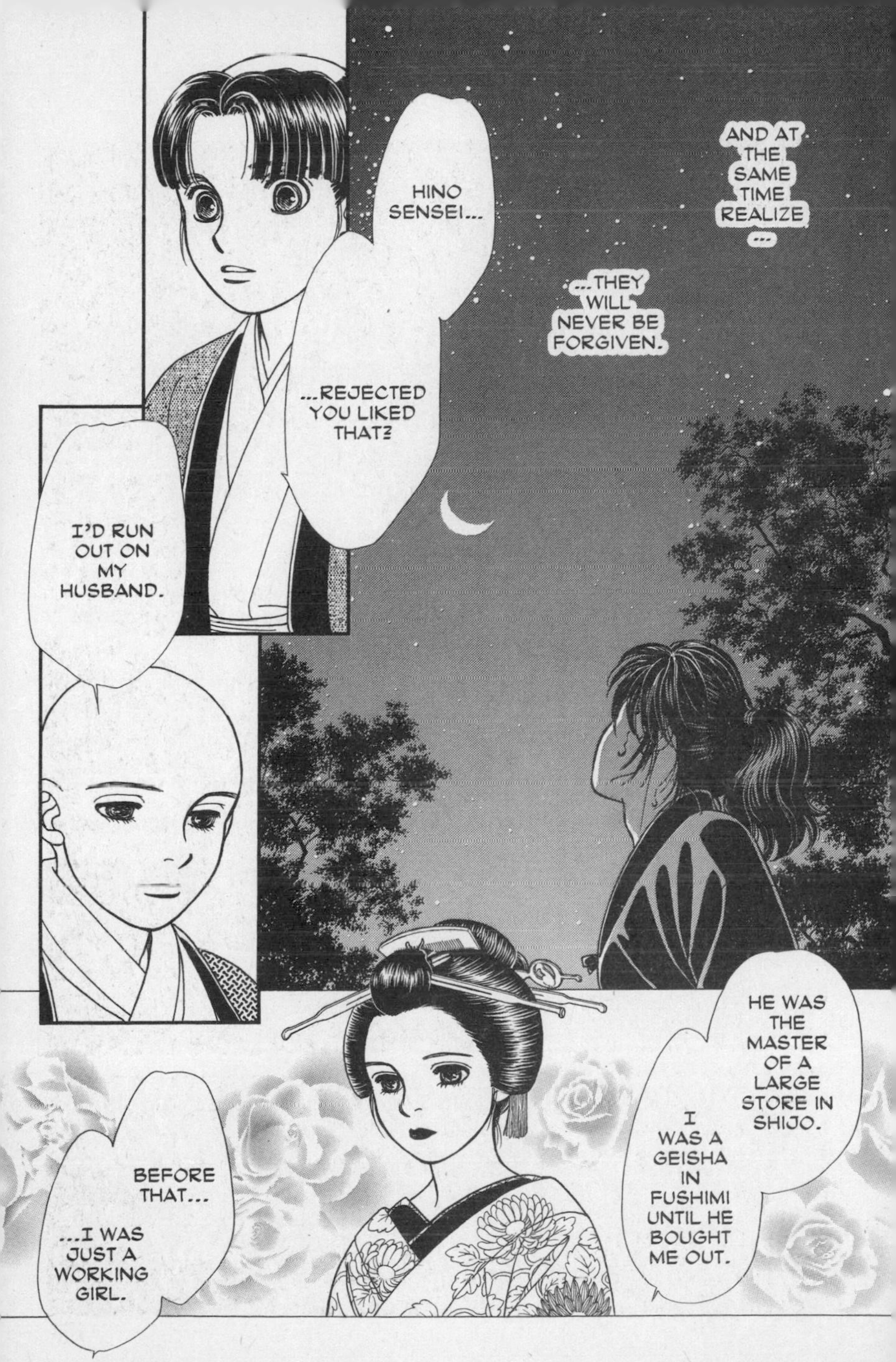
AND AT THE SAME TIME REALIZE ---
...THEY WILL NEVER BE FORGIVEN.
HINO SENSEI...
...REJECTED YOU LIKED THAT?
I'D RUN OUT ON MY HUSBAND.
HE WAS THE MASTER OF A LARGE STORE IN SHIJO.
I WAS A GEISHA IN FUSHIMI UNTIL HE BOUGHT ME OUT.
BEFORE THAT...
...I WAS JUST A WORKING GIRL.

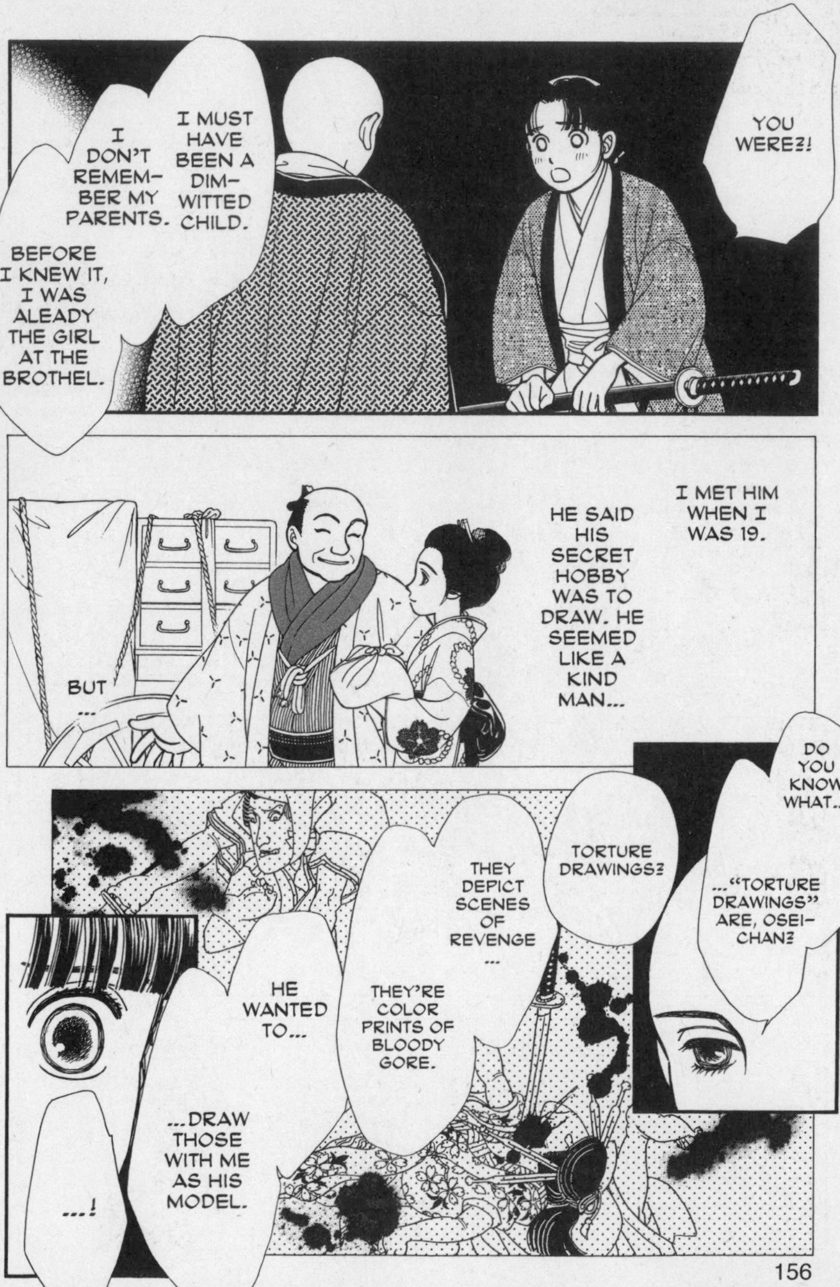
YOU WERE?!
I MUST HAVE BEEN A DIM-WITTED CHILD.
I DON'T REMEMBER MY PARENTS.
BEFORE I KNEW IT, I WAS ALEADY THE GIRL AT THE BROTHEL.
I MET HIM WHEN I WAS 19.
HE SAID HIS SECRET HOBBY WAS TO DRAW. HE SEEMED LIKE A KIND MAN...
BUT ...
DO YOU KNOW WHAT...
..."TORTURE DRAWINGS" ARE, OSEI-CHAN?
TORTURE DRAWINGS?
THEY DEPICT SCENES OF REVENGE ...
THEY'RE COLOR PRINTS OF BLOODY GORE.
HE WANTED TO...
...DRAW THOSE WITH ME AS HIS MODEL.
...!

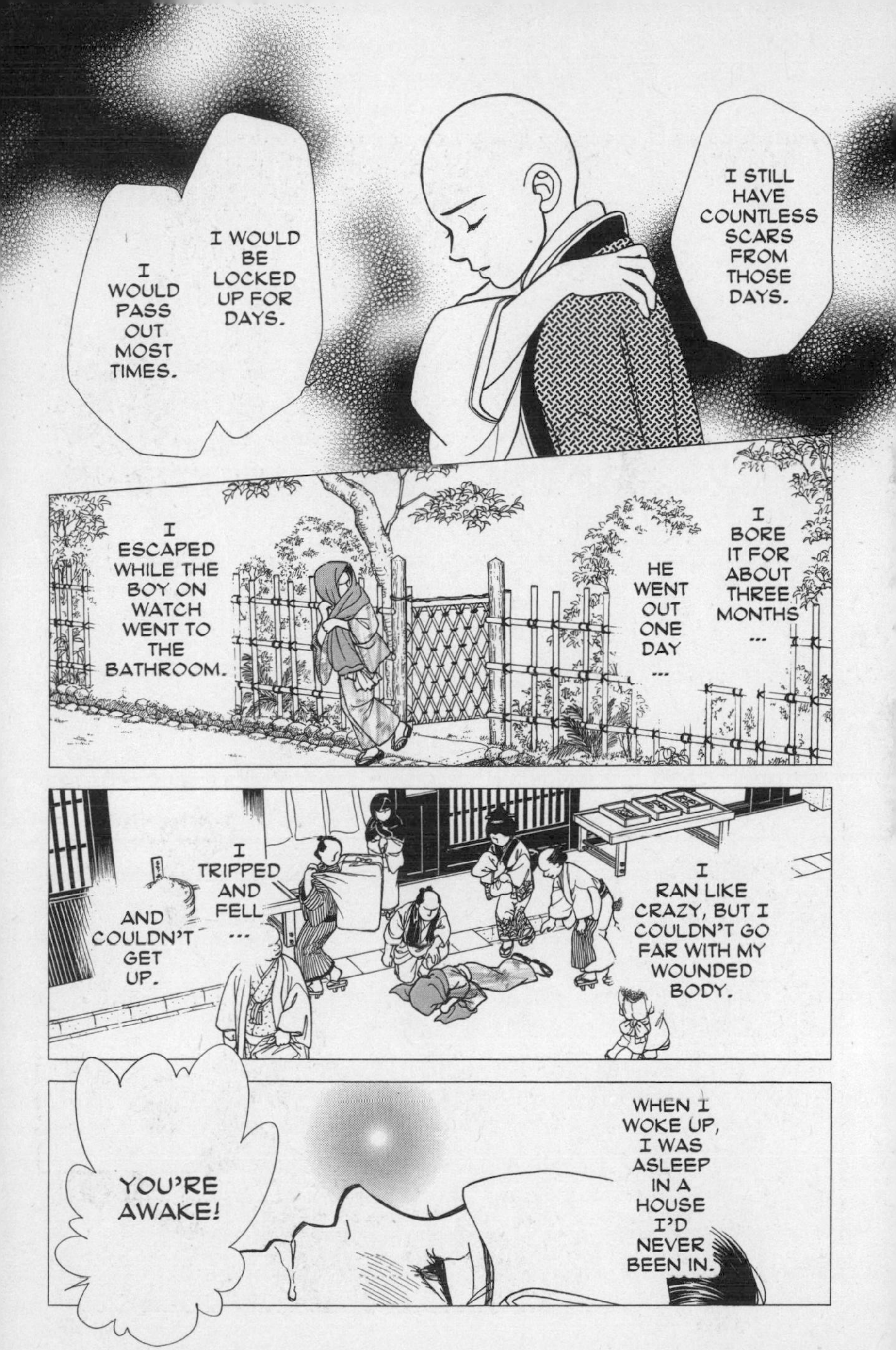
I STILL HAVE COUNTLESS SCARS FROM THOSE DAYS.
I WOULD BE LOCKED UP FOR DAYS.
I WOULD PASS OUT MOST TIMES.
I BORE IT FOR ABOUT THREE MONTHS ...
HE WENT OUT ONE DAY ...
I ESCAPED WHILE THE BOY ON WATCH WENT TO THE BATHROOM.
I RAN LIKE CRAZY, BUT I COULDN'T GO FAR WITH MY WOUNDED BODY.
I TRIPPED AND FELL ...
AND COULDN'T GET UP.
WHEN I WOKE UP, I WAS ASLEEP IN A HOUSE I'D NEVER BEEN IN.
YOU'RE AWAKE!

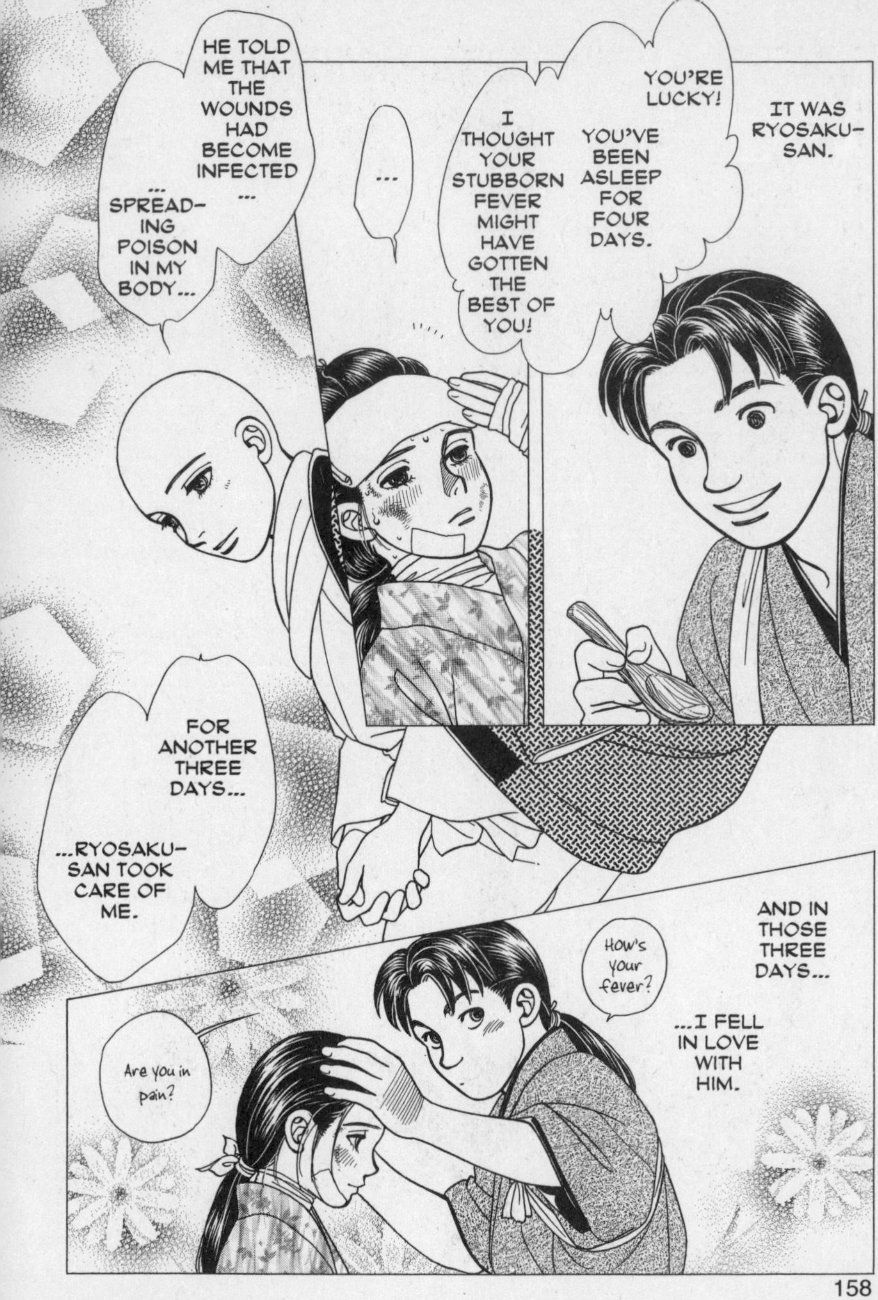
IT WAS RYOSAKU-SAN.
YOU'RE LUCKY!
YOU'VE BEEN ASLEEP FOR FOUR DAYS.
I THOUGHT YOUR STUBBORN FEVER MIGHT HAVE GOTTEN THE BEST OF YOU!
...
HE TOLD ME THAT THE WOUNDS HAD BECOME INFECTED ... ... SPREAD-ING POISON IN MY BODY...
FOR ANOTHER THREE DAYS...
...RYOSAKU-SAN TOOK CARE OF ME.
AND IN THOSE THREE DAYS...
How's your fever?
...I FELL IN LOVE WITH HIM.
Are you in pain?

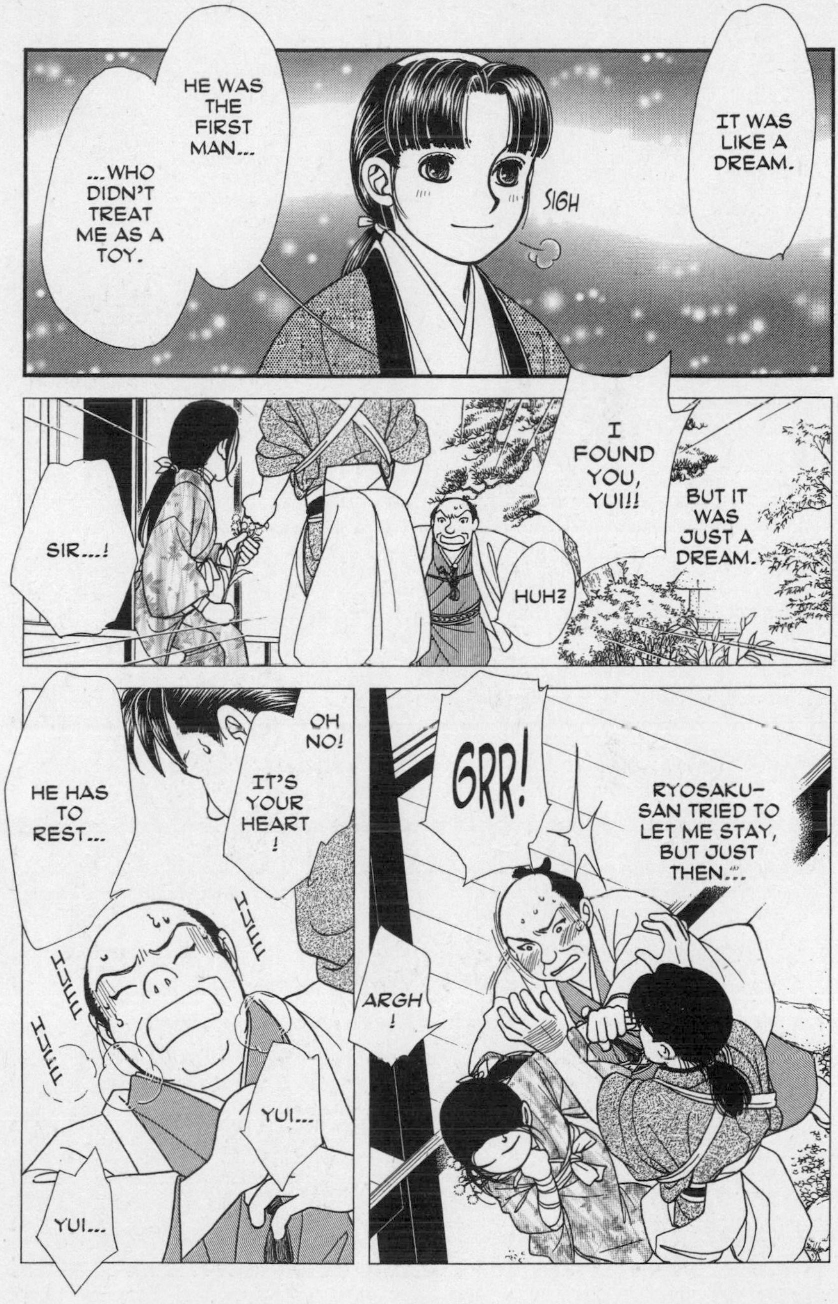
IT WAS LIKE A DREAM.
SIGH
HE WAS THE FIRST MAN...
...WHO DIDN'T TREAT ME AS A TOY.
BUT IT WAS JUST A DREAM.
I FOUND YOU, YUI!!
HUH?
SIR...!
RYOSAKU-SAN TRIED TO LET ME STAY, BUT JUST THEN...
GRR!
ARGH!
OH NO!
IT'S YOUR HEART!
HE HAS TO REST...
HUFF
HUFF
HUFF
YUI...
YUI...

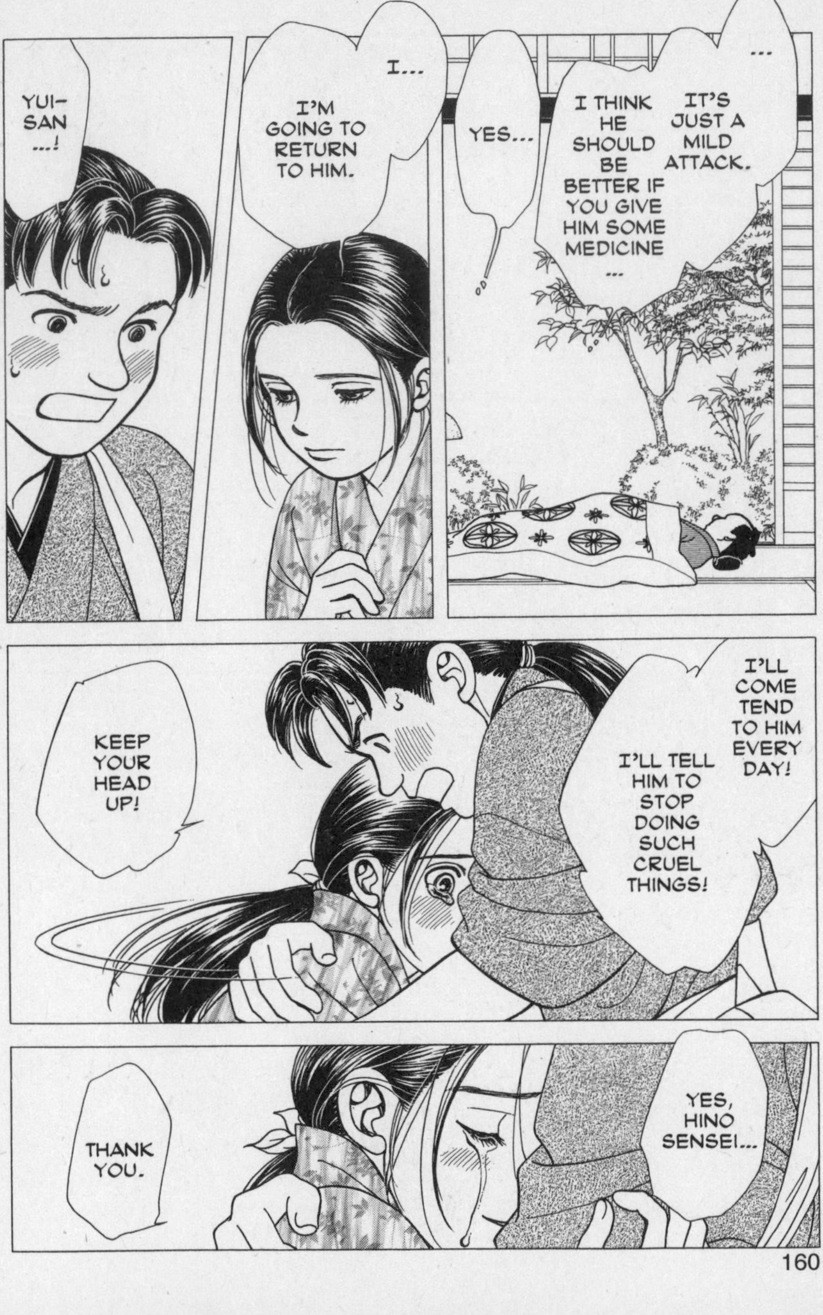
...
IT'S JUST A MILD ATTACK.
I THINK HE SHOULD BE BETTER IF YOU GIVE HIM SOME MEDICINE ...
YES...
I...
I'M GOING TO RETURN TO HIM.
YUI-SAN ...!
I'LL COME TEND TO HIM EVERY DAY!
I'LL TELL HIM TO STOP DOING SUCH CRUEL THINGS!
KEEP YOUR HEAD UP!
YES, HINO SENSEI...
THANK YOU.

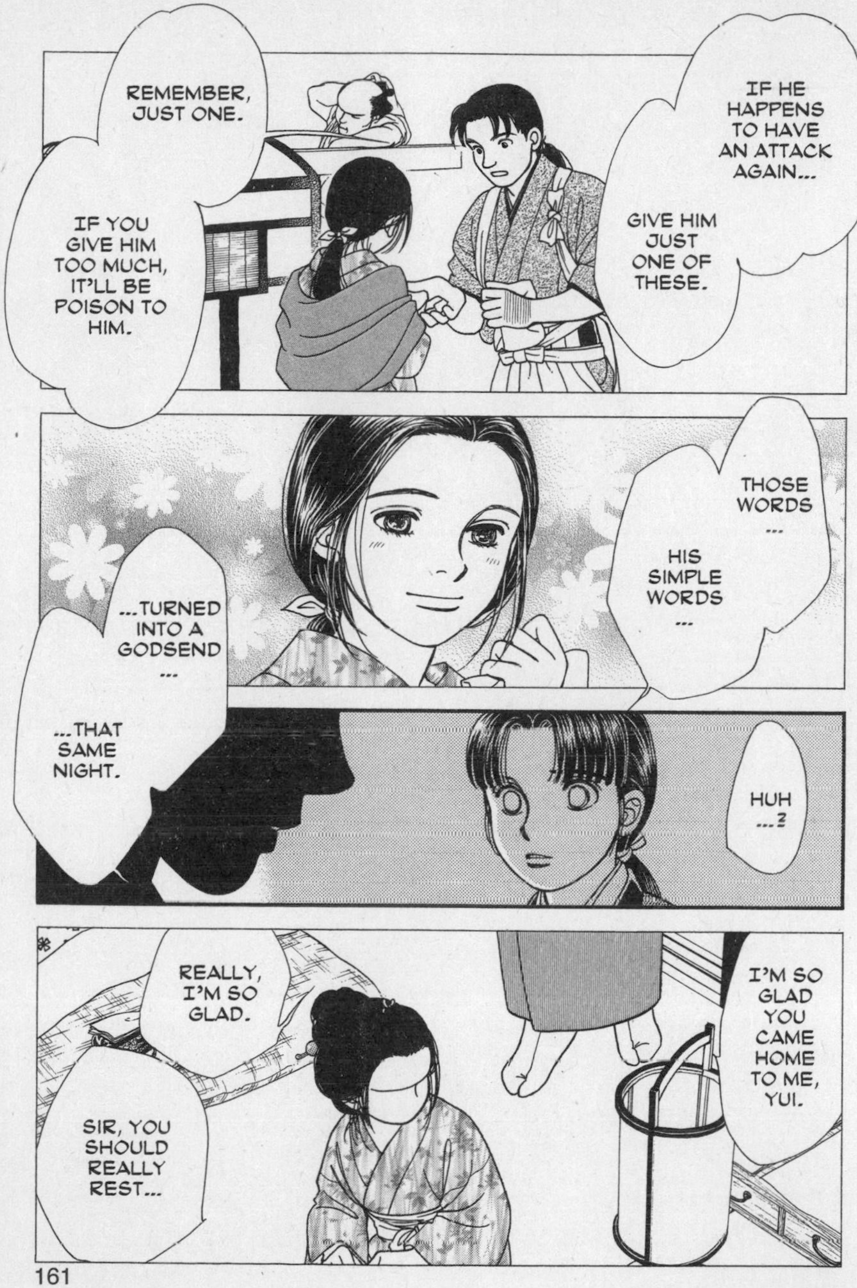
IF HE HAPPENS TO HAVE AN ATTACK AGAIN...
GIVE HIM JUST ONE OF THESE.
REMEMBER, JUST ONE.
IF YOU GIVE HIM TOO MUCH, IT'LL BE POISON TO HIM.
THOSE WORDS ...
HIS SIMPLE WORDS ...
...TURNED INTO A GODSEND ...
...THAT SAME NIGHT.
HUH ...?
I'M SO GLAD YOU CAME HOME TO ME, YUI.
REALLY, I'M SO GLAD.
SIR, YOU SHOULD REALLY REST...

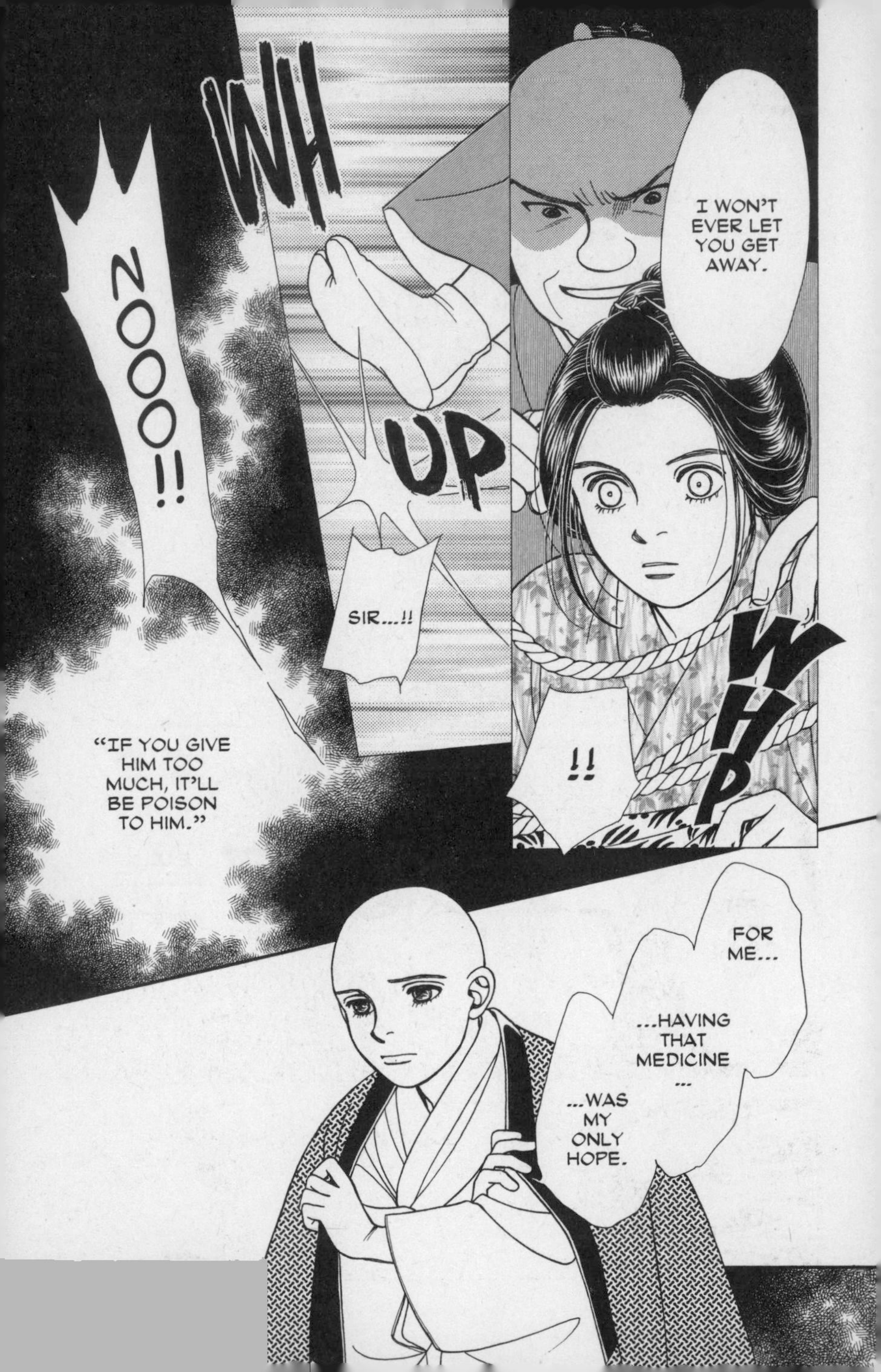
I WON'T EVER LET YOU GET AWAY.
WHIP
!!
WHUP
SIR...!!
NOOO!!
"IF YOU GIVE HIM TOO MUCH, IT'LL BE POISON TO HIM."
FOR ME...
...HAVING THAT MEDICINE ...
...WAS MY ONLY HOPE.

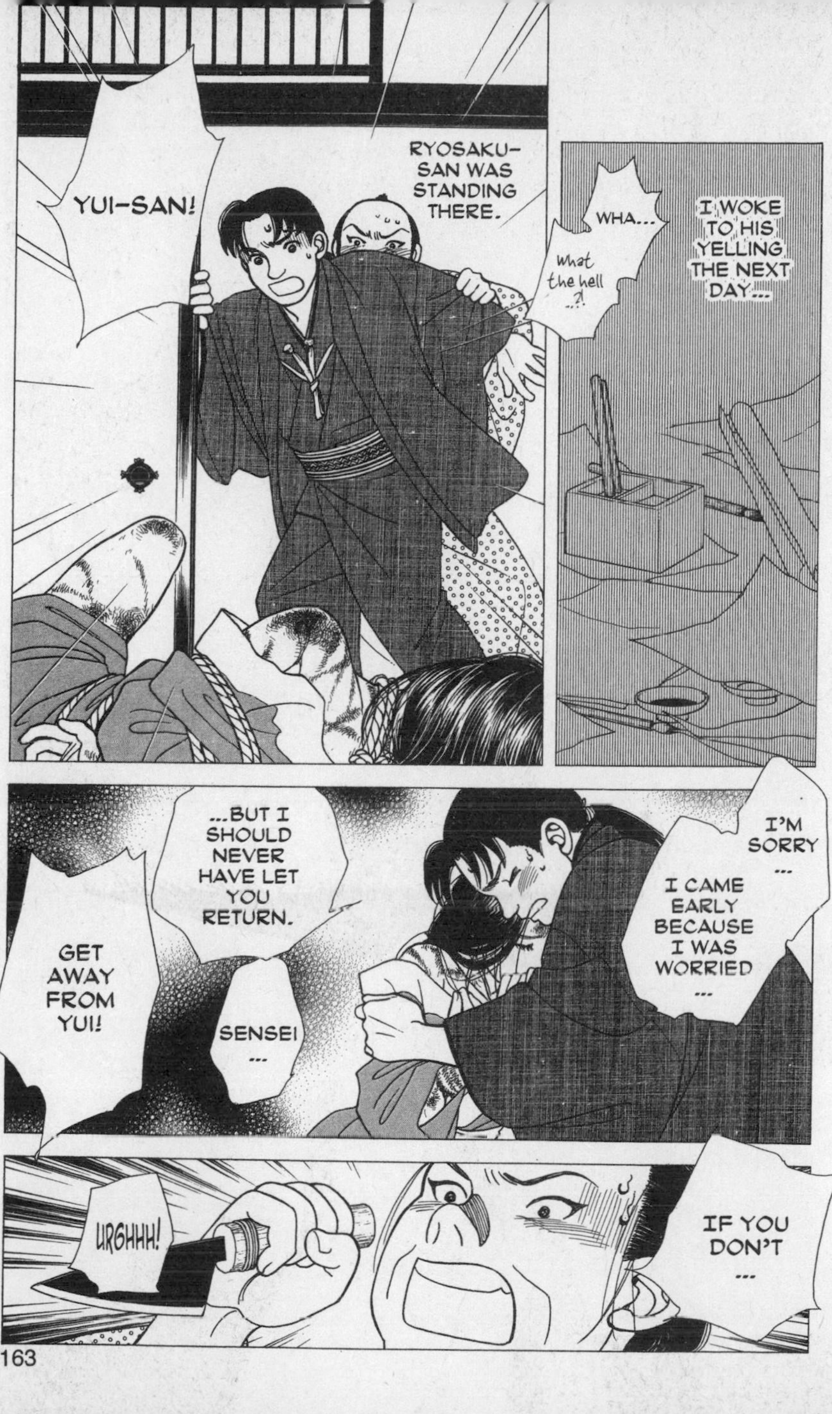
I WOKE TO HIS YELLING THE NEXT DAY...
WHA...
what the hell ...?!
RYOSAKU-SAN WAS STANDING THERE.
YUI-SAN!
I'M SORRY ... I CAME EARLY BECAUSE I WAS WORRIED ...
...BUT I SHOULD NEVER HAVE LET YOU RETURN.
SENSEI ...
GET AWAY FROM YUI!
IF YOU DON'T ...
URGHHH!

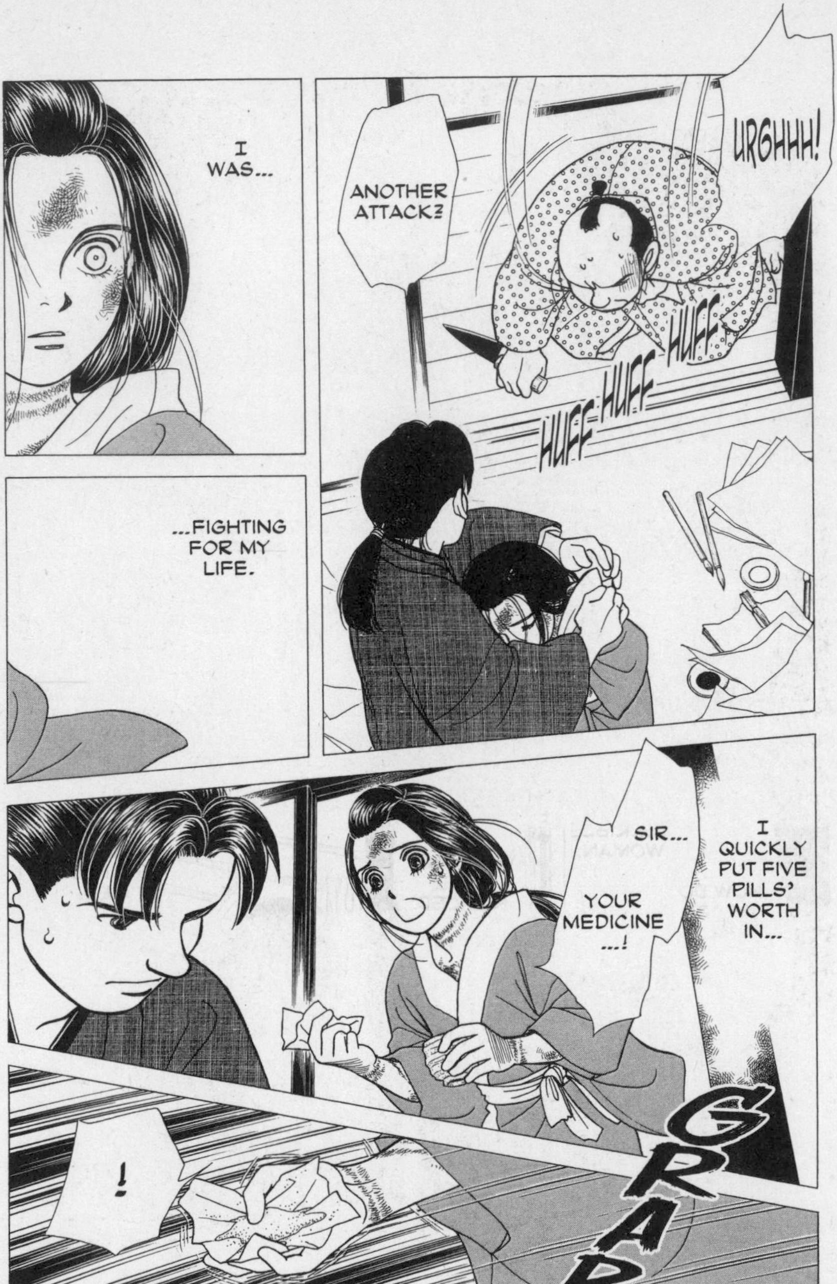
URGHHH!
ANOTHER ATTACK?
HUFF HUFF HUFF HUFF
I WAS...
...FIGHTING FOR MY LIFE.
I QUICKLY PUT FIVE PILLS' WORTH IN...
SIR...
YOUR MEDICINE ...!
GRAB
!

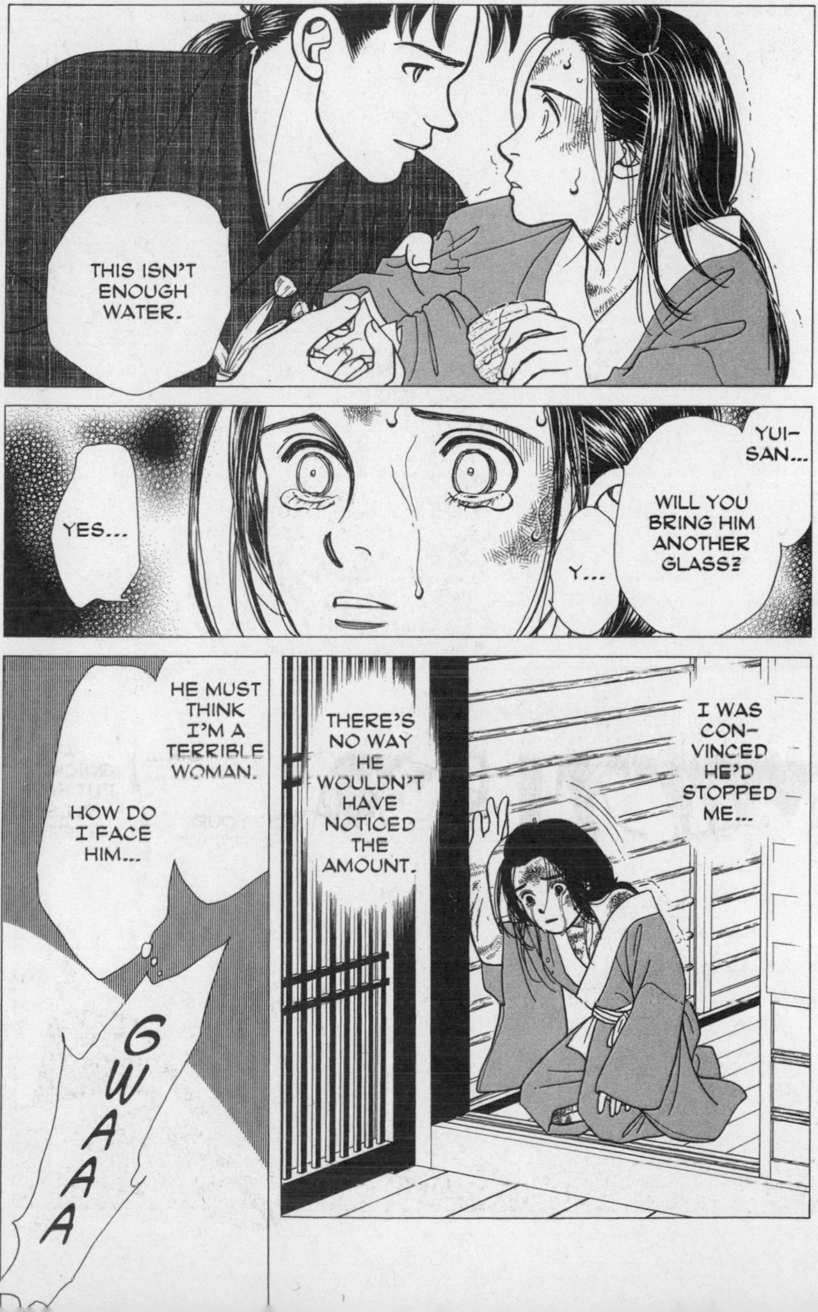
THIS ISN'T ENOUGH WATER.
YUI-SAN...
WILL YOU BRING HIM ANOTHER GLASS?
Y...
YES...
I WAS CON-VINCED HE'D STOPPED ME...
THERE'S NO WAY HE WOULDN'T HAVE NOTICED THE AMOUNT.
HE MUST THINK I'M A TERRIBLE WOMAN.
HOW DO I FACE HIM...
GWAAAA

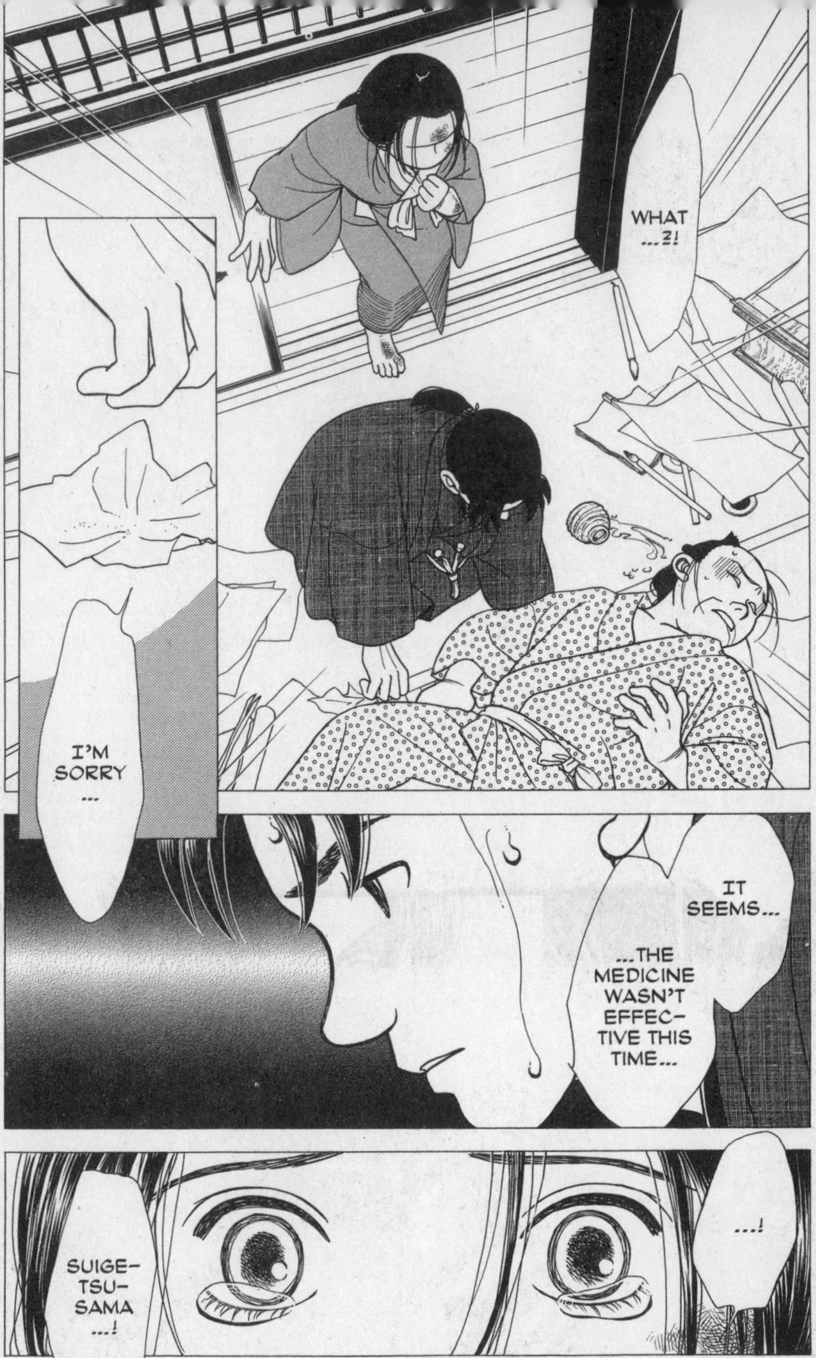
WHAT ...?!
I'M SORRY ...
IT SEEMS...
...THE MEDICINE WASN'T EFFECTIVE THIS TIME...
...!
SUIGETSU-SAMA ...!

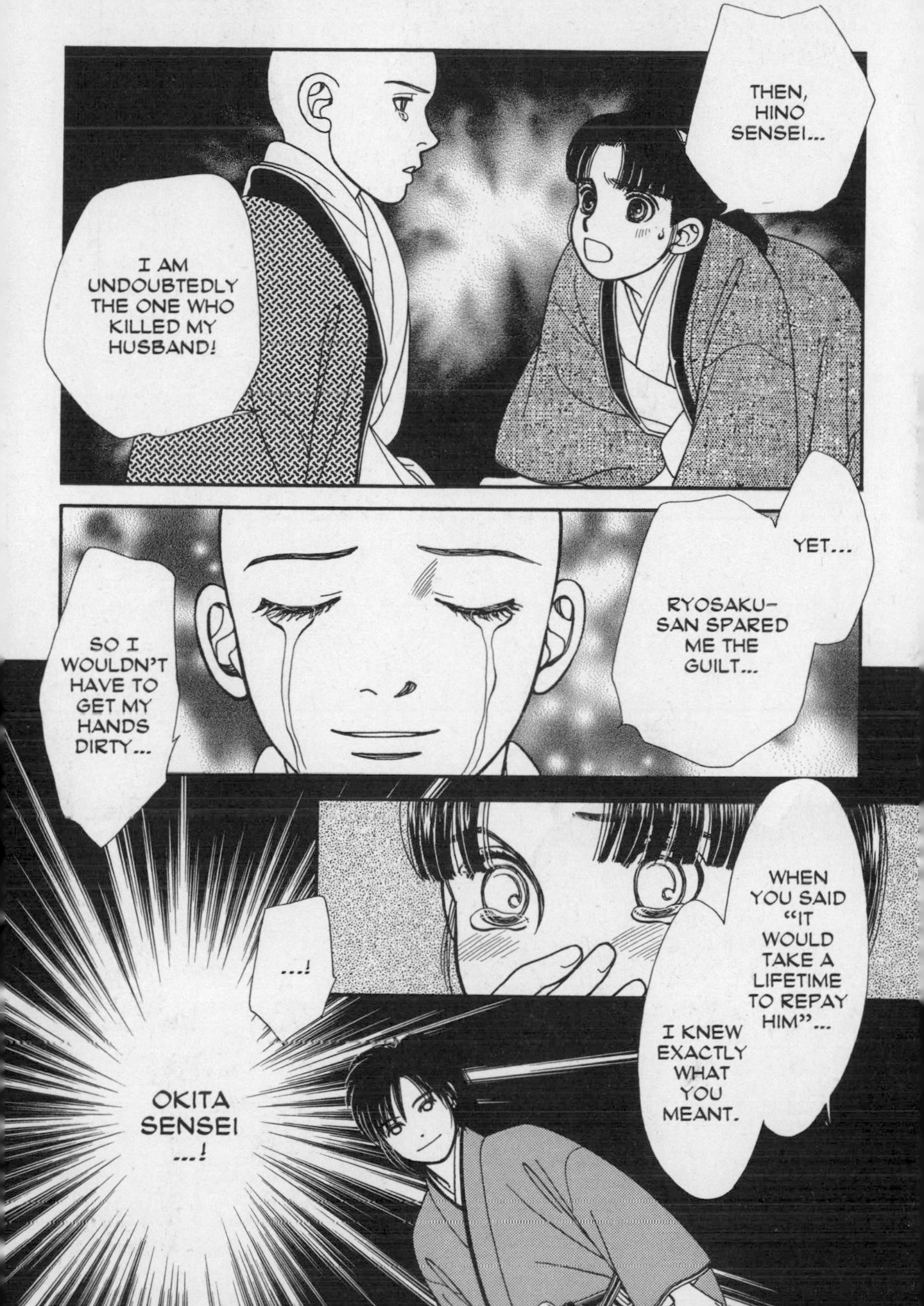
THEN, HINO SENSEI...
I AM UNDOUBTEDLY THE ONE WHO KILLED MY HUSBAND!
YET...
RYOSAKU-SAN SPARED ME THE GUILT...
SO I WOULDN'T HAVE TO GET MY HANDS DIRTY...
WHEN YOU SAID "IT WOULD TAKE A LIFETIME TO REPAY HIM"...
I KNEW EXACTLY WHAT YOU MEANT.
...!
OKITA SENSEI...!

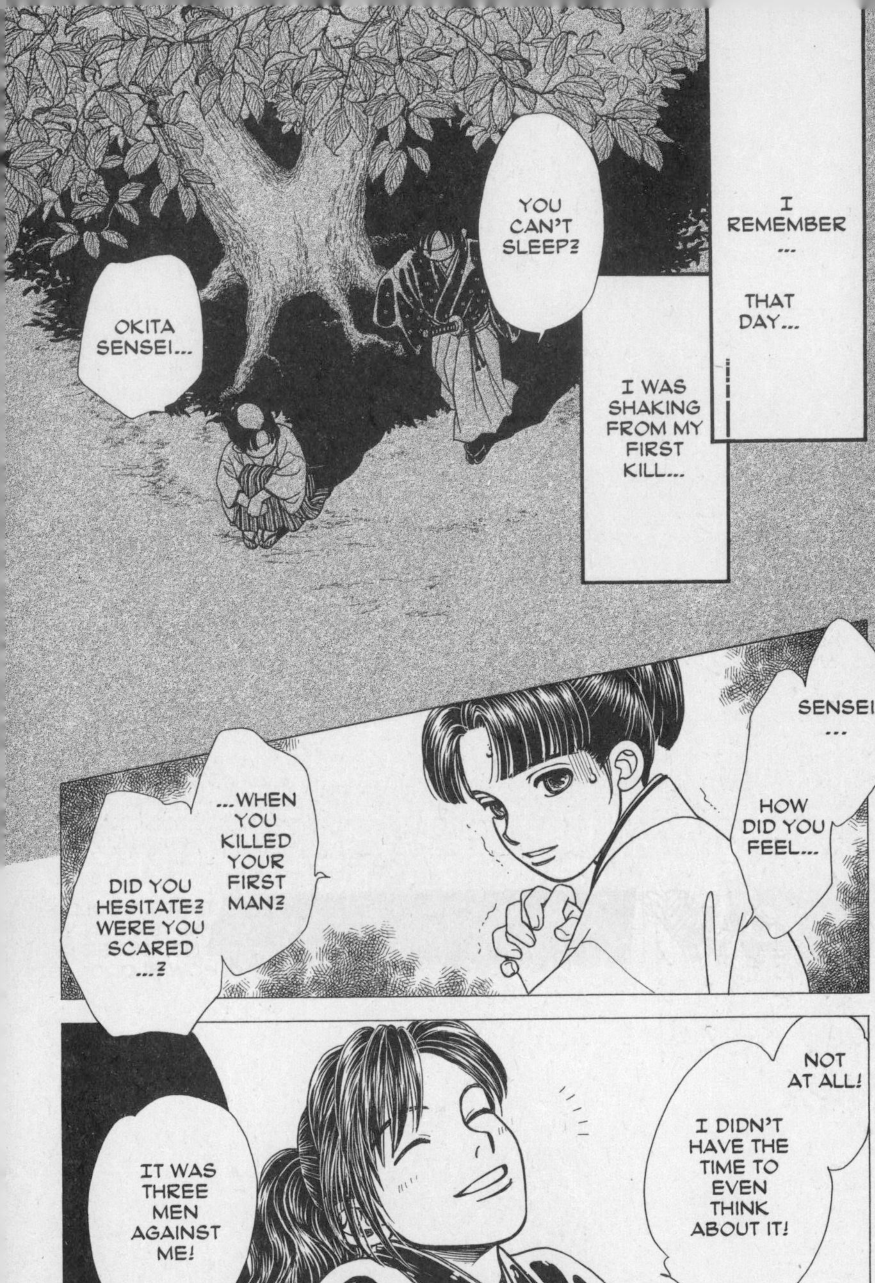
I REMEMBER ... THAT DAY...
I WAS SHAKING FROM MY FIRST KILL...
YOU CAN'T SLEEP?
OKITA SENSEI...
SENSEI... HOW DID YOU FEEL...
...WHEN YOU KILLED YOUR FIRST MAN?
DID YOU HESITATE? WERE YOU SCARED ...?
NOT AT ALL!
I DIDN'T HAVE THE TIME TO EVEN THINK ABOUT IT!
IT WAS THREE MEN AGAINST ME!

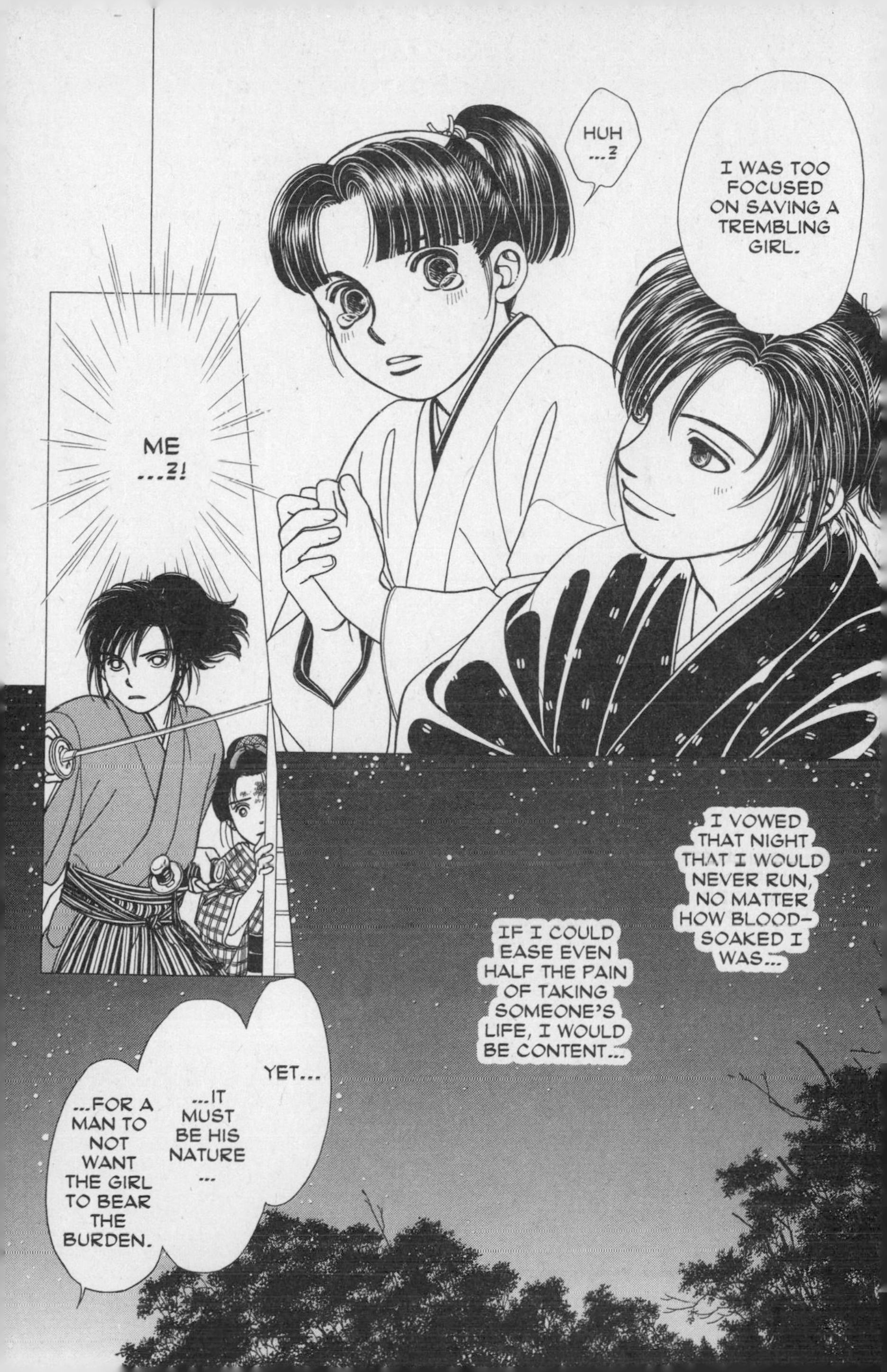
I WAS TOO FOCUSED ON SAVING A TREMBLING GIRL.
HUH ...?
ME ...?!
I VOWED THAT NIGHT THAT I WOULD NEVER RUN, NO MATTER HOW BLOOD-SOAKED I WAS...
IF I COULD EASE EVEN HALF THE PAIN OF TAKING SOMEONE'S LIFE, I WOULD BE CONTENT...
YET...
...IT MUST BE HIS NATURE ...
...FOR A MAN TO NOT WANT THE GIRL TO BEAR THE BURDEN.

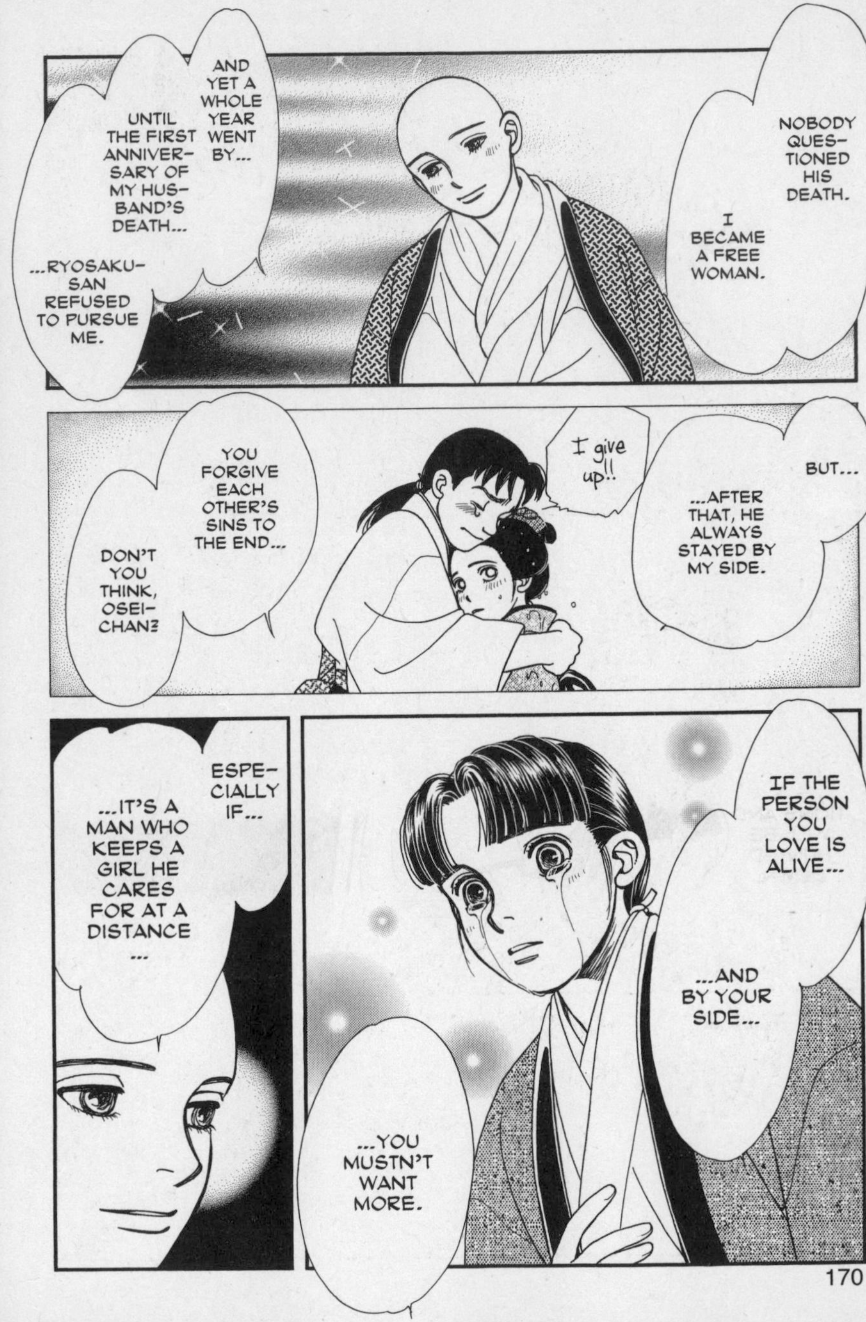
NOBODY QUES-TIONED HIS DEATH.
I BECAME A FREE WOMAN.
AND YET A WHOLE YEAR WENT BY...
UNTIL THE FIRST ANNIVER-SARY OF MY HUS-BAND'S DEATH...
...RYOSAKU-SAN REFUSED TO PURSUE ME.
BUT...
...AFTER THAT, HE ALWAYS STAYED BY MY SIDE.
I give up!!
YOU FORGIVE EACH OTHER'S SINS TO THE END...
DON'T YOU THINK, OSEI-CHAN?
IF THE PERSON YOU LOVE IS ALIVE...
...AND BY YOUR SIDE...
...YOU MUSTN'T WANT MORE.
ESPE-CIALLY IF...
...IT'S A MAN WHO KEEPS A GIRL HE CARES FOR AT A DISTANCE ...

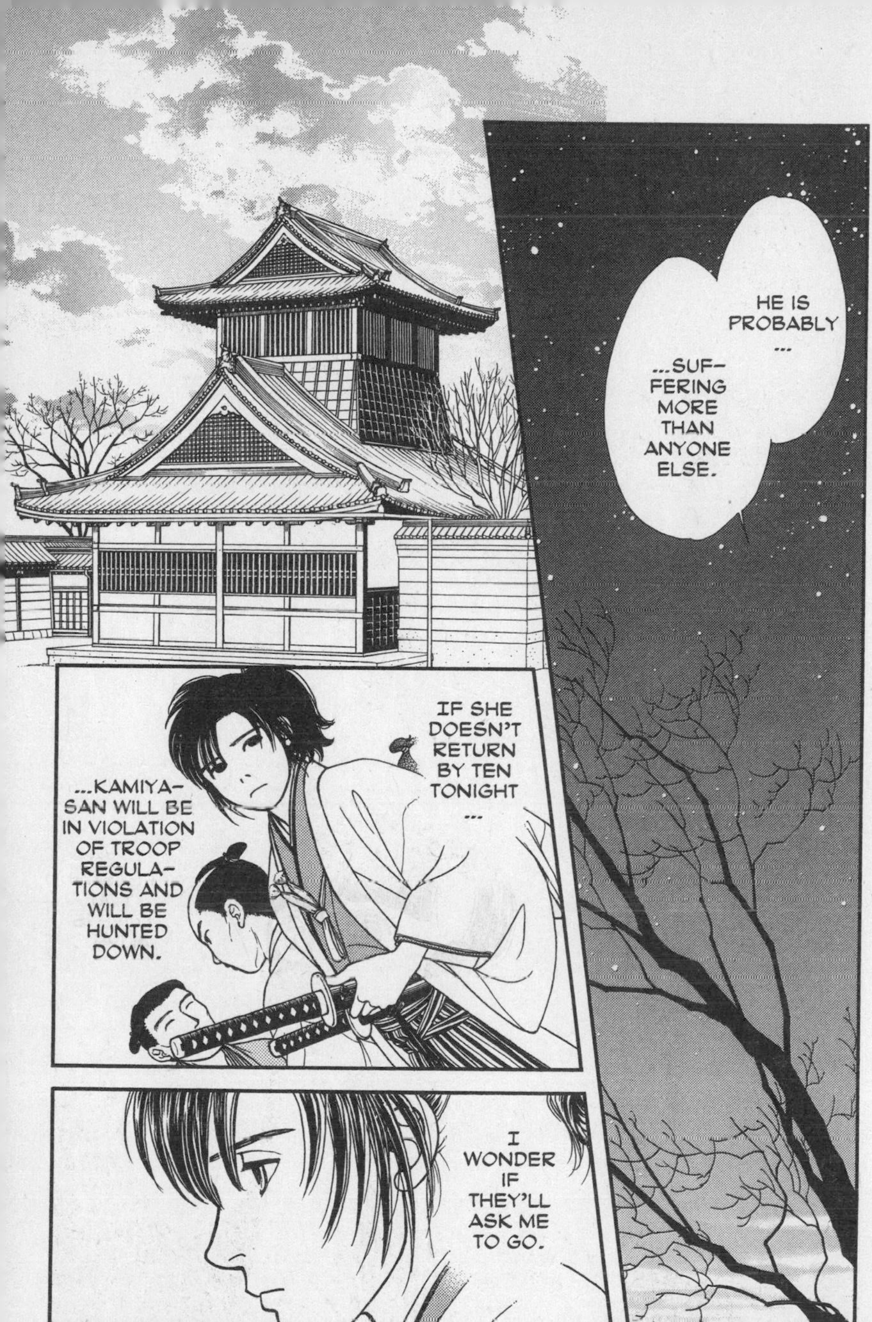
HE IS PROBABLY ...
...SUF-FERING MORE THAN ANYONE ELSE.
IF SHE DOESN'T RETURN BY TEN TONIGHT ...
...KAMIYA-SAN WILL BE IN VIOLATION OF TROOP REGULA-TIONS AND WILL BE HUNTED DOWN.
I WONDER IF THEY'LL ASK ME TO GO.

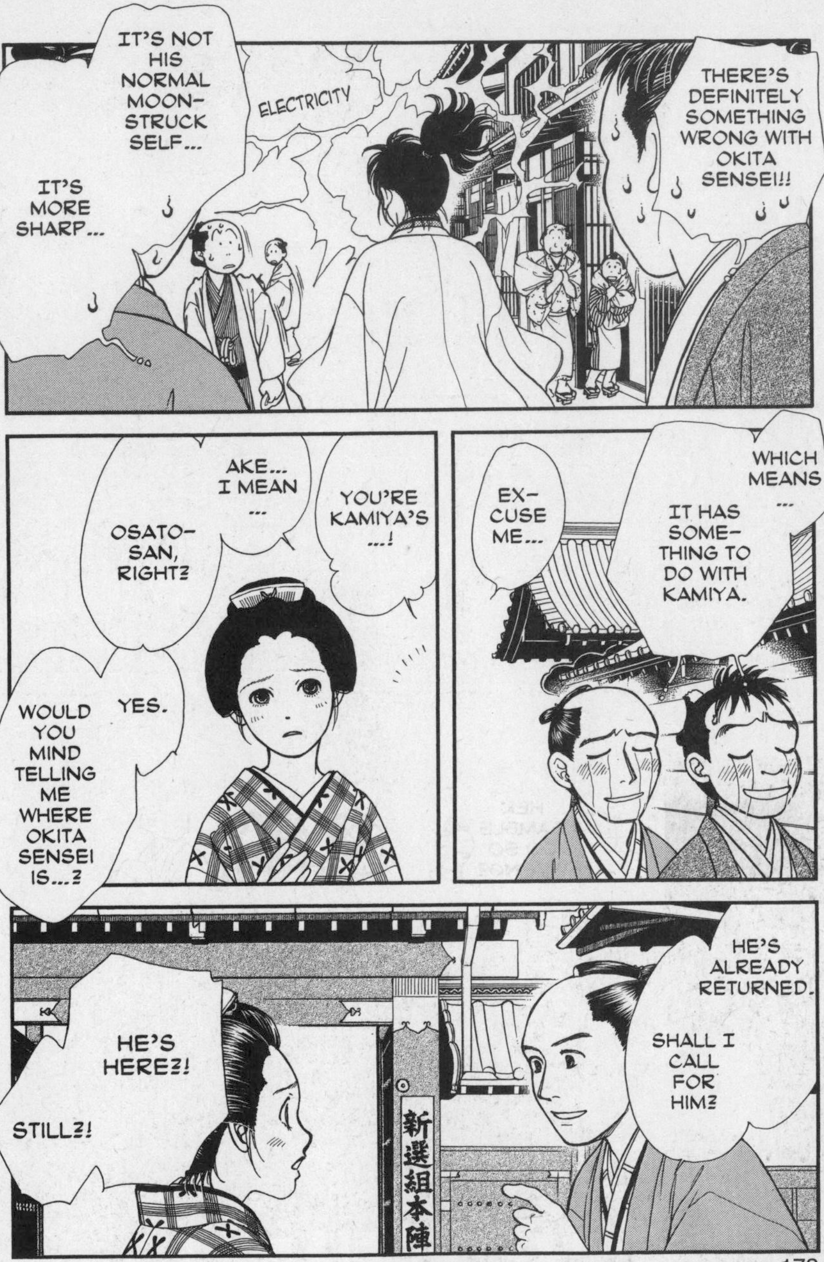
THERE'S DEFINITELY SOMETHING WRONG WITH OKITA SENSEI!!
ELECTRICITY
IT'S NOT HIS NORMAL MOON-STRUCK SELF...
IT'S MORE SHARP...
WHICH MEANS...
IT HAS SOME-THING TO DO WITH KAMIYA.
EX-CUSE ME...
YOU'RE KAMIYA'S...!
AKE... I MEAN...
OSATO-SAN, RIGHT?
YES.
WOULD YOU MIND TELLING ME WHERE OKITA SENSEI IS...?
HE'S ALREADY RETURNED.
SHALL I CALL FOR HIM?
新選組本陣
HE'S HERE?!
STILL?!

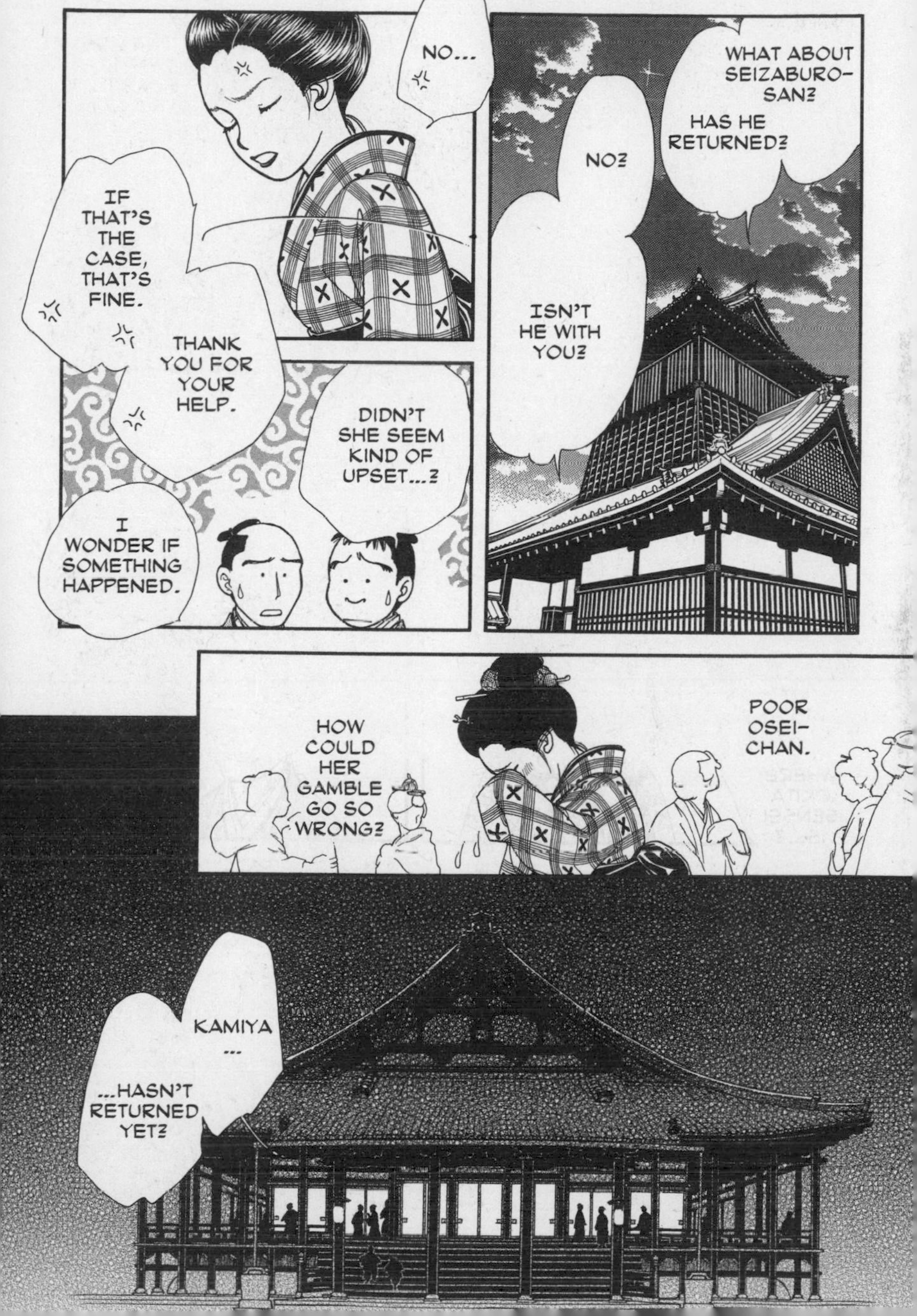
WHAT ABOUT SEIZABURO-SAN?
HAS HE RETURNED?
NO?
ISN'T HE WITH YOU?
NO...
IF THAT'S THE CASE, THAT'S FINE.
THANK YOU FOR YOUR HELP.
DIDN'T SHE SEEM KIND OF UPSET...?
I WONDER IF SOMETHING HAPPENED.
POOR OSEI-CHAN.
HOW COULD HER GAMBLE GO SO WRONG?
KAMIYA...
...HASN'T RETURNED YET?

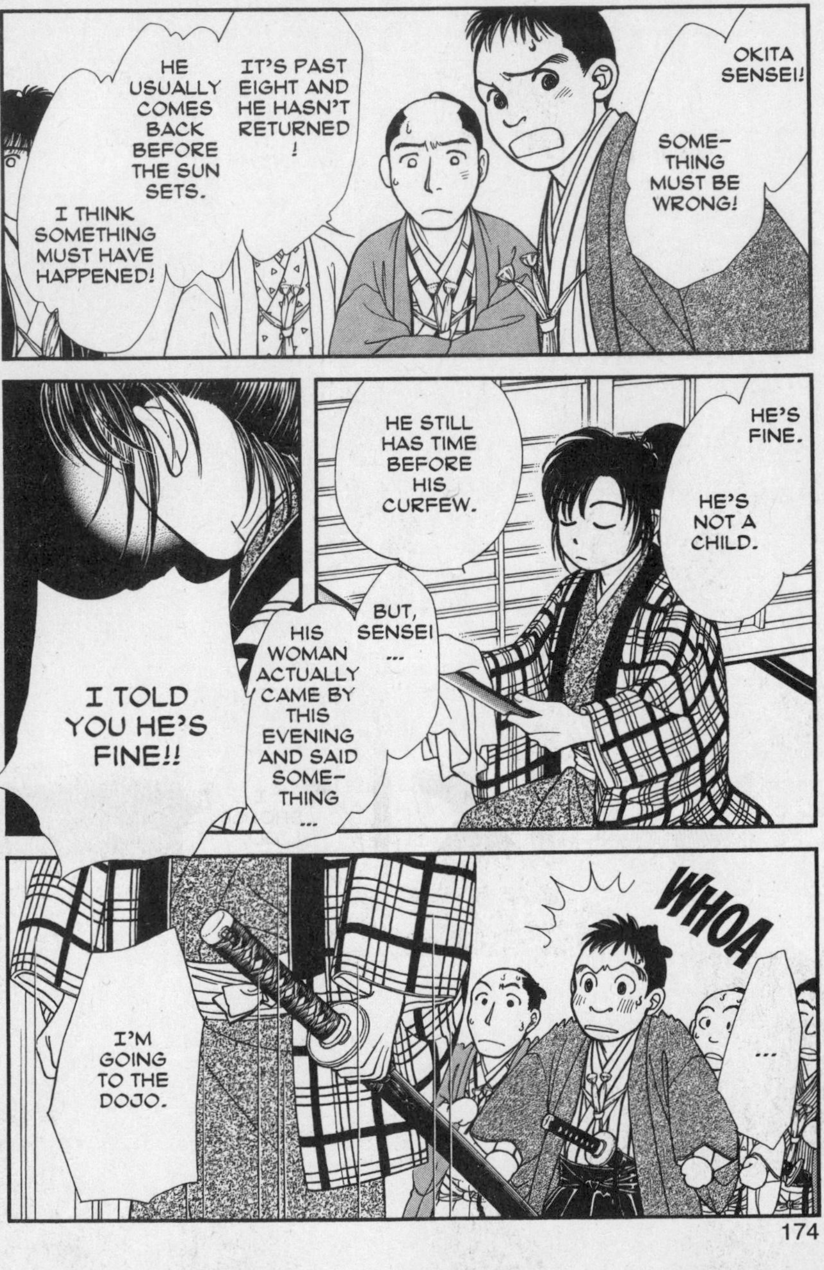
OKITA SENSEI!
SOMETHING MUST BE WRONG!
IT'S PAST EIGHT AND HE HASN'T RETURNED!
HE USUALLY COMES BACK BEFORE THE SUN SETS.
I THINK SOMETHING MUST HAVE HAPPENED!
HE'S FINE.
HE'S NOT A CHILD.
HE STILL HAS TIME BEFORE HIS CURFEW.
BUT, SENSEI...
HIS WOMAN ACTUALLY CAME BY THIS EVENING AND SAID SOMETHING...
I TOLD YOU HE'S FINE!!
WHOA
...
I'M GOING TO THE DOJO.

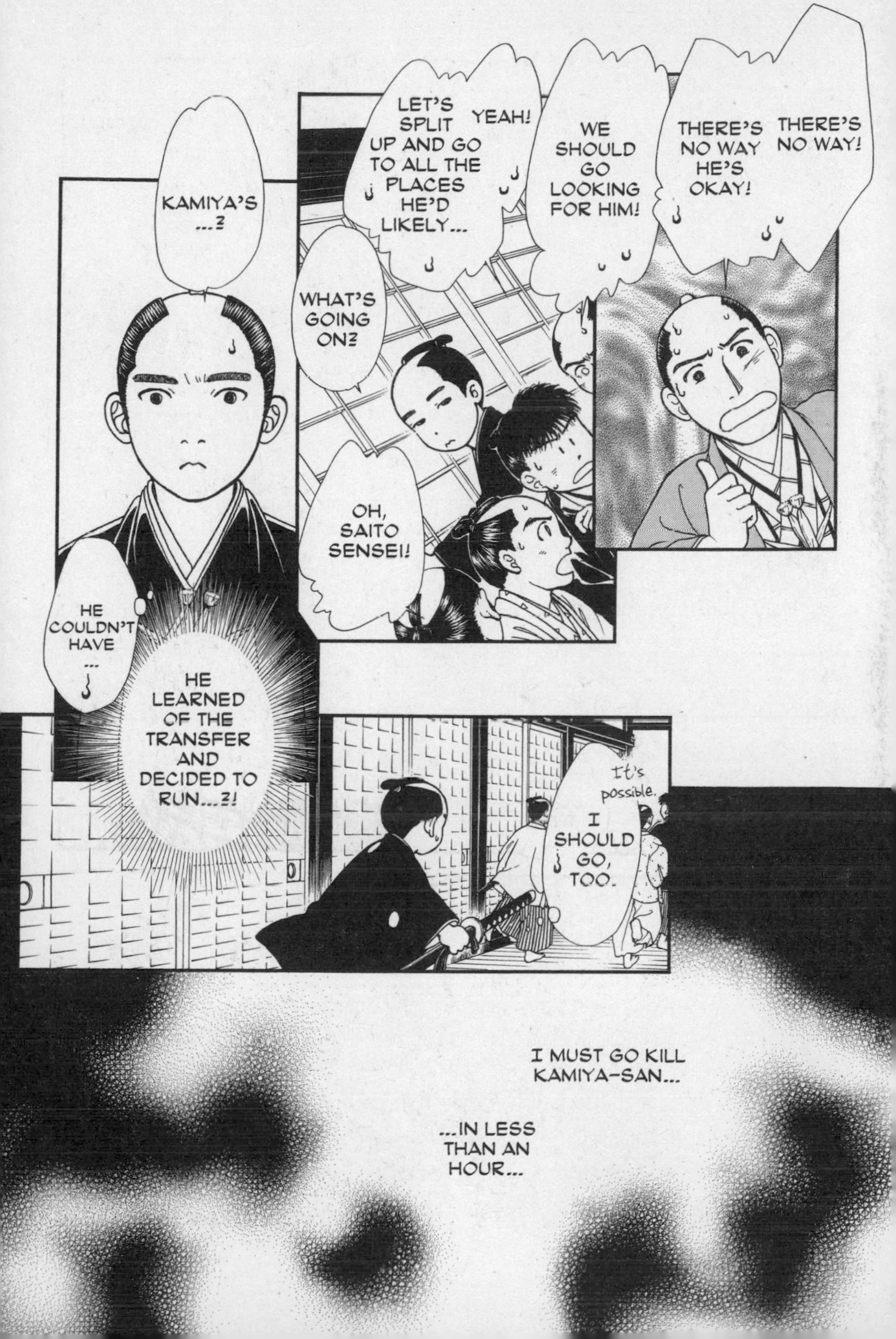
THERE'S NO WAY!
THERE'S NO WAY HE'S OKAY!
WE SHOULD GO LOOKING FOR HIM!
YEAH!
LET'S SPLIT UP AND GO TO ALL THE PLACES HE'D LIKELY...
WHAT'S GOING ON?
OH, SAITO SENSEI!
KAMIYA'S...?
HE COULDN'T HAVE...
HE LEARNED OF THE TRANSFER AND DECIDED TO RUN...?!
It's possible.
I SHOULD GO, TOO.
I MUST GO KILL KAMIYA-SAN...
...IN LESS THAN AN HOUR...

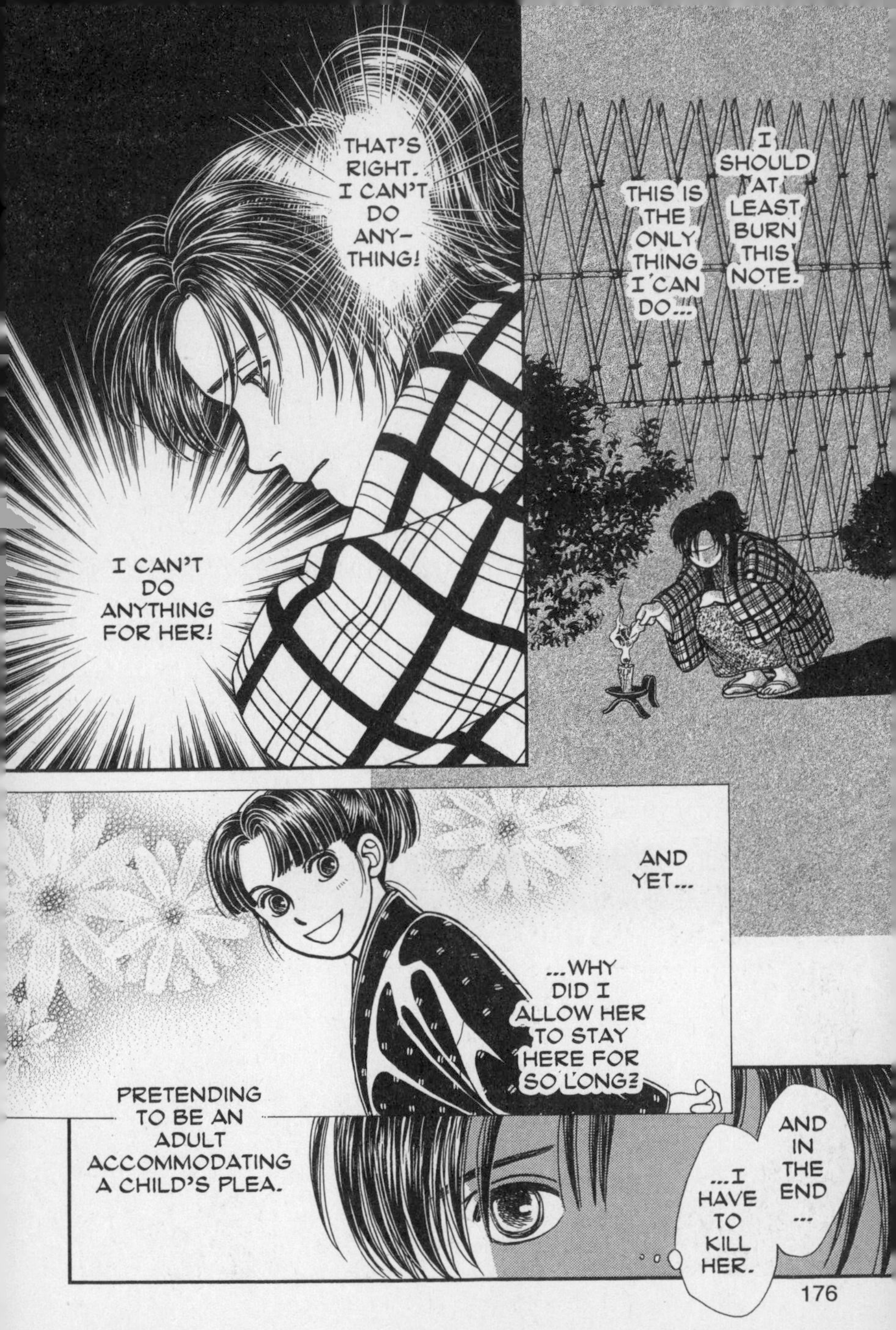
I SHOULD AT LEAST BURN THIS NOTE.
THIS IS THE ONLY THING I CAN DO...
THAT'S RIGHT. I CAN'T DO ANYTHING!
I CAN'T DO ANYTHING FOR HER!
AND YET...
...WHY DID I ALLOW HER TO STAY HERE FOR SO LONG?
AND IN THE END...
...I HAVE TO KILL HER.
PRETENDING TO BE AN ADULT ACCOMMODATING A CHILD'S PLEA.

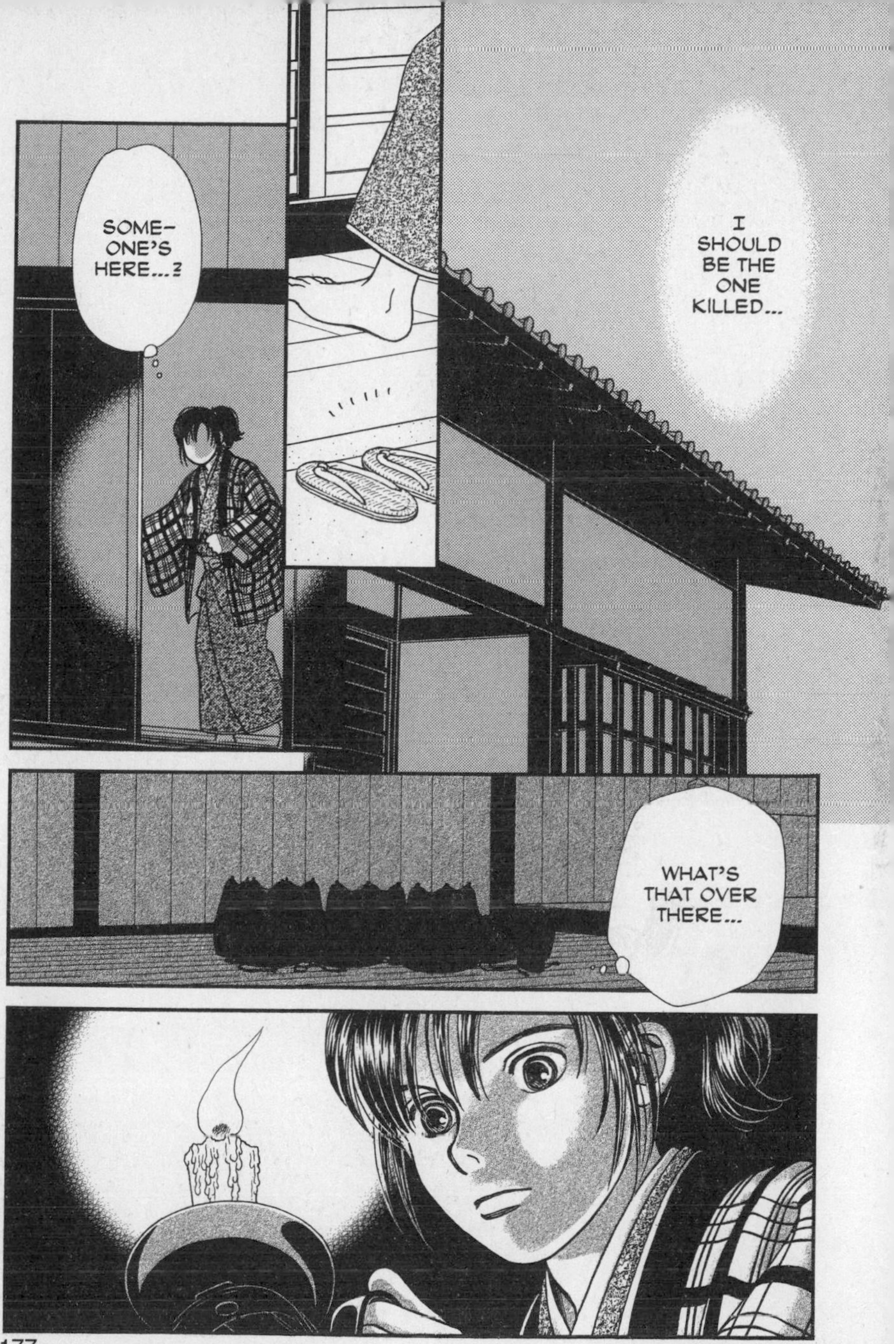
I SHOULD BE THE ONE KILLED...
SOME-ONE'S HERE...?
WHAT'S THAT OVER THERE...

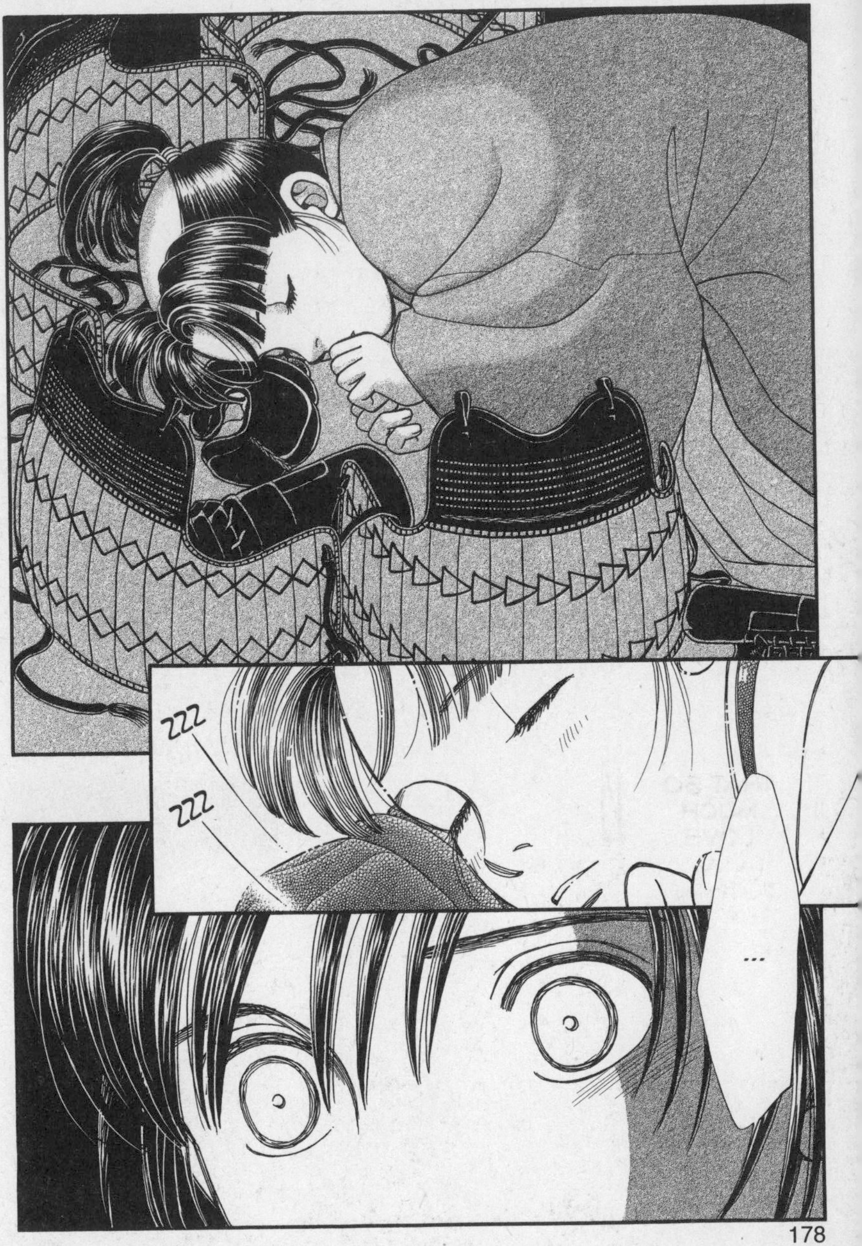
ZZZ
ZZZ
...

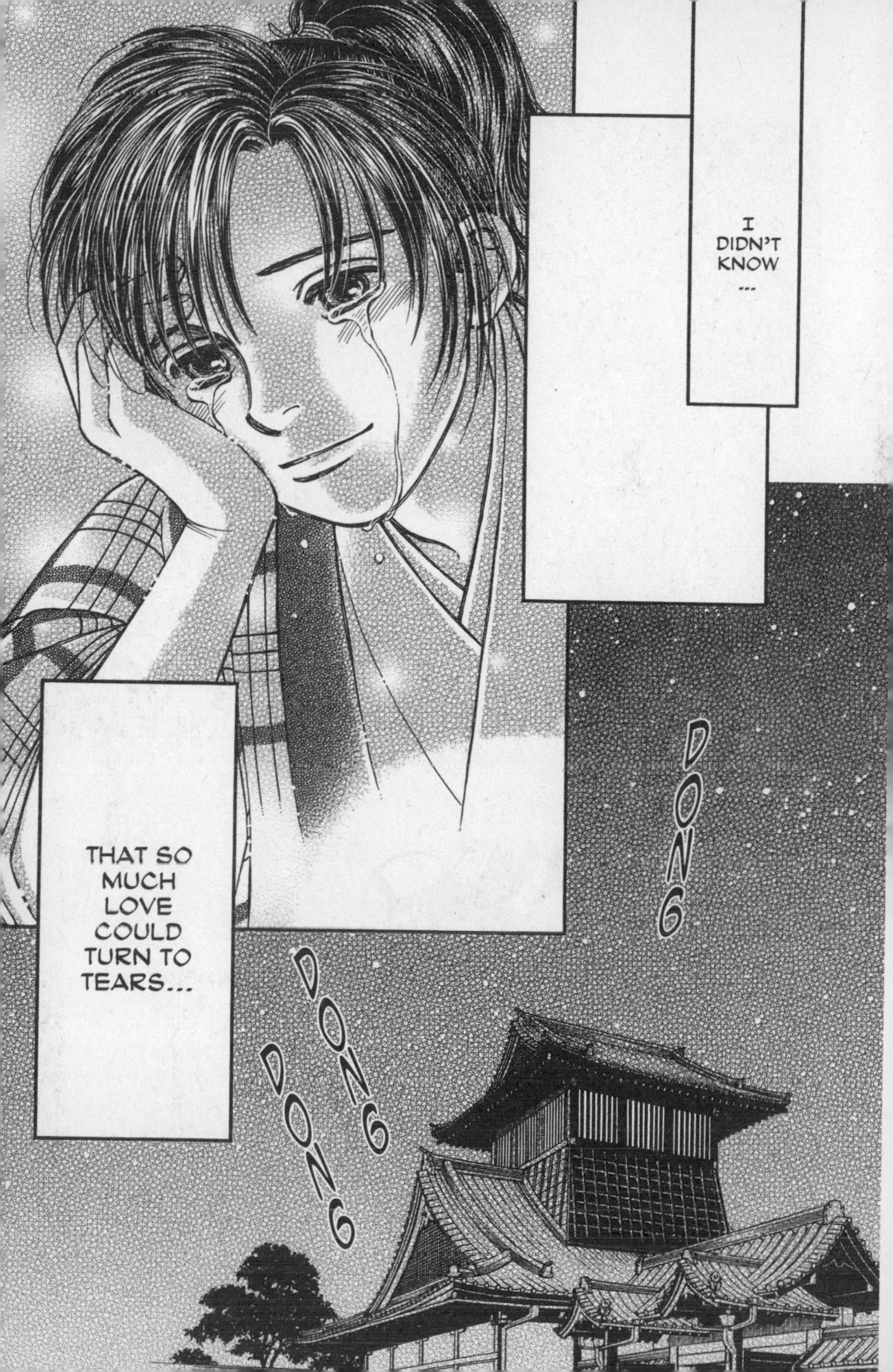

I DIDN'T KNOW ...
THAT SO MUCH LOVE COULD TURN TO TEARS...
DONG
DONG
DONG

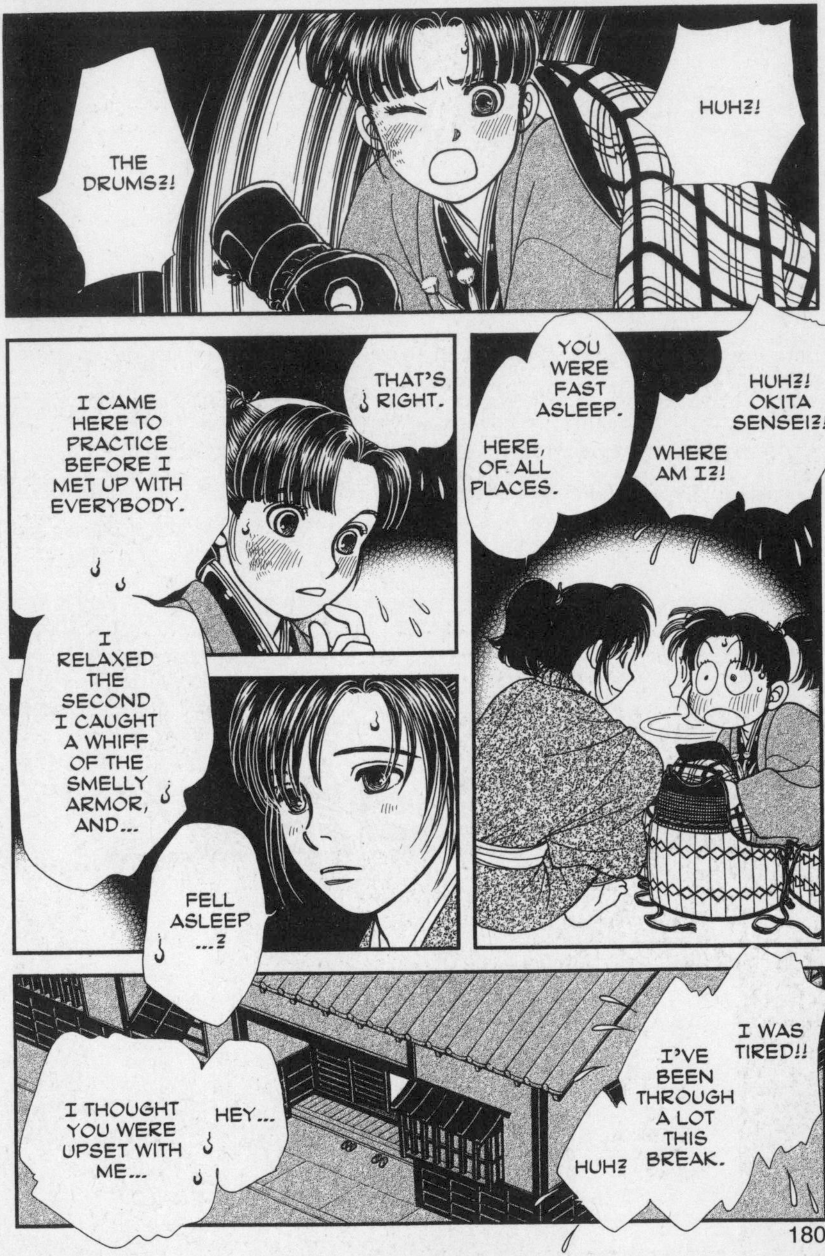
HUH?!
THE DRUMS?!
HUH?! OKITA SENSEI?!
WHERE AM I?!
YOU WERE FAST ASLEEP.
HERE, OF ALL PLACES.
THAT'S RIGHT.
I CAME HERE TO PRACTICE BEFORE I MET UP WITH EVERYBODY.
I RELAXED THE SECOND I CAUGHT A WHIFF OF THE SMELLY ARMOR, AND...
FELL ASLEEP...?
I WAS TIRED!!
I'VE BEEN THROUGH A LOT THIS BREAK.
HUH?
HEY...
I THOUGHT YOU WERE UPSET WITH ME...

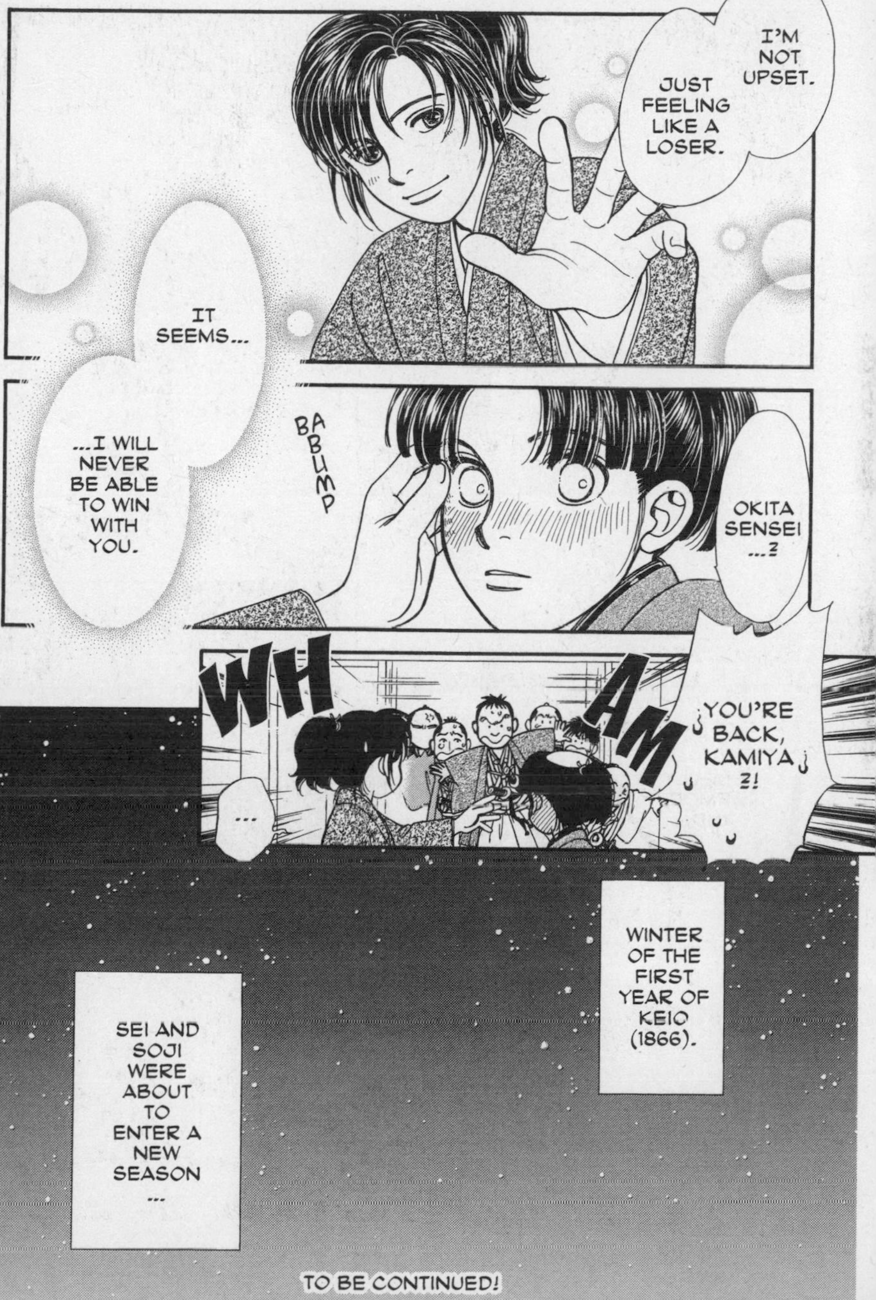
I'M NOT UPSET.
JUST FEELING LIKE A LOSER.
IT SEEMS...
OKITA SENSEI ...?
BA BUMP
...I WILL NEVER BE ABLE TO WIN WITH YOU.
YOU'RE BACK, KAMIYA?!
WHAM
...
WINTER OF THE FIRST YEAR OF KEIO (1866).
SEI AND SOJI WERE ABOUT TO ENTER A NEW SEASON ...
TO BE CONTINUED!

TAEKO WATANABE PRESENTS

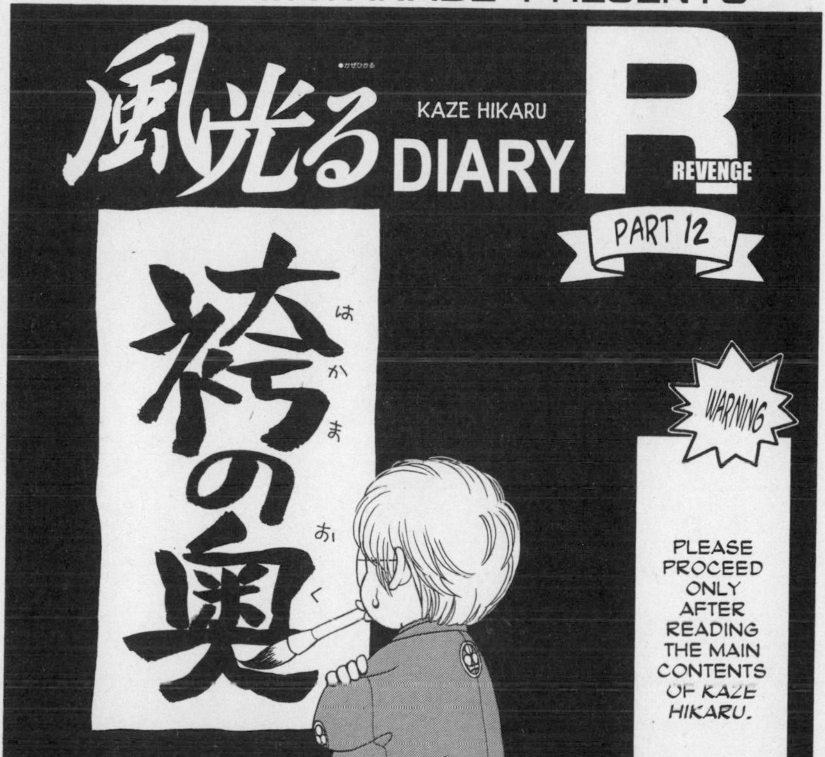
風光る
KAZE HIKARU
DIARY R
REVENGE
PART 12
WARNING
PLEASE PROCEED ONLY AFTER READING THE MAIN CONTENTS OF KAZE HIKARU.
袴の奥
*Sign: Unknown secrets of the hakama

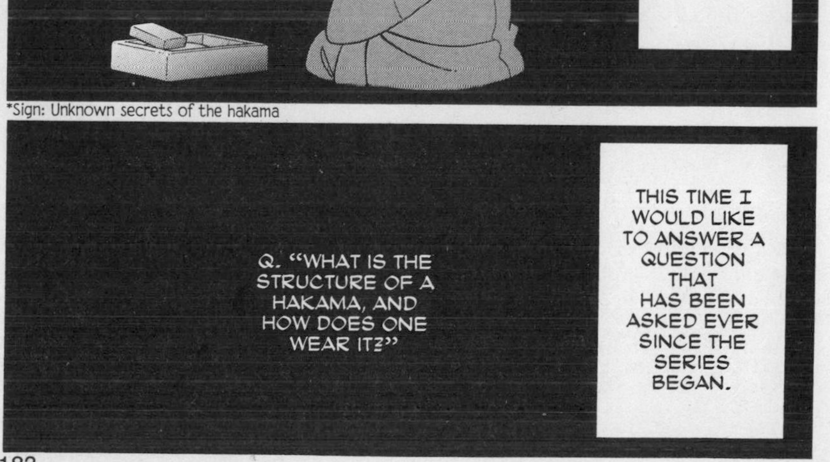
THIS TIME I WOULD LIKE TO ANSWER A QUESTION THAT HAS BEEN ASKED EVER SINCE THE SERIES BEGAN.
Q. "WHAT IS THE STRUCTURE OF A HAKAMA, AND HOW DOES ONE WEAR IT?"

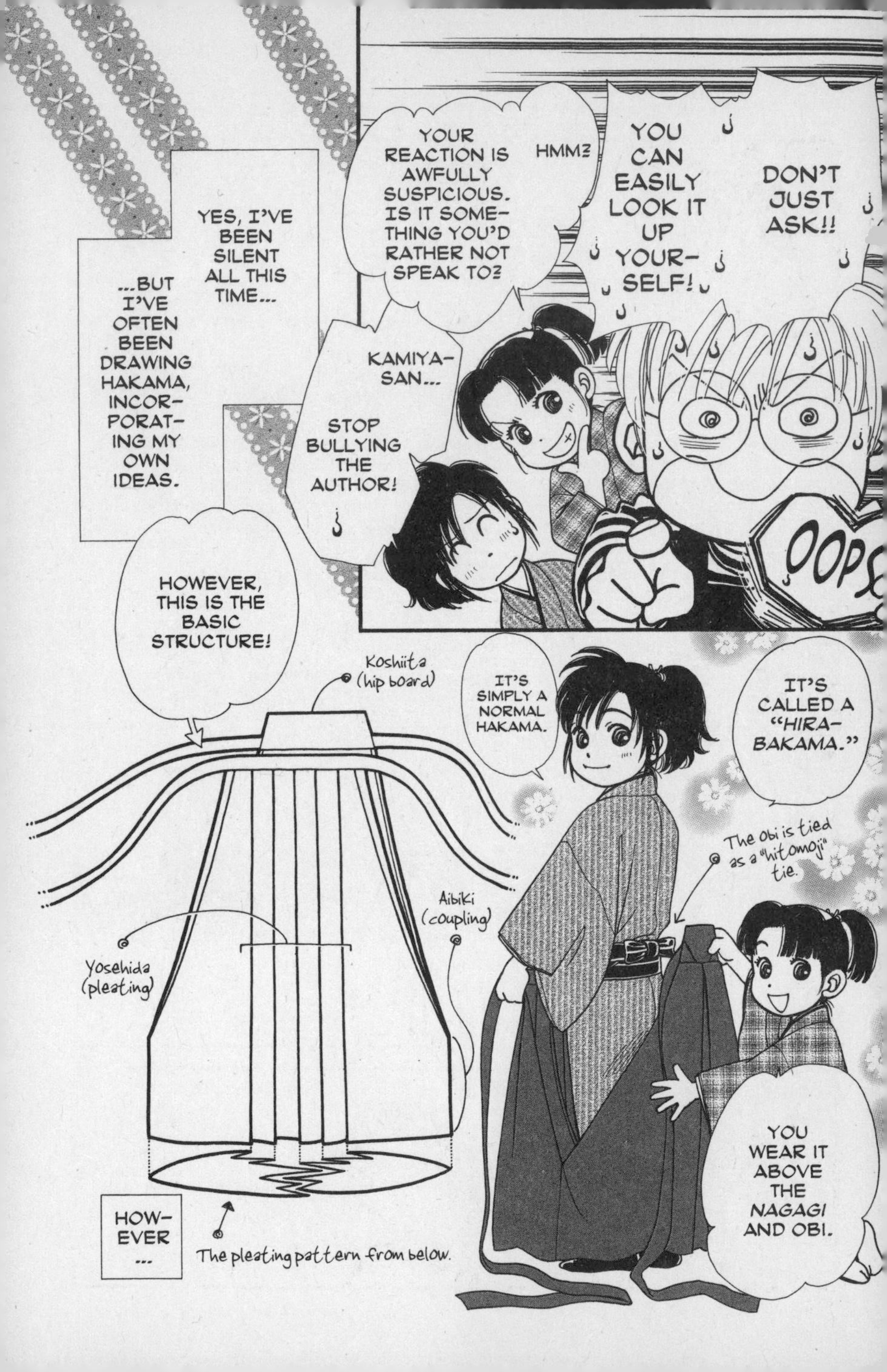
DON'T JUST ASK!!
YOU CAN EASILY LOOK IT UP YOURSELF!
HMM?
YOUR REACTION IS AWFULLY SUSPICIOUS. IS IT SOMETHING YOU'D RATHER NOT SPEAK TO?
KAMIYA-SAN...
STOP BULLYING THE AUTHOR!
OOPS
YES, I'VE BEEN SILENT ALL THIS TIME...
...BUT I'VE OFTEN BEEN DRAWING HAKAMA, INCORPORATING MY OWN IDEAS.
IT'S CALLED A "HIRA-BAKAMA."
IT'S SIMPLY A NORMAL HAKAMA.
The obi is tied as a "hitomoji" tie.
YOU WEAR IT ABOVE THE NAGAGI AND OBI.
HOWEVER, THIS IS THE BASIC STRUCTURE!
Koshiita (hip board)
Aibiki (coupling)
Yosehida (pleating)
The pleating pattern from below.
HOW-EVER...

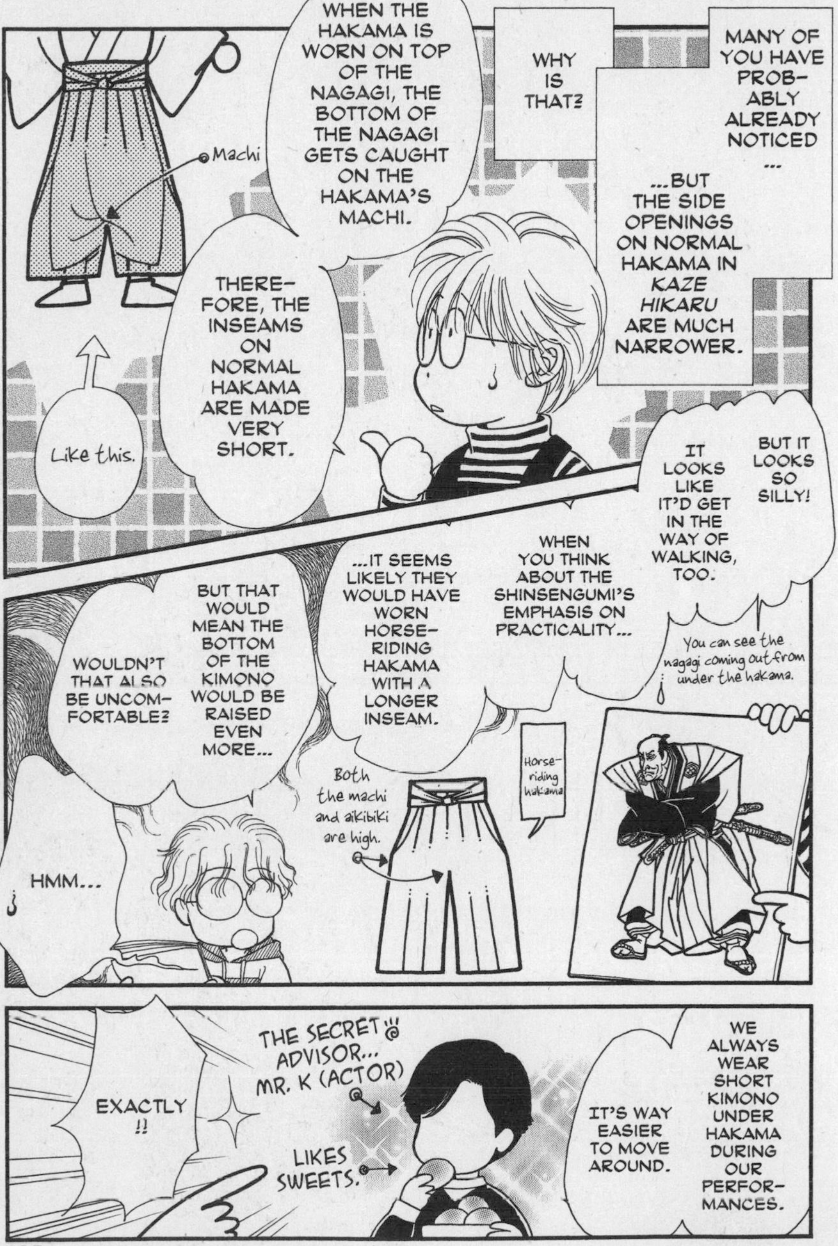
MANY OF YOU HAVE PROBABLY ALREADY NOTICED ...
...BUT THE SIDE OPENINGS ON NORMAL HAKAMA IN *KAZE HIKARU* ARE MUCH NARROWER.
WHY IS THAT?
WHEN THE HAKAMA IS WORN ON TOP OF THE NAGAGI, THE BOTTOM OF THE NAGAGI GETS CAUGHT ON THE HAKAMA'S MACHI.
THEREFORE, THE INSEAMS ON NORMAL HAKAMA ARE MADE VERY SHORT.
Machi
Like this.
BUT IT LOOKS SO SILLY!
IT LOOKS LIKE IT'D GET IN THE WAY OF WALKING, TOO.
You can see the nagagi coming out from under the hakama.
WHEN YOU THINK ABOUT THE SHINSENGUMI'S EMPHASIS ON PRACTICALITY...
...IT SEEMS LIKELY THEY WOULD HAVE WORN HORSE-RIDING HAKAMA WITH A LONGER INSEAM.
BUT THAT WOULD MEAN THE BOTTOM OF THE KIMONO WOULD BE RAISED EVEN MORE...
WOULDN'T THAT ALSO BE UNCOMFORTABLE?
Horse-riding hakama
Both the machi and aikibiki are high.
HMM...
WE ALWAYS WEAR SHORT KIMONO UNDER HAKAMA DURING OUR PERFORMANCES.
IT'S WAY EASIER TO MOVE AROUND.
THE SECRET ADVISOR... MR. K (ACTOR)
LIKES SWEETS.
EXACTLY !!

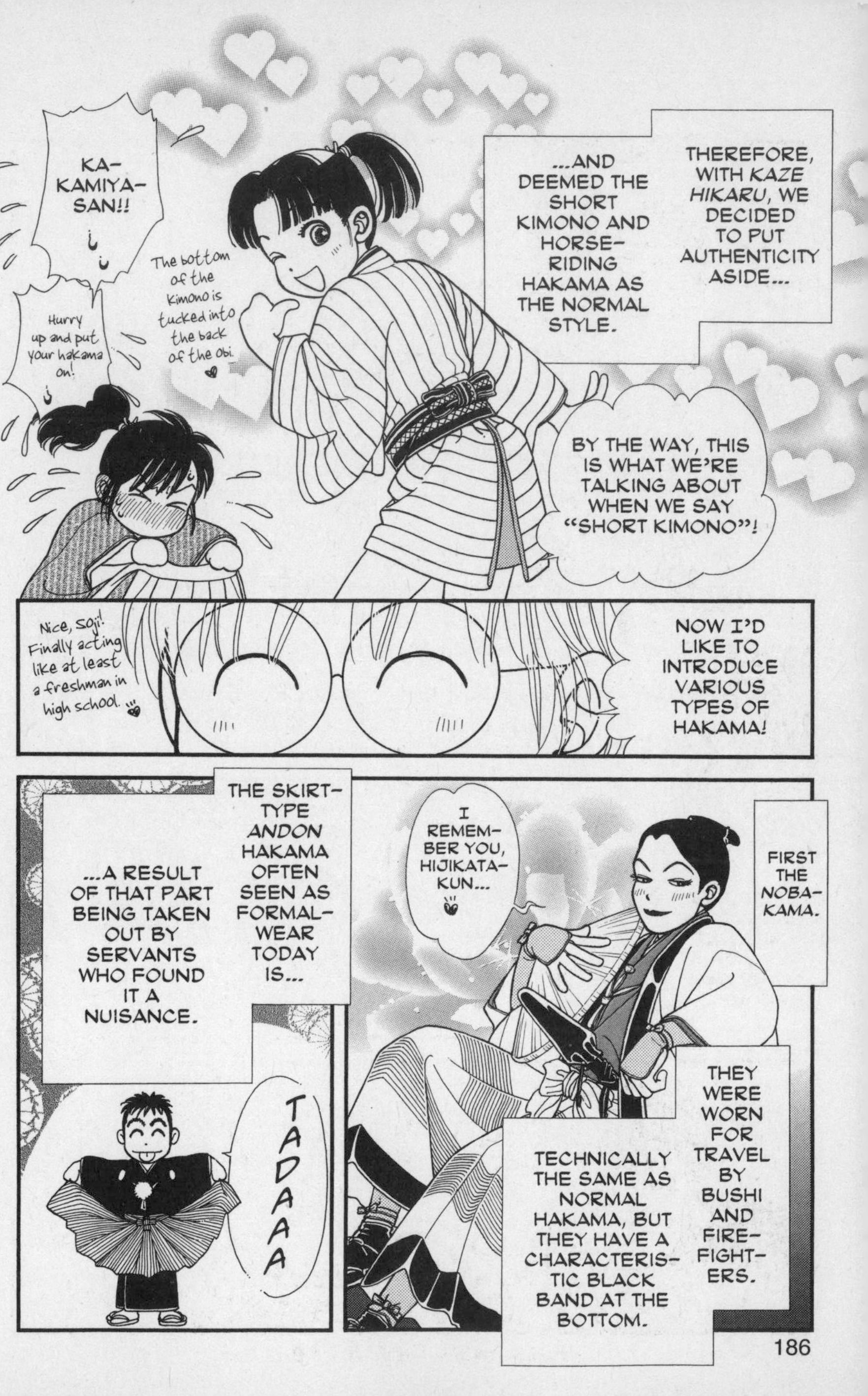
THEREFORE, WITH *KAZE HIKARU*, WE DECIDED TO PUT AUTHENTICITY ASIDE...
...AND DEEMED THE SHORT KIMONO AND HORSE-RIDING HAKAMA AS THE NORMAL STYLE.
KA-KAMIYA-SAN!!
The bottom of the kimono is tucked into the back of the Obi.
BY THE WAY, THIS IS WHAT WE'RE TALKING ABOUT WHEN WE SAY "SHORT KIMONO"!
Hurry up and put your hakama on!
NOW I'D LIKE TO INTRODUCE VARIOUS TYPES OF HAKAMA!
Nice, Soji! Finally acting like at least a freshman in high school.
FIRST THE *NOBAKAMA*.
I REMEMBER YOU, HIJIKATA-KUN...
THEY WERE WORN FOR TRAVEL BY BUSHI AND FIRE-FIGHTERS.
TECHNICALLY THE SAME AS NORMAL HAKAMA, BUT THEY HAVE A CHARACTERISTIC BLACK BAND AT THE BOTTOM.
THE SKIRT-TYPE *ANDON* HAKAMA OFTEN SEEN AS FORMAL-WEAR TODAY IS...
...A RESULT OF THAT PART BEING TAKEN OUT BY SERVANTS WHO FOUND IT A NUISANCE.
TADAAA

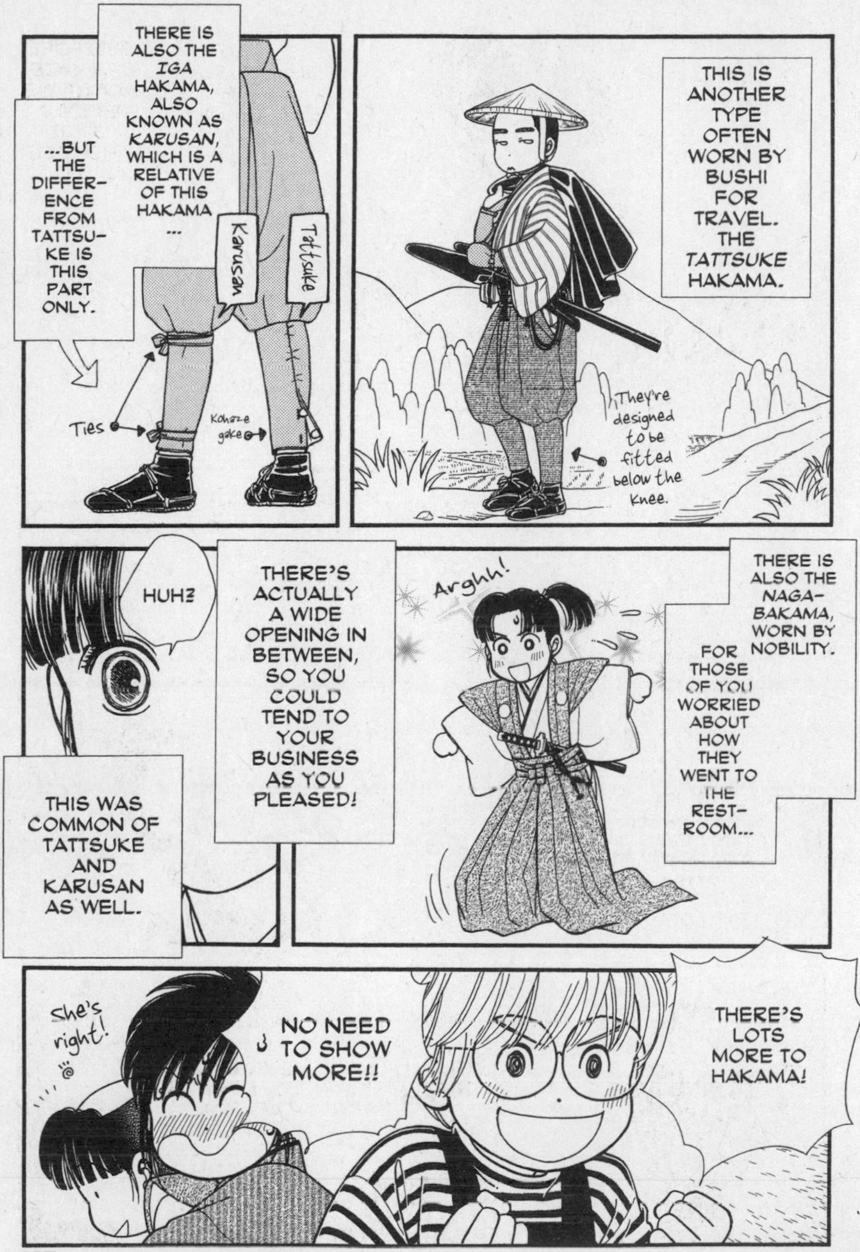

THIS IS ANOTHER TYPE OFTEN WORN BY BUSHI FOR TRAVEL. THE TATTSUKE HAKAMA.
They're designed to be fitted below the knee.
THERE IS ALSO THE IGA HAKAMA, ALSO KNOWN AS KARUSAN, WHICH IS A RELATIVE OF THIS HAKAMA...
...BUT THE DIFFERENCE FROM TATTSUKE IS THIS PART ONLY.
Tattsuke
Karusan
Ties
Kohaze gake
THERE IS ALSO THE NAGA-BAKAMA, WORN BY NOBILITY.
FOR THOSE OF YOU WORRIED ABOUT HOW THEY WENT TO THE REST-ROOM...
Arghh!
THERE'S ACTUALLY A WIDE OPENING IN BETWEEN, SO YOU COULD TEND TO YOUR BUSINESS AS YOU PLEASED!
HUH?
THIS WAS COMMON OF TATTSUKE AND KARUSAN AS WELL.
THERE'S LOTS MORE TO HAKAMA!
NO NEED TO SHOW MORE!!
She's right!

Kaze Hikaru Diary R: The End

Decoding Kaze Hikaru

Kaze Hikaru is a historical drama based in 19th century Japan and thus contains some fairly mystifying terminology. In this glossary we'll break down archaic phrases, terms and other linguistic curiosities for you so that you can move through life with the smug assurance that you are indeed a know-it-all.

First and foremost, because *Kaze Hikaru* is a period story, we kept all character names in their traditional Japanese form—that is, family name followed by first name. For example, the character Okita Soji's family name is Okita and his personal name is Soji.

AKO-ROSHI:
The *ronin* (samurai) of Ako; featured in the immortal Kabuki play *Chushingura* (Loyalty), aka *47 Samurai*.

ANI-UE:
Literally, "brother above"; an honorific for an elder male sibling.

BAKUFU:
Literally, "tent government." Shogunate; the feudal, military government that dominated Japan for more than 200 years.

BUSHI:
A samurai or warrior (part of the compound word *bushido*, which means "way of the warrior").

CHICHI-UE:
An honorific suffix meaning "father above."

DO:
In kendo (a Japanese fencing sport that uses bamboo swords), a short way of describing the offensive single-hit strike *shikake waza ippon uchi*.

-HAN:
The same as the honorific -*san*, pronounced in the dialect of southern Japan.

-KUN:
An honorific suffix that indicates a difference in rank and title. The use of -*kun* is also a way of indicating familiarity and friendliness between students or compatriots.

MEN:
In the context of *Kaze Hikaru, men* refers to one of the "points" in kendo. It is a strike to the forehead and is considered a basic move.

MIBU-ROSHI:
A group of warriors that supports the Bakufu.

NE'E-SAN:
Can mean "older sister," "ma'am" or "miss."

NI'I-CHAN:
Short for *oni'i-san* or *oni'i-chan,* meaning older brother.

OKU-SAMA:
This is a polite way to refer to someone's wife. *Oku* means "deep" or "further back" and comes from the fact that wives (in affluent families) stayed hidden away in the back rooms of the house.

ONI:
Literally "ogre," this is Sei's nickname for Vice Captain Hijikata.

RANPO:
Medical science derived from the Dutch.

RONIN:
Masterless samurai.

RYO:
At the time, one *ryo* and two *bu* (four *bu* equaled roughly one *ryo*) were enough currency to support a family of five for an entire month.

-SAN:
An honorific suffix that carries the meaning of "Mr." or "Ms."

SENSEI:
A teacher, master or instructor.

SEPPUKU:
A ritualistic suicide that was considered a privilege of the nobility and samurai elite.

SONJO-HA:
Those loyal to the emperor and dedicated to the expulsion of foreigners from the country.

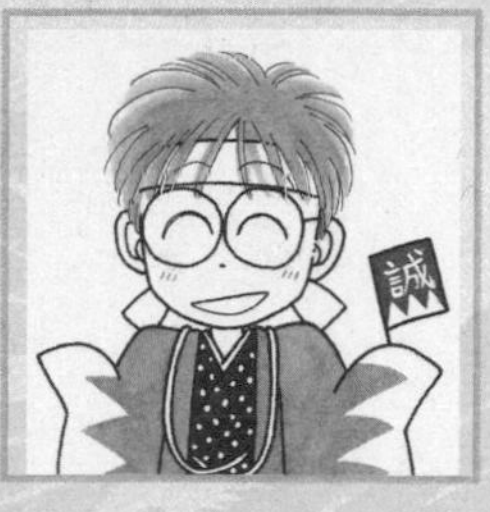
誠

I'm sure you feel that there's something strange with our two heroes, but the theme for this season's cover illustration will be a secret until volume 24 (heh). Why, you ask? Because this theme will be part of a series. Perhaps that hint was enough for some of you to figure it out, but in any case, please pray that the series doesn't get canceled between now and volume 24 (heh).

So, the seasonal word for this spring is "camellia." Some say camellias were considered ominous for bushi because the blossom falls off the tree as a whole flower, suggestive of beheadings. However, I'd like to believe that true bushi would not have feared it. Camellias in bloom are a truly awesome sight—ending their life so suddenly in the height of their grace and beauty... Arguably, the ideal way to go (heh).

Taeko Watanabe debuted as a manga artist in 1979 with her story *Waka-chan no Netsuai Jidai* (Love Struck Days of Waka). *Kaze Hikaru* is her longest-running series, but she has created a number of other popular series. Watanabe is a two-time winner of the prestigious Shogakukan Manga Award in the girls' category—her manga *Hajime-chan ga Ichiban!* (Hajime-chan Is Number One!) claimed the award in 1991, and *Kaze Hikaru* took it in 2003.

Watanabe read hundreds of historical sources to create *Kaze Hikaru.* She is from Tokyo.

KAZE HIKARU
VOL. 21
Shojo Beat Edition

STORY AND ART BY
TAEKO WATANABE

KAZE HIKARU Vol. 21
by Taeko WATANABE
© 1997 Taeko WATANABE
All rights reserved.
Original Japanese edition published by SHOGAKUKAN.
English translation rights in the United States of America and Canada arranged with
SHOGAKUKAN.

Translation & English Adaptation/Mai Ihara
Touch-up Art & Lettering/Rina Mapa
Design/Veronica Casson
Editor/Megan Bates

Printed in Canada

Published by VIZ Media, LLC
P.O. Box 77010
San Francisco, CA 94107

10 9 8 7 6 5 4 3 2 1
First printing, August 2013

www.viz.com

www.shojobeat.com